GW00361202

For Those In Peril

By the same author

FICTION

We Joined The Navy
We Saw The Sea
Down The Hatch
Never Go To Sea
All The Nice Girls
HMS Leviathan
The Fighting Temeraire
One of Our Warships
Good Enough For Nelson
Aircraft Carrier
The Good Ship Venus
A Drowning War
Polaris Fears And Dreams

NON-FICTION

Freedom's Battle: The War at Sea 1939–1945
The Forgotten Fleet
The Little Wonder: The Story of the Festiniog Railway
Sir Walter Raleigh
Air Power at Sea 1939–1945
Hurrah For the Life Of A Sailor: Life on the Lower Deck of the Victorian Navy
The Victoria Cross At Sea
War In The Pacific: Pearl Harbor to Tokyo Bay
Sink The Haguro!
Hands To Action Stations!: Naval Poetry and Verse of WW2
Find, Fix and Strike: The Fleet Air Arm at War 1939–1945
Below The Belt: Novelty, Subterfuge and Surprise in Naval Warfare
Jellicoe
Captains & Kings: The Royal Navy & The Royal Family 1902–1981
Convoy: The Defence of Sea Trade 1890–1980
The Death of The Scharnhorst
The Little Wonder: 150 years of the Festiniog Railway (Revised Edition)
Carrier Glorious: The Life & Death of an Aircraft Carrier
Air Power at Sea 1945 to Today
Warrior: The First and Last
ULTRA At Sea
The Naval Heritage of Portsmouth

FOR THOSE IN PERIL

Fifty Years of Royal Navy
Search and Rescue

JOHN WINTON

ROBERT HALE · LONDON

First published in Great Britain 1992

ISBN 0 7090 4917 X

Robert Hale Limited
Clerkenwell House
Clerkenwell Green
London EC1R 0HT

Digital Equipment Co. Ltd, a major supplier of computer systems to the Ministry of Defence, including the computers in the Royal Navy Sea Harrier, Sea King and Lynx aircraft, is delighted to contribute towards the author's research costs of this book.

Photoset in Times by
Derek Doyle & Associates, Mold, Clwyd.
Printed in Great Britain by
St Edmundsbury Press Ltd, Bury St Edmunds, Suffolk.
Bound by WBC Bookbinders Ltd, Bridgend, Glamorgan.

Contents

Acknowledgments

My grateful thanks are due to the many who gave me interviews, did research for me, corrected my drafts, flew me on helicopter flights, and sent or lent me letters, photographs, diaries, newspaper cuttings, logbooks, reminiscences:

Sub Lt Ian Adams RN.

Cdr P.E. Bailey RN, Lt Cdr John Baker RN, Lt Keith Blount RN (771 NAS), Rear Admiral A.S. ('Ben') Bolt CB DSO DSC, Rear Admiral Peter Branson CBE, Mr Alan Bristow, Lt (A) W.N. Brown RNVR, Mrs Jean Burbury, Cdr David F. Burke MBE RN.

Captain E.S. Carver DSC RN, Lt Cdr Mike Caws RN (Editor, *Flight Deck*), Major V.B.G. Cheesman DSO MBE DSC RM, Mr Ray Colbeck, Lt Cdr Ray Colborne RN, Lt Cdr R.R. Crayton RN, Chief Photographer M.P. Cunningham.

Rear Admiral Roger Dimmock CB, Sub Lt Jes Dixon RN.

Lt Cdr D.W.F. Elliott MBE RN, Fleet Chief Ken Enticknapp, CGM RN.

Lt Cdr Timothy Fletcher RN, Lt Cdr Neil Fuller RN.

Mr M.J. Green, CPOACMN J.P.R. ('Smiler') Grinney.

Captain David Hart Dyke CBE RN, Midshipman Geoffrey Hayward RN, Brigadier Frank Henn CBE (COS, United Nations Forces in Cyprus).

Mrs Yvonne Jerome (Shipwrecked Mariners' Society), Surg Cdr Rick Jolly OBE RN.

Mr Paul Kemp (Imperial War Museum).

Mr John Lansdown, Lt Cdr Mike Lawrence RN (CO 771 NAS), Vice Admiral Michael Layard CBE, Midshipman Robert Lee RN, Captain S. Leonard OBE RN, Lt Roy Lewis (819 NAS), Mrs Mary Lickford, Captain John Lippiett MBE RN.

Radio Supervisor Sam Macfarlane, Cdr Ian McKechnie DSO RN, Midshipman Kevin Meads RN, Midshipman Robert Milligan RN, Lt Cdr Ivor Milne RN, Mr Graham Mottram, Mr Eric Myall, ARAeS.

Lt Darrell Nelson USCG, Mr Iain Nethercott, DSM.

Lt Cdr Chris Parry RN, Lt Cdr John Passmore MBE RN, Lt Cdr William P. Powell RN.

Mr Ken Reed, Cdr Gordon Roberts OBE RN, Mrs Christine Robinson-Moltke.

Cdr E.G. Savage DSO DSC RN, Cdr G.J. ('Tank') Sherman MBE RN, Cdr Vic Sirett RN, Cdr Richard E. Smith MBE RN, Sub Lt Tony Snell RN, Cdr H.R. Spedding MBE RN, Midshipman Derek Spicer RN, Cdr Ian Stanley DSO RN, Cdr S.H. Suthers DSC DFC RN.

Lt Cdr Nigel Thomson RN, Mr John Tucker (Editor, *Navy News*), Mr M.J. Tupper DSM RN, Cdr R. Turpin MBE RN.

Lt Cdr V.A. Walker RN, Lt Cdr Jack Waterman RD RNR, Sub Lt Tim Watkins RN, Lt Cdr Peter West RN, POACMN Stephen Wright.

Cdr Tim Yarker RN.

Illustrations

1 Of Shoes ... and Ships ... and Shagbats

There is a faint but unmistakeable flavour of World War Two about it. They actually do 'Scramble', just as they did during the war. The duty Search and Rescue (SAR) aircrew come on at breakfast time and stay on call for twenty-four hours, until they themselves are relieved next day. They sit all day long in their ready room. They smoke, they chat, they brew cups of tea, they watch TV or a video. After a meal they play Cameroons with poker dice – loser washes up. But, most of all, they wait.

They might wait for hours, which stretch into days, while nothing happens: all calm and peaceful, not a cloud in the sky, not a squawk from any radio. Meanwhile, the normal work and activity of a busy airfield – HMS *Seahawk*, Royal Naval Air Station (RNAS) Culdrose, in Cornwall, is the biggest helicopter base in the UK – goes on around them.

Then, suddenly, the emergency telephone rings. All ready room conversation stops. The klaxon goes. 'Scramble the SAR!' is the cry. While most of the crew double out to the aircraft, one stays behind: a brief description of the emergency, a few facts, a scribbled map reference, a voice says 'Yes. Got that!' and then they are off – two pilots, an observer, an aircrewman and a diver, all sprinting full pelt across the airfield tarmac, fastening their helmet straps as they go.

They climb into the Sea King helicopter, a big bulky ten-ton aircraft, with its Ace of Clubs squadron insignia on its nose and its fuselage startlingly painted like a fair-ground organ in slabs of bright red and grey. Soon the engines are running and the huge rotor blades are swinging, faster and faster – 'burning and turning', as they say. A quick signal from the handler on the tarmac and within minutes of the 'Scramble' the Sea King is away, warning lights flashing and engines thundering like some great agricultural threshing machine in the sky as it wheels out over the Cornish fields and cliffs towards the sea.

As they fly towards their objective, even the crew's radio conversation, in clipped stereotyped phrases obscured and blurred in crackling static, is exactly like the sound track of one of those films starring Kenneth More, Robert Donat, Jean Kent and William Hartnell – only now the target is not the Luftwaffe or the Italian battle fleet. This is more domestic than epic, though just as urgent – a swimmer in difficulties, a dog cut off from its distraught owner by the rising tide, a holiday-maker with a broken leg after falling from a cliff face, drugs to be taken to a hospital.

Sometimes it sounds more serious – a report of what looks like a body seen floating face down in the sea, a smashed car at the foot of a cliff, a trawler with a badly injured crewman who needs to be taken to hospital urgently, a capsized sailing boat, a coaster whose cargo has shifted in a gale and whose crew are thinking of abandoning ship, a ship aground and breaking up in heavy seas.

Occasionally, there is a touch of comedy: a fat heifer who has strayed off her cliff pasture and fallen into a crevice. A shot of sedative, a large net, hoist on the winch and Buttercup is safe again. A delighted farmer later rings up to say 'Thank'ee. I'm glad to say Buttercup 'er's on 'er feet and eatin'.'

Astonishingly, not all the rescued are as grateful as that farmer. The SAR crews are no longer surprised or very much hurt by the attitudes of some of their 'clients'. Picnickers near the scene of a rescue complain that the down draught of the rotor blades blew sand into their sandwiches. One woman, rescued from a dangerous spot on a cliff face where she had been marooned by the tide, complained afterwards that her dress had been dirtied.

Another lady was spotted waving from an inflatable rubber raft, rapidly skimming out to sea on an offshore wind, next stop the Azores. Somebody rang up the Coast Guard, out came the SAR helicopter, and all was smiles. But the Captain of Culdrose later received a very stiff letter from the husband, asking why the helicopter man had rescued his wife but left her new beach shoes behind.

According to one famous Culdrose story, one husband sent the station the bill for dry-cleaning his wife's dress after she had been rescued. Commander (Air) replied that the bill would certainly be paid – 'as soon as Culdrose's account (please see enclosed) for £700 for the use of the Wessex helicopter had been settled'.

But the great majority of the rescued are very grateful, being well aware that somebody else's skill, training and dedication have saved them from an awkward and sometimes a potentially fatal predicament which was often their own fault. A file of letters, telephone calls, some Christmas cards and the odd bottle of whisky left at the main gate, all testify to how much so many owe to the SAR crews.

Risks and wrecks as old as seafaring history. But the idea of rescue, on an organised, systematic and permanent basis, is comparatively new. For centuries, people living by the coast – and especially the Cornish coast – were, if left to themselves, more interested in wrecking than rescue, and much more concerned with looting than lifeboats.

The first lifeboat was built in 1785 by a Mr Lionel Lukin, a coachbuilder and later Master of the Worshipful Company of Coachbuilders. Encouraged by the Prince of Wales (later George IV) Lukin converted a Norwegian yawl into what he called an 'unimmergible' by fitting a projecting cork gunwhale, air chambers at bow and stern and a false keel of iron. In 1786, Lukin converted a coble into a 'safety boat' for Archdeacon Sharp of Ripon. The boat was employed for some years in saving life from shipwreck at Bamborough, thus qualifying as the first ever life-boat station.

Public interest in lifesaving was aroused by the fate of the *Adventure* which ran aground in a gale off Newcastle in 1789. She was only 300 yards from shore and a huge crowd watched helplessly as her crew dropped one by one into the sea and were drowned. Public money was raised for the design of a lifeboat, the best being by Henry Greathead, a boatbuilder from South Shields.

In 1824 Sir William Hillary, an MP who had himself taken part in saving over 300 lives along the coast of the Isle of Man, founded the Royal National Institution for the Preservation of Life from Shipwreck, which became the Royal National Lifeboat Institution (RNLI), probably this country's most senior charity today. The RNLI developed over the years from a primitive venture owning a few rowing boats to an extensive country-wide organisation covering the whole coast of the United Kingdom, with specially designed and built self-righting lifeboats capable of operating in virtually any weather conditions.

Her Majesty's Coastguard (HMCG) was formed in 1820, as its name suggests, to guard the coast in the post-Napoleonic era. Although this was its chief role, HMCG inevitably became involved in coastal and inshore rescues. The duties of HMCG were rationalised at the end of the First World War and

Search and Rescue in the Victorian Navy: 'Man Overboard' from HMS *Shannon* on her way out to the Far East, 1857. Able Seaman William Hall, the black sailor standing up, won the Victoria Cross during the Indian Mutiny

the Service was reformed in 1925 under the Board of Trade primarily as a rescue service. Originally it operated through look-outs placed at frequent intervals around the coast. Keeping a lookout is still an important function of HMCG but today the principal watch is maintained on radio.

In the Royal Navy, rescue has always been an accepted, commonplace aspect of Service life. In the days of sail and into the era of the Victorian ironclad, falls from aloft were frequent and 'Man overboard!' was a regular cry. When the new and experimental 51-gun steam frigate HMS *Shannon*, commanded by Captain William Peel VC, was commissioned in 1856, she was fitted with a quick-acting 'Clifford's boat-lowering gear' which was used in earnest four times in 1857 during the ship's passage out to the Far East (where her Naval Brigade won immortality at the Siege of Lucknow in the Indian Mutiny).

With the coming of aircraft, rescue was at first, as it always had been, a matter of improvisation. Possibly the first ever rescue at sea by aircraft was in the North Sea during the First World War. On 5 September 1917, a De Havilland D.H.4 and a Curtiss H.12 'Large America' flying boat, No.8666, attacked a German Zeppelin L44, over the North Sea off Terschelling Island.

The Zeppelin escaped, having put a bullet in the radiator of the D.H.4 which had to ditch with engine trouble. Although 8666 also had trouble with its port engine, its pilot Lt Vincent Nicholl went back to pick up Fl Lt A.H.H. Gilligan RNAS, the pilot of the D.H.4 and his observer, Fl Lt. G.S. Trewin.

8666's starboard wingtip float was broken off during the landing and the hull was strained and began to leak. Gilligan and Trewin abandoned their

Curtiss H-12 'Large America' flying boat

sinking D.H.4 and swam across to 8666. With two extra above its normal crew of four, one defective engine and a damaged float, 8666 was unable to take off, so Nicholl taxied on one engine over an extremely rough sea towards the coast, fifty miles away, until his fuel ran out.

There was no food on board, and only the water in the radiators to drink. A watch-bill was arranged with five men baling continuously, while the sixth 'rested' by clinging to the port lower mainplane to keep the damaged starboard wing out of the water. Everybody was sea-sick. Their only hope were four carrier pigeons, which were released in pairs, at an interval of 48 hours.

The second pair each carried the message '3 pm. Very urgent. Seaplane 8666 to CO Air Station Great Yarmouth. We have sighted nothing. The wind has been drifting us WNW ever since we landed so we may have missed Cromer. We are not far from the coast as we keep seeing small land birds. Sea is still rough. Machine still intact. We will fire Very's lights every 45 minutes tonight. V. Nicholl.'

One of the second pair of pigeons was found, apparently exhausted, lying on a beach near the air of station and its message was retrieved. The aircraft had now been missing for three days and the rescuers had given up the search. But the Captain of the torpedo boat *Halcyon* worked out where the flying boat would be likely to have drifted, steered for the spot, and duly found 8666 some 100 miles north-east of Yarmouth. All six men were rescued and the flying boat towed in to Great Yarmouth.

The body of the pigeon, official number NURP/17/F/16331, was preserved at Yarmouth, displayed under a plaque 'A Very Gallant Gentleman', and is now on show at the RAF Museum, Hendon.

Between the wars, when the amount of flying at sea increased enormously, rescue had to be more specifically organised. Thus, an aircraft carrier always had an attendant 'Plane guard' destroyer, and sometimes two of them, keeping station with a sea-boat manned on the carrier's quarter while

'The time has come,' the Walrus said,
'To talk of many things –
Of pusher screws and "Shagbats"
And strutted, swept-back wings.
I'm an aeronautical wonder
And if that is not enough
Then I've wheels that I can land on
When the sea's a bit too rough.'

flying was in progress. Later, carriers had one or more 'ship's flight' Walrus amphibians, for use as air taxis and for air-sea rescue.

The Vickers Supermarine Walrus, or 'Shagbat' as it was known, was the air-sea rescue work-horse of the Second World War. Despite its homely, even comical, appearance, with its 'pusher' propeller, turned-up nose and boat-shaped hull, the Walrus proved itself reliable and resilient under punishment from sea and weather.

One of the earliest Walrus rescues of the war was by an aircraft of 710 Naval Air Squadron (NAS) who flew daily anti-submarine patrols out to sea and along the African coast from the seaplane carrier *Albatross* based at Freetown, West Africa.

On 14 January 1941, the 7,472 ton Blue Funnel cargo-liner ss *Eumaeus*, commanded by Captain J.E. Watson, was on passage to the Far East around the Cape of Good Hope with a draft of some 200 naval officers and ratings and one RAF sergeant when she sighted the Italian U-boat *Commandante Cappelini* on the surface.

Captain Watson increased speed and altered course to enable the gun on the ship's poop to bear. After a somewhat one-sided gun battle, in which all *Eumaeus*'s ammunition was expended, Watson decided to abandon ship. The U-boat then closed and torpedoed and sank her. Although there were casualties on board, and some of the lifeboats were damaged, many of the ship's company and passengers were able to get away in lifeboats or clinging to wreckage.

Meanwhile a Walrus of 710 NAS (pilot Lt. V.B.G. Cheesman, Royal Marines, observer PO Knowles, and Ldg Tel M.W. Dale as aircrewman) took off at 7 am tasked to search for and attack a submarine which had been reported as attacking ss *Eumaeus*. Finding nothing at the datum, 'Cheese' Cheesman turned north and heard reports from other aircraft that they had attacked the submarine. Eventually he sighted survivors in the distance, circled over them and saw many men in lifejackets hanging on to small pieces of debris, and others packed into lifeboats. Dale dropped the rubber dinghy near some of them.

Cheesman had fuel for ninety minutes and the return journey would take seventy, so he had twenty minutes to spare. He landed near one lifeboat with two men in it which had drifted some two miles from the rest, intending to tow it back to the main group. The sea was rough with a long swell, and before Cheesman could manoeuvre the Walrus near the two men, they both dived into the sea and swam across. Hauled on board, one man was in good condition but the other was exhausted.

Taxying to the main group, Cheesman found that some boats had wounded men in them. While they were transferring medical stores to one lifeboat, the Walrus' port wing-tip float and the lower mainplane were damaged, making take-off impossible.

Another Walrus of 710 NAS now appeared overhead and Knowles signalled to it by Aldis lamp asking for a course to steer to the nearest empty lifeboat. Cheesman taxied as near as he could to it and then, as neither Knowles nor Dale were strong swimmers, stopped the Walrus' engine and swam to the boat with a line which he tied to the lifeboat's painter. He swam back, restarted the engine and towed the boat to the survivors.

He then asked for three volunteers to man the lifeboat whilst he towed it round picking up survivors. Seven men manned the boat but misunderstood Cheesman's intention and cut the tow. However, they got out the oars, rowed round and picked up several survivors from floating debris. Meanwhile, other Walruses flew overhead, dropping supplies.

Knowles was sitting on the upper mainplane keeping lookout. At about 12.30 pm he sighted smoke to the north and shone his Aldis lamp in that direction. Soon two anti-submarine trawlers, *Bengali* and *Spaniard*, appeared and began picking up survivors. When they had all been recovered, the Walrus was taken in tow, at about 3.15.

By now Cheesman and his crew were, as he said, 'feeling slightly the worse for wear'. There was no reason for them all to stay in the Walrus so he decided to transfer them to one of the trawlers. But Dale was so keen to stay Cheesman kept him on board while Knowles and the two survivors went across in the last lifeboat.

During the long tow back, Cheesman and Dale took turns to pump out continuously. They existed on iron rations and water bottles, with a tin of fruit and cigarettes dropped by another Walrus. They finally arrived at 3.45 am the next morning, after 22 hours in the aircraft. They used the last of their petrol to start the engine and motor alongside *Albatross* and be hoisted on board, with water streaming out of the Walrus' damaged hull.

Of 300 men on board *Eumaeus* only 23 were lost. The last three survivors, the RAF sergeant and two sailors, were picked up still clinging to a mast by a destroyer the next morning.

'Cheese' Cheesman was awarded the MBE, Sub Lt W.C. Broadburn, the pilot of the second Walrus, was mentioned in dispatches, and Mick Dale, though he modestly said he 'really hadn't done anything to deserve it', the BEM. Captain Watson was appointed OBE and awarded Lloyd's War Medal for Bravery at Sea. (Ironically, as a footnote to this incident, *Bengali* and *Spaniard* were both sunk after a petrol explosion and fire at Lagos on 5 December 1942).

Walrus aircrew were impartial as to whose side, ours or theirs, they rescued. After the TORCH landings in North Africa in November 1942, 700 NAS was at Base d'Hydravions, near Algiers, on anti-submarine search and harbour protection duties. On 17th, a Walrus of 700 NAS piloted by Sub Lt Roy Blatchley took off in answer to a call from the RAF concerning a surrendered U-boat, 40 miles off Algiers.

Earlier that day a Hudson of No 500 Sq RAF piloted by Sq Ldr Patterson had surprised U-331 on the surface and bombed it. The U-boat dived at once but while it was diving one bomb blew its forward hatch open, so that the fore ends of the submarine began to flood. The captain, Kap Lt von Tiesenhausen, one of the most experienced U-boat commanders (he had sunk the battleship HMS *Barham* a year earlier) brought the U-boat to the surface, where it was bombed again by another Hudson.

Bombed several times and harassed by machine gun fire, von Tiesenhausen was compelled to surrender and hoisted a white flag. But while the Hudsons were orbiting gleefully over their prize, and preparing to escort it to an Allied port, to their utter dismay and consternation a Fairey Albacore with some Wildcat fighters from the carrier *Formidable* arrived, torpedoed U-331 and sank it.

Blatchley landed in a roughish sea and picked up sixteen of the U-boat crew. Unable to take off again, he taxied with his passengers until the arrival of the destroyer *Wilton* who recovered Blatchley and his crew and all the U-boat survivors, from the Walrus and from the sea. But the Walrus later sank under tow.

From early beginnings in the English Channel during the Battle of Britain the RAF developed a large, well organised and very efficient Air-Sea Rescue service, using mainly High Speed Launches (HSLs), which operated not only in home waters but world-wide, as far as the Mediterranean and the coasts of India and Burma.

Coastal Forces also used Rescue Motor Launches (RMLs) from harbours along the south and east coasts and there were many dramatic rescue actions. For example, on 15 July 1942, two HSLs and two RMLs from Dover to the crash scene some seven miles south-east of Boulogne where a very famous fighter pilot, Wing Cdr 'Paddy' Finucane, DSO DFC, had been shot down.

Finucane did not survive the crash. But meanwhile his would-be rescuers themselves came under attack from ten Focke Wulf Fw 190 fighters as they crossed the Channel. HSL 140 was hit, with one man killed and one wounded and HSL 138 was set on fire, with one man killed and several wounded, including her CO F/O W.E. Walters.

The German fighters then turned to ML 139 (Lt A.R.S. Hodgson RNVR), making five runs over her and setting her on fire. The fires were put out by Ch. Motor Mech. Leslie Adams and AB Guy Sandford (who both won the Conspicuous Gallantry Medal) and ML 139 went to help the burning HSL 138, taking three survivors from the water.

ML 141 (Lt Patrick Williams RNR) rescued seven more of 138's survivors from their liferaft and sank the blazing wreck with depth-charges. She herself was engaged by six Fw 190s who killed one officer and wounded three ratings. But ML 141 shot down one of the fighters and drove off the rest. MLs 139 and 141, and HSL 140 all reached harbour safely. Williams, who had already been mentioned in dispatches for air-sea rescue work from Dover a year earlier, was awarded the DSC. Hodgson also received the DSC, for services in ML 139, a year later.

In May 1944, several naval aircrews were appointed to No. 275 Sq RAF to carry out air-sea rescue during the invasion of France. They rescued a number of aircrews who had been shot down by enemy fighters and had baled out over

Rescue Motor launch of World War Two: RML 529, wearing the Royal Standard, with HM King George VI embarked for the review of the D-Day Normandy Invasion Fleet in the Solent, June 1944

the Channel. One Walrus picked up the entire crew of a B-17 Flying Fortress and, unable to take off again because of the extra weight, had to taxi towards home, passing so close to the island of Alderney that the aircraft came under fire from shore.

An operational Fleet Air Squadron had to be ready to undertake an SAR sortie, at any time, and despite whatever else they happened to be doing. In 1944, when 837 NAS, flying Fairey Barracudas, were at HMS *Owl*, RNAS Fearn, Ross & Cromarty: 'Several of us were in the wardroom bar at about midnight,' said Lt Cdr Jack Waterman RD RNR, 'having sandwiches and a beer after taking part in the Station production of 'I Killed The Count' – and still in various strange bits of stage costume (myself, for example, in a footman's green suit) and make-up.'

'The door opened – not the Officer of the Day come to close the bar – but our CO who fairly smartly told us all to get airborne, make-up or no make-up. A Wellington had gone in on the Skerries off Lossiemouth (which was then an RAF Wellington OTU); we were the only squadron in the area equipped for flare-dropping; and time was of the essence. So, about 1 am three aircraft took off. We dropped flares at intervals for about an hour, but sadly saw nothing. Even sadder, the aircraft was found after daybreak, with no survivors.'

Late in 1944 and early in 1945, Walrus and Sea Otters of 1700 and 1701 NAS went out to the Far East, to serve ashore in Ceylon and in India, and in escort carriers of the East Indies Fleet, for air-sea rescue and minesweeping operations. Two Walrus, nicknamed 'Darby' and 'Joan', were embarked in the carrier *Illustrious* primarily for air-sea rescue duties with the British Pacific Fleet. They flew sorties to look for ditched aircrew along the Sumatran coast and to a lake inland after the air strikes against Japanese oil refineries at Palembang in Sumatra on 24 and 29 January 1945.

But the main air-sea rescue effort for the Palembang strikes was carried out by the fleet's own destroyers, who rescued the crews of seven Avengers, two Corsairs and two Seafires. The submarine *Tantalus* was on station in the Malacca Strait and one aircraft ditched within twenty-five miles of her, but she had no calls for help and the aircrew were not recovered.

It was the submarine HMS *Tactician* who carried out what was very probably the first SAR rescue dive in British naval history. On 16 April 1944, the Eastern Fleet led by Admiral Sir James Somerville flying his flag in the battleship *Queen Elizabeth* with *Valiant* and the French battleship *Richelieu*, the battlecruiser *Renown*, carriers *Illustrious* and the American USS *Saratoga*, six cruisers (including one New Zealand and one Dutch) and fifteen destroyers (including four Australian, three US and one Dutch) sailed from Trincomalee to carry out Operation COCKPIT, an air strike against the harbour and oil storage tanks at Sabang, an island on the north coast of Sumatra.

The force arrived off Sabang early on 19th and began to fly off aircraft at dawn. Aircraft from *Illustrious* and *Saratoga* attacked from different directions at 5.30 am and achieved complete surprise. Twenty-four Japanese aircraft were destroyed on the ground, and three out of four oil tanks bombed and set on fire.

One Grumman Hellcat fighter from *Saratoga* piloted by Lt Dale 'Klondike' Kahn was hit by flak while strafing a shore battery and ditched in the sea near *Tactician*, who hastened at full speed to the spot. The Hellcat was just disappearing beneath the surface, with the pilot still in it.

Two of the best swimmers in *Tactician*'s ship's company, PO LTO Iain Nethercott and Ldg Stoker Frank Mustard, had been chosen as 'swimming party'. Neither had had any formal training as free divers (although Nethercott had qualified as a 'hard helmet' diver) nor did they have any special equipment such as masks and flippers, nor any briefing as to how a Hellcat's, or any other aircraft's, cockpit opened.

'We steamed as fast as we could towards the sinking aircraft,' said Nethercott, 'and the shore batteries were getting very close (afterwards the starboard lookout swore that one shell went between the periscope standards) as the Skipper jinked the boat in towards the plane in the water. As we neared it the nose dipped and it slowly sank. The plane had practically sunk, with only its tail showing. We came alongside just as the tail was disappearing. As we smashed alongside, 'Now' yelled the Skipper and Frankie and I jumped into the water from the starboard ballast tank almost on top of the plane's canopy.'

'We swam down and at about ten feet down we reached the cockpit canopy. We could see the pilot inside, in an air bubble presumably, desperately trying to open the canopy, and it seemed to have flooded up inside. I tried pulling the canopy back but it wouldn't shift. I pulled out my diver's knife, intending to try and hack my way in, when suddenly Frankie, who was on the other side, found an emergency release lever of some kind and we pulled the canopy back. The chap was OK and had already undone his webbing harness. The plane must have been sinking fast as it was getting darker. I was nearly out of air. I estimate we were passing through twenty to thirty feet on release. We dragged him out between us. He was struggling, probably drowning. We kicked our way to the surface. Was I glad! My lungs were bursting. McNally of the casing party dived in and grabbed him, and he was dragged aboard.'

'Frankie and I swam onto the ballast tank and lay there gasping. The Skipper leaned over the side of the conning tower and yelled at us, words to the effect that when we had finished our bathe would we get inboard as he would like to dive the boat. Our air escort gave us the all-clear, we dived away and made for the open sea.'

Nethercott heard afterwards that 'the Americans had wanted to give some of us a medal, but that the Admiralty had declined the offer, stating that we were only doing our job. This was true'. However, *Tactician*'s CO, Lt Cdr Anthony Collett, was made a Commander of the US Legion of Merit for this rescue later in the year.

When the British Pacific Fleet moved up to take part in air operations off the Sakishima Gunto, between Okinawa and Formosa, efficient air-sea rescue was a most important factor in maintaining aircrew morale and elaborate arrangements were made for it, using the Fleet's Walrus, American flying boats codenamed 'DUMBO', and 'LIFEGUARD' submarines waiting on the surface.

An American LIFEGUARD submarine, USS *Kingfish*, picked up Lt Cdr F.C. Nottingham RNVR, the CO of *Illustrious*' 854 NAS. Nottingham's Avenger was hit by flak on 27 March 1945 while making a bombing run over an airfield on the island of Miyako. One wing caught fire and then disintegrated. The observer and air gunner had no chance, but Nottingham baled out and after an anxious search as dusk was falling by *Illustrious*' Corsairs, was found in his dinghy by the submarine.

Four days later, on 31 March, *Kingfish* was in action again to retrieve the CO of *Indomitable*'s 857 NAS, Lt Cdr W. Stuart RNVR, whose Avenger was also hit by flak. Stuart ditched successfully and his whole crew were recovered. Stuart joined Nottingham in *Kingfish*'s wardroom which was now resembling a home for Fleet Air Arm gentlemen in reduced circumstances.

Off the Sakishima Gunto, 'Darby' and 'Joan' were normally embarked either in *Illustrious* or *Victorious*. To assist rapid take-off in rough weather, they were fitted with Jet Assisted Take Off (JATO) gear borrowed from the Americans (a modification unknown to and unauthorised by the Admiralty at home).

Their crews were once again called upon to make some daring rescues. On 16 April 1945, an Avenger of 848 NAS from *Formidable* was hit by flak over the same airfield on Miyako as Nottingham, and crashed in the sea close to the shore. The pilot and air gunner were lost, but *Victorious'* Walrus (with a fighter CAP overhead) landed and picked up the observer whilst actually under fierce small arms fire from shore.

SAR services could always be improvised. On 23 February 1945, the submarine HMS *Telemachus* was on her last patrol before going home, in the Java and South China Seas, when her Engineer Officer Lt Cdr (E) H.T. Meadows was badly injured, almost severing his right hand at the wrist, while working on the port main engine. In an impromptu SAR operation, an RAAF Catalina flying boat landed alongside *Telemachus* and took Meadows off to hospital in Australia.

After the war the Walrus was very largely replaced for air-sea rescue duties by the similar but slightly larger and faster amphibian Supermarine Sea Otter which had been embarked in some of the light fleet carriers of the British Pacific Fleet. The Sea Otter never quite achieved the same position in the affections of those who flew it as did the Walrus, but it was nevertheless a very successful air-sea rescue aircraft with many rescues to its credit.

The robustness of the Sea Otter and the resourcefulness of their crews were well demonstrated by an incident which began at 3 pm on 23 July 1948 when a

16th Carrier Air Group's SAR Walrus landing alongside and hooking on to HMS *Glory* (British Pacific Fleet 1945–47). Pilot Lt Eric Smitheringale, Obs. seen hooking on Lt Cliff Gould

message was received at HMS *Fulmar*, RNAS Lossiemouth, that all four engines of a Lancaster bomber from nearby RAF Kinloss had seemingly failed almost simultaneously and the aircraft had ditched in the sea 175 miles north-east of Lossiemouth, the crew's position being picked up from a 'Gibson Girl' transmission (portable transmitter in the dinghy survival packs of large aircraft).

At that time the Lossiemouth Station Flight consisted of one Hellcat (used as a high speed personal 'taxi' by the CO, Captain Caspar John), two Sea Otters for search and rescue, and a DH Dominie for additional search back-up. Apart from the Station Flight, and RAF Lancasters at Kinloss which could drop an airborne lifeboat, there was no airborne SAR service in the Cromarty/Fair Isle/Viking areas.

One of the Station Flight Sea Otters (pilot Lt(A) Stan Ellis, observer Lt(A) Gordon Roberts, TAG PO Jock Donaldson) was airborne at 3.15 with fuel for about 4½ hours flying. Two dinghies, with men waving from them, were sighted at 5.15, and Ellis prepared to land as close to them as he could. But, as so often, the swell was much greater than it had appeared from the air. As Roberts said, 'the landing was more like a ditching but Stan Ellis did a great job in controlling the 'bucking bronco' and we made it down safely with the aircraft engine still running. Manoeuvring alongside the two dinghies was very difficult as the sea was breaking over the aircraft but we eventually succeeded in getting them close enough to the rear hatch to haul the eight exhausted RAF personnel on board. (Apparently an earlier attempt by a Lancaster to drop an airborne lifeboat to them by parachute had failed).'

'There was very little room or comfort for the RAF crew as we had to spread them throughout the whole length of the Sea Otter but they seemed grateful to be in the dry even though their new home was only a little less sick-making than their dinghies.'

Heavy seas had put the radio out of action so Donaldson could not tell Lossiemouth that the RAF personnel had been picked up safely and that with eight extra bodies take-off was not possible. The choice was a long taxi, either to Norway or the Shetlands. They chose the latter and set off with waves breaking right over the aircraft and the strong possibility that the engine might be flooded and stop at any moment. The weight of water pressing on the rudder was so great that Ellis and Roberts had to combine their efforts to keep the rudder straight. One Flight Lieutenant was put in charge of the small hand-worked bilge pump and 'did a splendid job moving the tiny handle to and fro for several hours'.

At 9 pm a Lancaster appeared overheard and signalled by light for the Sea Otter to follow its line of flight. At 9.30, the Lerwick lifeboat and the aptly named Fishery Protection Vessel HMS *Welcome* came into sight. *Welcome* lowered her whaler, which with some difficulty and much bellowing through loud hailers, came alongside the Sea Otter and took the RAF crew and PO Donaldson back to *Welcome*.

The Sea Otter was now listing badly because the port float had been punctured and filled with water. Ellis and Roberts refused *Welcome*'s suggestion to sink their aircraft. Instead, they taxied close to the ship who passed over to them by line three ½ cwt. concrete sinkers which were hauled through the aircraft and lashed by Roberts to the starboard wing. With the aircraft thus 'more-or-less' on an even keel, a tow line was secured, and *Welcome* and the Sea Otter set off at about 6 knots.

They arrived in Lerwick harbour at 6 am the next day. There being no available slipway, they drained the flooded float by using 'sailor power' on the opposite wing to lift the float clear of the water. The engine started on the second try and, after taxying trials around the harbour, they took off. After stopping for fuel at Grimsetter in the Orkneys, they landed at Lossiemouth at 11.45, to find they had made headlines in the Scottish *Daily Mail* and *Daily Express*. Later, they had 'chocolate' signals from Flag Officer Scotland and Northern Ireland and from Air Officer Commanding 18 Group and, later still, were made honorary members of RAF Kinloss Officers' mess.

A Sea Otter went out to the Far East with the light fleet carrier HMS *Triumph* and was on board when the Korean war broke out in June 1950. *Triumph*'s Sea Otter carried out what was probably the last operational rescue by a flying boat on 19 July 1950 when an American Corsair pilot, Lt Wendell Munce USN, was shot down by North Korean ground fire off the west coast, about 120 miles north-west of *Triumph*.

Lt Peter Cane with CPO Gilbert O'nion as his observer took off and found Munce in his dinghy, with two other Corsairs circling overhead. The sea was very rough and conditions were theoretically over the limits for a Sea Otter landing. But Cane and O'nion decided that a man's life was worth the risk. The Sea Otter slammed into the oncoming waves, threatening to bury its nose permanently under the water. But Cane skilfully held the Sea Otter steady while O'nion hauled Munce through the after hatch and then sank the dinghy with his knife.

The take-off was just as difficult. 'I cannot remember how many waves we hit,' said O'nion. 'It felt like being in a roller coaster at a fairground. Seas were breaking over the top mainplane and the engine, which spluttered and caught again. The last wave we hit pushed us staggering into the air.'

Cane was later awarded the Air Medal (USA) and O'nion was mentioned in dispatches. Their Sea Otter left the Korean theatre when *Triumph* was relieved by HMS *Theseus* in October.

Theseus and later carriers off Korea were to see the operational debut of an aircraft which made obsolete the Sea Otter and all other fixed wing aircraft and all surface ships. Over the years this aircraft enabled Search and Rescue to evolve into its modern form, as a quick-response, flexible, wide-ranging, multi-functional, international service, for both military and civil purposes, effective over sea and land, by day and by night, in fine weather and foul, and for 365 days in every year.

2 From Da Vinci to Dragonfly

The helicopter has always been a flying paradox. Like the bumble bee, it is seemingly aerodynamically impossible. Its engine sound is one of the most irritating of all man-made noises, but when it is bound on an errand of mercy all is forgiven. By far the greatest share of the financial and technical impetus behind helicopter research and development has been by and on behalf of the military. But the helicopter has had a hundred civil uses.

Paradoxically, the helicopter was designed principally as a weapon platform, but it has also been a saver of lives par excellence. Helicopter design made major advances during the Second World War, but it showed its usefulness in emergencies from its earliest days; possibly the very first helicopter 'mercy mission' was on 3 October 1944, when a US Coast Guard Sikorsky R-4 flew blood plasma to a US destroyer after an explosion had injured more than a hundred of her ship's company.

This paradoxical pattern has continued ever since. Search and rescue was first provided for military purposes. Yet today over ninety per cent of search and rescue sorties are for civilians.

Leonardo da Vinci is credited, probably rightly, with the original concept of the helicopter, although men through the ages must have watched the spinning action of the falling sycamore seed, embodying the principle of the autogyro, every autumn in Europe. When da Vinci went to Milan, probably in 1481, he sent a letter which was in effect an inventor's prospectus or catalogue to Ludovico il Mori, Duke of Bari, uncle of the 13-year-old Duke of Milan and *de facto* ruler of the city.

In his letter da Vinci claimed to be able to build machine guns, breech-loading guns, tanks, armoured cars, mechanical bows capable of hurling flaming projectiles, contrivances for attack and defence at sea, devices for piercing enemy ships below the waterline, a ram for battering, a double hull so that a damaged ship could still stay afloat, diving suits, swimming belts – and flying machines.

One of the thirteen drawings of flying machines by Da Vinci, now in the Institut de France in Paris, 'Flying Machine with a man operating it' does appear to be a primitive form of pedal-powered helicopter with downward flapping wings. His 'helical screw' drawn in 1486, shows even more clearly the action of a helicopter's rotor blade.

However, in his notes da Vinci gave some sound advice: 'Make trial of the

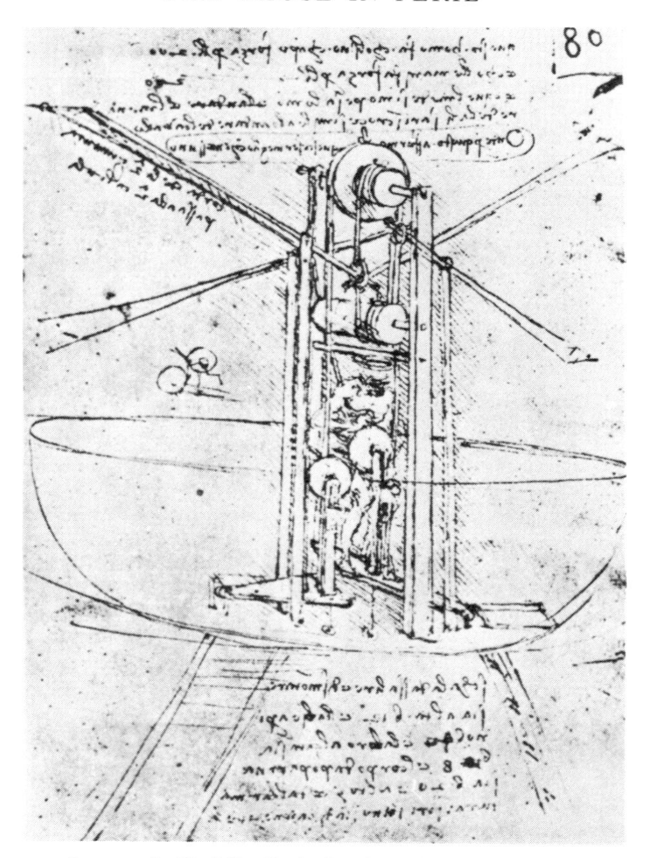

Leonardo Da Vinci's design for a flying machine

actual machine over the water so that if you fall you do not do yourself any harm'. But he soon realised that a normal man could not lift himself into the air by muscle power alone, and turned his attention to designs of machines for soaring and gliding.

Working models of helicopters were built in France and in Russia in the 18th century. In 1796 the French Academicians Launoy and Bienvenu devised a twin-rotor model worked by a bow-drill mechanism. Sir George Cayley, the 'Father of British Aeronautics', built a model on Launoy and Bienvenu's principles and flew it for short distances from the lawn of his house in Yorkshire. In 1843 he wrote the specification for an aerial conveyance which would have rotors for vertical lifting and airscrews for forward movement. In 1854 he made an aerial top with tinfoil blades worked by pulling a string. It looked like a child's plaything, but it was an early kind of helicopter.

In the 1860s, the word 'helicopter' was coined by the Viscomte Gustave de Ponton d'Amecourt, from the Greek words *helix – icos*, meaning a spiral, and *pteron*, a wing. But though there was now a Greek word for it, the lack of suitable propulsive power prevented any real progress until the beginning of the 20th century, after the invention of the internal combustion engine.

On 24 August 1907, at Douai in France, a helicopter designed and built by Louis and Jacques Breguet lifted Louis a few inches into the air. But this machine was steadied from the ground. When another, twin-rotor, machine designed by Paul Cornu took off from Lisieux in November, it was unaided, and must therefore rank as the first. In July a year later a machine designed by Louis Breguet and Charles Richet rose vertically and flew for a distance of 64 feet at a height of 15 feet. In Russia in 1909 Igor Sikorksy built a machine with two co-axial rotors. It was unsuccessful but its designer was to become a seminal figure in helicopter design.

In February 1921, Etienne Oehmichen told the French Academy he had managed flight in a machine weighing only 100 kilograms. It had two rotating wings and a 25 h.p. engine but no means of keeping it stable in flight. In 1922 a successful four-rotor helicopter, sponsored by the US Army, was designed and built in the United States. It had an 180 h.p. engine and weighed 3,600 lbs. It also lacked any real means of control in flight but it did fly, making about one hundred test flights, albeit all below 15 feet. On 4 May 1924, Oehmichen made the first one kilometre circuit in a helicopter, at Valentigney in France.

Meanwhile, on 9 January 1923 at Getafe, Madrid, the Spanish aviator Juan de la Cierva first flew his own invention known as the Autogiro. It had four rotor blades hinged to the rotor hub and lateral control was by means of ailerons. The autogiro was not a true helicopter; its rotor blades were not power-driven during flight and it was not capable of hovering. But it did have possibilities for use at sea which the Italian Navy was quick to perceive. The Cierva Autogiro Company's Chief Test Pilot, Reginald Brie, carried out trials in 1935, making several take-offs and landings on the cruiser *Fiume*, anchored, and underway at 24 knots off La Spezia.

These trials were successful enough to cause the British Admiralty to ask for them to be repeated for their benefit. Cierva agreed on condition that the Admiralty placed a firm order. In April 1935 Cierva himself came to this country to give a demonstration at Hanworth aerodrome of his C30 Autogiro. Its 3-bladed 37-foot diameter rotor had 'direct control' by which the 'disc' of the spinning rotor could be tilted in any direction about its vertical axis. This was a crucial technical advance in the development of autogiros and eventually of helicopters.

The Admiralty ordered two 2-seater C30 autogiros, which had 140 h.p. Armstrong Siddeley Genet engines. They were delivered to RAF Gosport and trials were carried out on board the carrier *Furious* in the English Channel.

Cierva was killed with 13 other people in a plane crash at Croydon on 9 December 1936 but his autogiros lived on after him. In 1938 the Admiralty ordered five C40 Cierva autogiros which were powered by 180 h.p. Salmson engines and did not require even a short run for take-off. They were delivered in 1939. Three went to France with the BEF to be flown for Army liaison and spotting by RAF pilots. The other two were to be used at sea in anti-submarine and gunnery spotting roles. But their further history, if any, is now obscure.

Meanwhile the design of helicopters progressed dramatically during the 1930s. On 26 June 1936 the Foche-Achgelis Fa.61, designed by Dr Heinrich K.J. Foche, took to the air for the first time. The Fa.61 was basically the fuselage of a Focke-Wulf FW44 Stieglitz (Goldfinch) trainer biplane, with the original 160 h.p. Bramo Sh.14A radial engine driving (through shafts and gearing) two 3-bladed 23 foot diameter rotors, rotating in opposite directions, mounted on steel tube pylon out-riggers. A small propeller in the conventional position at the front merely cooled the engine.

The Fa.61 soon established a series of helicopter records: distance in a closed circuit, 50 miles; distance in a straight line, 67.7 miles; speed over 20 kilometres, 76 mph; duration of flight, 1 hour, 21 minutes; height, 8,002 feet. In 1938 the Fa.61 pulled off a stunning publicity *coup* when the celebrated woman pilot Hanna Reitsch flew it on 14 successive evenings before audiences of 20,000, including foreign military and air attaches, *inside* the huge Deutschlandhalle during the Berlin Motor Show. In the same year another Fa.61 pushed the altitude record for a helicopter to 11,243 feet, and the distance to 143 miles.

The Kriegsmarine showed a consistent interest in helicopters for use in small ships and U-boats. During the Second World War they flew the Flettner F.1282 Kolibri (Hummingbird) and the Fa.223 Drache (Kite), the largest helicopter of the war, capable of lifting six people. A small rotary wing kite, the Fa.330 Bachstelze (Wagtail) was used for spotting from U-boats.

The idea of using a helicopter to raise a spotter's height of eye at sea also appealed to the Admiralty, who had noted the Fa.61's prowess. The Ministry of Supply offered to buy an Fa.61 but the Germans, understandably, hedged about delivery dates and asked for excessive prices and in the end no Fa.61 was ever forthcoming.

The Admiralty could soon have had their own helicopter. Mr C.G. Pullin, Cierva's chief designer, and the engineering firm of C. & J. Weir of Glasgow produced a helicopter, called the Weir W5, which first flew on 29 October 1939. It was an advanced and promising design but work on it lapsed under the pressure of wartime events in July 1940. Had development on the W5 continued, the Royal Navy might well have had operational helicopters at sea some years before they actually came into service.

Thus, the Royal Navy had to turn for its first helicopters to the United States and in particular to Igor Sikorsky, who had fled to America after the Russian Revolution. Sikorsky's VS-300 helicopter had made its first 'tethered' flight on 14 September 1939, and its first 'free' flight on 13 May the following year. But the US Navy could not at first see any future in helicopters. It was the US Army Air Corps who awarded Igor Sikorsky a contract to develop the VS-300.

In 1941, Captain Caspar John (a notable naval aviator and a future First Sea Lord) who was then Chief Naval Representative at the Ministry of Aircraft

Production and Director General Naval Aircraft Development and Production realised that the Fleet Air Arm's best chance, indeed its only chance, of getting the aircraft it needed would be from the United States.

John sent Brie (now Wing Commander) to America to investigate the possibilities of using autogiros in an anti-submarine role. Trials of the US Pitcairn Autogiro were carried out on board the merchantman *Empire Mersey*. They were satisfactory enough, but Brie also witnessed a demonstration of the VS-300 which made it clear to him, as to everybody else, that the future lay with the helicopter. Autogiros were dropped.

In October 1942 John himself set off for America representing the Admiralty in a joint Admiralty-Air Ministry Mission to Washington under the Minister of Aircraft Production, Oliver Lyttleton. Their task was to place the Air side of the British Admiralty Delegation to Washington upon a proper footing, to find out what the Americans were willing to provide, and to arrange it quickly. The result was the signing of a joint agreement setting out firm allocations of aircraft for the first six months of 1943, and provisional arrangements for the second six months.

Caspar John established very good relations with his opposite numbers in the States. 'From my first contact with the US Navy,' he wrote, 'I had nothing but help and cooperation, for which the Royal Navy owes a major debt of gratitude. We immediately established an organisation for procuring and distributing what was mutually agreed were our requirements surplus to the US Navy's needs. This involved organising the training of air and ground crews to fly and maintain the quite new and different types of US Navy aircraft'.

Amongst those new types of aircraft were to be helicopters. While Caspar John was in the States in 1942 he flew to the Vought-Sikorsky factory at Stratford, Connecticut, to meet Igor Sikorsky and see how his helicopter work was progressing. Sikorsky's new XR-4 had flown for the first time in January 1942, but the US Navy's Bureau of Aeronautics was still unconvinced the helicopter had a future at sea.

Caspar John took the opposite view. 'I was strolling with Igor Sikorsky one day,' he said, 'and I mentioned to him the problem of the anti-submarine war in the Atlantic. He had been an ardent supporter of the large flying boat, and I asked him if he could bring his talents to bear on rotary winged aircraft in the anti-submarine role. He seemed more interested in photography at the time but replied, "Yes, there are obvious advantages in stationary flight; you shall have one of my YR4A helicopters tomorrow for whatever tests you wish." '

This promise bore fruit when Caspar John returned to Washington in March 1943 as Naval Air Representative in the British Admiralty Delegation, representing the Fifth Sea Lord (who was responsible for naval air affairs on the Admiralty Board), and Naval Air Attache at the British Embassy. A joint Board for the Evaluation of the Helicopter in Anti-Submarine Warfare, with representatives from the US Coastguard and the Royal Navy, was formed early in 1943 to study the feasibility of operating helicopters at sea in all weather conditions, not just from aircraft carrier flight decks but from platforms fitted in other ships.

Empire Mersey had been sunk in October 1942, so a similar platform, some 90 feet by 40, was constructed on the tanker *Daghestan*. Trials with two XR-4s, with 180 h.p. Warner Super Scarab engines, were carried out in Long Island Sound. The XR-4s were unarmed, so there was no assessment of weapon capability, but these were the first series of flying and handling trials of a true helicopter at sea. Two XR-4s were embarked in *Daghestan* when the ship joined a convoy to the United Kingdom. One Navy pilot, two RAF pilots and a US Coast Guard pilot also embarked, to carry out flying trials on passage. But rough weather prevented any flying except for one take-off and landing by the US Coast Guard pilot in mid-Atlantic.

However, the Admiralty had seen enough and boldly ordered no less than 250 R-4Bs, which had a more powerful engine than the R-4. This was, as Caspar John said, 'a remarkable act of faith, not supported by the US Navy, but heavily backed by the US Army Air Corps, and by the US Coast Guard on whose airfield, Floyd Bennett, we established an international Helicopter Training School, with the White Ensign proudly flying'.

No. 1 Helicopter (Instructors) Course began at Floyd Bennett, near New York, in March 1944 with six RN pilots, two RAF pilots, and one Army pilot as students. The requirement was that all should have had at least 500 flying hours solo in fixed-wing aircraft but this was soon found to be excessive. An RN pilot

Hoverfly at HMS *Excellent*, Whale Island, Portsmouth 1945. Pilot Lt Albeury RNVR

who joined later had had only 60 hours on fixed-wing and did as well as anybody on that course. The course lasted four months with some 70 hours helicopter flying.

The war ended before R-4s came into full production and the Admiralty's 250 order was cancelled. But 52 R-4Bs, named Hoverfly I in the Royal Navy, were supplied under Lend-Lease. Some were retained at Floyd Bennett but some did cross the Atlantic. Nine Hoverflys were loaded on to the escort carrier HMS *Thane* at Newark, New Jersey, on 30 December 1944 and the ship moved to New York on 1 January 1945. *Thane* sailed on 3 January and arrived at Belfast on 14th when some aircraft were offloaded to Sydenham.

The ship sailed for Glasgow on 15 January but was torpedoed and irreparably damaged by U-482 off the Clyde Light Vessel the same day. She was towed into the Clyde estuary and anchored off Greenock, moving later to the Gareloch where the Hoverflys were flown off on 17 January, initially to Abbotsinch.

No. 1 Helicopter Flight was formed in January 1945 by Lt P. Allbeury and Lt Ken Reed and was stationed on the football pitch at HMS *Excellent*, the gunnery school at Whale Island. This, one of the first helicopter stations in the Navy, provided a taxi service to any of the Island's outlying establishments in the area, to Larkhill on Salisbury Plain and to HMS *Vernon*, the torpedo, mining and electrical school, which was then at Roedean School.

No. 2 Flight, with Lt Neil Fuller and Lt Alan Bristow, arrived in February 1945 at HMS *Tern*, RNAS Twatt, in the Orkneys where they were flown by 771 NAS for fleet communications and gunnery radar calibration. The first helicopter ditching in the Royal Navy occurred when a Hoverfly from *Tern*, piloted by Lt 'Dolly' Gray, had an engine failure and ditched in Scapa Flow while calibrating a battleship's gunnery radar. Gray and his passenger Cdr Dickson escaped but not until the helicopter had sunk to a depth of some 40 to 50 feet. Gray later reported that Cdr Dickson was considerably annoyed by the loss of his new hat while waiting to be rescued.

During 771's stay in the Orkneys, Lt Alan Bristow landed Hoverfly FT836 on 'A' turret of the battleship HMS *Anson* off Scapa Flow on 4 and 5 April 1945. These, the first helicopter landings on a capital ship in the Royal Navy, called for precise flying, 'B' turret having to be trained on the beam at Bristow's request. Even then there was little rotor blade clearance.

Other Helicopter Flights were formed, No.3 based at RN Radar Establishment, Haslemere, Surrey, No.4 based at HMS *Osprey*, Portland, No.5 at Admiralty Trials and Development Unit, HMS *Siskin*, RNAS Gosport, No.6 at Dartmouth for coastal hydrographic surveying, and No.7 at the Irish Army barracks at Tralee, also for hydrographic surveying.

After the war, the Fleet moved south from Scapa and 771 NAS moved too, its fixed wing aircraft to Zeals in Somerset and the helicopter flight to temporary quarters at Worthy Down. Lt Cdr Len Page RCN, who was in command of 771's helicopter flight, and Bristow flew their Hoverfly YR4Bs from Twatt to Worthy Down, 754 miles in twelve hours, spread over two days – an epic flight for helicopters in those days.

In September 1945 the Flight moved from Worthy Down to a hangar and slipway in Portland Dockyard. There the Flight, now commanded by Bristow, had four Hoverflys for gunnery spotting, radar calibration, airborne photography, anti-submarine warfare and helicopter pilot training.

Among experiments carried out at Portland were trials on the landing and handling of helicopters on small ships. On 5 September 1946, Alan Bristow with Lt Parkinson as his observer, landed his Hoverfly YR4B KK992, fitted with standard wheel undercarriage, on a wooden platform, 24 feet by 28 feet, specially fitted on the stern of the frigate HMS *Helmsdale* – the first helicopter landing on a frigate.

The first tail rotor failure of a Royal Navy helicopter occurred at Portland when Bristow was carrying out aerial photography of torpedo trials. Luckily, the helicopter was fitted with inflated rubber pontoons and Bristow was able to land it without damage in Portland harbour.

After Bristow was 'demobbed' in October 1946, Lt Cdr Parkinson and Lt Ken Reed joined 771 NAS at Portland (Reed being acclaimed in the Dorset Daily Echo as 'the Royal Navy's No 1 Hover-pilot'). On 1 February 1947, Reed flew his R-4 Hoverfly through a snow-storm to take mail to the battleship HMS *Vanguard* as she steamed down Channel, forty miles south of Portland, on her way to the Royal Tour of South Africa. The Royal Family were surprised and delighted when Reed landed his R-4 in brilliant sunshine on *Vanguard*'s quarterdeck.

Hoverfly R4B of 705 NAS landing on HMS *Vanguard*. Pilot Lt K. Reed

Four Motor Torpedo Boats had been stationed along Reed's route as navigational and to provide rescue if needed. However, there were no MTBs for the return flight with mail to Gosport where a courier was waiting to take it to Buckingham Palace and Reed had to fly through the continuing snow-storms by dead reckoning.

Later that year, 771's helicopters flew to Gosport to supply the nucleus of 705 NAS which reformed on 7 May 1947 as the Naval Helicopter Training Squadron, with Reed as its Commanding Officer. This was the true beginning of squadron helicopter flying in the Royal Navy.

The squadron's duties were wide-ranging: to train helicopter pilots, crewmen and maintenance personnel, to evaluate new helicopter equipment, to develop helicopter techniques, and to provide helicopters for special trials, Fleet requirements and Search and Rescue in the Gosport/Lee-on-Solent area.

The squadron had seven of the now familiar Hoverfly Is, with 180 h.p. Warner engines, a loaded weight of 2,530 lbs., a maximum speed of 75 knots, a ceiling of 8,000 feet and a range of 220 miles. Later there were also four Hoverfly IIs (Sikorsky R-6s). These had 245 h.p. Franklin engines, a loaded weight of 2,600 lbs., maximum speed 100 knots, and a ceiling of 10,000 feet. In practice they were little or no improvement on the Hoverfly Is.

Early experiments in Search and Rescue (SAR) took place in the late 1940s at the Air Sea Warfare Development Unit at RAF Thorney Island. Although there was a naval interest in the Naval Air Sea Warfare Development Unit (NASWDU) and SAR was officially one of 705 NAS commitments, in practice 705 did little in the SAR field because the Hoverfly was grossly under-powered. On a hot, still day it would barely lift its pilot, let alone the added weight of a casualty. Practical helicopter SAR in the Royal Navy had to await the arrival of the Westland-Sikorsky Dragonfly.

The Sikorsky S.51 as it was known in America, first flew in March 1946. Westlands, of Yeovil in Somerset, obtained a licence to manufacture them in December 1946. The first Westland-built Dragonfly flew on 5 October 1948, and the first production model on 22 June 1949. Sea trials with an American built Dragonfly on loan began in the light fleet carrier *Vengeance* in 1949. The first delivery flight took place on 13 January 1950 and the Squadron had taken delivery of 12 Dragonflies by June.

Trials continued with British-built Dragonflies on board the Royal Fleet Auxiliary *Fort Duquesne* in January 1951. In very rough weather in the Channel, when wind speeds gusted to 40 knots and the specially built helicopter platform on *Fort Duquesne*'s stern was sometimes rising and falling some twenty feet, Lt Cdr Sydney Suthers DSC and Lt Morton successfully carried out 183 landings in 20 days.

The Westland Dragonfly was the Royal Navy's first 'real' helicopter. With a crew of two – pilot and aircrewman – a loaded weight of 5,870 lbs, and a 550 h.p. Alvis Leonides 50 engine, giving a speed of 95 knots, climb rate of 970 feet/minute, service ceiling of 13,200 feet and a range of 300 miles, and fitted

Dragonfly HR1 operating from RAF *Fort Duquesne*

with a hoisting winch, it proved itself to be an excellent aircraft, quickly replacing destroyers as 'plane guards' for aircraft carriers. The first 'ship's flight' Dragonfly embarked in *Indomitable*, flagship of Admiral Sir Philip Vian, Commander-in-Chief Home Fleet, on 12 January 1951.

Dragonflies also replaced Sea Otters for air-sea rescue, which began to assume great importance as a role for helicopters from the very earliest days. It was quickly realised that SAR sorties were not just acts of good neighbourliness. They also had an immediacy and an urgency which was excellent training for the aircrews. SAR missions were 'for real', in a way no training exercise, however realistically staged, could ever be.

As early as the autumn of 1951 705 NAS also began to carry out research with RAF medical officers into SAR equipment, such as new immersion suits, and techniques, such as winching an injured or unconscious casualty up from a dinghy at sea.

On the morning of 17 April 1951, the submarine *Affray* failed to surface from an exercise dive in the English Channel. When the SUBSMASH signal (that a submarine was overdue) was made, one of the first searchers in the air

Dragonfly HR3 of the Station Flight, Ford, practising winching was a Sea Otter piloted by Lt V. Walker, the duty SAR pilot at RNAS St Merryn, who took off with CPO ('Donkey') Bray as aircrewman soon after 11.30 that morning. But no sooner had Bray switched on the aircraft's radar than the cockpit filled with smoke from a burning valve in the radar set.

At the same time Walker noticed his engine rpm dropping and soon afterwards he heard 'an almighty bang' as the propeller fell away to port. Although the 'Sea Otter was not a pleasant aircraft to fly and glided like a brick' Walker missed some overhead electricity cables, which he did not see until they were past, and put the aircraft down in a field of Cornish broccoli. Bray, who had not even had time to sit down, was unhurt but knocked himself out when jumping from the aircraft.

When the SUBSMASH signal was received at Gosport, nine Dragonflies of 705 NAS moved to Chickerell, a landing field near Portland. They took off at dawn the next day, 18 April, and flew an average of four hours each as part of a huge search and rescue operation, involving other submarines, more than twenty British, American, French and Dutch warships, a salvage team of tugs and lifting vessels, every lifeboat on the South Coast, and maritime patrols by naval and RAF aircraft. But nobody sighted anything throughout that day.

Affray had been expected to surface some 20 miles south-east of Start Point and the search began there. On 19 April submarines picked up faint hull-tapping sounds. Listeners in the submarine HMS *Ambush* thought they detected the code signal for 'We Are Trapped on the bottom'. A buoy marker was dropped, and 705's helicopters joined the crowd around the spot, which was ringed with vessels. Twelve grenades were fired, to inform *Affray*'s survivors that rescue ships were now on the surface nearby, and they could proceed with their escape.

Ships and helicopters waited in a state of high expectation. But nothing happened. Nobody appeared. It was a false alarm. 'It was the most disappointing time in our lives', said Mr D.W.F. Elliott, a Commissioned Pilot flying one of 705's Dragonflies that day.

The immediate search was called off on the evening of 19 April because there was no longer any great urgency to save life. *Affray* was actually found by an underwater TV cameras almost nine weeks later, on 14 June, lying near the edge of Hurd's Deep, 67 miles south-west of St Catherine's Lighthouse and 37 miles south west of her last reported diving position.

On 10 January 1952, two Dragonflies flown by Lt Cdr Suthers, now CO of 705 NAS, and Lt Farquharson set off from Gosport in appalling weather to try and assist the ship *Flying Enterprise*, adrift and sinking south-west of Ireland, with only her master Kurt Carlsen and Kenneth Dancy, mate of the tug *Turmoil*, on board her.

Farquharson's Dragonfly went unserviceable at Exeter airport. Suthers pressed on to reach Culdrose. He and Commissioned Observer J. Lambert took off in a 50 m.p.h. gale to reconnoitre *Flying Enterprise*'s position and if possible rescue the two men. Ten miles off the Lizard, when the ship's last reported position was still some thirty miles further on, Suthers realised his

Dragonfly could never reach the ship and return safely in that weather, and so wisely turned back.

In 1952 detached units of 705 NAS embarked in *Ocean* and *Campania* who sailed from the United Kingdom in June for the British atomic bomb tests at the Monte Bello islands, west of Australia. On 3 October 1952, the first British atomic bomb detonated above the frigate *Plym*, vapourising the ship in a colossal fire ball and a towering 'mushroom' cloud of smoke.

An hour later a Dragonfly flown by Lt Cdr D.T.J. Stanley, MBE, DFC, flew over the scene, dipping a container on a length of line into the sea to collect water samples. A second Dragonfly flown by Lt R. Leonard flew over the ground zero of the explosion to retrieve the heads of rockets which had been fired through the 'mushroom' cloud. If nothing else, these two sorties showed the Navy's, and the crew's, faith in the reliability of the Dragonfly and its engine.

On 29 October 1952, 848 NAS was formed under Lt Cdr Suthers from a nucleus of 705 NAS. Lt Cdr H. Spedding took over command of 705. On 21 November, 705 NAS led the Fly Past when Her Majesty Queen Elizabeth II visited Home Air Command, Lee-on-Solent. In December, 705's helicopters winched off four of the crew of the Danish motor torpedo boat *Havoernen* which ran aground on the Scrobie Sands off Great Yarmouth.

These stories were all well covered in the national press. But, in January 1953, 705 NAS took part in a huge international rescue operation which put helicopters firmly into the public eye.

3 Dutch Floods, Malayan Bandits and Greek Earthquakes

On the night of Saturday 31 January 1953, in the middle of a particularly hard and bitter winter, a combination of gale force north-easterly winds and a high spring tide breached the coastal defences on both sides of the North Sea. Hundreds of square miles of the lowest lying land in East Anglia and the Zeeland area of Holland were flooded by the sea. Over 300 people were drowned in England and over 1,300 in Holland, together with countless numbers of livestock. Thousands of people were made homeless. All power supplies failed, road and rail communications were disrupted and water contaminated in the affected areas.

The first call for helicopter assistance was at 6.30 am on Sunday 1 February, for two helicopters to rescue a small party of people marooned on the eastern end of the Isle of Sheppey. The CO of 705 Squadron, Lt Cdr H.R. Spedding, was called from his home at 6.40 am. Two Dragonflies, one flown by Spedding himself and the other by Lt G. Perks, took off from Gosport at 7.40 am.

The weather was appalling, with high winds and very poor visibility in frequent snow squalls. When they arrived, the helicopter pilots were told that the rescue had already been made and were ordered to fly to Manston. After a day of 'standing by', the two helicopters made a reconnaissance of the north Kent coast and landed at West Malling for an overnight stay.

By now, the full force of the gale and the spring tide had struck Holland. Enormous breaks were torn in the dykes and the sea flooded the islands of Over Flakkee, Schouwen and Tholen and huge areas of the mainland. The Dutch government requested helicoper assistance. That Sunday night the duty air officer at Gosport received an urgent signal:

UNCLASSIFIED
OPERATIONAL IMMEDIATE
FROM ADMIRALTY
TO FO AIR (HOME)
INFO C-IN-C PORTSMOUTH C-IN-C NORE NAS LEE-ON-SOLENT NAS GOSPORT BNA HAGUE
PREPARE ALL AVAILABLE HELICOPTERS FOR SERVICE.

FOUR ARE TO BE PREPARED TO PROCEED TO HOLLAND (GILZE-RIJEN) AS SOON AS READY TOMORROW FOR RESCUE SERVICE. CONFIRMATORY SIGNAL REGARDING FLIGHT WILL BE MADE. REMAINDER TO BE RETAINED AT SHORT NOTICE FOR HOLLAND. C-IN-C NORE IS TO RETAIN CONTROL OF THE TWO ALREADY LENT UNTIL FURTHER INSTRUCTIONS ARE ISSUED.

Two more Dragonflies left Gosport for West Malling at 7.30 am on Monday 2 February. The weather was still bad and at least once they lost their way, having to descend and check their position by reading the name on a Southern Railway platform, before finally landing at West Malling.

At 9.30 the CO and three others left for Holland, flying in and out of persistent snow storms in atrocious flying conditions. At one point they had to fly sideways, looking through the open doors of the helicopters, because snow was freezing on the windscreens and obscuring the view forward. Again, they were lost in a snow storm after crossing the Dutch coast and had to land in a field. The farmer, who could not speak English, was shown a map and pointed the direction of Gilze-Rijen, their destination.

But the bad weather forced them to divert to Woensdrecht, an airfield near Antwerp, where they refuelled and ate cheese sandwiches. They flew onwards to arrive at Gilze-Rijen, the Dutch Air Force base, at 2.50 pm. Apart from a Royal Netherlands Navy S.51 and a Bell from SABENA, the Belgian airline, these were the first helicopters to arrive.

24 January 1953, Grand Harbour, Malta. Two Dragonflies replaced the Sea Otter in the SAR role. Pilot of Sea Otter, Mr Chaplin, pilot of Dragonfly, Lt Cdr Paterson

The Dutch authorities had still not realised the full magnitude of the disaster which had struck their country. They knew that for nearly two days large areas of the countryside, almost half of Holland, had been cut off, but they had not yet been able to assess the scale or nature of the assistance required. Communications between the mainland and the islands had been completely severed. The only means of finding out conditions locally was by fixed-wing aircraft reconnaissance flights.

The first helicopter sorties were to take radio operators and their equipment to strategic points in the flooded areas. With darkness coming on, the helicopters had to return direct to base after unloading their cargoes.

Gilze-Rijen was some 45 to 50 minutes flying time by helicopter from the centre of the flooded area. Woensdrecht was about 30 miles nearer. It was suggested, and decided, that Woensdrecht be used as an operating base during the day, with the helicopters returning to Gilze-Rijen at nightfall.

During that first night 705 NAS maintenance personnel arrived by air from Gosport and removed passenger seats and non-essential loose fittings and equipment from inside the helicopters.

The aircrews were briefed at 7 am on Tuesday 3 February and the four helicopters were airborne by first light. The priorities were to take urgently needed radio equipment, food, drugs and medical supplies to isolated communities.

After that, 705 NAS went straight into rescues, picking up whoever they saw wherever they saw them. Sorties were flown all day and some 40 people were winched to safety from house-tops and other inaccessible places. There was little or no briefing for these first sorties. It was, as Senior Commissioned Pilot Doug Elliott said, 'just a question of using your loaf'.

Another five Dragonflies of 705 NAS flew over on Tuesday 3 February. The helicopters flew over a desolate, apparently lifeless scene, more sea than land. Here and there the threads of dykes and flooded roadways showed up through the water surface, with the occasional solitary windmill, standing like a ship becalmed. There were floating corpses, of horses, cattle, pigs, dogs and cats, by the hundred. There were surviving animals, huddled on higher ground wherever they could find shelter from the severe weather.

Everything was in shades of grey: grey troubled waters, whipped by the northerly winds, grey threatening skies bearing ever more grey snow-clouds, and grey stretches of land marooned in wastes of water. The very shape of Holland had vanished. The island of Schouwen-Duiveland, for instance, had virtually disappeared. Helicopters flew to the town of Oosterland, where many of the houses were almost submerged.

One of the first on the scene was piloted by Lt Ron Crayton. 'It was a sight I shall never forget', he said. 'You see pictures of floods in this country and you think, what are they worrying about? It's nothing compared to this. Here the whole countryside was under water. It was just a mass of water as far as you could see, with dykes sticking up here and there. Quite frightening'.

There were early difficulties over maps. The pilots were, of course,

Dutch floods, February 1953

unfamiliar with a landscape which, in its flooded state, was in any case almost featureless. As Lt 'Dick' Turpin said, 'We didn't know where we were picking them up from. We didn't know where we were taking them to. When we had dropped somebody off we didn't know where to go, to go back to where we got them from in the first place! So we tended to separate families from each other which caused a bit of distress'.

There were also difficulties over language. It was disappointing for the helicopter crews to land in a village where help was obviously needed and to find that the Dutch could not make themselves understood. Many of the country people had never seen a helicopter in their lives before. The young were fascinated, but the old were often terrified. Some did not realise why the helicopter had come and it was hard to persuade them, using only sign language, to come on board. These difficulties were partly resolved with the help of English-speaking Dutch naval officers, who went along in the Dragonflies to interpret and to reassure the rescued. This solved the problem and many people owed their lives to these young Dutch officers.

The pilots tended to look first for those on roof-tops or waving from windows – people on their own or obviously injured or in distress. Priority was given to the very young and the very old, to mothers with babies, to the sick and injured. A crowd who had gathered together on the top of a dyke or on a dry patch of land would usually be left for the time being, to be dealt with later.

At the end of the first day, some 200 people had been flown to safety and the nine helicopters had flown 63 hours. Luckily, flight distances were small and sorties were generally short. People were taken to the nearest place which had communications with the sea. An armada of boats and small shipping was waiting to evacuate them to Rotterdam and other large towns.

Landing sites were organised by clearing trees and other obstructions. In some places people were quick to learn and cleared sites and marked them with white strips. Typical sites were on the roads running along the tops of dykes, and jetties alongside small canals leading from the sea. Where a village was completely flooded, the only suitable landing place was often the church square.

On Wednesday 4 February, helicopters once more took off at dawn, with food, medicines and radio equipment. When these had been landed, the helicopters searched for survivors, concentrating on the island of Schouwen where the villages of Oosterland and Neiuwerkerk were evacuated. A total of 210 people were rescued, about 40 of them by winch, in 64 flying hours.

Not all the Dragonflies had winches, so pilots listened out on common radio frequency. If a pilot flying a winchless helicopter came across a situation needing a winch, he could call for a winch-fitted helicopter to assist.

There were some harrowing stories. One helicopter landed in a foot of snow to recover a young boy of about fourteen. He had seen his father, mother, and three brothers and sisters all disappear in the raging flood waters, so that he was now the sole survivor of his family. A mother gave her baby up to be rescued, saying she herself would wait for the next flight. When the helicopter returned she was nowhere to be seen, having probably died of cold and exposure. One old lady and her husband were rescued, but when they came to lift her out of the helicopter she was dead.

It was seldom possible to send a crewman down to assist the rescued, who thus had to work out for themselves how to put on the strop. On one flight Turpin saw people waving agitatedly to him from the top storey of a house. He lowered the strop and, to his consternation, saw it taken through the window into the house.

Hovering above, Turpin began to grow anxious. 'I moved out away from the house to try and see what was going on', he said. 'All of a sudden Reggie (Lt R. Hart, his observer and crewman) said 'There's somebody coming out of the window!'. And this lady, probably in her mid-sixties, dressed all in black, shot out of that window like a cork out of a bottle and came swinging out on the wire! She had very bad grazing on her legs, and she had the strop on the wrong way round, so that the harness was up her back, but she was cheerful enough and very glad to get into the helicopter. It was very fortunate that she wasn't lost'.

Occasionally conversation between rescuers and rescued took on a surrealist note. When Commissioned Pilot R. Williams embarked a very stout lady, clearly to him in an advanced state of pregnancy, he told her she was the first pregnant woman he had ever rescued. 'But I am not pregnant,' she said. 'You're not rescued yet', he said, gallantly.

There were surprisingly few accidents. The only fatality was an unwary Dutchman who was killed when he walked into the tail rotor of a Bristol

An old lady being helped to safety after helicopter rescue in Dutch floods of February 1953

Sycamore which had come to rescue him.

That Sycamore was one of several which arrived on Wednesday 4 February, from the Bristol Company's works at Filton, from the Ministry of Supply's experimental establishment at Boscombe Down and from the Army's Experimental Helicopter Unit at Middle Wallop. There was also a Dragonfly from British European Airways, which had lately started a passenger service from Cardiff to Liverpool, and helicopters from Belgium and S.55s from US bases in Europe. In fact, every available helicopter in Europe had flown to Holland to lend a hand.

On Thursday 5 February, the aircraft were once again off at first light although one had to return with severe rotor-head vibration – the only major unserviceability of the whole rescue operation. Some 200 people were evacuated that day from the village of Nieuwe-Tonge, on the island of Over Flakkee. There were only three landing sites in the village, each with enough room for only one helicopter at a time. Sometimes, there were between fifteen and twenty helicopters circling overhead, queueing for their turn to land. As Spedding said, 'it was rather like Piccadilly Circus!'

The sole accident to a helicopter was on 8 February, when Lt Crayton was flying out some radio operators and had to land on Acthuisen, on Over Flakkee. 'It was snowing and blowing hard,' he said. 'By that time there were small helicopter pads on the dykes so I decided to get down on one of them until the weather cleared. I landed and began to shut down. But unknowingly I landed on a sheet of ice. The wind was very strong and as the rotor slowed down the wind blew the helicopter backwards. I tried to wind the power on again but the tail rotor struck a post. I lost the tail rotor. The helicopter spun round and landed in about twelve feet of water. We (myself and a Dutch officer) had to get into the rubber dinghy'. They were recovered later in the day by an American Sikorsky S.55. The Dragonfly was retrieved some days later.

On Thursday 5 February Lt E. Spreadbury of 705 took Dutch officials for a tour of the flooded area, to search for survivors and to test the strength of the dykes. On the Friday, the helicopters made an early start and searched the island of Tholen. Nobody was seen in need of help. By midday it was snowing hard and visibility had dropped to 200 yards. The crews were thankful when flying was cancelled for the day.

By that Friday, 'Phase One' of the rescue was complete. Every pilot had flown up to 8½ hours a day in the most tiring conditions. 705 NAS had flown 225 hours 55 minutes, to rescue 734 people, three dogs and one cat. By the end of the week everyone cut off by the floods had been rescued, although there were still livestock by the thousands, starving and dying, although surrounded by water, of thirst.

All the usual limits and constraints on flying were disregarded while the emergency lasted. For instance, the centre of gravity was critical in a Dragonfly in flight. Lead weights were carried which could be transferred from forward to aft, to adjust for passengers. But these were soon dispensed with, the pilots often flying with the cyclic on the limits of its stops.

Officially a Dragonfly carried three or four: pilot, crewman, and one or two passengers, depending upon the seat configuration. 705 Dragonflies routinely carried five or more, the record being eight, albeit three of them children – and a dog.

Flying in such consistently cold and rough weather was very uncomfortable. There was no cockpit heating and the doors were always open. Thus greatcoats were the rig of every day, even in the air. The Dragonfly was essentially a 'handraulic' aircraft, with all manual controls, and flying it was very tiring, physically and mentally. As they said, 'you couldn't take your hands off the controls for a moment, not even to scratch your nose'. Nevertheless, those in 705 who smoked did smoke constantly, regardless of regulations, whilst flying on rescue work (the Dragonfly used high octane avgas!).

The Dragonfly, like the Hoverfly before it, was grossly under-powered. The consistently strong winds, of 15 knots or more, and the cold air temperature were ideal for helicopter flying but to get their overloaded aircraft off, pilots often had to employ a technique known as 'milking': lowering the collective with the left hand, twisting open the throttle and lowering the pitch thus allowing the r.p.m. to build up, then raising the collective and using the increased inertia in the rotor head to give added lift, then repeating the process, with left hand and then right hand – hence the term 'milking'.

In Holland, 705 discovered what a robust and reliable aircraft the Dragonfly was. Certainly they pushed it well beyond its official design limits. Aircraft flew beyond the laid-down hours for engines and air frames. Unserviceable instruments were ignored. 'You couldn't see someone down there in distress,' said Crayton, 'and say "I'll come back for you later". You just piled them in'. 'As long as the rotors would go round and you had an oil pressure', said 'Dick' Turpin, 'you flew – from first light until last light every day'.

There were at that time only a handful of helicopter pilots in the Royal Navy. Many of them had about 50 hours in helicopters, although others such as Doug Elliott, who had begun as a Rating Pilot in 1938, had as much as 380 hours on Dragonflies. Some of the pilots in Holland were still students, on their initial helicopter training course with 705. Commissioned Pilot Mr Richard Williams, for example, was a very experienced fixed-wing pilot, but he had only joined the helicopter course at Gosport on 8 January. But by the beginning of February he was flying 'live' SAR sorties over Holland. He was 'thrown in at the deep end' and, like the rest, had to evolve and perfect SAR flying techniques as he went along.

On 9 February Dick Turpin had the honour of flying Queen Juliana on a tour of the flood-devastated areas. The Queen had been very concerned about the plight of her people and this trip (her first ever in a helicopter) gave her a chance to see for herself. Next day, Bob Spedding himself flew HRH Prince Bernhardt on a similar tour. The whole Squadron were entertained, and thanked for all their efforts, by Queen Juliana and Prince Bernhardt at the Royal Palace at Soesdyke on 17 February.

At the request of the Dutch Government 705 NAS stayed until 19 February because exceptionally high spring tides were expected again on Sunday and Monday 15th and 16th. The main dykes had been weakened by the initial flooding and if there were strong westerly winds again with the high tides, a very large area of the mainland would have been inundated.

Three helicopters were available every day until Saturday 14 February when the whole Squadron came to readiness until the following Tuesday. However, the weather was fine, the dykes held and the helicopters were not needed.

Dragonfly, Dutch floods, February 1953

Whilst in Holland, the aircrews and the maintenance crews lived in huts on the airfield at Gilze-Rijen. They existed principally on coffee, Dutch cheeses, and bread – curiously garnished with 'hundreds and thousands' normally seen decorating childrens' birthday cakes. There were also hard-boiled eggs. Competitions were held in the evenings to see who could consume the most.

When this diet palled, as it soon did, 705 appealed to their alma mater at Gosport for fresh supplies. An aged but eagerly awaited Avro Anson staggered through the snow storms to Woensdrecht. But it was found to be full of loaves of bread.

There was another competition, besides eating hard-boiled eggs – for who could rescue the most people. This was, regrettably, somewhat accentuated in the press. Lt R.A. Thurstan, Senior Pilot of 705 NAS, was credited with 102 rescues in a single day's continuous flying, including one family of seven people recovered from a strip of land only ten yards long by seven wide. Bob Spedding's personal score was 110. But the undoubted overall winner was 705's 'Crab', Flt Lt D.C.L. (Danny) Kearns RAF, who rescued a total of 147 in five days' flying.

However, comparisons were unfair. Winching survivors took much longer than landing to pick them up. Not all the Dragonflies in Holland were fitted with winches (only two of the first four had winches). The Squadron as a whole rescued over 800 people; 64 of them were winched up, most of them by Turpin and Crayton. The Squadron flew a daily average of over 60 hours for a total of 401 hours 55 minutes.

So ended a most successful operation, which had yielded priceless first-hand experience of how to handle SAR helicopters in bad weather and over unfamiliar territory, away from a properly-equipped base and over a period of time.

Some quarters in the rest of the Navy, the 'fish-head' Navy, still had to come to terms with helicopters. The only unpleasantness of 705's stay in Holland was an unexpected disagreement with the Commanding Officer of the Rhine Flotilla. His own ships were themselves doing invaluable relief work, but he demanded, first, that a helicopter be placed permanently at his disposal and, second, that he should have operational control over 705 NAS and their movements.

This was a classical example of the traditional Navy reacting to a new development. It was resolved by a short conference between the CO Rhine Flotilla and the CO 705 NAS. It took place in a staff car at Woensdrecht. Observers noted that the car windows were considerably steamed up, but Bob Spedding eventually emerged with his command of his own Squadron intact.

705 NAS were to have flown home on 19 February but were delayed by fog. They finally took off on 20th and landed at 5.05 pm that evening at Gosport (where, in spite of their exertions, they still had first to clear Customs).

The pilots who took part in the Dutch flood operations were Lt Cdr H.R. Spedding, Lt R. Turpin, Lt R.R. Crayton, Lt G. Perks, Lt P.Earl, Lt R.A. Thurstan, Lt E.C. Spreadbury, Senior Comd Pilot D.W.F. Elliott, Comd

Pilot R. Williams, Flt Lt D.C.L. Kearns RAF and Lt J. Reilly US Navy. The crewmen were Lt R.F. Hart, Sub Lt A. Bishop, Aircrewmen S. Craig, L. Stevens and A. Japp, and PO Tel G. Jones.

Vice Admiral J.A.S. Eccles, Flag Officer Air (Home), published a Special Order of the Day – the helicopter branch of the Royal Navy's first public commendation:

Service in Dutch Flood Disaster

Between the 2nd and 20 February 1953, 705 Squadron from RN Air Station Gosport was in Holland working under the Netherlands Territorial Command to carry out rescue and relief measures in connection with the flood. Testimonials to the good work of the Squadron have reached me from many quarters and have now received a full report of its activities I wish particularly to commend the following officers and ratings.

Lieutenant Commander H.R. Spedding – For initiative, energy and fine leadership in command of the Squadron as well as for flying very long hours and personally rescuing a large number of people. His ready acceptance of risk, sense of responsibility and devotion to duty were of the highest order.

Lieutenant R.A. Thurstan, Flight Lieutenant D.C.L. Kearns, Lieutenant E.C. Spreadbury, Lieutenant G. Perks, and Senior Commissioned Pilot D.W.F. Elliott – For outstanding devotion to duty and courageous flying under the most arduous conditions. Each of these officers flew for long hours and rescued many people.

Commander (E) R.H. Webber and Lieutenant Commander C.R. Bateman – for unremitting zeal and energy in sustaining the base task at Gosport.

Petty Officer Telegraphist G. Jones and Aircrewman First Class S. Craig – for consistent high morale and devotion to duty which were a fine example to all during a period of most difficult and trying conditions.

Chief Aircraft Artificer E.W. Bevis, Aircraft Artificer Second Class W.A. Davies, Petty Officer Airman Fitter H.E. Tampling and Naval Airman Mechanic First Class F.R.C. Osborn – for exemplary devotion to duty and cheerful acceptance of long hours of arduous work day and night as members of the Squadron Maintenance Party, whereby a 100% serviceability of aircraft was maintained. Signed J.A.S. Eccles, Vice Admiral.

It took 705 NAS no time at all to notice that there were two notable omissions from this list of names – Crayton and Turpin. In 705 NAS line-book, a copy of the Order was pasted in but with a photograph of Crayton and Turpin and an arrow pointing to the legend 'AND WE WERE THERE TOO!!!'

The Squadron also received official thanks, testimonials, and elaborate parchment scrolls from Holland, and many letters from individuals who had been rescued. But perhaps the most lasting reward for the helicopters' splendid performance in the Dutch flood disasters, and in flood relief at home, was the effect upon the minds of the general public. Whatever arms, missiles, rockets and torpedoes might be fitted to helicopters in the future, no matter how many helicopter 'gunships' went into action, helicopters would for ever more be chiefly associated with errands of mercy.

The Dutch flood operations had long-lasting effects on helicopters in the Navy. 'We certainly were breaking new ground then,' wrote 'Dick' Turpin, years later, 'the knowledge of helicopter operations, navigation etc. was really at the beginning of a new age. Most of those involved were very experienced fixed wing pilots – hence our capability to use our initiative and previous aviation experience to good effect. Every one of us was on his own, to deal with many new and unknown problems. Experiences gained in Holland under sad and difficult conditions helped to develop the background techniques and procedures that are in effect today. I guess we were all pioneers!'

For five years 705 NAS had been the Navy's only helicopter squadron. On 29 October 1952, a second Squadron, 848, formed at Gosport with pilots from 705 and Lt Cdr Sydney Suthers as CO. 848 NAS, the Navy's first operational helicopter squadron, was formed specifically for operations in Malaya and was equipped with the Sikorsky S.55, a very famous helicopter known as the Whirlwind.

705 NAS had been evaluating the Whirlwind, using an aircraft which Westland procured from Sikorsky's and loaned to the Navy. The prototype Whirlwind had first flown on 10 November 1949. It was a considerable advance in every way on the Dragonfly, being larger, faster (over 100 mph), and with a much greater carrying capacity of up to ten people.

In 1952, 12 Whirlwind HAR 21s (the equivalent of the US Marines' HRS-2) and 15 Whirlwind HAS 22s (the equivalent of the US Navy's HO4S-3) were delivered to this country under the Mutual Defence Aid Programme. The HAR 21s went to 848 NAS, while the HAS 22s equipped 706 NAS, the Navy's first anti-submarine helicopter squadron, which reformed at Gosport on 7 September 1953, becoming 845 NAS, the Navy's first operational anti-submarine squadron on 15 March 1954.

Meanwhile 848 NAS and their twelve American-built Whirlwinds embarked in the light fleet carrier *Perseus* on 9 December 1945, bound for Singapore where they disembarked on 8 January 1953 and established a base at Sembawang.

The 'Emergency', as it was called, had begun in Malaya in 1948, when the Communists attempted to take over the country, using guerilla tactics and terrorism instead of the ballot box. British troops trying to counter the terrorism and round up the terrorists were frequently at a disadvantage, because much of the country in which the Communists (CTs, as they were called) operated was difficult going, and sometimes virtually almost impenetrable, on foot. Troops might take days to hack their way through a few miles of jungle. Helicopters gave them instant mobility.

After a short 'work-up', 848 NAS were deemed operational on 24 January 1953 and from that date stationed three Whirlwinds at Kuala Lumpur, three at Sembawang, and the rest Front Line in Reserve (F.I.R.) with the maintenance personnel, also at Sembawang. Two Whirlwinds at Kuala Lumpur and two at Sembawang were kept at one hour's notice for flying from dawn to dusk.

Business was brisk from the start. One Whirlwind from Kuala Lumpur carried out a casualty evacuation – 'casevac' in SAR-Speak – the very next day, 25 January, picking up three wounded soldiers from a jungle clearing and taking them to the British Military Hospital at Kinrara. The Sembawang detachment flew their first 'casevac' two days later, winching an injured Gurkha soldier out of the jungle and flying him to the British Military Hospital in Singapore.

Flights were generally short, allowing fuel to be cut down, giving more capacity for carrying personnel. Landing grounds were nearly always mere clearings in the jungle, with no names, only map references, where trees often more than a hundred feet high had been cut down to give a space not much wider than the span of a Whirlwind's rotor blades. In such places winching was impracticable and the winching equipment was removed, to give an extra 100 lbs lifting capacity.

Helicopters carried troops to operational trouble spots, dropped hundreds of tons of supplies of all kinds, from ammunition to tractors, evacuated casualties, took tracker dogs to round up bandits, brought back to Sembawang live Communist (CT) POWs for interrogation, or the heads and hands of dead CTs for identification (most of the active CT terrorists were known by name and face to police and intelligence).

848 NAS Whirlwinds dramatically transformed the tactical situation on the ground. One Whirlwind could take a 'stick' of five fully-equipped soldiers from the 5th Malay Camp at Batu Lima, for example, and in twelve minutes fly them to a position in the jungle which would have taken them twelve hours to reach on foot.

The Squadron took part in two major operations in their first two months. In the first, Operation BAHADUR, five Whirlwinds took 75 Gurkhas to their Landing Zone in 20 sorties. The second, Operation CATO in March 1953, was carried out after an intelligence tip-off that a gathering of important Communist delegates was to be held in Benta in western Pahang. A full brigade of 650 men with 4000 lbs of equipment was flown into the area, requiring 183 sorties and 103 flying hours.

In the event, disappointingly few CTs were killed or captured but the Operation had been a most convincing demonstration of helicopter capabilities. Later in March, 205 troops were flown to seven different jungle clearings, in 51 sorties. In another operation in May, 1,800 men were carried in four days.

During their first five months, 848 NAS carried 4,000 troops on operational flights and 848's pilots amassed 1,500 flying hours. In the same period they had also taken 90 sick or wounded troops from the jungle to military hospitals; the speed of the evacuation often meant the difference between life and death for the casualty.

848 NAS, like 705, were leaders in a new field. 'The Squadron pioneered jungle operations,' wrote 'Jim' Suthers, 'developing techniques as we flew and this included hundreds of casualty evacuations, many at night and in atmospheric conditions which reduced engine performance by 15–20 per cent. That first year was completed without a single accident.'

848 NAS received the Boyd Trophy for 1953, presented annually for the outstanding feat of aviation in the Royal Navy. By the end of the year, their helicopters in Malaya had flown for over 6,000 hours, carried 18,000 personnel – troops, doctors, VIPs, SAS, aborigines – and 363,000 lbs of stores – explosives, guns, food, medical stores, and leaflets (one Whirlwind crew released 700,000 leaflets in one 2-hour operation over areas occupied by terrorists). They had evacuated over 500 casualties, including wounded terrorists and members of the public. The maintenance staff at Sembawang had kept up a very high rate of availability.

Sometimes 848 NAS went to the assistance of a sister service. On 18 May 1955, the RAF helicopter carrying Air Vice Marshal Edwards-Jones on a tour of inspection broke down in the jungle near Fort Iskander and the pilot appealed by radio for assistance. The CO of 848, Lt Cdr M.W. Wotherspoon, was returning to Kuala Lumpur with three SAS casualties. It was then late afternoon and by the time Wotherspoon had landed, refuelled at Sembawang, and taken off again it was after 7 pm and quite dark. The rescue had to take place by the light of torches and the Whirlwind's headlight.

Wotherspoon found the Air Marshal in a clearing which was only 70 yards by forty yards wide and surrounded by trees 150 to 200 feet high. He could not land, because the other helicopter was in the way, so he hovered while the

Westland Whirlwind of 848 Sq., Malaya

Air Marshal climbed on to an improvised platform some five feet high and clambered across into the cabin.

848 also undertook SAR sorties similar to those around the coasts of the United Kingdom. In August 1956 the Hong Kong owned 3,537 ton steamer *Metal Trader*, on passage from Britain to Japan and intending to call at Singapore for bunkering, ran aground at Pulau Kupur on the approaches to Singapore.

While efforts were being made to refloat the ship, her Third Officer Yik Choeng suffered an attack of acute appendicitis on 19 August and the ship asked for help. Lt Cdr Roy Wilson, with Lt Thomson as Observer, took off from Kluang, where 848 NAS had a detachment, in darkness before dawn on 20th, although Whirlwinds at that time were not equipped for night flying and technically were not cleared to do so.

Wilson landed at Sembawang, picked up Surg. Lt Willis and flew out to the ship. The doctor was winched down, Yik Choeng was put on a stretcher, hoisted up and flown to Singapore General Hospital.

The 'Emergency' was officially declared over in 1956, with a defeat for the Communists. By the time 848 NAS officially disbanded on 18 December 1956, they had flown 11,394 hours, (9,763 operationally), lifted 41,104 troops, 2,926 passengers and 819,710 lbs of freight, and made 764 casevacs and 85 bodevacs.

When 848 NAS finally withdrew from Malaya in January 1957, the Government of the Malayan Federation presented the Squadron with a silver *kris*, the curved dagger which is the country's national symbol. As an official statement said 'Wherever a task needed doing, 848 did it with good humour and tireless energy. If a pin was stuck at random anywhere in a map of Malaya, within a few miles of that spot a helicopter of 848 would have been operating'.

Lt Cdr Brian Paterson had taken over from Suthers as CO of 848 NAS in January 1954. Paterson had been involved in a major SAR operation in the previous summer, after severe earthquakes and tidal waves killed 1,000 people and rendered over 100,000 homeless in the Ionian Islands, off the west coast of Greece, in August 1953.

By then, helicopters had begun to replace fixed-wing aircraft in the SAR role at home and abroad. On 24 January, two Dragonflies replaced the Sea Otter for SAR with 728 Squadron at HMS *Falcon*, RNAS Hal Far, Malta. On 13 August, both Dragonflies, flown by Paterson and Lt Ronald Leonard, with Lt George Spetch as third pilot, embarked in the cruiser *Bermuda* in Grand Harbour, Malta. One Dragonfly was parked on 'Y' turret, the other on the quarterdeck.

Bermuda and another cruiser *Gambia* sailed from Malta later that day and arrived off Zakynthos, the major town on the island of Zante, early on 15 August. A base for the helicopters was established on a large field south of Zakynthos, with the assistance of assault landing craft from the USS *Rockbridge*, who landed personnel, stores and petrol, and the US Marine Corps, who provided tents.

In the next five days the two Dragonflies flew 72 sorties of 43½ flying hours, rescuing people injured or trapped in debris and flying them to the hospital at Zakynthos. On 20 August the helicopters were ordered to the next island of Cephalonia, some twenty miles north of Zante. The Squadron gear was loaded into three 3-ton Army lorries which were driven on board the ss *Humphrey Gale*, an LST chartered by the War Office. *Humphrey Gale* took lorries and squadron maintenance crews to Cephalonia. There, the helicopters operated from a former US Navy base in a field two miles from the town of Argostolion.

One Dragonfly was badly damaged on the first day, when it crashed on landing whilst Paterson was taking General Iatrides, the Greek army commander, on a tour of the island. The remaining Dragonfly carried on ferrying injured and wounded islanders from outlying districts to the improvised hospital site at Argostolion. The total was 42 sorties, for 31½ flying hours, between 21 August and 6 September.

The damaged Dragonfly was eventually recovered by a truly United Nations working party: Paterson himself; Commissioned Air Engineer Cuddeford; a shipwright, an engine-room artificer and seamen from *Bermuda*; a tank landing craft of the Greek Navy; a 5-ton truck with a winch and crew of two from the United States Marine Corps; and the local chief of police with thirty villagers.

Meanwhile the other Dragonfly was flown on board the light fleet carrier *Theseus*, some 30 miles south-west of Cephalonia, on 7 September. The ground party came off in a landing craft on 12th. Even now the rescue work was not finished. There were reports of another earthquake in Cyprus. *Theseus* sailed there and Paterson flew another 22 sorties. Thus the two Dragonflies flew a total of 136 sorties, and nearly 90 flying hours, between 15 August and 17 September, when *Theseus* arrived in Malta.

As so often, there were heart-felt testimonials from the rescued. The people of the village of Shkimatar wrote: 'With tears in our eyes, owing to the great danger and wounds we have sustained, we feel very grateful to Her Majesty Queen Elizabeth and to the polite Englishmen. You are the most generous and polite people and we wish you every prosperity and happiness'. Another wrote: 'Our community of Volimais is exceedingly thankful for the medical assistance and food received for the babies, as well as the sweetened milk for the people of Volimais, who number 2000 mouths. We request that are warmest thanks be conveyed to Her Majesty the Queen, the Government, and the friendly English people, who we pray will be watched over by God the All-loving to their great blessing'.

The Squadron personnel who took part in the rescue operations and on whom these thanks were showered were: Lt Cdr B. Paterson, Lt R. Leonard, Lt S. Holdaway, Lt G. Spetch, Commissioned Air Engineer B. Cuddeford, Senior Commissioned Photographic Officer J. Hanman, and twenty ratings. Paterson was also awarded the MBE.

4 Korea: *Triumph*, *Theseus*, *Glory*, *Sydney* and *Ocean*

Theseus, with Paterson, Leonard and the others who had flown SAR sorties so successfully in Greece and Cyprus, arrived back in Malta on 17 September 1953. There, they were joined in Grand Harbour by ships on their way home from the Korean War.

An armistice had been signed at the town of Panmunjon, on the 38th Parallel, at 10 am on 27 July, 1953, to come into effect at 10 pm that evening. So ended a bloody war which inflicted a total of nearly four million casualties, military and civilian, although ignorant politicians in the United Kingdom persisted in referring to it in the language of peacetime, as though it were a minor 'brush fire' affair.

The Korean War made the helicopter's reputation, world-wide. There was something that appealed greatly to the public in the images which emerged of helicopters – the 'handy andies', 'flying egg-beaters', 'gyrating angels' – thrashing and whirling down the valleys and across the paddy fields of Korea to pick up downed aircrew.

The image of the helicopter as a life-saver was given powerful stimulus by James A. Michener's novel 'The Bridges at Toko-Ri' and the subsequent film, with a memorable performance by Mickey Rooney as the carrier's S.51 helicopter pilot, complete with green top hat, green scarf and disrespectful attitude to authority (reputedly based on a real character, Chief Aviation Pilot Durne W. Thorin, who once rescued 118 officers and men from a stranded frigate).

Every pilot whose aircraft was hit by flak over Korea tried to reach the sea. The water was cold – in winter so very cold that aircrew had to be recovered within minutes before they froze to death – but it was still much better than a North Korean POW camp. At sea, there was always an excellent chance of being picked up by the SAR helicopters who could recover aircrew from the water in a fifth of the time taken by even the most alert and well-trained destroyer seaboat's crew – besides releasing that destroyer and her numerous ship's company for other duties.

In September 1950, a Corsair from the carrier USS *Boxer* newly-arrived off Korea suffered an engine failure on take-off and crashed into the sea ahead of the ship. The SAR helicopter had the pilot back on deck within three minutes. This was the standard SAR helicopters aimed to equal – or beat.

Later, the US Navy converted LST 799 into a helicopter base and floating landing pad – the first in naval history. She took station off Wonsan harbour, on the east coast of Korea, in April 1951 and eventually rescued 24 pilots – US Navy and Marines, British, and one South African – two by boat and the rest by helicopter.

With helicopters in the field, a wounded man could be picked up in the front line, a blood transfusion could be started before the helicopter left the ground and completed by the time the helicopter reached the Mobile Army Surgical Hospital (M.A.S.H., in a celebrated TV film series). Of every 1,000 wounded men who reached hospital alive in the Second World War, 45 died; in Korea, largely thanks to helicopters, only 25 of every 1,000 were lost.

Triumph (Captain A.D. Torlesse DSO, himself a very experienced Fleet Air Arm observer) was the first British carrier to take part in the Korean war. She had No 13 Carrier Air Group (Lt Cdr P.B. Jackson) embarked: 800 NAS (Lt Cdr I.M. MacLachlan) with twelve Seafire 47s, and 827 NAS (Lt Cdr B.C. Lyons), with twelve Firefly Is. *Triumph* and the American carrier USS *Valley Forge* flew off the first air strikes of the Korean War early on 3 July. On 19 July 1950, when *Triumph* was operating with *Valley Forge* in the Yellow Sea, her SAR Sea Otter made what was very probably the last operational Sea Otter rescue at sea.

But the first British SAR of the Korean War was carried out by the sea-boat from the frigate HMS *Alacrity* (Cdr H.S. Barber). On 12 July the crew of an American B-29 bomber baled out and landed in the estuary of the Seoul river, an area which had scores of small islands, with shoals and mudbanks running thirty miles out to sea.

Over-flights by an American flying boat found nothing. It was thought possible the B-29 aircrew might have been picked up by friendly junk or sampan, but a cautious search (the last hydrographic survey of those waters had been 68 years before) by the destroyer HMS *Cossack* also revealed nothing. However, *Alacrity* picked up seven of the ten-man crew on 16 July. Commander Barber was later awarded the Bronze Star Medal by the grateful Americans.

Off Korea, *Triumph*'s aircrew soon learned that in a war zone people shot first and asked questions later. On 28 July, Commissioned Pilot D.R. White of 800 NAS was vectored out to investigate a radar contact which showed 'unfriendly'. It was a B-29 bomber which shot him down into the Yellow Sea – 'for no apparent reason', according to *Triumph*; because of his own absent-mindedness, according to the Americans. White was picked up, suffering from burns, by an American destroyer and returned to *Triumph* later that day.

On 29 August Ian MacLachlan, the CO of 800 NAS, was killed in a bizarre accident when a Firefly, landing on, tipped onto its nose. The propellor shattered and a large fragment smashed through the island scuttle of the operations room and struck MacLachlan on the head, inflicting wounds from which he died.

Despite these set-backs, and the short-comings of her old and short-ranged aircraft, and troubles with a leaking shaft stern gland, *Triumph* continued to fly sorties against targets ashore and CAPs for the blockade and covering forces for the landing at Inchon in September.

Triumph sailed from Sasebo in southern Japan on her way home on 25 September. She was relieved by HMS *Theseus* (Captain A.S. ('Ben') Bolt, DSC*, another very experienced Fleet Air Arm observer – *Warspite*'s observer at Matapan in March 1941) who arrived at Sasebo on 5 October, with No 17 Carrier Air Group (Lt Cdr F. Stovin-Bradford) embarked: 807 NAS (Lt Cdr M.P. Gordon-Smith) with twenty-one Sea Fury XIs, and 810 NAS (Lt Cdr K.S. Patisson) with twelve Firefly Vs. She had a Sea Otter but no helicopter.

Theseus, wearing the flag of Rear Admiral W.G. Andrewes, Flag Officer Second in Command Far East, and the British force commander at sea, sailed from Sasebo with other ships on 8 October. That afternoon, a Firefly jumped both crash barriers after landing and wrecked itself and two other Fireflies in the deck park – thus wiping out a quarter of 810 NAS total strength. However, the remaining nine Fireflies kept up a high serviceability rate.

On 9 October, *Theseus'* first day of operational flying off the Korean coast, the Fleet Aviation Officer (Cdr E.S. Carver) flew ashore to the Tactical Air Control Centre (TACC) at Kimpo, near Seoul, to make sure that they knew Admiral Andrewes' general intentions, and what types of aircraft *Theseus* would be operating. He also obtained information about the American helicopter rescue flight based at Kimbo and the means of getting in touch with them.

Carver's visit was well worthwhile, because TACC knew nothing of any British carrier operations in the Yellow Sea, and because the helicopter SAR flight was soon needed. The next day, 10 October, Lt S. Leonard of 807 NAS took off in a Sea Fury as No.2 to Stovin-Bradford for an armed reconnaissance of an area some fifteen miles south of the coastal town of Chinnampo, about 70 miles behind enemy lines. After strafing targets along a road they found a camouflaged store and made two attacks.

The second attacking run was a mistake because by then the North Korean defenders had had time to man their guns. The two Sea Furies met an intense burst of light flak from the hill opposite and from two innocent-looking haystacks. Leonard's aircraft was hit and badly damaged. He was forced to land in a paddy field in a valley some five miles away where his aircraft broke up. He put his Mae West on the wing to show he was still alive.

Another pair of Sea Furies, piloted by Lts A.C. Beavan and Austin, were ordered to strafe anyone approaching, while Stovin-Bradford climbed to 14,000 feet and reported the 'down' to *Theseus*. The American 3rd Air Rescue Squadron sent a helicopter escorted by a US Tigercat to the scene. Meanwhile Austin kept at bay four North Koreans who tried to reach Leonard. The Sea Furies flew Rescue Combat Air Patrols (RESCAPs) until a helicopter with a doctor arrived from Kimpo an hour later.

The doctor, Lt Col John C. Shumate, USAF, and the helicopter pilot,

Lt Stanley Leonard RN, 1950

Lt Col John C. Shumate USAF

Captain Dave McDaniel

Captain David C. McDaniel, USAF, dragged Leonard, who was badly hurt, out of his cockpit while under small arms fire from a farmhouse nearby. McDaniel gave covering fire with a machine gun as Leonard was lifted into the helicopter.

On the return flight McDaniel radioed the USMC Hospital Ship *Consolation* while Shumate gave Leonard a blood transfusion and morphia. The helicopter landed on the beach at Inchon, where another doctor and an ambulance were waiting, and transferred Leonard to the *Consolation*. Stovin-Bradford flew to Kimpo with some clothes for Leonard and a bottle of whisky for McDaniel and Shumate. Two days later Leonard was in hospital in Tokyo.

This, the Royal Navy's first helicopter SAR incident, was an extremely brave rescue by the American helicopter team, whose courage and efficiency were, in Stovin-Bradford's words, 'beyond praise'. Through the recommendation of Captain Bolt, and his and Leonard's persuasive urgings thereafter, Shumate and McDaniel were both awarded the Military Cross. In due course they were presented with their MCs by the British Ambassador in Washington DC.

Before the next patrol *Theseus'* Sea Otter was sent across to the repair and ferry carrier HMS *Unicorn* for a new engine to be fitted. An American Sikorski S.51 took its place – the first SAR helicopter embarked in a British carrier. Its pilot, Chief Aviation Pilot Dan C. Fridley, US Navy, of Santa Cruz, California, and his crew became, in 'Ben' Bolt's words, 'more British than the British. They painted 'Royal Navy' and 'HMS Theseus' on the aircraft and nothing was too much trouble for them.' (They also painted the sardonic slogan 'The Thing?' on the helicopter fuselage.)

Leonard's sortie and rescue set a pattern. 'We had a CAP of two Sea Furies when operating in the Yellow Sea,' said 'Ben' Bolt, 'with two more in readiness on deck. When an aircraft went down it was reported by his mate who stayed to protect him. Meanwhile the two stand-by Furies were immediately flown off to take over RESCAP and to protect the rescue helicopter. This system worked well.'

The whisky also set a precedent. 'As an inducement I awarded a bottle of Scotch to the pilot and doctor of any helicopter which brought one of our aircrew back to *Theseus*. The message quickly got around and there was quite a competition to get to our chaps first – very good for morale.'

On the west coast *Theseus*' operating position was normally in the Yellow Sea about 70-80 miles offshore. The increased range and endurance of her Sea Furies and Firefly Vs were a great advantage, compared with *Triumph*'s obsolescent Seafires and Firefly Is which, by the time the ship left, were almost on their last legs.

But the high rate of flying rendered *Theseus*' catapult reeving unusable. For her second patrol, unable to launch fully loaded aircraft with bombs, rockets or drop-tanks, six Fireflies were landed at Iwakuni. The remaining aircraft were restricted to flying CAPs over the ship herself and the American minesweepers off Chinnampo.

Theseus then went down to Hong Kong for repairs but was recalled in a hurry after the Chinese counter-attack across the Yalu river on 27 November 1950. She was back on station for intensive flying in December when her aircraft flew 630 accident-free sorties in seventeen flying days. However, on Christmas Eve a Sea Fury suffered engine failure after take-off and ditched four miles ahead of the ship. The pilot, Lt D.W.P. Kelly, was recovered unhurt by the Canadian destroyer HMCS *Sioux* after thirteen minutes in the icy water.

In winter a rescue destroyer, known as a 'Bird Dog', was stationed about halfway between the ship and Inchon. The first 'Bird Dog' destroyer was HMS *Consort* who took up her duties on 14 January 1951. When Lt Cdr M.P. Gordon-Smith, who had taken over as Air Group Commander, ditched after his aircraft was damaged by AA fire on 27 January, the 'Bird Dog' was the Canadian destroyer HMCS *Nootka* (Cdr A.B. Fraser-Harris DSC*, RCN, himself a distinguished aviator). When *Nootka* came alongside *Theseus* to transfer Gordon-Smith, Fraser-Harris signalled: 'Your bird, sir. My tail is wagging'.

Less lucky was Lt Beavan who was killed on 26 January when his Sea Fury crashed into the sea while on CAP. The destroyer HMS *Comus* searched the area but could find only two small pieces of wreckage.

The North Korean gunners were improving with practise. On 28 January, Lt P.L. Keighly-Peach was reconnoitring roads north and north-east of Seoul when his Sea Fury was hit by anti-aircraft fire and he decided to force-land. The cockpit hood temporarily stunned him as it was jettisoned and the cockpit filled with smoke, but the aircraft landed in a narrow valley near Tongduchon-ni and slid along for about 200 yards, the tailplane breaking off, before coming to rest in a small copse. Keighly-Peach got out of the wrecked aircraft and hid in a ditch. The rest of his flight flew RESCAPs until an American helicopter arrived 90 minutes later. Its crewman, Corporal Carl W. Pool, USAF, was awarded the DSM.

On 3 February, *Theseus*' aircraft were bombing and strafing targets in the Inchon area while the American cruiser USS *St Paul* and the destroyer USS *Hank* were carrying out a bombardment. In one sortie, when an armoured fighting vehicle was destroyed and two more damaged, Lt J.M. Pinsent's Sea Fury was hit by small arms fire and ditched alongside *St Paul* whose helicopter recovered him from the water within a few minutes.

Unfortunately, the hoist wire parted and Pinsent fell back into the sea. However a second attempt was successful and Pinsent was soon on board *St Paul*, very cold but unhurt. He was transferred to HMCS *Cayuga* and returned to Kure in Japan in her.

Not all the losses were caused by the enemy. On 14 February the front gun of a Firefly fired as the aircraft caught an arrester wire while landing on. PO Airman J.F. Wigley, who was working in the forward deck park, was fatally wounded. He was buried at sea with full naval honours the next day.

But enemy flak was growing steadily more dangerous. In March, *Theseus* carried out bombardment spotting and CAPs for the cruiser HMS *Kenya*, and continued to attack enemy communications such as road and rail bridges. On 12 March, the Firefly of Lt D.L. James was severely hit by flak and James was very lucky to reach Suwon airfield, 25 miles south of Seoul. The next day, another Firefly was shot down while bombing a railway bridge near Sariwon. Examination of the wreckage later showed that the crew, Lt G.H. Cooles, and Flt Lt D.W. Guy RAF, must both have been killed instantly.

For her last operating period in April 1951, off the east coast of Korea, *Theseus* embarked a US Navy Sikorsky S.51 fitted with an 'anti-coning' device which enabled it to operate from the flight deck in wind speeds up to 35 and 40 knots instead of only about 22 knots.

April was the busiest SAR month for *Theseus*. Five Sea Furies and one Firefly were lost or badly damaged. On 10th two Sea Furies were attacked in error by US Marine Corsairs. One was set on fire and very badly damaged but its pilot Lt Leece managed to struggle back on board. On the same day, another Sea Fury was shot down by flak. The pilot, Pilot III R.H. Johnson, was taken prisoner. A third had to make a forced landing with flak damage at Kangnung airfield. The pilot, Lt H.G. Julian, had minor injuries and shock.

On 12 April a Firefly of 810 NAS flown by Commissioned Pilot F.D.B.

Sikorsky S51 of HU-1 US Navy. Off Korea over HMS *Theseus*

Bailey was hit while attacking a bridge near Songjin. Oil pressure failed, the engine stopped, and Mr Bailey had to ditch about ten miles north-east of Hungnam, some 40 miles from *Theseus* and the American carrier USS *Bataan*. The helicopter from *Theseus* rescued Bailey, and *Bataan*'s recovered his observer Aircrewman Loveys, after they had both spent 40 cold minutes in their dinghies.

Next day, Lt J.S. Humphreys' Sea Fury was hit by flak during a reconnaissance over Hamhung and he crashed-landed in a small paddy field. Fortunately, the aircraft skidded into a dried-up river bed which gave Humphreys cover from small arms fire. The remaining aircraft of the flight flew RESCAPs while two other Sea Furies in the area escorted a helicopter from the cruiser USS *Manchester* off Wonsan, some 40 miles away. Humphreys was picked up after some 38 minutes and taken to *Manchester* with severe head injuries and a badly broken ankle.

On the third day, 14 April, a Sea Fury flown by Lt I.L. Bowman was hit by flak south-west of Hungnam but force-landed successfully. The other aircraft flew RESCAPs despite heavy anti-aircraft fire in the Hungnam area whilst, once again, *Manchester*'s faithful helicopter flew to the scene. Being overloaded, it had to ditch cameras and stores en route but it landed under intense ground fire, recovered Bowman, and took off again with itself and Bowman both unscathed.

For these two particularly gallant rescues *Manchester* was presented with a commemorative plaque by *Theseus*. Of *Manchester*'s helicopter crews, Lt Roger J. Gill, USNR, won a DSC, and Aviation Pilot Henry Cardoza, USN, AM3 James H. Hicks, USN and Aviation Mechanician's Mate Thomas C. Roche, USN, won DSMs. (Nine American helicopter crewmen of the US Navy and US Air Force won British medals for bravery in Korea).

On the afternoon of 18 April, a Sea Fury piloted by Lt T.R.S. Hamilton was returning from a sortie which had attacked and wrecked stone-crushing machinery and vehicles in a quarry near Yonan when it ditched in the sea about 60 miles from *Theseus*. Hamilton failed to clear his dinghy as he left the aircraft before it sank. By the time *Theseus*' helicopter reached him, he had been in water at a temperature of about 42°F for 55 minutes. He was almost unconscious, but recovered within 24 hours.

Theseus was relieved by HMS *Glory* on 24 April 1951 and went home to the United Kingdom. For their achievements in Korea her 17th Carrier Air Group received the Boyd Trophy for 1950, the first time the Trophy had been won by an Air Group. (The Trophy is a silver model of a Fairey Swordfish, first presented in 1946 in commemoration of the work for naval aviation of Admiral Sir Denis Boyd KCB, CBE, DSC, and awarded annually to the

Captain Ben Bolt of HMS *Theseus* embarking in 'The Thing?' piloted by Chief Aviation Pilot Dan C. Fridley US Navy, off Korea

pilot(s) or aircrew(s) who in the opinion of Flag Officer Naval Aviation achieved the finest feat of aviation in the previous year).

In the 1951 New Year list, *Theseus*' Executive Officer, Cdr F.W.R. Larken, and her Commander (Air), Cdr F.H.E. Hopkins, were promoted to Captain. Stovin-Bradford, the Air Group Engineer Officer, Lt Cdr (Ops) and the Navigating Officer were all promoted to Commander. Ben Bolt himself was awarded the DSO.

Glory (Captain K.S. Colquhoun DSO) had the 14th Carrier Air Group (Lt Cdr. S.J. Hall) embarked: 804 NAS (Lt Cdr J.S. Bailey), with twenty-one Sea Fury XIs, and 812 NAs (Lt Cdr F.A. Swanton) with twelve Firefly Vs. She also had a US Navy S.51 helicopter, also known as 'The Thing'.

Glory began her first patrol off the Korean coast on 27 April 1951, her arrival coinciding with the opening of the Chinese spring offensive. Low cloud and fog delayed flying which finally got off to a discouraging start late on 28th. After fifteen sorties, the weather clamped down. A Sea Fury on CAP, piloted by Lt E.P.L. Stevenson, disappeared into thick cloud at 900 feet and was never seen again.

Glory coordinated some of her aircraft strikes with the anti-Communist North Korean 'Leopard' Guerilla organisation ashore. On 2 May, on the last detail of the day, Sea Furies rocketted a large tin-roofed building which guerillas had given as the target. After the attack, one Sea Fury flown by Lt(E) P. Barlow developed engine trouble. Barlow had to land in a stream north of the bomb-line in enemy territory. An American helicopter picked him up and took him back to Seoul, none the worse for wear. His Sea Fury was strafed and set on fire.

'The Thing', piloted by Lt P. O'Mara USN, made its first rescue on 14 May. One of the bosun's party, Able Seaman MacPherson, fell overboard whilst the ship and the Australian destroyer *Bataan* were refuelling from the RFA tanker *Wave Premier*. The helicopter was actually in the air at the time, with a naval photographer, Mr E.J. King, taking newsreel pictures of the replenishment. Mr King took part in the rescue by jumping into the sea to assist MacPherson, who was wearing oilskins and sea-boots, into the sling.

Next day, a Sea Fury was hit by flak and ditched in the sea. The pilot, Lt J.A. Winterbottom, was picked up by a friendly Korean sampan and taken ashore. He was later evacuated by an American helicopter from LST 799. Three days later, on 18 May, a Firefly piloted by Lt R. Williams was hit by rifle fire from the ground. Williams ditched in about three feet of water some 70 miles north of *Glory*. He and his observer, Aircrewman 1st Class K.L.J. Sims, were helped by two sympathetic South Koreans in a fishing sampan until they were picked up by 'The Thing'. Williams was unhurt but Sims was wounded in the arm.

In June 1951 the United Nations army was advancing steadily northwards. But meanwhile the North Korean anti-aircraft gunners continued to improve with practise. When *Glory* took over from the American carrier *Bataan* for her next patrol on 3 June, the weather was good and her aircraft successfully strafed and bombed enemy troop movements.

But more and more aircraft were hit by flak. A Sea Fury ditched after engine failure off Chodo island on 4 June. The pilot, Lt(E) P.A.L. Watson, was picked up uninjured by the sloop HMS *Black Swan*. But on 7 June a Firefly was damaged by enemy fire while on an armed reconnaissance and came down in the sea ahead of *Glory*. Pilot III S.W.E. Ford, did not get out and was lost.

On the same day, another Firefly was hit in a nacelle tank and began losing fuel rapidly. The pilot, Lt R.E. Wilson, headed for the coast and ditched in the sea off the island of Paengyong-do. A shore-based helicopter was overhead in only four minutes to recover him and his observer Sub Lt L.R. Shepley. 'The Thing' arrived to return them to the ship.

Flying had to stop on 11 June because of contamination in the aviation fuel. There were rumours in the newspapers of sabotage. In fact the fault was in a seldom used and corroded supply pipe in the RFA tanker *Wave Premier*.

Helicopters were very good for the morale of aircrew, who knew that there was now a rapid and efficient rescue service in the event of trouble. Helicopters could do in minutes what a destroyer could not do in an hour. When no helicopters was available for *Glory*'s next period off the coast, from 23 June to 2 July, a destroyer had to be detached from *Glory*'s screen to act as plane guard for most of the day. Captain Colquhoun was concerned enough to shift *Glory*'s flying-off position some 30 miles to the north of the normal, so as to be nearer a shore-based helicopter.

It was a good patrol and *Glory* kept up a striking rate of over 50 sorties a day until an accident to the catapult. Rocket Assisted Take Off Gear (RATOG) had to be used for the last two days. But aircraft were still suffering constant damage from flak and several had to land at Suwon for repairs before flying back to the ship.

Only two were lost. A Firefly was shot down in flames after bombing targets in the Chinnampo area; Lt J.H. Sharp and Aircrewman 1st Class G.B. Wells were killed. One Sea Fury ditched just ahead of the ship after a catapult strop broke out during launching. The pilot was rescued by the 'Plane Guard' destroyer.

By the time *Glory* arrived for her next patrol, on 11 July, the Chinese spring offensive had been defeated and truce talks had begun. There had been a report on 9 July of a MiG jet fighter, shot down in shallow water, some 40 miles north of Chodo. The wreck was awash at low tide and the tail fin was spotted on 11th by Lt W.R. Hart from *Glory*. Two days later Lt D.A.M. McNaughton sighted the rest of the aircraft. On 18th, *Glory*'s helicopter accurately laid two buoys to mark the positions of the tail and fuselage, and the MiG was successfully lifted and salvaged.

In the meantime, the hectic war in the air went on. Thirteen of *Glory*'s Sea Furies and six Fireflies were damaged by flak and one Firefly was damaged when landing on. Four aircraft were lost. On 16 July, a Firefly crashed and burned out in enemy territory after a bombing attack on Sariwon, a north Korean town about halfway between Seoul and the northern capital of

Pyongyang. Lt R. Williams and Sub Lt I.R. Shepley, who had both survived previous ditchings, were both killed.

The next day, Lt Hart had engine trouble in his Sea Fury and had to ditch south of Choppeki Point on the west coast. He was picked up unhurt almost at once by the ROK frigate *P.F.61*.

In the first Sea Fury strike of 18 July, on buildings and railway sidings near Osan-ni on the west coast, two aircraft flown by Lts P.G. Young and P.S. Davis were hit by flak. A shell exploded in the cockpit behind Young but he returned to the ship safely. (Young had transferred to *Glory* from *Theseus* and completed his 100th sortie on his last mission).

Davis had to ditch further south, off Choppeki Point. He had some trouble with his Mae West, and his dinghy did not inflate properly. He spent 1½ difficult hours swimming and supporting himself in the water until *Glory*'s helicopter arrived to rescue him.

On the same day, another Sea Fury piloted by Mr T.W. Sparke, Commissioned Pilot, was hit by flak, again over Sariwon, and crashed in flames.

Glory was back on patrol on 1 September. Occasionally her helicopter had its own troubles. During the last detail of the day on 9 September, and the last of that operating period, a Firefly flown by Lt P.G.W. Morris, with Lt Legg as his observer, was hit in the oil system by flak while carrying out a dive-bombing attack and was forced to land on a mud flat in enemy territory near Haeju. The helicopter went out but had a faulty fuel gauge, ran short of fuel, and had to make a precautionary landing on a small island. *Glory* stayed in the area overnight. Petrol in cans was taken in by a destroyer next morning. Helicopter and Firefly crew were recovered, and the Firefly was set on fire and destroyed.

From 16th to 20 September *Glory* operated on the east coast, returning to the west coast on 21st for what were to be the last days of her last patrol. By this time her catapult was giving trouble. Fully loaded and bombed aircraft had to be launched by RATOG (Rocket Assisted Take-Off Gear). On 22 September, the RATOG on Commissioned Pilot J.P. Hack's Firefly failed to fire and the aircraft went straight into the sea. Mr Hack was recovered by the helicopter but sadly his observer, Act. Sub Lt. R.G.A. Davey, went down with the aircraft and was not seen again.

The last ditching was made by *Glory*'s Air Group Commander himself, Lt Cdr Hall, whose Sea Fury suffered engine trouble whilst attacking junks in the Chinnampo area on 25 September. Hall's flight headed for the island of Chodo and then turned south, hoping to reach the ship. But Hall was forced to ditch some miles south of Chodo. He made a good ditching but then had to spend an hour in the water which, by that time of year, was already getting very cold. *Glory*'s helicopter picked him up, beating a Dumbo flying boat from shore, which was taxying out to the scene, but the sea was too rough for it to make a landing.

Glory was relieved at the end of September 1951 by the Australian light fleet carrier HMAS *Sydney* (Captain D.H. Harries, RAN, himself a World War Two fighter pilot) who had No. 21 and part of No. 20 Carrier Air Groups (Lt Cdr M.F. Fell) embarked: two squadrons of Sea Furies, 805 NAS (Lt Cdr W.G. Bowles, RAN), of 20 CAG, and 808 NAS (Lt Cdr J.L. Appleby) and one of Fireflies, 817 NAS (Lt Cdr R.B. Lunberg). She also had a USN helicopter, 'Shine Angel', for SAR duties, captained by Lt P. O'Mara, USN.

Sydney's first operational sortie, led by Fell himself on 5 October 1951, made her the first Dominion carrier to send her aircraft into action. *Sydney* overtook *Glory*'s record of 89 sorties in a day on 11 October, ending with an attack by sixteen Sea Furies on 2,000 enemy troops caught digging in on the hills covering the beaches.

Sydney's next patrol was from 18th to 28 October. She celebrated Trafalgar Day 21 October with an attack on a fleet of junks in the Yalu Gulf. But 28 of *Sydney*'s aircraft were damaged by flak during the patrol and three were shot down. On 25 October two Sea Furies were hit. One ditched off Chinnampo and the other landed at Kimpo. The pilots, Lt C.M. Wheatley RAN, and Lt Cdr J.M. Appleby, 808's CO, were both recovered.

A third Sea Fury, piloted by Sub Lt N.W. Knappstein RAN, was hit on the following day and crash-landed on a mudflat in the Han River estuary. Knappstein was quickly picked up by HMS *Amethyst*'s sea-boat, which also salvaged remnants of his Sea Fury.

Later the same day, 26 October, there was a notable helicopter rescue. That afternoon, five Fireflies were attacking tunnels ten miles south of Sariwon when they ran into intense light flak and one was shot down. The pilot, Sub Lt N.D. MacMillan RAN, made a skilful crash landing in a field.

MacMillan and his observer, Observer 1st Class J. Hancox, were unhurt, but they were still in a very dangerous situation. They were in enemy territory, actually only three miles away from the target they had just been attacking. It was late in the day, and it was doubtful if *Sydney*'s helicopter could reach them and get clear before nightfall.

However, Captain Harries decided to try – a decision, he said, 'received with enthusiasm' by the helicopter crew – Aviation Device Chief Arlene K. Babbitt and Aviation Mechanician's Mate Callus C. Gooding. This news was conveyed by Fell who flew low over MacMillan and Hancox to tell them the helicopter was on its way. But in so doing Fell's Sea Fury was also hit and he had to land at Kimpo.

Sea Furies flew RESCAPs over the crash and were joined by R.A.A.F. Meteors of No. 77 Squadron. Below, the two aircrew were surrounded by North Korean troops whom they kept at bay with short bursts from their Owen sub-machine-guns. The Meteors had to leave at 5.15 pm. The Sea Furies, too, were ordered to leave, being at the limit of their fuel endurance, but the pilots, Lts J.H.G. Cavanagh and J.R.N. Salthouse RAN, decided to hold on for a few more minutes.

Ten minutes later, 'Shine Angel' arrived and touched down, having flown at a good 20 knots more than its accepted maximum speed. Gooding jumped out and shot two of the enemy who had crept up to within fifteen yards. MacMillan and Hancox were taken on board and 'Shine Angel', with its escort of Sea Furies, landed with the last of the daylight at Kimpo.

It was more than anybody could reasonably have expected. 'It is felt that the ship's guardian angel had a very hardworking and successful day,' wrote Captain Harries, while commenting on the 'fine performance of the helicopter's crew'. For this rescue, Babbitt and Gooding were both awarded well-earned DSMs.

Captain Harries studied the whole question of rescue very carefully. He introduced high-visibility fluorescent panels, to be carried by all aircrew. They were immediately successful. Twice, after aircraft had crashed in enemy territory, the rescuing aircraft sighted the panels long before they saw the crews.

By November 1951, armistice talks were in progress at Panmunjon, but the situation on land was stalemated. On her next patrol, which began on 5 November, *Sydney* suffered her first fatal casualty when the Sea Fury of Lt K.E. Clarkson RAN failed to pull out of a dive while attacking enemy transport and Clarkson was killed.

Sydney's December patrol began with another tragedy. On 7th, a Sea Fury piloted by Sub Lt R.P. Sinclair RAN was hit by flak north-west of Chinnampo. Sinclair bailed out but hit the tailplane as he jumped and was killed. His body was recovered by helicopter and later committed to the deep with full naval honours.

Four other aircraft were damaged that day but only one pilot, Sub Lt A.J.B. Smith, was forced down and landed on the island of Paengyong-do. He was unhurt and was recovered by helicopter. On 13 December, Fireflies attacked a village on the Ongjin peninsula and rail bridges between Wonto and Allyong reservoir. When Lt D.J. Robertson RAN returned from this sortie, his Firefly was marshalled into 'Shine Angel' putting the helicopter out of action for the rest of the patrol.

SAR duty was taken over by 'Pedro Fox', a helicopter based on Paengyong-do, who went into action at once. During an attack on box cars north of Chinnampo, Lt P.B. Cooper RAN's Sea Fury was hit and he had to bale out. His flight flew RESCAPs until he was picked up uninjured by 'Pedro Fox' and taken to Paengyong-do.

During that afternoon, Lt Cdr W.G. Bowles RAN, CO of 805 NAS, was hit by the same guns had downed Cooper earlier in the day. He baled out safely into shallow water where a friendly junk picked him up and took him ashore. RESCAPs were flown by the rest of his flight, and by the Fireflies after they had completed their missions, until 'Pedro Fox' arrived. The destroyer HMAS *Tobruk* collected both pilots during the night but the very high winds, rough seas and snow showers which prevented flying from *Sydney* also kept Bowles and Cooper on board *Tobruk* until 16 December.

Sydney's next, and what was to be her last, patrol off Korea began on 28 December and had mixed fortunes. One catapult broke down on 1 January

1952 and on the 2nd a Sea Fury on CAP piloted by Sub-Lt R.J. Coleman RAN got separated from his leader and was lost. An air and sea search by Fireflies and by one of the destroyers from *Sydney*'s anti-submarine screen, USS *Hanson*, continued for the rest of the day. A wide area was searched, but no trace of Coleman or wreckage was seen. However, on the next day, Sub-Lt Macmillan made the 2000th operational deck landing on *Sydney*.

The year of 1952 opened with continuing stalemate on land, while the armistice discussions dragged on with no appreciable prospect of progress. There were accusations by the Communists of germ warfare by the United Nations. At sea on the west coast, the main preoccupation was the protection of the so-called 'strategic' islands, which stretched from the Han river estuary up to Chinnampo.

Sydney left for Sasebo and eventually Australia on 25 January 1952, after a sustained performance by her ship's company and air group which Rear Admiral A. Scott-Moncrieff (who had relieved Andrewes in April 1951) described as 'quite excellent'.

On 6 February, *Glory* arrived off the west coast for the first patrol of her second tour of duty in Korea. She began flying operations as if she had never been away, averaging over 50 sorties a day, although six of her Firefly pilots had been disembarked before sailing to Iwakuni, the United Nations Air Base some twenty miles from Kure in Japan, for deck landing practise.

The gun batteries along the whole coast had been strengthened in *Glory*'s absence but she lost only two aircraft during this patrol. On 12 February, Lt A.M. Knight's Sea Fury suffered loss of oil pressure after being hit and Knight made a forced landing at Paengyong-do, one of the 'strategic' islands. *Glory*'s helicopter retrieved him, uninjured, later that day.

On the next day another Sea Fury piloted by Lt R.J. Overton was hit after attacking a gun position and ditched near another 'strategic' island, Chodo. Overton was picked up after only a few minutes by the ROK Auxiliary Minesweeper *501* which had got under way very promptly to go to the rescue.

The next patrol, during which the 5,000th deck landing of the commission was recorded, began on 24 February. On 1 March Lt J.R. Fraser's Sea Fury suffered loss of oil pressure, probably caused by small arms fire, while returning from a Target CAP (TARCAP). Fraser did get back to the ship, but his engine cut out after he had joined the landing circuit and was flying up the starboard side of the ship to land on. The ship's helicopter recovered him in the record time of 60 seconds – ditch to deck.

Overton's luck ran out in the next patrol. On 15 March his Sea Fury was hit by AA fire on a strafing run in the Chinnampo area, crashed into a hillside near the Amgak peninsular and exploded. *Glory*'s final SAR incident on this tour was on 28 April, during a strafing attack on two villages in the Pungchon area near Chodo, when Act. Sub-Lt D.G.L. Swanson's Sea Fury had engine trouble, forcing him to ditch south of the island. He was picked up in fifteen minutes, unharmed in his dinghy, by an American helicopter from Chodo.

Glory left for Hong Kong and the Mediterranean, having made what

Scott-Moncrieff called 'an outstanding contribution to the prestige of British naval aviation. She will certainly be missed', he said, 'not least by the Communists ...'.

At Hong Kong, *Glory* turned over to another light fleet carrier, HMS *Ocean* (Captain C.L.G. Evans, DSO, DSC – Charles 'Crash' Evans, a famous FAA character both in the war and after) who had No. 17 Carrier Air Group (Cdr A.F. Black) embarked, with Sea Furies of 802 NAS (Lt Cdr S.F.F. Shotton) and Fireflies of 825 NAS (Lt Cdr C.K. Roberts). These squadrons had come out to the Mediterranean in *Theseus* and changed ships at sea off Malta on 12 February.

Ocean began her first patrol on 11 May 1952 and kept up a furious striking rate, flying 87 sorties on her first day and averaging 76 a day over a period of seven and a half flying days. On 17 May she flew 123 sorties, surpassing *Glory*'s previous record of 105 sorties in a day, and setting up a new record for light fleet carriers.

Such activity had its price. Two aircraft were lost through unexplained engine failure on 11 May: a Sea Fury flown by Lt H.M. McEnery, who was unhurt, crash-landed on Paengyong-do, and a Firefly ditched in Haeju Bay; the crew, Lt S.G. Gandey and his observer Sub-Lt. A. Bishop, were picked up suffering from shock by an American Grumman Goose amphibian provided by the Joint Operations Centre (JOC), Korea.

Five aircraft were lost to enemy action. On 11 May one Sea Fury was damaged and came down in the sea; the pilot, Lt M.E. Scott RAN, was picked up by the American destroyer USS *Lowry*. On 14 May another Sea Fury was hit by flak and crashed on the Amgak peninsula. The aircraft exploded on impact with the ground and the pilot, Lt(E) Kenneth Macdonald, was killed.

Lt Cdr Roberts, CO of 825 NAS, and his observer Lt W.G. Cooper ditched to seaward of the ship on 16 May and were recovered by a JOC Grumman Goose, as was Lt N.E. Peniston-Bird on 18th, when his Sea Fury was set on fire during a low level attack. On the following day, a Firefly was hit whilst giving close air support to the Commonwealth Division, crashed and exploded. Lt Cdr T.J.C. Williamson-Napier and Aircrewman 1st Class L.M. Edwards lost their lives.

Not all the accidents happened in the air. As always, a flight deck was a most dangerous place. On 19 May an aircraft handler was blown overboard when a RATO ignited prematurely. The destroyer USS *March* quickly lowered a boat but the man sank before it could reach him. His body was never found.

Ocean's second patrol was from 29 May to 6 June. One Sea Fury and one Firefly made forced landings on the beach at Paengyong-do. In the Firefly's case, the cause was the failure of an engine connecting rod. *Ocean*'s Fireflies had suffered three such failures in the previous three months and three ditchings had very likely been due to the same cause. In his Report of Proceedings, Captain Evans was rightly incensed that his aircrews 'should have to fly over enemy territory in aircraft powered by such unreliable engines'.

Ocean had arrived in the Far East with a Sea Otter for SAR but had taken over *Glory*'s helicopter in Japan. It carried out its first rescue on 4 June when the engine of McEnery's Sea Fury failed as he was approaching the ship. He requested an emergency landing but had to ditch. On the same day, Sub-Lt Swanson (who had transferred from *Glory*) was rescued again by a US helicopter after the tail had been shot off his Sea Fury and he had baled out at 1,000 feet, landing in the sea 200 yards off the enemy coast, but near the friendly island of Chodo.

There was a sadder outcome a month later, on 4 July, when Lt R.C. Hunter and his observer Lt R.J.A. Taylor took off for a test flight in a Firefly. The engine failed shortly after take-off. Hunter had to ditch near the ship. Both men got clear of the aircraft before it sank. The helicopter was overhead at once and picked up Taylor. But in the four minutes which was all the helicopter took to land Taylor on board and return, Hunter disappeared. He was not seen again, in spite of an extensive search.

On 25 June 1952 the war had entered its third year, and a fortnight later the armistice talks – now virtually suspended – began their second. The carriers on the west coast, alternating their patrols with American carriers, continued the familiar routine: CAPS, TARCAPs, flak suppression, air strikes, and bombardment spotting.

Ocean was on patrol again from 21st to 31 July. On 24th, Lt Cdr R.A. Dick who had recently relieved Shotton as CO of 802 NAS, was shot down over the Taedong river and killed. He was succeeded by Lt. Cdr. P.H. London. Later that day, Gandey and Bishop force-landed again in their Firefly, west of Chodo, and were rescued by helicopter.

Dick's death followed a melancholy historical pattern for COs of 802 NAS, an unusual number of whom were killed in action. Lt Cdr J.F. Marmont was lost when *Glorious* was sunk off Norway on 8 June 1940. Lt Cdr J.M. Wintour, flying from the auxiliary carrier *Audacity*, was killed in action with a Focke Wulf Kondor while defending the Gibraltar-bound convoy OG76 on 8 November, 1941. His successor, Lt (later Admiral) D.C.E.F. Gibson claimed to be the only CO of 802 to survive the war. Certainly his successor, Lt Cdr E.W. Taylour, flying from the escort carrier *Avenger*, was killed defending convoy QP18 on 13 September 1942 and *his* successor, Lt D.P.Z. Cox, was lost when *Avenger* was torpedoed and sunk by U-155 on 15 November 1942.

Enemy aircraft now made their first appearances. On 27 July, when *Ocean* was some 70 miles to the north of her usual operating area, four MiGs supported by ten others at various heights attacked three Fireflies who were escorting a fourth, badly damaged by flak, to the coast where it could ditch. Two Fireflies were damaged before escaping into cloud. The flak-damaged Firefly ditched half a mile west of Chodo, and the crew, Lt. P. Watkinson and Lt. C.J. Fursey, were picked up by small craft. Later that day a division of Sea Furies was attacked by four MiGs, but outmanoeuvred them and damaged the Mig leader.

Ocean returned to the coast on 8 August. So, too did the MiGs. Lt P.

Carmichael, leading four Sea Furies early on 9th, was attacked by eight MiGs north of Chinnampo. On MiG was shot down and was seen to explode on hitting the ground.

That afternoon, McEnery was leading four Sea Furies with three new RNVR pilots (all from 1832 NAS, based at Culham, Berkshire, who had volunteered for service in Korea) on a tour of the TARCAP area when they were attacked out of the sun by four MiGs. McEnery damaged one MiG with one long burst of fire, but one of the newcomers, Lt R.J. Clark RNVR, had a drop-tank set on fire. He jettisoned the burning tank, extinguished the fire by side-slipping and finally landed on after a highly dramatic debut in Korea. Meanwhile, two Sea Furies were being attacked by MiGs over Chinnampo. One, piloted by Lt R.H. Hallam, was severely damaged and had to make a wheels-up landing on Chodo, but Hallam was not hurt.

Clark was evidently one of those lucky pilots. On 14 August his Sea Fury stalled after a RATOG launch and fell upside down into the sea. Miraculously, he escaped and some 80-90 seconds after the accident came to the surface, where the helicopter was already waiting to return him to the flight deck with a bump on his head and bruises.

In the next patrol, on 27 August, a Firefly was hit in the radiator by flak and headed for the coast. The pilot, Lt W. Le G. Jacob, debated over the intercom with his observer, Aircrewman 1st Class C. Hearnshaw, DSM, whether to bale out or ditch. Hearnshaw, a very experienced aircrew CPO, who had won his DSM in *Formidable* in 1941, told Jacob he had been shot down seven times and did not much mind what Jacob decided so long as he made his mind up. Jacob ditched off Chodo, to make Hearnshaw's eighth.

The Firefly tipped over as it hit the water but came upright. Both men swam ashore. A massive RESCAP was flown by four F-86 Sabres from Kimpo, four US Marine Corsairs and four Sea Furies. Jacob swam back to retrieve secret equipment such as the gunsight from his aircraft which was lying in shallow water. He and Hearnshaw were returned to *Ocean* in Chodo's helicopter that evening.

Ocean began her tenth and last patrol of the tour on 23 October. On 27th, the Chodo helicopter was in action again when a Sea Fury piloted by Lt(E) D.G. Mather was hit by flak and Mather made for the coast. But the engine failed before the Sea Fury could reach the sea. Mather made a good landing in a paddy field a few hundred yards short of an extensive mud-flat, about fifteen miles north of the Taedong river estuary, an area where there were many enemy troops.

After an hour, and two attempts by the enemy to capture Mather, the helicopter, piloted by Lt Christy, US Navy, arrived and picked him up. Meanwhile, ten Sea Furies and two US Marine Corsairs flew RESCAPs. Mather's Sea Fury was destroyed.

The final rescue of this tour (for which *Ocean*'s 802 and 825 NAS were to win the Boyd Trophy for 1952) was on 30 October after Lt(E) C.M. Jenne's Sea Fury suffered a total engine failure shortly after take-off. In a short, sharp model evolution, Jenne ditched, got out of the aircraft before it sank, was picked up by the ship's helicopter and smartly returned on board.

That evening, *Ocean* left the Korean coast after holding a short memorial service at which wreaths were dropped overboard for the eight shipmates who had lost their lives during the operations.

Glory (Captain T.A.K. Maunsell, who had relieved Captain Colquhoun on 23 April 1952) sailed from Sasebo on 10 November 1952 wearing the flag of Rear Admiral E.G.A. Clifford (who had relieved Admiral Scott-Moncrieff on 23 September 1952) to begin her first patrol of her third tour; *Glory* and *Ocean* alternated off the Korean coast from January 1952 until after the Armistice in July 1953.

Glory had embarked 801 NAS (Lt Cdr P.B. Stuart) with twenty-one Sea Fury XIs, and 821 NAS (Lt. Cdr. J.R.N. Gardner) with twelve Firefly Vs. She also had an SAR Dragonfly with a Royal Navy pilot, Lt A.P. Daniels. Almost all the aircrew were new to Korea.

Despite bitter fighting on land, especially towards the end of 1952, the stalemate continued. But for the carriers at sea there was a heavy flying programme, mostly flown in bad weather, of close support to the troops defending the islands, attacks on bridges, tunnels, railway lines and enemy troops.

The North Korean anti-aircraft gunners had lost none of their zeal or accuracy, in fact the weight and intensity of the flak seemed to increase the longer the war went on. In *Glory*'s first patrol, nine Sea Furies and six Fireflies were damaged by flak and one Firefly by a shell exploding in her gun.

Two aircraft were lost. On 18 November a Sea Fury was shot down while attacking a railway bridge south of Sariwon. The pilot, Lt R. Nevill Jones, was killed. The same day, a Firefly was hit in the port radiator by flak. The engine cut out while still over the land, but the pilot Lt(E) D. Robbins ditched in Tatong Bay, about two miles from the coast. He was picked up from the water (having failed to inflate his dinghy) by the helicopter from Paengyong-do.

On the next patrol, nine Sea Furies and one Firefly were damaged and there were four deck landing accidents. In the freezing weather, the Fireflies began to suffer engine coolant problems. On 6 December a Firefly piloted by Lt S.G. Marshall suffered engine failure from this cause and ditched about sixteen miles east of *Glory*. The weather was fine, with no swell and very little wind, and Marshall put his Firefly down so smoothly it stayed afloat for 40-50 seconds (compared with the usual eight). He was picked up by *Glory*'s helicopter, piloted by Daniels, after fifteen minutes in his dinghy.

Captain Maunsell having fallen sick, Captain E.D.G. Lewin ('Drunkie' Lewin, another very notable naval aviator, who had flown *Ajax*'s spotting Sea Fox floatplane at the Battle of the River Plate in December 1939) assumed command of *Glory* at Kure on 14 December and the ship sailed for the west coast the next day.

Daniels had made a good start on 6 December but ten days later, on 16th, there was a disaster. Daniels was in the Dragonfly on the flight deck, with the

WG706 Dragonfly HR3, HMS *Glory*. Taken off Korea. Pilot A.P. Daniels killed in accident, 16 December 1952

engine running and rotor turning, when strong turbulent winds around the forward end of the island superstructure threatened to blow the helicopter over the ship's side to starboard.

Daniels tried to make a 'snatch' take-off and did get airborne but the helicopter was unstable and crashed into the sea, minus its tail rotor boom which broke off. Daniels and Aircrewman 1st Class E.R. Ripley were both killed.

These were the first operational RN fatalities in an SAR helicopter crew, although not the first RN helicopter deaths: Lt Ockelford of 705 NAS was killed flying a photographic sortie over Devon in 1948, when his Hoverfly flew into overhead power cables – a perennial hazard for helicopters.

In that patrol of December 1952, *Glory*'s aircraft concentrated upon bridges and railway rolling stock. Close support was given to the Commonwealth Division on 22 and 24 December. But losses were heavy. On 18 December there was an explosion in the port inner gun bay of a Sea Fury piloted by Lt A.J. Leahy, who had to force-land on Paengyong-do. Two days later there was an explosion in the wing of a Firefly attacking a junk offshore. The Firefly crashed into the sea and the pilot, Lt P.G. Fogden, was killed.

The sea was now very cold. Ditched aircrews' lives virtually depended upon their dinghies. In a strike on the Haeju area on 21 December, a Sea Fury flown by Lt V.B. Mitchell was hit in the engine. Mitchell had to ditch about a mile offshore. He sat in his dinghy for an hour until a Grumman Goose from 3rd USAF Rescue Group landed alongside and picked him up, cold but surviving. The sea water temperature was 35°.

The saddest loss of the year was on Christmas Day. Lt R.E. Barrett was killed when his Firefly was shot down while attacking a bridge north of Haeju. *Glory* left the area on Boxing Day but was back for her first patrol of the New Year of 1953 on 4 January.

It began very badly. On 5 January a Sea Fury piloted by Lt Mather was hit by flak and caught fire after an attack on a railway bridge north of Chaeryon. Mather baled out, but his parachute was lost out of sight before it reached the ground. Aircraft flew RESCAPs for 90 minutes and a USAF helicopter, escorted by two Sea Furies, came out to look for him, but had to turn back because of bad weather. One of those escorting Sea Furies, piloted by Sub-Lt B.E. Rayner, lost R/T contact and was not seen again. Mather became a prisoner-of-war.

Later on this dreadful day, Sub-Lt J.M. Symonds RNVR was trying to form up on his divisional leader at 3,000 feet when his Sea Fury got into a spin from which it did not recover. The aircraft disintegrated and burst into flames when it hit the ground.

The first rescue of the year was on 6 January, after a Firefly flown by Lt W.R. Heaton was hit by small arms fire. The engine began to vibrate violently, as though it were trying to shake itself to pieces, and the cockpit filled with smoke. Heaton managed to ditch successfully five miles off the enemy coast, north of the friendly island of Kirin-do. A USAF helicopter from Paengyong-do rescued him after he had been thirteen minutes in his dinghy and returned him to *Glory*.

There were more losses in February. On 9th a Firefly piloted by Sub-Lt P. Millett swung to starboard on landing and went over the side; Millett and his passenger, Captain Bury RA, were picked up by a destroyer. Later that day, Sub-Lt Hayes' Sea Fury was hit by flak which severed an oil pipe, causing the engine to fail over the Taedong river estuary. Hayes ditched a mile south of Chodo and was picked up by a USAF helicopter. On the following day, 10 February, a Firefly ditched soon after taking off because of an engine coolant leak. The pilot, Lt P.D. Dallosso, and Sub-Lt R. Harrison, were picked up by an American destroyer in the screen, USS *Hanna*.

There were two fatal casualties. On 11 February, Lt C.A. MacPherson was killed when his Sea Fury was hit while making a low-level strafing attack on a stores dump, crashed on a hillside, exploded and burst into flames. Another Sea Fury was lost on 14th when its engine cut out and the pilot, Sub-Lt D.R. Bradley, ditched close to the ship. The aircraft hit the sea nose down at about 145 knots, broke in two and sank in ten seconds. The screen destroyers were on the spot at once, but could not find Bradley.

These were the last casualties until 25 April, when two Sea Furies were lost, with their pilots. Lt J.T. MacGregor was dive-bombing a railway bridge when his Sea Fury went into a spiral dive, probably caused by flak damage, and crashed into the ground. An hour later, Sub-Lt W.J.B. Keates was dive-bombing a cave entrance, tried to pull out of the dive, but lost control and the Sea Fury burst into flames when it hit the ground.

On 5 May 1953, *Glory* began her last patrol, and her twenty-fifth in all. By this time the Armistice talks were progressing and the Korean coast was in a state of what Captain Lewin called 'unnatural calm'. One Firefly ditched off Yong Pyong Do with engine failure, probably caused by small arms fire. The pilot, Lt W.R. Sherlock, was rescued uninjured by HMS *St Bride's Bay*.

Glory held a memorial service for the twelve shipmates who had given their lives on 14 May, and left Korea for the last time that evening. She was relieved by *Ocean* (Captain B.E.W. Logan, himself an observer) who arrived at Sasebo on 17 May. Embarked in *Ocean* were 807 NAS (Lt Cdr T.L.M. Brander) with twenty-one Sea Fury XIs, 810 NAS (Lt Cdr A.W. Bloomer) with twelve Firefly Vs, and an SAR Dragonfly.

Although the air war, if anything, intensified as the prospect of an Armistice seemed to come nearer, *Ocean* had very few losses. On 29 June, a Firefly ditched after flak damage and the next day a Sea Fury ditched after engine failure. The Firefly pilot, Lt B.V. Bacon, and the Sea Fury pilot, Sub-Lt C.C.B. Hill, were both picked up by the helicopter from Paengyong-do.

By July, *Ocean*'s catapult was giving trouble and, to keep to the flying programme, strikes had to be flown off using RATOG. The ship's own helicopter made its first rescue on 15th, the first flying day of a new patrol, when it picked up Lt J.J. Mulder R. Neth.N. who fired his Sea Fury's RATOG rockets too early, failed to gain flying speed, and went into the sea ahead of the ship.

The first Firefly that day crashed into the sea immediately after take-off. The observer, Lt K.M. Thomas, went down with the aircraft. The pilot, Lt A.J.D. Evans, was recovered alive by the American destroyer USS *Southland* but he failed to respond to prolonged artificial respiration, never regained consciousness, and died on board.

At the end of flying that day, a combined memorial service for Thomas and Evans was held in *Ocean*. As dusk fell, the screening destroyers, USS *Buck* and *Southland* and HMS *Cockade*, closed in astern and on *Ocean*'s quarter to take part. These were the last aircrew casualties. The Armistice was agreed on 27 July 1953.

Glory had done three tours of duty off Korea, *Ocean* two, *Triumph*, *Theseus* and *Sydney* one each. Between them, their aircraft had flown around 25,000 sorties. Twenty-two aircrew were killed in action, mostly shot down by anti-aircraft fire, and fourteen were killed in accidents.

The losses would have been higher but for the helicopters. At various times RN aircrew were rescued by helicopters operating from US Air Force airfields, from LST 799, from US bombarding cruisers at Wonsan and Inchon, and from their own carriers.

Despite their value and their effect on morale as short-range rescue aircraft, as well as other tasks such as mine-spotting, mail delivery and personnel transfer, ship-borne helicopters had severe limitations as to their radius of action over the sea. A 30-knot head wind reduced a helicopter's ground speed to not much more than that of a surface ship. VHF communications were unreliable, night- and instrument-flying were things of the future, and dead reckoning navigation was always liable to large errors. There is no doubt many fewer RN aircrew would have been rescued had it not been for the USAF helicopters operating from shore bases along the Korean coast.

Nevertheless, Korea showed that, 'E & OE' ('Errors and Omissions Excepted') the helicopter had proved its worth.

5 Sproule Net and Suez, November 1956

In the 1950s, SAR steadily broadened its outlook and improved its techniques. Originally devised and carried out by servicemen for the rescue of their fellow servicemen, SAR increasingly catered for civilians. There were improvements in organisation and equipment. A Rescue Co-ordination Centre was set up in Plymouth, to collect and disseminate information and to co-ordinate and direct rescue assets; other Centres followed, around the rest of the country. Links were established between SAR units and the Coast Guard.

One of the earliest aids to Search and Rescue was the 'Sproule Net'. Lt Cdr John Sproule had qualified as a pilot before the war and joined the Fleet Air Arm as a Sub Lt (A) RNVR in 1940. He took the helicopter conversion course – known as SMAC20, 'Special Miscellaneous Air Course No 20' – and qualified in December 1948. He accepted a permanent commission in 1950 and in 1953 was appointed CO of the newly-formed SAR Flight at HMS *Peregrine*, the Royal Naval Air Station, at Ford in Sussex. The Flight had two S.51 Dragonflies, with two pilots and to aircrewmen. Their 'parish' ran roughly from Selsey Bill in the west to Beachy Head in the east.

At first Sproule was 'not too pleased to be confronted with SAR duties, which sometimes dwell rather heavily on the sadder aspects of aviation'. But soon, like every SAR crew ever since, he discovered that he 'had been given the best flying job in the peacetime FAA'.

A man of inventions, Sproule constructed a 'scoop' from a frame of 1 inch steel tubing, about five feet square, suspended on four cables from the helicopter hook. His crewman, CPO S.W. Lock, a very experienced telegraphist/air gunner ('small and wiry, fast on *The Daily Telegraph* crossword', as Sproule said) rigged a net inside the framework with cod-line and sailor's knots.

The idea was literally to 'scoop' the casualty out of the water, making rescues less reliant on the rescued being able to handle the usual strop. It worked and an improved Mark IV net became standard equipment in all SAR flights.

Sproule himself carried out one of the neatest 'net' rescues. He was airborne one morning on a 'warming up the engine' local sortie when air traffic told him that a Firefly from a carrier in the Channel was in difficulties and was about to ditch. He headed to intercept.

'Commander Baldwin, the Commander Air, was also airborne for his weekly trip in a Vampire and being very much faster he soon located the Firefly about six miles off Littlehampton. Very shortly I was relieved to spot the two aircraft flying low over the water and we had a grand stand view of the Firefly ditching. With the Dragonfly fairly rattling along at maximum speed, I made encouraging remarks on the radio to its worried pilot. Within 30 seconds of immersion a very surprised Lt Foulkes RN was in our net and being winched up to the helicopter where, cold and wet, he sat shivering until we delivered him to the front door of the sick bay at Ford: to this day I get a Christmas card from him each year.'

Fifteen naval air stations and nine aircraft carriers were given Dragonfly Flights during the early 1950s. They flew HR3s, with all-metal rotor blades and hydraulic servo controls, and later HR5s, with increased engine power and improved instrumentation. As the decade went on, the Dragonfly was replaced by the Whirlwind, the first Ship's Flight to receive a Whirlwind HAR Mk3 being *Ark Royal*'s, in the summer of 1955. More Flights converted to Whirlwinds as aircraft and crews became available.

The annual pattern of 1950s SAR sorties has remained virtually unchanged

981FD Dragonfly HR3. Ford Station Flight using its 'Sproule' net to recover crewmen

over the years. In winter and rough weather, ships took the ground or took in water, their cargoes shifted, crew members were sick or injured. Ashore, in hard winters, helicopters flew pregnant women and casualties out, food for people and fodder for livestock in.

At Easter, the 'Silly Season' – as SAR crews called it, then as now – begins with falling cliff climbers and walkers, holiday-makers injured, lost or cut off by tides, swimmers, canoeists, dinghy sailers and yachtsmen in difficulties, sailing boats and yachts sinking, dismasted or capsized.

In May 1953 there was one of the first – possibly even the very first – of the 'holidaymaker' helicopter rescues of which there were to be literally thousands around the coasts of the United Kingdom in the decades to come.

Two brothers from Newcastle-on-Tyne were exploring a cave on Asparagus Rock, virtually an island in Kynance Cove on the Cornish coast, when one of the boys, 18-year old David Kaye, fell heavily, injuring a leg and fracturing his skull. The other boy pulled his unconscious brother onto a ledge and when the tide went down took him down a steep rocky slope to the beach. The injured boy would have to be moved before the tide came in again or he would drown.

The boys were spotted by Mr Harry Harris, a cafe proprietor from Kynance Cove who informed the Coastguard. Three Coastguards reached the scene and two of them, Mr G.F. Timothy and Mr C.R. Cook, waded the two hundred yards out to the Rock. Some civilians had also paddled out with blankets.

Mr Timothy decided to ask for a helicopter and signalled by semaphore, holding a white cap in each hand, to his colleague Mr Wheeler ashore: 'Ask Culdrose helicopter for injured man'. The message was passed at 3.28 pm and in only thirty minutes a Dragonfly from Culdrose had arrived.

'When we arrived there,' said the pilot, Lt W.P. Powell, 'we saw the boy lying on the grass on the little island, there were about half a dozen or so people round him. I endeavoured to land on the island, but the space was not large enough.'

'The doctor shouted to me that my front wheels had touched down, but that my rear wheels were still four feet off the ground. The doctor jumped out and attended to the boy. Meanwhile I moved away and tried to come back in again but it was impossible to land on that spot.'

'It was marvellous,' Mr Timothy said later. 'On the steeply shelving rocky surface the pilot made an attempt to land but it was too risky. On the second time around he hovered, steadied the machine, and a naval surgeon lieutenant jumped about four feet to give medical aid to the injured man.'

After one unsuccessful attempt to lift the boy into the helicopter, the doctor put a harness on him and he was winched up. 'It was one of the finest things I have ever seen,' said Mr Timothy. 'The pilot tipped the machine at the right moment so that Kaye was hauled through the aperture cleanly. The timing was splendid.' The boy was flown to Culdrose sick bay and then onwards to the Royal Cornwall Infirmary.

Possibly the first SAR holiday-maker rescue by a helicopter. Mr David Kaye being picked up by a Dragonfly from RNAS Culdrose at Kynance Cove, Cornwall, May 1953

The stories of those Fifties rescues can still be found in Squadron line-books, in private scrapbooks and old press cuttings. Occasionally, one particular rescue stands out from the rest, because of its difficulty and its unusual circumstances. On 29 September 1954, the United States transport *General Maurice Rose* was in the English Channel off Start Point, on passage from New York to Bremerhaven, when her Captain signalled that the four-year-old son of an Army sergeant in Germany had contracted polio. He requested that the sick boy should be landed as quickly as possible. But a second signal said that the boy's condition was worsening and an iron lung would be needed to save him.

At 5 am on 30 September the Rescue Co-ordination Centre in Plymouth asked Flag Officer Air (Home) if there was a helicopter available to take the iron lung out to the ship, hoist the boy into the helicopter, and put him into the iron lung. At 7.20 a Whirlwind took off from Gosport (Lt Cdr G.C.J. Knight, pilot, with Lt Adams and Senior Commissioned Observer Peter Rowsell) to fly to Eastleigh airfield, where an iron lung had been taken by road from Southampton Chest Hospital.

Knight took off with the iron lung, the hospital's night supervisor and a nurse embarked, to rendezvous with the ship 20 miles south of Portland Bill. The weather was not encouraging for such a potentially tricky mission. There was a very strong south-westerly wind blowing, and the visibility was poor in rain and low cloud.

Once over the ship, Knight took the Whirlwind down to mast-head height, but the helicopter was buffeted from side to side by violent winds made even more unpredictable by the eddies and turbulence caused by the ship's superstructure. Knight had to lift up well clear of the masts, and consequently the winch wire had to be operated at its maximum length.

Rowsell went down on the wildly swaying wire, to reach the deck, where the ship's doctor told him the boy was now too ill to be moved. Knight decided to lower the iron lung down to him. But it was too heavy to lower in one piece, and if it fell or was damaged it might be rendered useless. All the effort would be wasted and the boy would die.

While Knight fought to control the helicopter in the air pockets, the medical staff dismantled the iron lung until it could be lowered in two sections, each wrapped in a blanket. Knight had twice to risk the air turbulence and the scything sweep of the ship's masts, and descend until each section could land firmly on the deck, where it was unhooked.

The ship signalled thanks and said that no further help was needed. Rowsell had to stay on board, while Knight and the rest of the crew were very glad to be able to fly away, after a most anxious and nerve-racking half an hour's hovering over the ship. Few such rescues had been attempted at that time, and very little was known about the effects upon a helicopter's handling of such violent air disturbances over a large ship.

General Maurice Rose signalled that she was proceeding up Channel and intended to discharge the patient in calmer waters, off the Nab Tower. The iron lung with the boy in it was taken ashore to hospital. The boy recovered and on Christmas Day that year Knight talked to his parents in a 'Round the World' broadcast link.

This episode had favourable repercussions for helicopters in high places. The Commander-in-Chief United States Naval Forces, East Atlantic and Mediterranean, Admiral John H. Cassady, wrote to Admiral of the Fleet Sir Rhoderick McGrigor, the First Sea Lord, 'to express my personal appreciation to you for the vital assistance rendered by the Royal Navy in this emergency. It is my understanding that the helicopter operation was conducted with utmost skill. I would like to extend to all who participated my highest esteem'.

The year 1956, an important one for the naval helicopter, opened with a

Sea Hawk ditching off the east coast of Scotland on 9 January. The pilot Keighly-Peach (home from Korea and now a Lieutenant Commander) was recovered by the Lossiemouth SAR Dragonfly piloted by Senior Commissioned Pilot A.W. Webb. Two days later, Webb took a mother and her sick child to hospital in what was very probably the first night Casevac in the United Kingdom.

At about 4 am on the morning of 3 February, the 9,862 ton Norwegian vessel *Dovrefjell* struck a reef a mile south-south-east of Muckle Skerry Light in the Pentland Firth. It was blowing a Force 9 gale from the south, and the ship lay beam on to the rocks with heavy seas breaking over her. Her engine-room was holed and flooding, and her rudder and both propellers had been carried away. Lifeboats were launched from Longhope in the Orkneys and Wick but were unable to approach the ship.

Dovrefjell's SOS was picked up by Wick radio and broadcast to all shipping. At 6 am the ship's master, Captain H.A. Hansen, signalled that their position was dangerous. Flag Officer Scotland, Vice Admiral W.G.A. Robson CB DSO DSC was at sea in the destroyer *Wizard* making a farewell tour of his command before being relieved, and personally took charge of the rescue. At 7.31 he signalled to Lossiemouth for helicopters to stand by for rescue operations.

The first Dragonfly, piloted by Lt R.H. Williams, who had taken part in the Dutch flood rescues, with Acting PO Tel R. Moneypenny as his aircrewman, arrived over *Dovrefjell* at 8.15. The wind was blowing at 45 knots and solid spray was reaching a height of 100 feet. Robson thought it too dangerous for helicopter rescue and ordered Williams to return to Wick and wait for further instructions.

But on the way back Williams met the second Dragonfly from Lossiemouth, piloted by the Flight's CO, Lt J.R. Palmer, with CPO A. Japp as his crewman. This Dragonfly had in fact been unserviceable on the ground but after a splendid effort by the Flight's ground crew, led by Air Artificer Buck, it was ready to fly in 40 minutes.

Both Dragonflies returned to the ship. Palmer came down to 40 feet over the bridge, where he could see most of the crew had mustered, and made what Admiral Robson later called a 'bold decision to lift in the weather and sea conditions prevailing'. Because of the ship's aerials and the general air turbulence, winching had to be done from a height of 50 feet, which was near the limit for a Dragonfly. But Japp lowered the sling and the first of the Italian crew was hoisted up.

Palmer moved away and flew in a tight circle while Williams closed the ship and lifted one man. Palmer then returned to lift a second man. Williams did the same. Both helicopters flew to an improvised landing field in the grounds of a Hotel at John O'Groats.

In the next three hours, both helicopters made eight sorties, lifting two crew members each time. They were joined by an RAF Sycamore of 275 Squadron from Leuchars in Fife, flown by Flt Sgt V. Kyrke-Smith, with Flt

Sgt R.W.R. Briggs as crewman, who flew four sorties and rescued eight men. Between them, the three helicopters lifted all 31 Italian seamen, the eight Norwegian officers and finally, and reluctantly on his part, Captain Hansen.

Dovrefjell was at that time the largest helicopter rescue at sea, in terms of the numbers rescued. The helicopter crews were deluged with praise from all sides. 'Hovering Heroes – Six Save 40' proclaimed the headlines. 'The whole operation was most efficiently and quickly performed,' signalled Admiral Robson. 'Well done indeed'. King Haakon of Norway sent the First Sea Lord, Admiral the Earl Mountbatten, a telegram expressing his appreciation of the helicopter crews' 'extraordinary fine deed and bravery'.

Palmer and Williams were both awarded the MBE. Japp and Moneypenny received the Queen's Commendation. Palmer was also made a Chevalier of the Norwegian Order of St Olav. Williams, Japp and Moneypenny were awarded the Norwegian Medal for Heroism. The crews of the two helicopters of Lossiemouth SAR Flight won the Boyd Trophy for 1956.

This was the first time the Trophy had been awarded for helicopter rescues in this country. When awarding it the Flag Officer Air (Home), Vice Admiral Sir Caspar John, said that he had 'given particular attention to the deservedly strong claims made on behalf of all those who took part in the Suez operations'.

There were indeed contenders for the Boyd Trophy in the Suez operation. A period of growing international tension in the Middle East had come to a climax on 26 July 1956, when Lt Colonel Gamel Abdel Nasser, President of Egypt, combined financial expediency with personal satisfaction by 'nationalising' the Suez Canal.

Considerable forces were used in the Anglo-French attempt to regain the Canal: on the British side, 45,000 men, 12,000 vehicles, 300 aircraft and 200 warships; on the French, 34,000 men, 9,000 vehicles, 200 aircraft and 30 warships. But this force took months to assemble and train.

The Egyptian Navy was not a major force, having only four destroyers, some escort vessels, a dozen Soviet P. 6 and five ex-British Fairmile MTBs. But the Egyptian Air Force was the largest in the Middle East, with several splendid airfields taken over from the RAF under the Anglo-Egyptian Treaty of 1954, and some squadrons of Russian MiG-15s which outperformed all the RAF's and Fleet Air Arm's current fighters except the Hawker Hunter 5s of Nos 1 and 34 Squadrons RAF, based in the United Kingdom.

Of the British aircraft carriers, *Bulwark* was training and trials carrier in home waters. In a few hectic days she was stored and ammunitioned for war, brought up to full complement, embarked three Sea Hawk Squadrons, 804, 810, and 895, and arrived in Malta on 13 August. *Albion* was at Portsmouth, due to start working up in October. Her programme was hastened, so that she arrived in the Mediterranean on 17 September, with two Sea Hawk squadrons, 800 and 802, 809 NAS of Sea Venoms and 'B' Flight of 849 NAS Skyraiders.

The only British carrier actually in the Mediterranean in July was the large fleet carrier *Eagle*. Although a somewhat accident-prone vessel, she had been in commission since 1955 and had an all-purpose air group in a good state of training. As ground attack and army support were to be the main roles at Suez, her Gannet Squadron, 812, disembarked to Hal Far in Malta, and was replaced by 893 NAS Sea Venoms, who had been working up to join *Ark Royal* (at Devonport for extensive refit to cure the 'teething troubles' of her first commission). Thus *Eagle* was to have two Sea Hawk Squadrons, 897 and 899, two Sea Venom, 892 and 893, a Westland Wyvern Squadron, 830, and 'A' Flight of 849 NAS Skyraiders. *Eagle* and *Albion* had Whirlwind 3s for Ship's Flight and plane guard duties.

The three carriers began an intensive work-up programme, based on Malta, with a visit to Toulon late in September for consultations and flying exercises with the French Navy, who were to provide another two carriers: *Arromanches* (ex HMS *Colossus*) with two squadrons, 14F and 15F, of F4U Corsairs, and *Lafayette* (ex USS *Langley*) with one squadron, 9F, of Avengers.

In October, the training programme began to include helicopter drills. For Suez, the British carrier squadron, commanded by Vice Admiral Sir Manley Power, had five carriers: *Eagle* (flagship), *Albion, Bulwark*, and *Theseus*, with seven Whirlwind HAS.22s of 845 NAS, and *Ocean*, with six Whirlwind HAR.2s and six Sycamore HC.14s of the Joint (Army and RAF) Experimental Helicopter Unit, known as JEHU ('Experimental' was dropped for the operation 'to reassure the customers'), normally based at Middle Wallop in Hampshire.

Operation MUSKETEER, the seizure of the Suez Canal, was planned to take place in three stages: air attacks by RAF aircraft from Cyprus and Malta, and by the carrier air groups off shore, to neutralize the Egyptian Air Force; an airborne landing by the British 16th Independent Parachute Brigade and the French 10th Airborne Division; and a sea-borne assault by the 3rd Commando Brigade, supported by one regiment of 48 Centurion tanks. Later would come the British 3rd Infantry Division, sailing from the United Kingdom, and the French 7th Division Mecanique Rapide, from Algeria.

Whilst political controversy grew, at home and at the United Nations, the carriers continued to exercise for their roles in an operation which, by the end of October, seemed as if it was never going to happen. But at 5 pm on 29 October Israeli paratroopers dropped at the eastern end of the Mitla Pass, the gateway into Sinai. Israeli armoured columns crossed the border into Egypt that night.

The British and French governments later made unconvincing denials of any fore-knowledge of the Israeli attacks. That morning, 29 October, the three British carriers left Grand Harbour, Valetta, and put to sea, ostensibly for an Exercise, codenamed BOATHOOK, but steaming eastwards at ominously high speeds of over 20 knots.

Eagle suffered a very serious mishap when flying began that day. At 8.15, the main reeving wire of the starboard catapult broke during a launch and sent a Sea Hawk into the sea, where the ship passed almost right over it. The pilot, Lt L.E. Middleton of 897 NAS, went down some depth with his aircraft before he succeeded in getting out. He had the presence of mind to blow out bubbles, as he said, 'to see which way was up'. He surfaced after three minutes under water, and was picked up by *Eagle*'s plane guard Whirlwind. (A month earlier, Middleton's Sea Hawk caught fire as it was being launched by the catapult; again he crashed into the sea ahead of the ship and he was recovered, unconscious, by the Whirlwind).

The starboard catapult was put out of action, beyond *Eagle*'s ship's staff capacity to repair. All now depended upon the port catapult which was itself reaching the stage when its wires would have to be replaced – normally an eight-day task. Thus from the outset of MUSKETEER there was the possibility that the flagship, with her large and balanced air group, might not be able to operate any of her aircraft except her Skyraiders – and her Whirlwind, of course.

The carriers expected to fly off their first strikes at 4.30 am on 31 October, when an ultimatum to the Egyptian and Israeli governments calling on both sides to withdraw expired. But there was then an anti-climactic delay, while the British and French carriers and their screening ships waited all day for the signal for action.

The first Sea Hawk and Sea Venom strikes were launched early on 1 November, to attack airfields in the Cairo and Canal area. The carriers soon established a steady rhythm, turning into wind and flying off fresh strikes every 65 minutes. By noon on the next day, all the main airfields had been bombed and strafed, some 70 aircraft had been destroyed and 90 damaged, and it was decided that the Egyptian Air Force had been virtually eliminated.

The slower turbo-prop Wyverns were then allowed to fly further inland. The main target was Huckstep Camp, a huge military transport depot east of Cairo, where over a thousand vehicles including armour, parked in neat rows in the open, were worked over with bombs, rockets and 20 mm cannon shells.

There was no air opposition, but the anti-aircraft gunners in the Nile delta, as in Korea, improved with practise. One Sea Venom of 893 NAS was hit by flak during an attack on an airfield. The observer was injured and the hydraulic supply to the undercarriage severed. The pilot Lt Cdr Wilcox made a copybook wheels-up landing on board *Eagle* but his observer Fl Lt Olding later had to have his left leg amputated above the knee.

While *Albion* withdrew to replenish on the next day, 3 November, the other two carriers kept up the pressure on airfields and Huckstep Camp. Sub Lt C.J. Hall's Sea Hawk went over *Bulwark*'s side on landing and Hall was lost.

Eagle's air group made a special effort against Gamil Bridge, a solid causeway west of Port Said which was the coastal link to Alexandria. One Wyvern of 830 NAS was hit during a dive-bombing attack on the Bridge, but flew out to sea where the pilot Lt D.F. MacCarthy ejected and came down in the water some 4,000 yards from shore batteries which opened fire. Aircraft from *Eagle* and *Bulwark* flew RESCAPs overhead while others engaged the

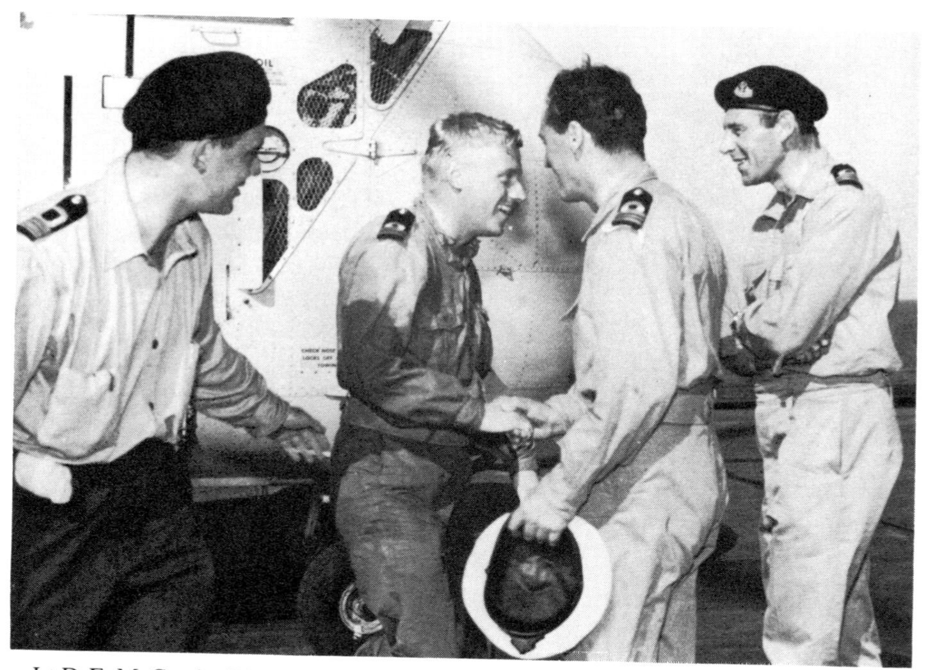

Lt D.F. McCarthy RN, of 831 *Wyvern* NAS (2nd from left), who was shot down by Egyptian anti-aircraft fire during a strike on Gamil Bridge, being welcomed back on board HMS *Eagle* after stepping down from the Whirlwind which rescued him

shore batteries until the Whirlwind, piloted by Lt Cdr P.E. Bailey, arrived from *Eagle* some 70 miles away. MacCarthy eventually returned on board after two hours, unhurt.

On Sunday 4 November, it was *Eagle*'s turn to replenish. During the day a CAP from *Bulwark* sighted four Egyptian MTBs off Alexandria. The following strike sank one with rockets, set two on fire and damaged the fourth.

Early on 4 November, three companies of the 3rd Battalion the Parachute Regiment dropped on Gamil airfield, getting down in ten minutes, and securing the airfield in about forty-five minutes more, with slight casualties. Meanwhile French paratroopers dropped on Port Fouad, opposite Port Said, and secured that side of the Canal.

Air cover was provided by 'cab ranks' of twelve to sixteen Sea Hawks and six Corsairs from the carriers, aircraft being called down to attack targets as needed by the soldiers. *Eagle* lost another Wyvern in a strike against the Coastguard Barracks, a solid modern building, stoutly defended, which bombing and rocketting had failed to subdue, on the western side of Port Said.

The strike leader, Lt Cdr W.H. Cowling, placed his 1000 lb delayed action bomb precisely on the ground floor and gutted the building, but was hit and had to bale out using his ejection seat about ten miles out to sea. Once again, the faithful Whirlwind, with Bailey in the chair, was there to pick him up and take him back to the ship.

In fact, Bailey and other helicopter pilots had been supporting the paratroops on Gamil. About 90 minutes after the landing, the paratroops reported that they were short of wireless batteries and asked if the carriers could supply them. Batteries were flown in by helicopter, followed by medical supplies.

Helicopters landed their stores, picked up wounded, and flew them out to the ships, in round trips of some 100 miles. While destroyers took over plane guard duties out at sea, the Whirlwinds established a regular shuttle service between ships and shore, with the helicopters bringing in a doctor, and various stores and comforts including a thousand gallons of fresh water, bars of 'nutty' (chocolate) and cartons of cigarettes (Senior Service, of course). They also evacuated thirty-seven wounded, including some French flown in from their landing area at Port Fouad.

By nightfall on 5 November the invasion armada was on its way to Port Said. Covered by carrier aircraft and after a bombardment by the warships offshore, 40 and 42 Commandos, Royal Marines, landed from LSTs in Port Said early the next morning and began to fight their way through the streets.

Meanwhile, 45 Commando had been waiting to land by helicopter from *Ocean* and *Theseus* some seven miles offshore. The first helicopter carrying the CO of 45 Commando, Lt Col Norman Tailyour DSO, reconnoitring for a suitable landing place, was hit but not discouraged. By 6.30 am helicopters were approaching in waves to land their troops under somewhat troublesome sniper fire on a patch of waste ground beside De Lesseps' statue, near the Canal.

The whole of 45 Commando, some 425 officers and men and 23 tons of stores, were brought ashore, faultlessly, in 91 minutes, in this the first helicopter-borne assault landing in history. 'Two squadrons whipped the men ashore in record time', wrote Captain E.F. Pizey DSO, commanding *Theseus*, in a letter to the Admiralty describing what he called the 'wonderful job' performed by the helicopters in ferrying the Commandos from ship to shore. 'The helicopters, after the initial lift, returned in groups of five to reload within about a minute, and after every second flight they were refuelled in four minutes.'

'While all this was going on, the first casualties from the Parachute Regiment, which was dropped the previous day, were being received in the *Theseus* from HMS *Eagle*, also brought in by helicopters. After our assault had been landed, the "choppers" turned their attention to Commando casualties and in fact one Royal Marine Commando who landed with the first wave was back on board and in bed within twenty minutes. Very soon we had about thirty casualties on board. We were in fact acting as the forward casualty clearing station and the rear receiving station, since the "choppers" could do the job so quickly and efficiently.'

'The main Army medical unit was on board the *Theseus* and at one time as many as eleven doctors were working on the casualties as they came in. The speed of helicopter casualty evacuation showed up very strongly the imperfections of boat transport. When we entered harbour and had a French hospital ship near us, it took far longer to transport Frenchmen by boat to her than it had taken the "choppers" to bring them from shore. I am sure the helicopter assault carrier, with hospital accommodation, is here to stay.'

Captain Pizey noticed one 'really splendid rescue'. 'Three helicopters were returning from HMS *Eagle* when one of them had to ditch about a mile from the ship because of shortage of fuel. On board the helicopter with the pilot were two French paratrooper stretcher cases. The pilot [Lt J.A.C. Morgan, of 845 NAS] hauled one of them out through the escape hatch, saw him swimming, and then went to the door of the cabin. He opened it as the helicopter was sinking and somehow heaved out the second man, who was floating in his stretcher. The pilot then kept both casualties afloat until they were rescued by another helicopter with winch lifting gear. Two minutes later the pilot was picked up and landed on HMS *Theseus*.'

The carriers flew constant 'cab rank' sorties over the beach-head during that day, but had surprisingly few calls for assistance. Armed reconnaissances

Whirlwinds from HMS *Theseus* taking the first of 45 Royal Marine Commando into action

were flown along the Port Said-Ismalia road. *Eagle* lost another Sea Hawk during an attack on an army camp at El Kantara. The pilot, Lt Donald Mills of 897 NAS, ejected and landed in the desert about 30 miles inland and ten miles east of the Canal, not far from El Kantara. British and French fighters flew a RESCAP over him until Peter Bailey and his whirling chariot arrived from *Eagle*.

'When I was within about ten miles of Don's position,' said Bailey, 'I could see carrier aircraft orbiting. There were Corsairs from the French carriers and Sea Hawks from our own, keeping all ground forces approaching Don well away. He'd twisted an ankle on landing but other than that was OK. On the return flight to *Eagle*, a northerly wind had increased to over 30 knots and direct flight became marginal. *Bulwark* was detached posthaste to the south. That gave me the reserve I needed – landed on, and took on a few gallons to return to *Eagle* without incident. We toasted Don's safe return in champagne that night.'

By the close of that day, fourteen LSTs had discharged troops, vehicles and stores ashore. British and French troops had linked up. Advance units had begun to probe southwards towards El Kantara and Ismalia. The leading Centurions were well on their way towards Suez.

But a ceasefire came into effect at 11 pm. *Eagle*'s port catapult had made

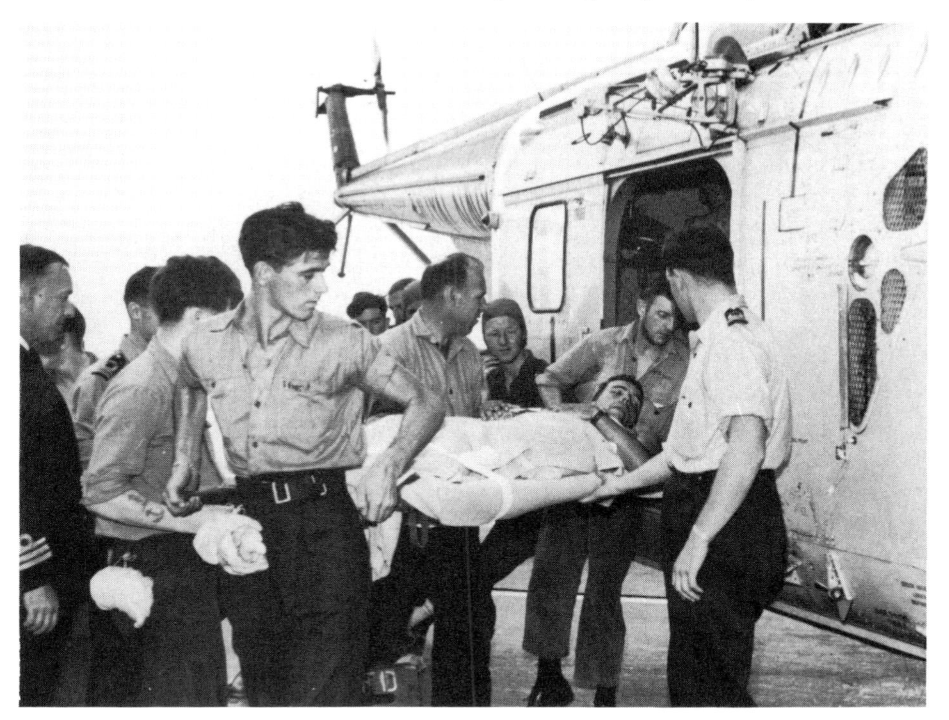

A wounded soldier on a stretcher being lowered out of the Whirlwind which had flown him to HMS *Eagle*

631 launches and was looked 'frayed'. Admiral Power and his staff transferred by helicopter to *Bulwark* on the afternoon of 7th and *Eagle* left for Malta. For her, and indeed for everybody, MUSKETEER was over, although there were many weary weeks ahead of occupation of Canal Zone, mine and obstruction clearance, and operations offshore, as well as a continuing political furore.

While the politicians who had themselves been largely responsible for it continued to bemoan the 'Suez debacle', those who had had to carry it out continued to regard MUSKETEER as a success. Certainly, it was yet another score for the helicopter in this new role, first used at Suez, of carrying assault troops ashore from a specially converted and fitted-out 'Commando' aircraft carrier.

Amongst the awards for Suez, there were DSCs for the COs of 830 NAS (Lt Cdr C.V. Howard) and 893 NAS (Lt Cdr M.W. Henley) in *Eagle*, 802 NAS (Lt Cdr R.L. Eveleigh) in *Albion*, and 810 NAS (Lt Cdr P.M. Lamb) in *Bulwark*. The COs of 897, 899, 892, 800, 809, and 804 NASs were all Mentioned in Dispatches. For the helicopters, Bailey of *Eagle* and the CO of 845 NAS Lt Cdr J.C. Jacob were Mentioned in Dispatches. Lt John Morgan, of 845, was awarded the MBE (he was later to lose his life in Borneo).

Meanwhile, far away, on the other side of the world from the heat and dust and controversy of Suez, other Whirlwinds were carrying out their usual search and rescue functions in the cold and ice of the South Atlantic. On 9 November 1956, HMS *Protector* (Captain J.V. Wilkinson DSC GM), a netlayer converted to an Ice Patrol Ship, crossed over the Antarctic Circle, to equal the record (set up by a Norwegian whaler in 1893) for the earliest date of crossing in the Wedell and Bellingshausen Sea areas during the Antarctic 'summer season'.

Protector's first task on her return to the Antarctic was to rescue a sledging party of the British Antarctic Expedition who were marooned on Roux Island. On 9 November the ship's two Whirlwinds made five sorties of about forty miles each way, to pick up two men, by hovering over the pack ice, and return them to their base on Lent Island. Equipment and specimens were also lifted off, together with nine husky dogs – who were reasonably docile, even whilst being hoisted.

6 'The most savage, bloodthirsty, treacherous tribe in Borneo'

On 25 September 1958, *Victorious* (Captain Charles P. Coke, DSO) was in the English Channel, preparing to fly on the first fixed-wing squadrons of a new commission. The ship had recommissioned at Portsmouth on 14 January that year, after a refit and modernisation in Portsmouth Dockyard which had lasted over eight years – the longest, most complicated and most expensive such conversion of modern times. She had spent much of the year on sea and flying trials but was now ready to become operational.

The first Squadron to embark that day were 803, who had reformed with Supermarine Scimitar fighters at Lossiemouth on 3 June. Having flown down via Yeovilton, the Scimitars were to fly on board in pairs, the first being led by the Squadron CO, Cdr J.D. Russell (who was Mentioned in Dispatches as CO of 800 NAS in *Albion* at Suez).

Cdr Russell's Scimitar landed but failed to catch a wire and went over the port side into the sea. The plane guard Whirlwind, piloted by Lt R. Duxbury, with Lt G.R. Fyleman and Ldg Seaman R. Brown, was overhead almost at once. Brown, armed with an axe, went down on the wire to assist Russell who could clearly be seen from the ship still sitting in his closed cockpit, although the aircraft was beginning to sink. Despite Brown's efforts, the cockpit canopy was apparently jammed and remained shut. Russell, who had been unable to free his legs from his straps, went down with the aircraft and was drowned.

The aircraft seemed to take an age to sink, in full view, very close to the ship. It was, of course, fully photographed, and there was much resentment in the Fleet Air Arm at what was thought to be insensitive media handling of the incident.

But good did come out of it. Cdr Russell's much publicised death served to highlight a serious situation. Between 1955 and 1961, 69 naval aircraft crashed into the sea, with the loss of 56 aircrew. Ditchings were only 12% of major Fleet Air Arm aircraft accidents but 52% of them were fatal and they made up a third of the total fatalities on land and sea.

The incident led to the provision of naval diving equipment in aircraft and the training of aircrewmen as divers so that a crewman could go down to or with the sinking aircraft and assist the occupants to escape. Also it led to the

Fatal accident to Cdr Russell CO of 803 NAS *Victorious*, September 1958

development of barometrically operated ejector seats in aircraft. While improvements were being made to ejection seats and canopy release systems, the first helicopter diving team was formed in 1961.

The plane guard destroyers and helicopters were, in a sense, the first naval units specifically and regularly dedicted to search and rescue. But any ship could be called upon to render aid at any time. While *Victorious* was suffering her private tragedy, another carrier *Bulwark* (Captain Percy D. Gick OBE DSC*) was just completing what the Admiralty called 'one of the finest salvage operations of recent times' thousands of miles away.

On the night of 12/13 September 1958, the Liberian tanker *Melika*, 20,551 tons, and the French tanker *Fernand Gilabert*, 10,715 tons, collided in the Gulf of Oman and both ships caught fire. *Melika*'s upper deck was engulfed in flames and tons of burning oil spread over the sea.

Bulwark, who was exercising with the frigate *Loch Killisport* some 150 miles to the north, picked up distress signals at 7 am on 13 September. She recovered her aircraft, except for one Skyraider which flew off to locate the stricken ships, and with *Loch Killisport* headed for the scene at 23 knots, as did the frigates *Puma* and *St Bride's Bay* who were also in the area.

When *Bulwark*'s Skyraider arrived, one of the tankers could be seen to be down by the bow, burning fiercely forward, and covered with dense smoke which made identification impossible from the air. The Swedish tankers *Ceres* and *Sira*, and the British tankers *Anglican Diligence* and *Border Hunter* were picking up survivors.

The tankers with survivors were asked to close *Bulwark*, who was steaming towards them, so that the Whirwind HAS.7s of 845 NAS could fly in doctors and medical aid as soon as the ships were in range. *Bulwark* herself joined the tankers about an hour later, and the ships steamed southwards, while 845 NAS's helicopters ferried injured survivors to *Bulwark* and landed *Bulwark*'s Executive Officer, Cdr R.H.H. Brunner, and a small firefighting party on board the burning tanker, which was about 12 miles away from *Bulwark* (and had by now identified by a relief Skyraider as *Fernard Gilabert*).

Meanwhile, there was no sign of *Melika* but reports from survivors and the other ships indicated that she had continued to steam southwards after the collision at some speed, although she had been abandoned by her crew. She was found an hour later by a Skyraider, listing and on fire, some 25 miles from the scene of the collision.

Soon afterwards *Bulwark*, steaming south with the injured survivors, passed close to *Melika* who was on fire amidships. Helicopters transferred *Bulwark*'s First Lieutenant, Lt Cdr P.P.R. Dane, and a small firefighting party to the forward section of *Melika*. *Bulwark* herself then steamed towards Masira to fly off a Skyraider and three helicopters with injured survivors to the RAF base there, for onward flight to Bahrein and hospital.

By the time *Bulwark* returned to *Melika*, *Puma* had put a firefighting party on board the after section of the tanker, but they were unable to join *Bulwark*'s party because they were cut off by the fire raging amidships.

Melika was an impressive and daunting sight as *Bulwark* closed her to try and pass a tow. She was ablaze amidships, her gunwhale was awash and the sea was spouting up in geysers through the mid-deck hatches.

There was a swell running and both ships were rolling considerably, so boat work was difficult and hazardous. At one point a seaboat was caught under *Bulwark*'s counter and two of the boat's crew were injured. Then *Melika*'s bows holed *Bulwark* above the waterline. A tow was secured at last but progress was very slow as *Melika* was yawing wildly and the tow parted after two hours.

In the meantime Cdr Brunner radioed that all the fires in *Fernand Gilabert* were out and that *St Bride's Bay* and *Loch Killisport* were standing by her. *St Bride's Bay* took the tanker in tow by the stern and began to tow her to the shelter of Ras al Hadd. But this tow parted after only a few hours, and then bad weather prevented another being passed. *Bulwark*'s helicopters ferried a party of engineers over to *Fernand Gilabert*.

At last, tows were successfully passed to both tankers. *Loch Killisport* took *Fernand Gilabert* to Karachi, while *Bulwark* towed *Melika* to Muscat, with *Puma* secured to *Melika*'s stern to act as a kind of sea anchor. For operations in the Persian Gulf and for their part in the *Melika* salvage, *Bulwark*'s 845 NAS were awarded the Boyd Trophy for 1958. It was accepted by Lt Cdr H.M.A. Hayes, who had been CO of the Squadron until just before the incident, and

Whirlwind of 845 NAS, HMS *Bulwark*, rescuing survivors after tanker collision, Gulf of Oman, 15 September 1958

Lt Cdr C.M.A. Wheatley RAN, who was temporary CO at the time.

Towards the end of the 1950s Whirlwinds began to suffer reliability problems. There were some ten incidents spread over a period (although cynics said they were 'once a fortnight') of Whirlwinds ditching after loss of power, rough running, or engine and rotor failures. On 23 September 1958, a Whirlwind of 824 NAS embarked in *Victorious* ditched in high seas during a 'rotors running' refuelling exercise. Another Whirlwind picked up the crew of three, one of them, Leading Seaman Phillips, being 'heave-hoed'. This, the SAR last resort, was a modified block and tackle, manually operated by the crewman of the SAR helicopter. Very possibly this was the first emergency use of the 'heave-ho'.

The 1960s brought a new helicopter, still regarded by some who flew it as the SAR aircraft *par excellence*. It was the Westland Wessex, the replacement for the Whirlwind. Developed from the piston-engined US Sikorsky S-58, the Wessex was the first Fleet Air Arm helicopter designed from the outset as an anti-submarine aircraft. It had an automatic pilot and could operate by day or night in all weathers. It was the first helicopter powered by a free gas turbine to be produced in quantity anywhere in the world. With a crew of four – two pilots, an observer and an aircrewman – the Wessex was a handy, reliable and robust aircraft. In its troop-carrying role it could carry up to sixteen fully-equipped marines. It could be readily manoeuvred into confined spaces and was easy to handle near cliff faces.

The Wessex's Napier Gazelle gas turbine had a number of advantages. It gave a higher power-weight ratio, so that the helicopter could carry a greater disposable load. It was smoother and marginally less noisy, and it could be airborne from cold within 45 seconds. It burned kerosene which meant that ships need no longer carry avgas (petrol) – a highly inflammable and unpopular fluid – at sea.

The first Yeovil-built Wessex made its maiden flight on 20 June 1958 and evaluation by 700H Flight began at Culdrose in June 1960. The first front-line Wessex squadron were 815, who commissioned at Culdrose on 4 July 1961 and embarked in *Ark Royal* in September 1961.

The second operational Wessex squadron, 819, formed at Eglinton in Northern Ireland on 5 October 1961 and pulled off the first major SAR operation by a Wessex, on 4 December when an SOS message was picked up from the Dutch *Steintje Mensinga*, which had run aground in a gale near Eagle Island, on the west coast of Ireland.

A Wessex of 819 was scrambled, with the CO Lt Cdr J.R.T. Bluett, and Lt P.J. Judd as pilots. They flew across country in appalling weather and despite high seas took off six of the crew from the sinking ship. Another four, who refused to leave the ship, were drowned. Bluett and Judd received a Special Order of the Day Commendation.

Steintje Mensinga was, in fact, the second half of a notable SAR 'double' for Bluett. Flying a Whirlwind HAS.7, when he was CO of 719 NAS Joint Anti-Submarine School Flight at Eglinton, he and his observer Lt G.R.

Fyleman, and his crewman Ldg Seaman A.L. Barker all received the Greek Ministry of Mercantile Marine Silver Medal (2nd Class) for the rescue of the crew of the Greek ship *Argo Dilos* on 20 October 1960. The pilot of a second Whirlwind from 719, Lt F.H. Simpkin, his observer Lt P.R. Lloyd, and his crew received the same medal, as did the Captain, Cdr R.G. Gaunt, and members of the ship's company of the frigate *Leopard* who assisted in the rescue.

Almost a year later, on 29 November 1962, in the Indian Ocean, there was the first night rescue by a Wessex. It was an aircraft of 815 NAS, embarked in *Ark Royal*, with Lt V. Sirett as pilot, Lt C. Brown co-pilot, observer Lt M. Palmer and PO Barker as aircrewman. They were in fact a very experienced crew, having all been members of the Wessex Initial Flying Trials Unit (IFTU) at Culdrose, where they had pioneered procedures for night rescues.

Sirett and his crew were airborne, exercising the night rescue techniques they had evolved, and had done three practise circuits, when Palmer told Sirett that he had just heard what sounded like a SARBE (Search and Rescue Beacon) giving the emergency code over the radio. Sirett stopped the exercise and started to home on the beacon. The ship informed them that the crew of a Sea Vixen had just baled out.

Sirett saw a light in the water – actually on the Mae West of the Sea Vixen pilot. Using the very procedure they had just been practising, Sirett carried out 'an automatic let down on the flight control system, down to a Doppler hover over the sea. But the aircraft was fairly unstable. The sea was quite rough and whilst I managed to get close to the survivor I couldn't position the aircraft over him. There was quite a lot of spray about. The aircraft was rocking, some twenty degrees nose up and nose down, sitting in the hover, thirty feet above the sea'.

'By lowering the sonar body into the water and putting the flight control system into the 'cable mode', so that the aircraft stayed steady over the cable, we managed to establish a stable hover, with the survivor about twenty yards away at two o'clock. In the light of the downward indication light, shining on the water, we indicated to the survivor to get out of his dinghy and come underneath the aircraft'.

'He paddled his dinghy over, got out of it, but grabbed hold of the sonar cable! Obviously he couldn't see much of what was going on in the dark and the spray. He gave the cable several yanks. This made it shake a bit. The aircraft was doing all sorts of funny gyrations. So we started to wind in the sonar cable and the survivor let go. We then lowered the winch and picked him up. The observer was afterwards picked up by one of the plane guard helicopters'.

'That was without doubt the most demanding rescue I have ever been involved in,' Sirett said, 'because it was so dark, the sea was so rough, and because at that stage we were all relatively inexperienced in night search and rescue'.

In the early 1960s, there were the usual SAR disasters, domestic and dramatic. They were always unexpected, in that nobody knew what was to come when the 'Scramble' telephone rang, but they tended to follow a familiar pattern. Their bald descriptions read like a collection of press cuttings. In May 1962 a man fell over a cliff at Porthleven; a Dragonfly flown by Lt D.B. Ferne from Culdrose lifted him to the top where an ambulance took him to hospital. Next day, a Whirlwind of 771 NAS retrieved two canoeists stuck in the mud on the River Fleet. On 30th, a man capsized his dinghy off Perranutloe and was picked up by the same Dragonfly and pilot from Culdrose.

In January 1963, in the middle of one of the hardest winters of modern times, the CO of 705 NAS, Lt Cdr P.J. Craig, and other members of his Squadron air and ground crews returned a week early from their Christmas leave to fly food and fodder to villages and farmsteads cut off by deep snow drifts on Dartmoor.

Later that month, a Sea Vixen of 893 NAS crashed on the round-down of *Centaur* during a night landing. The pilot Lt Cdr Fieldhouse and his observer Lt Swift were both killed; the plane guard helicopter could only find the body of Fieldhouse.

In August, two Sea Cadets and a man were stranded whilst cliff walking at Marloes on the Welsh coast and were picked up by the SAR Flight Whirlwind from HMS *Goldcrest*, the Naval Air Station at Brawdy in Pembrokeshire. In October, the 600-ton Spanish coaster *Juan Ferrer* ran aground in Mount's Bay and all 15 crew took to the water. A Dragonfly from Culdrose recovered the bodies of several of the eleven men who drowned.

In February 1964, twenty sheep were driven over a cliff at Pwllcrochan Bay, St Nicholas, but were all safely gathered in by the Whirlwind from Brawdy. In July, Brawdy's Whirlwind rescued two Belgian ornithologists who slid 90 feet down a slope and then fell 30 feet on to a rocky beach on Skomer Island.

Occasionally, one SAR event stood out dramatically. On the night of 18/19 March 1965, Lt Richard Smith was piloting a Wessex V of 707 NAS, the Culdrose Squadron which gives advanced and operational training to commando pilots before they enter the front line. Smith was taking part in a night exercise involving clandestine landings from canoes by the 22nd Special Air Service on the Castlemartin ranges in South Wales.

Smith's task, of deploying SAS pickets along the cliffs to detect the incoming canoeists, was finished and he had flown back to base on the range, when the SAS Squadron commander asked if he could fly a search along the coast for some canoes which had failed to arrive.

Smith's crewman, Chief Air Fitter Robert Kentsbeer, said he thought he had seen a red flare beyond the range boundary. Smith took off again and found three canoes, rafted together, about 3-4 miles off St Govan's Head. Smith made a slow fly past and saw the canoeists 'wet, exhausted, very unhappy and gesticulating particularly towards one of their number lying across the foredecks of the rafted craft'.

It was a rough, overcast night, with fleeting shafts of moonlight. The aircraft had a radio altimeter which gave only a poor indication of height below 50 feet, its starboard generator had failed ('pilots notes recommended flight termination as soon as possible').

The Wessex V had no throttles for the engines, which were controlled by computers with a 'tendency to object violently to a reduction in overall voltage and evinced their displeasure either by freezing the power at that set or, worse still, reducing power to zero or increasing it to maximum'. Neither Smith nor his crew had any special training in night SAR.

Nevertheless, they unanimously decided to 'have a go'. Kentsbeer dropped marine smoke markers in the form of a large 'T', with its vertical pointing towards the canoes. Smith flew by the 'T', guided by Kentsbeer's commentary from the back, while the co-pilot, Lt John ('Daisy') Adams, kept his eyes 'glued' to the altimeter, with orders to haul up on the collective if they ever dropped below 30 feet, when they would climb ahead and go round again.

They had to do that several times before they winched up one man 'in a bad way' but able to tell them that the man lying across the foredecks was dead. The rescue had taken 75 minutes. After refuelling (and reassurance from the ground crew that the generator *was* delivering its full voltage despite the red warning light which continued to 'glare balefully' from the panel) Smith took off again and rescued a second man, also in a bad way, while the two remaining canoeists fit enough to do so gestured that he should be taken ashore at once.

The Tenby lifeboat had been called out and later recovered two survivors and two bodies. Smith was appointed MBE for Gallantry. Adams and Kentsbeer received Queen's Commendations.

SAR sorties were, of course, flown all over the world. In March 1965, a Wessex of 820 NAS from *Eagle* ditched while transferring personnel off Singapore. *London*'s Wessex Flight scrambled in under four minutes, picked up the crew of two and returned them to *Eagle*. Next day *London*'s Flight took a sick aborigine from Sempai to Gompak Hospital. In April, in the same waters off Singapore, a Sea Vixen of 893 NAS from *Victorious* suffered an engine fire and both crew ejected. A Wessex of 814 NAS winched up the pilot, Lt Anderson, and the observer, Sub Lt Rainsbury, who was apparently unconscious and in fact died on board.

Eagle and *Victorious* had been taking part in the last stages of 'Confrontation'. This was nothing less than an undeclared war, which was deliberately played down in the media by both sides, so that few who did not actually take part in it ever knew its extent or duration.

In March 1958 the last Flag Officer Malaya hauled down his flag in Singapore, after the formation of the Federation of Malaya, which was to have included Brunei, whose Sultan had accepted the principle of federation. But on 8 December 1962, an armed revolt by the 'North Borneo Liberation Army', who opposed the Federation, broke out in Brunei and in nearby Sarawak and later in North Borneo.

Wessex HAS 1 of 845 NAS, Nanga Gaat, Borneo

The Sultan of Brunei appealed for British help. An advance party of 42 Commando Royal Marines was flown in from Singapore. In one daring sortie, one company of Commandos rescued the Resident and European nationals who were being held hostage in the town of Limbang, some ten miles up the Limbang river.

Meanwhile the aircraft carrier *Albion*, which had just finished a conversion to the helicopter commando role that year, was on passage eastwards from Mombasa to Singapore with two Commando helicopter Squadrons, 845 NAS (twelve Wessex HAS.1s) and 846 NAS (six Whirlwind HAS.7s), and 40 Commando embarked. Ordered to the trouble scene 'with all dispatch', she called at Singapore to embark HQ 3 Commando Brigade and arrived off Borneo on 14 December, after a 3,000 mile passage at high speed.

Aircraft of 845 and 846 flew ashore to the racecourse at Kuching, on the east coast of Borneo. Supported by the helicopters and by the minesweepers at sea, the Commandos had the situation under control in a week. Later, destroyers, frigates, minesweepers and tank landing craft brought up more troops and fire power. All the major towns of Brunei and Sarawak were cleared of rebels by February 1963.

Albion left for Singapore early in January 1963, leaving a detachment of 846 NAS at Labuan in northern Borneo. In mid-January, there was serious flooding in north Borneo and 846 paused from their military duties to fly relief sorties.

By April, the emergency in Brunei was over, but there were ominous rumblings from Sarawak. At Easter, on 12th April, there was an armed attack on a police station and armoury at Tebedu near the Indonesian border. Once again *Albion* sailed from Singapore in a hurry with 845 NAS, and 40 Commando, recalled from weekend leave, while 846 NAS transferred from Brunei to Kuching.

Once again, the situation was brought under control, but this was really only the beginning of 'Confrontation'. In September 1963, a new independent State of Malaysia was proclaimed, formed from the Federation of Malaya, the State of Singapore, British North Borneo (renamed Sabah), and Sarawak – but without Brunei, chiefly because of a failure to reach agreement over the Sultanate's oil revenues.

The new Federation was violently opposed in Indonesia, whose President Sukarno had openly sympathised with, and covertly supported, the North Borneo Liberation Army. Sukarno refused to recognise the State of Malaysia and threatened 'a terrible confrontation'. In Indonesia itself there were anti-British riots, with the burning of the British Embassy in Jakarta, and the looting of British citizens' homes and destruction of property. Malaysia, which Sukarno had sworn to 'crush before the sun rose on 1 January 1965', broke off diplomatic relations with Indonesia.

Indonesian guerilla attacks and infiltrations began to increase along the 970-mile border between Malaysian Sarawak and Indonesian Borneo, known as Kalimantan. Surveillance and police operations on this border, which ran through thick jungle and had never been accurately mapped, was the task of a small British Security Force, commanded by Major General Walter C. Walker – with the traditional help from the Navy.

The helicopters resumed their roles, familiar from Malaya a decade earlier, of transporting and supporting the troops ashore, in a climate of high temperatures and humidity, and a countryside of mangrove swamps, rubber plantations, rice paddyfields and virgin forest with trees reaching 200 feet in height. There were almost no roads and, until the advent of the helicopters, transport had since time immemorial been by river longboats or, very laboriously, on foot.

There were many helicopter adventures, some of them demanding outstanding flying skills from the aircrews, in conditions which would have been regarded as unreasonable at home. In September 1963, the Senior Pilot of 845 NAS, Lt Cdr Digby Lickfold, took off in a Wessex with a doctor to keep a jungle rendezvous with a Gurkha platoon who had been in action with the enemy and had one Gurkha badly wounded.

When Lickfold arrived there were no Gurkhas at the rendezvous. Short of fuel, he had to leave the doctor behind and fly back to base to refuel. The weather was worsening but Lickfold took off again in poor light, pouring rain and low cloud – conditions officially described as 'normally totally unacceptable' – to pick up the Gurkha and take him to hospital. Lickford was appointed MBE for Gallantry.

Although the helicopters were intended principally to support the military, winning 'Hearts and Minds' was part of the overall military strategy. Whenever possible SAR missions were flown on behalf of the people of Borneo.

The countryside was not as remote as was believed. Helicopter crews were taken aback to find, in areas where helicopters had never flown before, the local population tuned into 'The Archers' on their transistor radios. Early in 1963 one of the nomadic Punan tribe (reputed to be very shy and rarely seen by the outside world) was evacuated by a helicopter flown by Lt Cdr David Burke, CO of 846.

Burke found that the tribesmen 'approached without any fear the helicopter I had flown into a forward landing site, ignoring the noise and considerable disturbance to indicate politely that they would welcome a lift to Kuching hospital to get treatment for one of their number – rather like catching the No 96 bus to town'.

The helicopters' flying effort, over difficult jungle terrain, often through torrential rainstorms, with inadequate maps, radar and radio aids and weather forecasts, was truly prodigious: in 1963, 846 NAS's Whirlwinds flew 3,750 operational sorties, won the Boyd Trophy for the year. David Burke was awarded the MBE and, subsequently, accelerated promotion to Commander.

Early in 1964 there was trouble in Sabah, which had previously been quiet. *Albion* disembarked 846 NAS to Tawau and 845 NAS to Sibu in Sarawak, and continued to support them both although the distance by sea between them was almost 1,000 miles.

In March 1964, at Aden, *Albion* was relieved by her sister ship *Bulwark* (who had been the first carrier to be converted to the Commando role). *Bulwark* took over *Albion*'s stores and equipment and her assault landing craft. She also received from *Albion* six Wessex which, combined with 706B Flight, became 845 NAS. *Bulwark* arrived in Singapore on 2 April 1964.

The situation in Sarawak required that half of 845 NAS be permanently detached ashore. The other half remained on board at first, the groups changing places every three months. At its peak 845 NAS had twenty-six helicopter pilots, flying nineteen Wessex, two Whirlwinds ('liberated' from 846 when it disbanded) and three Hillers.

As the Squadron CO, Lt Cdr 'Tank' Sherman, said, the Whirlwinds 'were very useful for saving the whole lift of a Wessex when a one/two person casevac was required. The Hillers were also useful for flying the Colonel around without similarly wasting a Wessex'.

While eleven Wessex, and one or two Hillers remained in *Bulwark* to maintain the Commando ship role, the Borneo detachment, of eight Wessex, two Whirlwinds and one or two Hillers, was stationed in three places, at Sibu, the capital, and in two forward bases, at Simanggang, and at Nanga Gaat, 150 miles up country and only 30 miles from the Indonesian border.

The main base was at Sibu, in some cramped bungalows near the small airfield, which was named HMS *Hornbill*, after the national bird. This detachment supported all the military activity in the Third Divisioin of Sarawak, an area the size of Wales, mostly mountainous and almost entirely covered in jungle.

The Simanggang detachment was withdrawn in June 1964, but Nanga Gaat remained the Squadron's permanent forward base, deep in the eastern half of the Third Division, from where the whole Division was within the 100-mile radius of action of the Wessex.

At Nanga Gaat, life among the Iban tribes people had a flavour all its own. Very soon the aircrews developed a deep respect and affection for the Ibans and became virtually part of their community. Many learned the Iban language, some eventually spoke it fluently.

The aircrew lived in *attap* huts and dressed for dinner in the evenings at the local 'pub' – the Anchor Inn – informally, in a necklace presented by an Iban friend, and a sarong. The sailors were often invited to spend a night in a native longhouse – an unforgettable experience, with pints of *tuak*, the ferociously potent Iban rice wine, and songs by Iban maidens.

A London *Evening Standard* cartoon by Jak in August 1964 represented 845 NAS as 'the most treacherous, bloodthirsty tribe in Borneo', and an Admiral described them as 'those pirates', but the respect and affection were returned in full by the Ibans. They offered to send 300 warriors to defend Nanga Gaat air base should the Indonesians ever attack it. Helicopters were added to Iban tribal tattoo designs. The Iban Temonggong Jugah, the Federal Minister of Sarawak, whose home was in Nanga Gaat, adopted one of the Squadron's Royal Marine pilots as his son. An Iban mother, who was taken to hospital by helicopter when complications set in during child-birth, named the resulting baby boy Helicopter Anak Manjan.

Besides their support for the Army, 845 ran what amounted to a Flying

'We're the most savage, bloodthirsty, treacherous tribe in Borneo' (courtesy of the *Evening Standard*)

Doctor service for the local people. They once flew 100 Ibans to hospital during a cholera epidemic. On 19 August 1964, Lt Malcolm ('Cosh') Kennard, Lt Lindsay MacPherson and PO Edward Smith, flew a night sortie to a place called Nanga Entabai to pick up a young Iban, Kumbang Anak Badan, whose head had been pierced by a harpoon during a fishing trip with a friend. He was rushed to hospital and recovered. Luckily, the missile had penetrated a 'silent' part of the brain.

This was only one of many such sorties. Just before midnight on a Sunday in February 1964 a message was received at Sibu from the Gurkhas at Song, a village about 100 miles up river, that an Iban had been seriously injured. (Later, it transpired that two Ibans had been fighting with parangs – machetes. The 'Tuai Rumah' headman being away, his 17-year-old son had attempted to intervene but had received very bad slashes for his trouble. One hand was almost severed at the wrist).

Sherman, who took the message, asked, 'What is the weather like at Song?'

'It is clear,' said the Gurkha informant.

Doubting that, Sherman asked, 'Can you see the stars?'

After a long pause, 'No we can see no stars.' (In other words, it was totally overcast).

'Is it raining?'

'No. It is not raining.'

'Can the man wait until the morning?'

'No. He will die by then.'

The final question, but it had to be asked – 'Will he die anyway?'

'No, we do not think so if he is rescued now.'

Sherman took off five minutes later, to find a cloud base down to 1,000 feet and getting lower the further he went, with steady drizzling rain underneath. Visibility was so poor he had to follow the line of the river rather than fly direct. The journey, he said, 'was about the worst I have ever flown. The visibility at Song was so bad I almost flew past without seeing it. I eventually saw a few torches waving on the padang in front of the school where the trees had been cleared and, inwardly cursing the Gurkhas' idea of 'clear weather', I landed'.

The doctor said that the patient had only an hour to live. Short of time and fuel, Sherman had to climb out on instruments to 3,000 feet, higher than any of the surrounding hills, and make a bumpy flight back, using dead reckoning and guesswork. Fortunately he was able to 'let down' until making visual contact with the airfield, when 'it was all plain sailing'. An ambulance took the Iban to hospital where a Chinese surgeon was waiting. The Iban lived, with an arm as good as new, 'thanks to a brilliant Chinese surgeon and a wildly inaccurate Gurkha weather report!'

The Squadron was supported from the sea by *Bulwark*, who closed the shore of Sarawak, but did not anchor. Instead, she steamed up and down the coast, darkening ship every night.

Such intensive flying over such terrain ran the risk of accidents. 845 had a very good record, despite 'bending' several Wessex and suffering some material failures, until one period between February and April 1965 when they lost five aircraft, three pilots, two aircrewmen and eleven soldiers. Nevertheless, in 1964 845 NAS flew 10,000 operational hours, transported 50,000 passengers, lifted out 500 casualties, ferried millions of lbs of stores and ammunition, and won the Boyd Trophy for 1964. The CO, 'Tank' Sherman, was appointed MBE and awarded the Order of the Star of Sarawak. The Senior Pilot Lt Cdr B.C. Sarginson was also appointed MBE.

In June 1965, *Albion* arrived in the east again, bringing 848 NAS (Lt Cdr G.A. Andrews) with their new Wessex HU.5s to relieve 845. 848 NAS divided into an HQ Flight and four sub-flights to operate as required, and as intensively as their predecessors had done, in the jungle. They were not to be reunited until August 1966 when they all embarked in *Albion* for the passage home.

Bulwark recommissioned in April 1966 and returned to the Far East, in time for the ending of Confrontation, with the signing of an agreement after the ousting of Sukarno. 845 NAS were the last to operate in Borneo. Their farewell celebrations with the Ibans in Nanga Gaat lasted several memorable days. The last detachment of Wessex V's of 845 embarked in *Bulwark* at Labuan on 7 October 1966. Four years of extensive, and intensive, helicopter flying in the Malaysian Borneo States of Sarawak and Sabah, and the Sultanate of Brunei, had come to an end. It had been nearly four years since the whole of 845 NAS were embarked together.

The fighting might be over, but the emergencies went on. In January 1967, there was serious flooding in the Malaysian State of Trengganu. A landing party from *Bulwark* and helicopters of 845 NAS went to the area to help with the recovery of casualties and the distribution of food.

At home, the 120,000 ton Union Oil tanker *Torrey Canyon*, flying a Liberian flag and manned by an Italian crew, ran aground on the Seven Stones Reef, off Land's End, on 18 March. A Dutch tug, of the Wijsmuller salvage company, and the St Mary's lifeboat were first on the scene. The destroyer *Barrosa* also arrived, followed by the minesweeper *Clarkeston* with 1,000 gallons of detergent on board. A Wessex from Culdrose winched Lt Michael Clark with a portable radio set down to *Torrey Canyon*'s deck, to report on the situation.

Next day, nine of the crew were taken off by the St Mary's lifeboat. But the weather was worsening and the swell increasing. The Captain, Pastrengo Rugati, asked for a helicopter to take off another nine men. Culdrose sent two helicopters, the first winching up five men, the second four.

On 21 March, after unsuccessful attempts to pull or float the ship off, there was a huge explosion on board which blew Hans Stal, Wijsmuller's senior salvage expert overboard. He was picked up and brought back on board. Culdrose sent a helicopter which winched a doctor down to the tug *Titan* to examine Stal. He was badly injured and died on board *Titan* while he was being taken to Penzance. Captain Rugati and the remaining members of his crew abandoned the ship that afternoon.

Attempts at salvage were given up on 28 March. The ship was later bombed

Whirlwind HAR 1, 705 NAS passing a towline from HMS *Acute* to the burning German coaster *Vormann Rass*. Start Point, 11 March 1959

into a wreck by Sea Vixens, Buccaneers and RAF Hunters, and much of it disappeared below the water. But the oil spilled caused massive pollution along the beaches of Cornwall and Devon and eventually in northern France.

Many SAR sorties required the most precise flying, in the most difficult conditions of weather and poor visibility. On the night of 16 April 1968, Culdrose received a request from the Trinity House office at Penzance for a helicopter casevac of a man suffering from a crushed shoulder and severe head inujuries from the Longships Lighthouse, just off Lands End.

A Wessex of 706 NAS (Lt David Blythe, second pilot Lt Richard Saker, PO ACMN Anthony Mills, Medical Assistant Barry Norton, and Lt Cdr Michael Cudmore, an air engineer who volunteered to go along to help if needed) took off at 10 pm, on a pitch black night, with sweeping rain and a 30 knot wind gusting up to 40 knots.

The first attempt, to winch Norton down from a height of 130 feet above the sea, had to be abandoned as too dangerous because of the lack of visual reference points at that height and the severe wind-buffeting the helicopter was experiencing.

Blythe then decided to lift the casualty from the gallery, a three-foot platform running round the top of the lighthouse, below the lamp. He achieved a safe and steady hover, with his wheels only five feet above the aerials on the lighthouse. He himself could not actually see where he was because the lamp was directly below him and out of sight and its light, reflected from the boiling waves below, created a blinding glare. He had to rely on Saker to give him their precise height from the instruments and on Mills in the back for his sideways directions.

Mills lowered the winch, while keeping up a steady flow of directions, as the casualty, already strapped into a Neil Robertson stretcher, was lifted up and over the gallery rail and swung clear. While Norton and Cudmore looked after the injured man, Blythe flew him to Culdrose. From there he was taken on by ambulance to the Royal Cornwall Hospital.

Two days later, the Prime Minister, Mr Harold Wilson, was present for Culdrose's 21st Birthday celebrations. He told his audience that 'Culdrose has inscribed new honours on its great record by this remarkable rescue. I know I am speaking for all your guests when I express to those concerned the congratulations of us all on this wonderful feat of airmanship, at night and in a gale, to bring off from that difficultly situated lighthouse a man suffering from severe injuries'.

Blythe was appointed MBE and the others all received the Queen's Commendation for Brave Conduct.

7 Into the Seventies: *Merc Enterprise*

The British helicopter industry, overshadowed by Sikorsky, continued to develop helicopters, albeit more in hope than in anger, throughout the 1950s. Late in 1957 sea trials of the Fairey Ultra Light jet-powered helicopter were carried out in the frigate *Grenville*. The English Channel was very rough, with winds up to 62 knots, but the helicopter landed and took off successfully some seventy times from a small platform while the ship was pitching ten to twelve feet and rolling up to 14 degrees to either side.

In 1959 trials of the Saunders-Roe P.531 were carried out in the destroyer *Undaunted*. Nothing more was heard of the Fairey Ultra Light, but the P.531 eventually became the Westland Wasp.

The Initial Flying Trials Unit for Wasps (700W NAS) formed at Culdrose on 4 June 1963, and finally disbanded on 4 March 1964. The following day 829 NAS commissioned as the 'parent' Headquarters Squadron for all Ship's Flights, moving to RNAS Portland in December 1964.

The Wasp had a crew of two and provision for three passengers, a top speed of about 120 mph, and a range of some 300 miles. Although it was not long before it came to seem too small and too low-powered, the Wasp was in its day a game and willing little aircraft which gave every frigate captain his own air arm.

With the Ship's Flights – Wasps in the frigates, Wessex in the *County* Class destroyers – the helicopter may be said to have to have come into its own in the Royal Navy. It fulfilled all the requirements of 'organic' airpower, being versatile, controllable and, above all, instantly available. Furthermore, the ship's helicopter flight brought Fleet Air Arm equipment, methods, personnel and terminology intimately into the Navy's surface ships. Never more would the air branch be a 'trade' apart, known only in aircraft carriers and air stations.

A helicopter extended the range at which a ship could sight and attack a target. It also, of course, greatly increased the range and scope of SAR sorties. One of the very first Wasp SAR sorties was by the Ship's Flight of the Type 81 frigate *Gurkha* in the Persian Gulf in November 1965. *Gurkha*'s Wasp, piloted by Lt D. Anderson of 829 NAS went to the assistance of the dhow *Fathal Khair*, in difficulties some 150 miles east of Bahrain. Thirteen men and a Lieutenant RN were drowned but the Wasp did winch up one man with leg injuries to safety.

Two years later, on 3 November 1967, a Shackleton aircraft of RAF Coastal Command ditched in the South China Sea, 400 miles west of Sumatra. The Ship's Flight Wasp of the Type 12 *Leander* Class frigate *Ajax*, piloted by Lt M. Atrill of 829 NAS, searched for some 6½ hours. The Flight Engineer, a signalman and a Flight Sergeant were rescued, injured but alive. Two bodies were also recovered.

Ten days later, on 13th, the destroyer *Fife*'s Ship's Flight Wessex ditched during an exercise. Three of the crew of four were picked up by the Wasp of the Type 12 frigate *Juno*, piloted by Lt J.J.D. Knapp of 829 NAS.

But *Fife*'s Wessex carried out a notable rescue on 23 October 1968, after the MV *Tui Lau* struck rocks in the Pacific, 100 miles east-south-east of Suva. The Wessex, piloted by Lts N.G. Truter and J.A. Holt of 829, with Leading Seaman Walker as crewman, lifted off 87 passengers and crew and took them to *Fife* who landed them at Suva.

The 1970s were the busiest decade yet for SAR. Some idea of the scale and variety of SAR operations, major and minor, at home and abroad, can be seen in a selection of incidents from one year, 1970. In January, a Wessex 3 of 706 NAS ditched in Falmouth Bay after a fire warning light illuminated whilst in the hover. A Sea King of *Ark Royal* rescued the crew and marked the sunken Wessex with buoys so that it could be recovered later. Ten days later, on 19th, a Whirlwind from Lossiemouth was called out by the Mountain Rescue Team to look for a team of four climbers lost on Ben Nevis in atrocious weather conditions; one man was found alive, and three bodies.

On 22 January, *Ark Royal*'s SAR Wessex transferred crew members from the coaster *Friesland* to the MV *Nordhaven* whose engines had broken down 40 miles north-west of Culdrose; there were no casualties and the Wessex pilot, Lt Clarke, was afterwards interviewed on BBC TV 'Spotlight'. On 28th, the frigate *Hermione*'s Ship's Flight Wasp, flown by Lt De Hartog, was launched to look for a man overboard, A.B. McGovern, but nothing was found.

On 1 March an RAF Canberra crashed in Lyme Bay. Three parachutes were reported to have been sighted. The SAR Flight from Portland RNAS was scrambled, and the frigate *Dido*'s Wasp, which was airborne on a test flight at the time, was diverted to search. One survivor was picked up, and one body; the third crew member was never found. On 9th, Brawdy's SAR Whirlwind picked up 18-year-old Matthew Hutchon, seriously injured after falling 120 feet down a cliff at St Goven's Head, and flew him to hospital in Carmarthen.

So far the year's main SAR incidents had been at home. On 15 March, the Royal Yacht *Britannia* was on passage across the Cook Strait from Wellington, North Island, to Picton in South Island, New Zealand, with HM The Queen and the Duke of Edinburgh on board. A southerly gale was blowing with 60 knot winds whipping up huge seas.

As *Britannia* cleared Wellington Heads that morning and steamed south, she met the full force of the gale. Crockery and glass on board were broken

Chf Shprt David Lindsay, who is still being given artificial respiration, being carried down the gangway of HMNZS *Waikato* in Wellington, 15 March 1970. The frigate's Wasp is in the background. (Courtesy of the *Evening Post*, Wellington, NZ.)

and *Britannia* had to reduce speed to four knots. Lt Cdr D.J. Bird and a rating were trapped up forward in the 'eye' of the Yacht's fo'c'sle by heavy seas and both were injured.

At about 7.30 a.m. a sudden enormous freak wave broke over the escorting frigate, HMNZS *Waikato*, and swept three men off her fo'c'sle into the sea. *Waikato* dropped lifebelts overboard, but was unable to turn at once because of the sea state and the limited sea room. She had to return behind the shelter of the headland before flying off her Wasp, piloted by Lt Nigel Burbury RN, who began a systematic search of the stormy Strait waters, although conditions at the time were marginal for Wasp flying.

By then, the three men had been in the water for nearly forty minutes, but Burbury found two of them, Lt Cdr John J. Maire and PO George Morley, in the first ten minutes, winched them up and flew them back, unhurt, to the ship.

The third man, Chief Shipwright David Lindsay, had suffered severe head injuries and was recovered unconscious by the Wellington Harbour Board launch *Tiakina* which took him alongside *Waikato*. Artificial respiration failed to revive him and he was pronounced dead by the doctor when the ship arrived back at the Overseas Terminal in Wellington. HM The Queen sent *Waikato* a message of condolence.

Burbury was a very experienced pilot, who had flown in Borneo and was on two year loan service with the Royal New Zealand Navy. He had already carried out one remarkable rescue in the previous December, after the LORAN (Long Range Navigation) Station on tiny Tern Island, in the French Frigate Shoals, 500 miles north-west of Hawaii, was swept by 50-foot waves which wrecked most of the buildings and equipment and forced the US Coast Guards manning the Station to take refuge on a roof.

Waikato, on her way to Singapore, turned back and flew off her Wasp at dawn on 2 December. In three hours almost continuous flying, Burbury took off nineteen Coast Guard, three Alsatian dogs, and a quantity of personal gear and equipment. He received an aptly-worded signal of congratulation from Rear Admiral D.C. Davies, commanding the US Navy's Hawaii Sea Frontier, quoting Psalm 69, verse 2: 'I sink in deep mire, where there is no standing: I am come into deep waters, where the floods overflow me'. For the Cook Strait rescue, Burbury received the Air Force Cross.

On 9 May 1970, when the cruiser *Blake* was in Australian waters, a small motor-boat was sighted drifting off the Great Barrier Reef. A Wessex 3 of 820 NAS was launched to winch up the occupants who, it transpired, had had no food or water for three days. They were taken on board, fed and then flown ashore.

The frigate Wasps were still busy, *Jupiter*'s to look for and find a missing boat in the Channel on 1 June. On 1 August 1970, the inter-island ferry *Christena* sank off St Kitts in the Caribbean, with great loss of life. *Sirius*' Wasp, flown by Lt France of 829 NAS, coordinated the search for survivors and bodies. Over 250 bodies were sighted, many of them mauled by sharks, but there were 92 survivors.

By August, the 'Silly Season' was in full swing at home. On 21st, *Ark Royal*'s Wessex, again piloted by Lt Clarke, rescued a man and three children stuck on cliffs at Caerhays Beach. On 27th, Brawdy's Whirlwind picked up and took to hospital a Mr P.J. Christian who had first fallen 15 feet down a cliff and suffered minor injuries and had then been cut off by the tide at Stackpolewarren. Two days later, a dinghy was reported missing off Nare Head and black objects were sighted in the water. A Wessex of 771 NAS was scrambled and found the dinghy safe.

In September Lt Clarke was in action again, recovering a seaman who fell overboard from *Ark Royal* on 7th. By October, the 'Silly Season' was over and the autumn weather was causing ship casualties. On 3rd, a Sea King HAS.1 of 824 NAS from *Ark Royal* picked up three of the crew of the Federal German coastal freighter MV *Leda*, drifting and listing off the coast of East Anglia, and took them to HMS *Ganges* at Shotley. The ubiquitous Lt Clarke lifted another four of *Leda*'s crew to safety, just before the ship sank.

On the evening of 9 November 1970, *Ark Royal* was taking part in a NATO Exercise, LIME JUG, in the Mediterranean. She was about 110 miles west of Crete, preparing to launch Phantoms, and was being closely shadowed, as she had been since first light that day, and every other day, by a Russian SAM *Kotlin* Class destroyer.

Ark Royal was steering into wind and had just launched the first aircraft when the Russian destroyer *Kotlin 365*, on the carrier's starboard bow, suddenly turned as though to cross her bows from starboard to port. When the Russian was about a mile away, *Ark Royal* signalled 'You are standing into danger' but *Kotlin 365* stood on.

Ark Royal's engines were put hard astern, but the two ships collided. Some damage was done to *Ark Royal*'s bows on the port side. The *Kotlin*'s port side was badly scraped and her superstructure damaged. Seven of her sailors were thrown, or jumped, over the side.

A sea and air search began at once, by the frigates *Yarmouth* and *Exmouth*, the RFA oiler *Tidesurge*, another Russian ship, and *Ark Royal*'s Wessex, piloted by Clarke. Boats from *Ark Royal* and *Yarmouth* picked up five Russian seamen. Two were not found.

On 8 December a Buccaneer crashed into a hillside in Morayshire, but both crew ejected. A Whirlwind from Lossiemouth picked up the pilot, Fl. Off Warren, and the body of the observer, Pilot Off. Paines. Finally, on New Year's Eve, Lossiemouth's Whirlwind was called out to look for a skier who had been missing for 24 hours in the Aviemore area. The man was found in reasonable condition and flown to hospital.

But each year there were SAR incidents which stood out. On 6 February 1971, *Eagle* was at anchor in Gibraltar Bay when fire broke out in the Cypriot merchant ship *Byzantium* alongside the Detached Mole. *Eagle*'s Wessex ferried fire-fighting personnel and equipment to the ship. The fire was brought under control and extinguished by the teams from *Eagle*, from the guided

Rescue of Wolf Rock lighthousekeeper, 2 August 1971

missile destroyer *London*, and from the Gibraltar Port Authority.

Late in June 1971 *Bulwark* was involved in another SAR incident in an unusual way. New entry trainee sailors from HMS *Raleigh* at Torpoint were taking part in a sailing race for cutters and whalers from Plymouth to Fowey. The weather worsened and visibility decreased markedly during the day. Some of the boats were overturned by squalls and others were driven ashore under high cliffs at Whitesand Bay near Port Wrinkle.

A massive SAR operation was launched from Culdrose. There was every likelihood of a major disaster, but fortunately not a single life was lost. But by the time the helicopters had recovered all the crews from the water, the weather had clamped in at Culdrose and it was impossible for the helicopters to land there.

Bulwark, who was then doing a week's self-maintenance in Devonport Dockyard, had an emergency signal to prepare her flight deck to receive aircraft. She acted as an emergency landing strip, and fuelling and overnight stop, for four Sea Kings and two Wessex Mk 5s.

That autumn *Eagle*'s helicopters carried out a major rescue which earned 826 NAS the Boyd Trophy for 1971. At 3 pm on the afternoon of 7 October, when the ship was in the South China Sea, on passage from Singapore to Subic in the Philippines, an SOS message was received from the American freighter *Steel Vendor* with a cargo of cement which had run aground on Loai Ta Reef, some 55 miles south of *Eagle*.

Typhoon Elaine had passed through the area two days before and the weather was still unsettled, with a huge southerly swell and winds up to 40 knots. *Eagle* had in fact stood down from flying stations that forenoon because of the weather. It took nearly an hour to range and fly off two Sea Kings, 140 and 145, because the ship's rolling made all deck movements and rotor engagement hazardous.

The wind was still blowing at gale force, and the ship had drifted before it. She was holed on her port side, listing to starboard and being pounded on to the reef by sea and swell when the Sea Kings arrived overhead.

145's crewman, CPO TASI M.W. Bush, was lowered down to the ship's bridge to discuss the situation with the Master, Captain Lambert. Bush was winched up again to report that Captain Lambert wished to abandon ship, as she was in an impossible situation, badly holed and breaking up.

Bush was lowered down again to take charge of the rescue and 145 started to take up survivors, while 140 hovered high overhead as radio link and radar beacon. In *Eagle* two more Sea Kings were ranged and launched.

145 lifted sixteen survivors and moved away, to be replaced by 140, who took off fourteen. By that time the two more Sea Kings had arrived and took off the remaining ten survivors, making 40 in all. One survivor had fallen down a ladder and was semi-conscious. He also weighed about sixteen stone and it was impossible to move him away from a doorway so further winching by that Sea King had to be discontinued. Luckily there was another Sea King available to come in and winch up the last five men.

Sea King over *Steel Vendor*, October 1971

Survivors were lifted by strop, with Bush briefing them and ensuring that they put the strop on correctly. The last two up were Bush and Captain Lambert, using a double lift harness, so that Captain Lambert was the last to leave his ship.

In the following year there was another superb rescue, which was virtually a solo virtuoso effort by a Wasp pilot. On 12 July 1972, the frigate *Yarmouth* was ordered to go to the assistance of the SS *Oriental Falcon*, aground on the Pratas Reef in the South China Sea, some 150 miles south-east of Hong Kong.

The ship arrived on the scene late in the day and immediately launched the Wasp, piloted by Lt R.P. Seymour of 829 NAS, to reconnoitre. The wind was blowing force 7, the sea was rough at State 6, and continuous rain was reducing visibility to about three-quarters of a mile. The *Oriental Falcon* was hard aground on the reef, lifting slightly to the largest waves.

In spite of the weather conditions and the failing light, Seymour decided to begin winching up the Chinese crew at once. The only area he had to work on was a hatch cover 40 feet by 26 feet just forward of the bridge superstructure and surrounded on three sides by tiers of containers up to 24 feet high. The hatch was illuminated, but the containers were not.

With these difficulties, and in heavy drenching rain, which hampered visibility and piloting in the open-sided cockpit, as well as causing intermittent failure of the Wasp's generator, Seymour winched up thirteen men, transferring three or four men at a time to *Yarmouth* in 2½ hours of continuous flying. By that time it was completely dark. The rescue was temporarily suspended and *Yarmouth* returned to Hong Kong to land those who had been rescued.

While *Yarmouth* was in Hong Kong news was received that the weather was worsening and the rest of the crew of the *Oriental Falcon* had called for immediate assistance. *Yarmouth* went back to the reef and in weather as bad as before Seymour winched up the remaining 29 men, the last of them the Chinese master, in another 2½ hours of intensive and difficult flying, with the Wasp right on its limits. Seymour was awarded a very well-earned Air Force Cross.

At home the SAR capability around the coasts of the UK was augmented in October 1972 by the arrival of 819 NAS at the recently established HMS *Gannet*, the old USAF air base at Prestwick, on the Ayrshire coast of Scotland. 819 NAS had been at RAF Ballykelly in northern Ireland, flying Wessex HAS.1s, and then HAS.3s with more advanced radar and sonar systems, since 1961. Besides their main anti-submarine warfare commitment, they had carried out several notable SAR operations (including the crew of *Steintie Mensinga* in December 1961).

When RAF Ballykelly closed in 1961, 819 NAS disbanded until February 1972, when they reformed at Culdrose with the Sea King HAS.1. At Prestwick, 819 NAS had the unique experience, for the Fleet Air Arm, of operating from a civil airport under VFR conditions and the control of non-service personnel. Their main task was as before to provide helicopter support for anti-submarine operations. But, as before, they also had an SAR capability and from April 1975 819 NAS had a Department of Trade tasking to provide a Sea King at 90 minutes' readiness for SAR.

Each year's record of SAR incidents bore what could be called a strong family resemblance to the last. Certain types of rescue occurred again and again, in a time-honoured sequence. But SAR remained a chapter of uncertainties. SAR crews still lived from day to day, from hour to hour, waiting for the telephone to ring.

In spare moments SAR crews sometimes pondered on the causes of accidents. There seemed no consistency to them. The weather played a major part, of course, and the time of year, and the time of day. But 'scrambles' were called in clear fine weather, with not a breath of wind. Yet another day, of howling wind and lowering skies from dawn to dusk, might pass without any incident. SAR crews might spend an entire Bank Holiday weekend playing cards and watching TV, and might then be called out twice or three times on the Wednesday or Thursday, when everybody should have gone home.

Nor by any means were all or even the majority of 'scrambles' for holiday-makers, or 'grockles' as they were known in the West Country, in difficulties. A good many of them were for local people who perhaps should have known better and should have taken proper precautions. But 'It will never happen to me' remained a sure-fire hostage to disaster.

Every SAR Flight kept a 'Search and Rescue Incident Log', usually a large heavy book, like a Squadron Linebook or a midshipman's journal. Brief details of every sortie were noted, with times of take-off and landing, and the pilot's report of the incident and its outcome. By the early 1970s SAR reporting and recording had become more formalised. SAR Incident Reports had to be written on a standard form, known as a Form 'R', which was filled out for every SAR sortie. It formed the basis of a later signal to a wide range of addresses. including the Ministry of Defence, the Board of Trade, the Rescue Co-ordination Centres in Plymouth and Edinburgh, Flag Officer Naval Aviation, the nearer Royal Naval Air Stations and the relevant RAF Group. The detail in the entries required, from A to S, showed that bureaucracy had already gained a firm grip:

A Classification of incident (eg aircraft, shipping, coastline, land false alarm, medevac) and date of incident
B Subject of SAR action, operator or operating base, or address if known
C Time military search or rescue unit left base
D Nature of incident
E Initial distress message received by whom, by what means and at what time, from what source
F Agency requiring SAR assistance
G Rescue Coordination Centre (RCC) concerned and time distress message or request for assistance received at RCC
H Position of incident (latitude and longitude for all military incidents)
J How located and time
K How rescued and time
L Survivors or casualties
(1) Involved
(2) Rescued
(3) Recovered dead
M SAR forces employed
(1) Fixed wing aircraft: type and mark, unit, dates flown, hours for each date
(2) Helicopters: type and mark, unit, dates flown, hours for each date
(3) Land rescue teams: unit, manhours involved on each date, MT type and miles run
(4) Surface craft: type (for RAF Marine Craft only), unit, hours sailed on each date
N Survival equipment dropped (show vocabulary, reference, nomenclature and quantities)
O Radio, visual or audio distress signals made by survivors, range of first contact and altitude of search vehicle, if aircraft

P Communication with adjacent RCCs. Show other RCCs with which communication established and medium used

Q Transfer of Control. Where control passed from one RCC to another, indicate RCCs concerned and time of handover

R Termination of search. Where survivors are not found, and search is terminated, show on whose authority or agent with whose agreement search was terminated

S Narrative (amplifying important parts points with special reference to the degree of success or failure in the employment of equipment).

For the SAR Flight at HMS *Daedalus*, RNAS Lee-on-Solent, in the summer of 1973, form-filling was a major and time-consuming undertaking. The Flight was formed in February that year to fill the gap left by the departure of the RAF helicopters from Thorney Island. But unlike the RAF, the Solent Flight was also tasked by the Department of Trade and Industry, on behalf of HM Coastguard, to provide civil SAR service at 15 minutes notice from dawn to dusk throughout the year, covering an area from Beachy Head, 57 miles east of Lee-on-Solent, to Start Point, about 100 miles west.

This was high profile SAR, giving aid to the public in the full public eye. The Solent was crowded with holiday-makers, swimmers, surf-boarders, yachts, dinghies and sailing boats of all sorts, ferries and passing warships.

Their first 'Silly Season' began early that year of 1973 and ended late. Between March and September, their Whirlwind Mk 9 flew 114 sorties, and nearly 130 for the year as a whole.

The Incident Log captures the flavour of an English summer season, its mishaps and its false alarms: small boat sighted sinking off Old Castle Point, Cowes; small dinghy sighted sinking off Clarence Pier, Southsea; yacht in difficulties off Western Shore, Southampton; two 11-year-old boys missing from Yarmouth, Isle of Wight in a 12-foot boat 'coloured blue or pink with a dirty white top'; man stuck in mud at Langstone; four-year-old boy over cliff at Culver; medevac of woman with ruptured aorta from Newport Hospital; 'body' seen in water off Ventnor Pier (actually a log); motor boat in difficulties off Bognor Regis; patient with severe spinal injuries taken to Stoke Mandeville Hospital; five canoeists in difficulties south of Atherfield Point, Isle of Wight; two elderly ladies fallen over cliff east of Seaford ...

The Whirlwind crew were always quick to react, often being airborne inside 60 seconds. When they took as long as three minutes the pilot felt impelled to explain the circumstances (e.g., the duty helicopter had been fitted with blade cuffs and all but one of the ground crew were in the hangar and did not hear the 'scramble' alarm).

When SAR crews returned from a sortie, their rewards were the characteristically high adrenalin flow and exhilaration of a successful rescue, and the occasional letter of heart-felt thanks. From a lady in Halifax, Yorkshire: 'I apologise for not writing to you before this to express the deep appreciation of myself and my family for your very prompt action when our chartered yacht sank after 'bumping' into the yellow Admiralty Buoy off

Yarmouth I.O.W. On reflection my two young sons were thrilled at their trip in your helicopter, because you appeared so swiftly on the scene of our disaster, none of us realized how tricky the whole situation could have been'.

From a lady in Guildford (it often was the wife who wrote): 'I just had to write both from my husband and myself, to thank you from the bottom of our hearts for rescuing our daughter from the sea at Hayling Island last Friday. If it had not been for your wonderful swift and efficient action, I just don't know what we would have done, we both feel we can never thank you enough. Certainly we will never forget you'.

Sometimes, thanks took a tangible form. From a man picked up from a fishing boat with a badly bleeding arm, after his arm had healed: 'I did appreciate the help you and your colleagues gave me, and I hope you will accept the enclosed (£5 which went to the welfare fund) with my thanks and have a drink on me'.

Not all the rescues were successful, but people still wrote: 'May I express my sincere thanks to you and your men for their very prompt response to the emergency call-out on Sunday last and their attempts to save the life of my fiancé (a diver drowned while diving in Freshwater Bay). Though this time it was "in vain" it was extremely reassuring to see the helicopter arrive so very quickly and know that everything possible was being done to help, and that your men were fully capable of coping with the emergency'.

From an army major at Middle Wallop: 'I am writing to thank you for the very gallant effort made to find our son last week. The fact that Kelvin was the only one of the party lost reflects highly on your integrity and skill. Being in the business myself I appreciate the problems and am sure the rescue attempt could not have been in better hands'.

The summer of 1973 gave way to a particularly stormy winter, with at least one SAR incident, subsequently to become famous, which tested even the Sea King's limits.

The Westland Sea King, with the basic airframe of the Sikorsky S-61B, first flew in 1969 and entered operational service with 824 NAS, who formed at Culdrose on 24 February 1970. The Sea King HAS.1 was not just a helicopter. It was a fully-integrated, all-weather, hunter-killer anti-submarine weapon system, with radar, sonar, automatic flight control in the hover and a crew of four (two pilots, observer and sonar operator/aircrewman – plus a diver for SAR). It also had some new features for British helicopters: a power-folding five-bladed main rotor, retractable undercarriage and boat-shaped hull with side sponsons.

As the Fleet Air Arm's fixed-wing element withered away in the late 1970s, the Sea King emerged as the Navy's major front-line aircraft. At 21,000 lbs, or nearly ten tons fully loaded, it is a large helicopter, with a cruising speed of 130 mph and a range of nearly 800 miles. Able to fly six- to seven-hour sorties (more than twice as long as a Wessex) and cover a search area four times greater, it is an excellent SAR aircraft, as it demonstrated in the *Merc Enterprise* rescue, of January 1974.

On the forenoon of 16 January, the 480-ton Danish merchant vessel *Merc Enterprise*, which had sailed from Liverpool with a cargo of barley the day before, ran into a Force 11 gale whilst rounding Land's End, with winds of 50 knots, gusting to 70 knots, and waves from 30 to 50 feet high.

The cargo shifted and the ship began to list to starboard. By midday the list had increased to thirty degrees, *Merc Enterprise* was constantly shipping green seas and her holds were filled with water. The Master, Captain Jan Fedderson, realised that the situation was hopeless. At 12.42 pm he broadcast an SOS 'May Day' signal, giving his position as approximately 25 miles south of Plymouth.

There were nineteen people on board: Captain Fedderson and his crew of 15, including a young boy, and three wives including Fedderson's who had come along for the trip. It seems that most of them got away from the ship, in two lifeboats, two dinghies and a life-raft, but these were overturned almost at once by the tremendous seas running, and all the occupants were pitched into the water.

Fedderson's SOS was picked up by Coastguard HQ at Falmouth, by Coastguard stations at Rame Head, Brixham and Land's End, by seven other ships in the Channel, and by the RAF Rescue Co-ordination Centre at Mountbatten, Plymouth, who immediately called Culdrose.

The position given in the signal meant a round trip from Culdrose of some 150 miles – beyond the feasible distance for Whirlwinds, especially in that fierce weather. Clearly it was a task for the long-range Sea Kings. '592' of 706 NAS (Lt H.F. Hatton and Lt P. Shaw, observer Lt K. Flemons, and aircrewman PO D. Jackson) had taken off by 1.55 pm and was quickly followed by '596' (Lt Cdr D. Blythe and Lt K. Lamprey, observer Sub Lt D. Keaney, and aircrewman PO D. Fowles). The third Sea King was from the Royal Naval Foreign Training Unit (R.N.F.T.U.), a Federal German Navy aircraft 'Germany 5' (Lt Cdr D. Mallock and Kap Lt O. Reiners, observer Lt A. Tremelling, and aircrewman Lt z s. Schuler). Fourth was '051' from 824 NAS (Lt A. Baker RAN and Lt V. Ratcliffe, observer Lt R. Winchcombe, aircrewmen Ldg Sea B. Sharpe and AB A. Williams).

Another 'Mayday' call had been received from a position west of Land's End and a second R.N.F.T.U. Sea King 'Germany 8' (Lt R. Ellis and Kap: Lt O. Smogrovics, observer Lt N. Crocker, and aircrewman Ober Lt M. Kopp) was sent to investigate. But it proved a false alarm and 'Germany 8' flew back to join the others.

'592' arrived over *Merc Enterprise* first, at about 2.15 pm. The situation was not promising. Huge rollers some seventy to a hundred feet in height were sweeping in from the south-west. Their sides were so steep and high that Hatton had to 'fly' the Sea King up and down as though crossing a range of hills. The sea itself was streaked white with wind-driven foam for as far as the eye could see. Below, the ship had capsized and had almost sunk so that only the shape of the keel and the bottom of the upturned hull were visible.

Lifeboats could be seen, and debris and a discernible oil slick and, through the spray, what looked like two survivors in life-jackets. In those conditions,

The *Merc Enterprise* rescue, 16 January 1974

Hatton found it impossible to hover normally above the survivors so he flew down wind some distance, the winch line was paid out and '592' then flew back up wind, 'trailing' the strop across the sea, hoping the survivors could reach it. Miraculously they did, and these first two survivors were successfully winched up.

Two more survivors, a man and a woman, were seen and the strop was dragged towards them. But they could not or would not reach it, being either too exhausted or too terrified to let go of each other. So PO Jackson was lowered on a 'double-lift' harness downwind of the couple, and was towed through the sea towards them.

Jackson found that the man was almost unconscious from an ugly gash on the head, and both his legs were badly injured. The woman was hysterical with terror and, despite Jackson's pleadings, refused to let go of the man. Finally, Jackson had to use all his strength to break her grasp and then force the strop over her head. He and the woman were then winched up, although the woman continued to kick and struggle frenziedly until she was actually hauled into the Sea King.

Jackson now had to go down a second time for the man. He himself was beginning to suffer from the effects of the cold, the buffeting of the sea and his own intense physical efforts. Meanwhile, Hatton was still flying the Sea King to try and minimise the effect of the stupendous rise and fall of the waves. But such was the sea running that at one point Jackson looked across and saw the Sea King actually level with him, with the winch cable laid out horizontally between them. But the man was much more amenable and was speedily lifted up.

Flemons then spotted another survivor in his lifejacket. Jackson went down for the third time and a fifth survivor was safely gathered in. All were in desperate need of urgent medical attention so Hatton flew directly to the Royal Naval Barracks, Devonport. Ambulances took the survivors to the Royal Naval Hospital, Stonehouse.

Meanwhile, the other Sea Kings were quartering over the area around *Merc Enterprise*'s hull, searching for survivors and sending down their crewmen. Blythe tried to hold '596' steady against the sudden and violent wind gusts while PO Fowles went down on the wire. Fowles reached the body of one man, who was very probably dead already, and actually had his clothing in his grip when a huge wave washed right over him, wrenched the body away and swept it some distance from him.

When Fowles tried to grasp the body again, another wave lifted him up and dropped him so suddenly that the winch cable entangled itself around Fowles' helmet visor and the winch hook dealt him a smashing blow on the face, knocking him nearly unconscious and causing a wound which later needed seven stitches.

Fowles tried again and again to swim towards the body but each time wind and sea took it further away. From above, the observer Sub Lt Keaney saw another man who might still be alive. Fowles was winched up, '596' moved overhead and Fowles went down again. But, as before, a rising wave produced yards of slack cable which then went bar-taut as the wave subsided. Fowles was hit on the mouth by the hook again. At last, Blythe could see that Fowles was weakening and had had enough. He was winched up, half hanging out of his harness. '596' flew back to Culdrose.

Lt Cdr Mallock in 'Germany 5', over to port of '592', had also been flying his Sea King up and down to match the troughs and crests of the waves. This motion was so violent that some of the crews began to feel literally air-sick. As the winchman OberLt Schuler went down to pick up a survivor, one giant wave passed only ten feet below the helicopter. Schuler was dragged under, the winch-wire tautened until it was almost horizontal, and the Sea King itself was checked by the drag of Schuler's body underwater. When Schuler went under the next wave, the winch-hook swung into his face and cut his eye.

Astonishingly, Schuler came to the surface near the survivor, grabbed him and held on as they were both swept under by the waves. The survivor, actually Captain Fedderson, ripped open the zip-fastener of Schuler's suit so that it filled with water, but he and Schuler were winched up. Another survivor was seen and despite the blood streaming down his face Schuler went down again to rescue a second man.

Schuler gathered in two dead bodies, one of them Mrs Fedderson. It now seemed probable that those left in the water would almost certainly be dead. Mallock had to balance the possibility of finding anyone else alive against the critical condition of his two survivors. He decided that it would be better to fly to Plymouth and did so, whilst he and his crew concealed from Captain Fedderson for the time being the fact that although his wife had been picked up she was dead.

Meanwhile, Lt Ellis in 'Germany 8' and Lt Baker in '051' were still looking for survivors. 'Germany 8' recovered two bodies, and '051' one.

Three merchantmen had arrived in the area and four more were on their way although all of them were having the greatest difficulty manoeuvring in the extreme conditions. The nearest ship was the 2,000 ton Russian stern trawler *Leningrad* whose crew actually saw four survivors clinging to wreckage. Thrown ropes and scrambling nets were of no avail, so, in an act of

Petty Officer Aircrewman David Jackson, awarded the Air Force Medal for the *Merc Enterprise* rescue

singular bravery, four of the Russian sailors went into the sea on the ends of ropes and each of them recovered one survivor.

Those were the last to be saved. '592' had five survivors, *Leningrad* had four, 'Germany 5' had two survivors and two bodies, 'Germany 8' had two bodies, and '051' one. Thus, of the 19 souls in *Merc Enterprise*, eleven had been picked up alive, with five bodies, and three missing.

To rescue so many in such conditions was a magnificent achievement by the Sea Kings and by *Leningrad*. But now there was a new and unexpected danger which threatened to make the rescuers need rescue themselves.

8 Cyprus 1974: 'Bottles, nappies and nippers ...'

Having delivered the two survivors and two bodies to the Royal Naval Barracks, Devonport, Lt Cdr Mallock in 'Germany 5' took off again and, in the fading light, headed back towards *Merc Enterprise*, where a new situation had developed.

Captain Gyemnady Beljaev, of the Russian trawler *Leningrad*, had signalled that he would not risk trying to reach Plymouth, a harbour strange to him, in the dark and in that weather. But, if the four survivors on board were not landed soon, they would almost certainly die without medical attention. Mallock decided to try and winch the survivors up into 'Germany 5'.

But the first run over the trawler showed that winching would be extremely hazardous. *Leningrad* was rolling prodigiously, her mast whipping from side to side through nearly 90°. Mallock was willing to try, but there were language difficulties. Mallock could not make Captain Beljaev understand that it was imperative that *Leningrad* steered as steady a course as possible, keeping the wind on one bow. In SAR, there is always a fine line between the possible and the suicidal. Mallock decided to abandon the rescue attempt.

Fortunately, Beljaev then changed his mind and decided to make for Plymouth after all. Mallock called off the helicopter rescue operation. With great relief, 'Germany 5' headed for Culdrose. It was 5 pm, 'Germany 5' had been airborne for three hours, and Mallock and his crew were bone weary.

But 'Germany 5' had been flying westward for barely three or four minutes when Rame Head Coastguard Station came on the air. There was anxiety about the Plymouth lifeboat, *Thomas Forehead-Mary Rowse*, which had been called out by Falmouth Coastguard HQ that afternoon, in response to *Merc Enterprise*'s "Mayday" call.

The lifeboat coxswain, John Dare, and his crew were all strong and experienced seamen, used to bad weather, but none of them had ever known wind and sea conditions as bad as they met as soon as they cleared Plymouth breakwater that day. Three of them were sea-sick – an almost unheard-of occurrence – and they all admitted later they were 'dead scared' at times.

Rame Head Station gave them the option of returning, because of the weather, but John Dare understood that at least seven of *Merc Enterprise*'s crew were still missing, and decided to press on.

But when the lifeboat reached the area, where *Merc Enterprise* had by now sunk, there was nothing to be seen. Dare heard that the helicopters had called off the search. With great care and difficulty in those seas, he turned the lifeboat for home and shortly afterwards, south of the Eddystone Lighthouse, 'Germany 5' was sighted, asking if all was well. Reassured, 'Germany 5' also turned for home, for the second time. The lifeboat went on, actually succeeded in sighting *Leningrad*, and escorted her into Plymouth.

Heading west from the Eddystone, 'Germany 5' had now been airborne for some three and a half hours, and had two hours' fuel left – ample to reach Culdrose in normal circumstances. But after about 15 minutes' flying, when 'Germany 5' was south of Dodman Point, about midway between Rame Head and the Lizard, the engines began to falter. In the gusts of tremendous air turbulence caused by the storm, there was a sudden unaccountable high frequency vibration, with disconcerting sounds like rapid machine gun fire.

Mallock reduced speed to 110 mph, which seemed to remedy the situation, but made a PAN call to Culdrose. Soon the fusillade of staccato sounds, like car engines back-firing, began again. Flames and sparks could be seen coming from the starboard engine. Mallock reduced speed further to 90 mph and, as 'Germany 5' flew slowly across Falmouth Bay, made a second PAN call to

Trophy from grateful locals, 1974

Culdrose, asking for stand-by SAR facilities in case 'Germany 5' had to ditch.

Lt Baker in '051' had just landed at Culdrose when the PAN signal was received. He took off again at once, sighted 'Germany 5' approaching the Lizard peninsula, and took up station half a mile astern. But '051' soon began to suffer the same alarming experience: air turbulence, extreme vibration, loud bangs, flames and sparks, and intermittent engine failures. Far from being able to assist 'Germany 5', Baker now had to try and save '051'.

Baker turned back and, as he passed over the coastline, '051' had a double engine surge and then both engines died. Baker prepared to make an auto-rotation landing, but as he neared the ground he saw a farmhouse in the landing lights, dead ahead. At that moment one engine fired again, Baker was just able to lift over the house and force-land in a field close by.

Meanwhile, Mallock was fighting to save 'Germany 5'. Both engines stalled at 750 feet and the aircraft began to fall towards the sea where, in that weather and at that point on a rocky coast-line, the crew would have almost no chance of surviving. Fortunately one engine recovered enough for Mallock to be able to pick the aircraft up and fly on slowly towards the land.

The poor visibility was made even worse by salt encrusted so thickly on the windscreen that Mallock could barely see out. Both engines failed again and the helicopter began to auto-rotate downwards, while the crew prepared for a force-landing. By the landing lights Mallock saw a ploughed field, sloping from left to right at a fairly steep angle. It was not ideal, but better than nothing.

Unfortunately nobody saw the power lines stretching across their approach. A brilliant blue flash lit up the stormy night sky for miles around as the Sea King severed the power lines, hit the ground and tilted over some 25° to starboard. Much relieved to be down in one piece, Mallock and his crew looked out upon the unusual sight of power cables thrashing the ground, as though in agony, and emitting showers of blue and orange sparks.

The Sea King had put out all the lights in the district, but Mallock and his crew found their way in the total darkness and still howling wind and rain across fields to a farmhouse where they were welcomed and given whisky until the road transport from Culdrose arrived.

All that now remained was to hold post mortems on the causes of the accidents. The clue lay in those heavily salt-encrusted windshields. The violence of wind and sea and the size of the waves generated around *Merc Enterprise* that day had whipped up quantities of salt-laden spray a hundred feet into the air. The Sea Kings' Rolls-Royce Gnome engines had therefore been sucking in heavily salt-impregnated air for hours on end. The salt had coated compressors and turbine blades and eventually clogged the engines, literally to a standstill.

Mallock and Baker both won the Air Force Cross, Jackson, Fowles and Aircrewman Adrian Williams of '051', the Air Force Medal. The other sixteen aircrew received Flag Officer Naval Air Command Commendations. John Dare was awarded the RNLI's Bronze Medal and had a letter of

The face of pain: an injured man from the MV *Shackleton* is hoisted up on a stretcher, with SAR aircrew man in attendance, 9 May 1974

gratitude from the Danish Mercantile Authorities. Mercandia Shipping Co of Denmark awarded RNAS Culdrose and Falmouth Coastguard HQ the Mercandia Blue Ribband. Lt Cdr David Mallock also won the Royal Aeronautical Society's Alan Marsh Medal for 1974.

The *Merc Enterprise* rescue crews might also have won the Boyd Trophy for 1974, but there was stiff competition for that later in the year.

Cyprus, a British colony since 1925, has been a strategically valuable island in the eastern Mediterranean since Roman times. After a four-year campaign of violence against British rule by the Ethniki Organosis Kyprion Agoniston (National Organisation of Cypriot Fighters), better known as EOKA, Cyprus became independent on 16 August 1960. Archbishop Makarios was elected president of the new republic.

The new constitution, a compromise between the British, Greek and Turkish governments, laid down that there should be no union of Cyprus with any other state. Partition, into Greek and Turkish zones, was explicitly ruled out. Britain, Greece and Turkey all reserved the right to intervene in Cypriot affairs, either jointly or singly, to guarantee the new constitution and the republic's independence.

Britain kept sovereignty over the two bases of Akrotiri and Dhekelia, in the south of the island. Greece had the right, which she exercised, to keep 950 troops in the island. Turkey also had 650 troops in Cyprus.

Such an arrangement was hardly a basis for a stable future. It did not satisfy the aim of the Greek Cypriots, held since the mid-19th Century, for *enosis*: the union of Greece and Cyprus. Nor did it resolve the ancient and mutual hatred between the 78 per cent of Greek Cypriots and the 18 per cent minority of Turkish Cypriots. After the murder of two Turkish Cypriots in December 1963, there was an outbreak of violence in Nicosia which quickly spread across the whole island.

Order was only restored by a partially effective ceasefire in 1964 and by the arrival of a United Nations Peacekeeping Force. But both sides continued to accumulate arms and to train men. Greek Cypriots and Turkish Cypriots effectively controlled their own areas of the island, defending them with their own armed forces, the Greek Cypriot National Guard and the Turkish Cypriot Freedom Fighters.

In an uneasy lull, punctuated by spasms of violence, the great danger was that Greek Cypriot extremists, always suspicious that Makarios was betraying their great dream of *enosis*, might gain the upper hand and provoke Turkey to take action.

On 15 July 1974, Makarios was deposed by a Greek nationalist coup and fled to London. Turkey responded on 20 July with an amphibious landing at Five Mile Beach, on the north coast, just west of the port of Kyrenia. The invasion site was judiciously chosen. The area from Nicosia to Kyrenia had the largest enclave of Turkish Cypriots in the island, so the local population there would be likely to welcome Turkish troops (they would also be protected from retaliatory massacre by Greek Cypriots).

The Turks landed across the beaches with three divisions, some 40,000 men in all, with tanks, airborne and helicopter borne assault troops, and close support from the Turkish Air Force. The Turks advanced extraordinarily slowly and cautiously, but the bombing and shelling started forest fires which spread vigorously in the intense summer heat. Many buildings were wrecked: a large £1½ million hotel, recently advertised in British newspapers, and only opened on 15 June, was totally gutted by fire. Casualties were comparatively low, but there were atrocities among the civilian population on both sides. Soon there were refugees.

The British refugees listened to the instructions broadcast by the British Forces Broadcasting Service and headed for Six Mile Beach, to the east of Kyrenia, or to the port itself. With their baggage limited to one suitcase each, they made for the beaches as though obeying some atavistic tribal tradition, as though the British as a nation firmly believed that no matter how badly things had gone wrong, no matter how hopeless the situation might seem, all they had to do was to make their way in as orderly a manner as possible down to the sea, and there the ships would be waiting.

Indeed, the ships were waiting. On 15 July the helicopter carrier *Hermes* (Captain Peter Branson RN) was on passage from New York, two days out from Malta, where she was due to land 41 Commando, when the news arrived

Turkish/Cypriot War, July/August 1974. Wessex V from 845 Sqdn picking up passengers to take to HMS *Hermes*

of the *coup* in Cyprus.

After making personnel changes and collecting stores by helicopter as the ship passed Malta, *Hermes* carried on eastwards, towards a position from where the Commando could be disembarked to support the British Sovereign Bases at Akrotiri and Dhekelia.

A naval Task Group now began to form, with *Hermes* as the nucleus. She was joined on the evening of 18th by the frigate *Rhyl*, as escort. The destroyer *Devonshire* and the frigate *Andromeda* were due to join on 20 July, the RFA *Olna* on 21st, and RFAs *Olwen* and *Regent* later. RFA *Gold Rover* had already sailed from Malta.

Russian ships were in the area and a Russian AG1 began trailing *Hermes* at first light on 19 July. That evening, there were reports of a large Turkish amphibious force making for Cyprus and it was learned in the early hours of 20th that they had landed in the Kyrenia area. *Hermes* headed for Larnaca Bay, on the south-east coast of Cyprus, close to Dhekelia, the likeliest place for landing the Commandos.

The Turks had given warning of Danger War Zones, from which shipping was to keep clear; these covered virtually all approaches to Cyprus except two 'corridors' to Akrotiri and Dhekelia. On the evening of 20th Captain Branson decided to station *Hermes* and *Rhyl* to watch the corridor to Larnaca and *Andromeda* that leading to Episcopi, near Akrotiri.

The Commandos were landed by helicopter to Dhekelia in three hours on

Sunday morning, 21 July, with the ship underway to get enough wind over the deck for heavy loads. *Hermes* then anchored to land heavy transport by lighter.

Devonshire and *Olna* had joined, and *Gold Rover* arrived that afternoon. *Hermes* stayed off Dhekelia until 40 Commando, who had arrived in Cyprus by air, had established themselves.

On Sunday afternoon *Rhyl*, followed by *Andromeda* and then by *Olna*, were detached via Cape Andreas, the easternmost 'finger-tip' of Cyprus, to proceed along the north coast so as to begin embarking UK and other 'friendly' nationals from the Six Mile Beach area at first light on Monday morning. But because of what Branson called 'an incredible volume of sounding-off noises in Ankara and Athens', the British Embassy in Ankara gave an undertaking that no evacuation would take place without Turkish approval. The Six Mile Beach plan was cancelled, which was as well because the area was subjected to constant air and sea bombardment throughout Monday 22 July.

Hermes spent 22 July off Akrotiri. In the evening four Wessex of 845 NAS were flown ashore to support 40 Commando, before *Hermes* herself headed eastward at 25 knots with *Devonshire* to join the frigates and, everyone hoped, begin the evacuation at first light on Tuesday 23 July.

The ships of the Task Group assembled off Cape Andreas at 2 am on 23rd and headed west, but, once again, there was a check; Captain Branson was ordered not to go past a point about sixteen kilometres east of Kyrenia. But once there the order came to proceed. A ceasefire was to come into effect that day, and the rescue could go ahead.

Obeying his instructions, to keep his main force some eight miles off the coast, Captain Branson sent helicopters to reconnoitre the beaches east of Kyrenia. *Andromeda*'s and *Rhyl*'s Wasps picked up observers of 814 NAS from *Hermes* and flew reconnaissances to find out where the refugees were. Lt Tim Yarker, flying *Rhyl*'s Wasp, 'found sixty British refugees at Six Mile Beach (where the main concentration of refugees was to be). This I reported to the Task Group Commander in *Hermes* and went on to recce Kyrenia itself.'

But the rescue continued to be hampered by diplomatic haverings. *Andromeda* had been sent in to investigate the situation in Kyrenia. Her Commanding Officer, Captain R.W.F. Gerken RN, intended to anchor as close as he could to the shore, to make the boat trip as short as possible and to give his ship a lee against the westerly wind which it was known would freshen as the day warmed up. On shore he could see a throng of people on an open space and on the verandah of the Dome Hotel, many of them waving and holding up a large Union Jack.

No sooner had *Andromeda* anchored and begun to lower her boats than, as a result of further diplomatic hesitations, Captain Branson had to order her to rejoin *Hermes* out at sea. Gerken signalled for permission to land but this was refused. So 'with thoughts of the virtues of the blind eye and a telescope' he reluctantly ordered the anchor weighed and the boats rehoisted. 'We could sense the disappointment of the crowd ashore,' he said.

Branson was just as disappointed and annoyed. As he said 'it was embarrassing on three counts: *Andromeda* had encouraged people to come down to the jetty to be taken off by boat; people on Six Mile Beach had seen ships and helicopters and now expected prompt action; and finally we were enjoying a calm spell ashore with no firing evident and therefore were wasting time. However, retire we duly did – shamefacedly and not without violent protests from Bob Gerken in *Andromeda*'.

However, at 8 am, after an hour's pause, Captain Branson was authorised to go ahead again and there were to be no more delays. *Andromeda* was able to go inshore again, lower her two sea-boats and begin the evacuation.

A very capable officer of the Army Air Corps, Major P.M. Gill, acted as liaison between Army and ships. Having visited *Hermes* to confer with Captain Branson, he was flown back to Camp Tjiklos where Finnish UN troops were based and from there he moved around the area reporting about 300 tourists including five wounded in the Dome Hotel, another 70 at the Hesperides Hotel and a further group, including 40 members of a Ukrainian dance troupe, at the Xenia Hotel.

Yarker flew *Rhyl*'s Principal Warfare Officer, Lt Robbie Kerr, ashore to Tjiklos to provide a radio link between Gill and the Task Group. The camp was on a spur 2,000 feet up which involved 'flying over both Turkish and Greek positions, which attracted unwelcome attention! Later I flew to west Kyrenia and pulled out 25 civilians from a hotel car park. On one trip I brought back a radiant young mother, nursing her tiny baby, overwhelmed that her ordeal was over. That was one of the biggest passenger loads ever carried by an RN Wasp. I managed to cram in seven on that trip'.

As the Wasps from *Rhyl* and *Andromeda* sighted refugees, they reported them to *Hermes* who plotted them in the military operations room, and then tasked individual helos for the evacuation – 'rather like a Commando operation in reverse', as Branson said.

Flying along the beach, *Andromeda*'s Wasp passed the gutted hotel. 'We found the occupants camped on rocks beneath the hotel,' said the pilot, Lt Ian McKechnie, 'with Union flags and the letters U.K. pricked out in sheets in the sand and rocks. Their reactions were out of this world. They were obviously so relieved we had found them and they leapt about waving and cheering so that we felt quite mean having to leave to radio in our reports of their whereabouts. United Nations forces were much in evidence and so was the fact that the ceasefire was being broken. We found many houses with the roofs destroyed or damaged by shellfire, others pockmarked by bullets and some burnt out. Tanks and fighting vehicles were lying around burnt out and the Turkish forces were there in strength and never could one feel totally confident that despite the Union flags fixed to the sides of our aircraft that they would know that they should not fire on us.'

Hermes' sixteen Commando-carrying Wessex 5s of 845 NAS and her four

ASW Sea Kings of 814 and *Devonshire*'s Wessex 3 began to lift off refugees from Six Mile Beach and take them out to *Hermes*. British armoured cars escorted convoys of cars laden with refugees to the embarkation area, whence the helicopters ran a day-long taxi shuttle service out to the ships.

The 'customers' were very impressed. 'Then a helicopter came over us, counting,' said one holidaymaker, Mr N. Harvey. 'More waves and cheers. More helicopters and a small naval landing party, including a UN officer, appeared and evacuation began. One of the smartest bits of taxi-work I have ever seen, as soon as one helicopter lifted off another was there. Some sixty of us, with a case apiece, were lifted off in what seemed like a matter of minutes. Yet there was no impression of hurry or strain.'

On board the ships, the sailors took charge of their unexpected guests, providing everything from hot showers to babies' creches, from hot tea to warm clothing. Tables with food and hot drinks were laid out in *Hermes*' hangar.

'Jack came up trumps as usual,' said McKechnie, 'feeding them his beer, cramming the kids with nutty and then playing with them while the parents slept on his bunk. I doubt if a single sailor did not give away his beer ration. And the dishes of sweets that they provided in their messes for the kids were quite an eye opener. When we disembarked them to Akrotiri that night they looked fine compared with the blank dazed faces that came aboard.'

There were soon, according to the *Western Morning News*, some 'heart-warming stories – of tables with food and coffee stuck among parked helicopters; of tough sailors who admitted to a lump in the throat as holidaymakers were whisked on board after huddling on beaches with battle raging round them; of the playroom for children with toys seemingly plucked from a magician's hat; of comforting survivors, young and old, frail and infirm, with frightening stories to tell'.

'Surgeon Commander Peter Bond said "We had three to four nurses who offered to help. We couldn't have got by without them. We had pregnant ladies, a two-day old baby, three women in their nineties and one who had had a heart attack that morning, a man recovering from a stroke, 20 to 30 with minor flesh wounds, plus three major cases, two of which were operated on that afternoon. It's not often a naval doctor at sea gets much to do".'

'*Hermes*' Executive Officer, Commander Anthony Hutton, said that there were lots of tears and emotion. Cabins were turned over to families and the cafeteria worked non-stop dispensing hot coffee. "There was an unceasing flow of questions. Bottles, nappies and nippers suddenly became our lot for 36 hours. I have never known the sailors in this ship to be more warm-hearted, more hospitable and more determined to go out of their way to help".'

Fortunately, the Turks appeared to have been briefed and did not fire as the helicopters came and went. *Andromeda*'s Wasp's first Casevac was an old lady of 94: 'I came close to emotional involvement to see someone so frail and incapable of looking after themselves being lumped into the back of a Wasp'.

Andromeda's Wasp, Cyprus, July 1974. Kyrenia Castle in the background

Another Casevac to *Hermes* was a Greek Cypriot woman with her two-day old baby girl; the mother was so moved and relieved to be rescued she christened her baby Hermoula, the feminine of Hermes.

The helicopter shuttle service from shore to ship was going well when there were the sounds of tank engines approaching and fighting from the outskirts of Kyrenia. 'We then really started rushing things,' said McKechnie. 'My aircraft takes four passengers and I was taking old people and nervous people who leapt in as if they always travelled on the floor of a helicopter with no doors on and when we had the four adults we put children in their arms. The emotional shock of getting away was just too much for some who simply burst into tears of relief once they were in the aircraft and parents who were terrified spent all their energies quieting children who were much less frightened than them. We shifted about 500 off from the town. We had 192 in *Andromeda* of whom about 45 had come off in the Wasp.'

Not everybody wanted rescue. In the afternoon, Yarker spotted a large banner 'British-Help', landed in a nearby olive grove, and sent his crewman Ldg Cook Smith 'to find out what they wanted. He returned with a letter for the Task Force Commander complaining about Turkish savagery, and a message for telegraphing home. Turkish aircraft had rocketed the cliff-top villa we had flown over earlier, killing the British owner, leaving his wife and neighbours to bury him. The telegram was a summons from the wife to her son to fly out and sort things out! No persuasion would shift these redoubtable expatriates, whom I last saw having tea by their pool!'

Devonshire's Wessex flew off another twenty refugees that evening. By about 5.30 pm the operation was over. In all the ships evacuated about 1,530 people. Altogether, the combined British services, Navy, Army, RAF, rescued 7,526 people – men, women and children, families, residents, holiday-makers, businessmen – 5,171 of them British.

On Wednesday 24 July, *Andromeda* was just beginning to refuel alongside *Gold Rover* when Captain Gerken heard that a Search and Rescue operation was in progress some twenty miles to the west. He broke off fuelling at once and made for the area hotly followed by *Gold Rover*.

The original message was that an aircraft had ditched and up to 36 survivors were in the water. But later it transpired that the survivors were from a Turkish destroyer which had been sunk by Turkish aircraft in an 'own goal' attack on 21 July. ('Before you split your sides with laughter,' McKechnie commented, 'I must also report that twice in one day we were overflown by Nimrods whilst in company with *Rhyl* and within half an hour received Flash signals to investigate two Turkish destroyers in the position we had then been in').

Nevertheless, the '*Kocatepe* Incident' was an extraordinary saga of incompetence. From the outset of their invasion, the Turks had been paranoiac about the possibility of a Greek counter-attack. When, on 20 July, there was a report of a Greek convoy of eight to eleven ships assembling at Rhodes and when, the next day, air reconnaissance reported ships heading for Cyprus, the Turks' worst fears were realised.

The air reconnaissance reports remained shadowy, never properly confirmed, and it seems the 'convoy' was never more than a chance grouping of merchant ships, but the Turks remained apprehensive and decided to attack it if it ever entered the prohibited zone. Two more reports from shadowing aircraft seemed to confirm the threat: the first, that several destroyers of a type provided by the US to both the Greek and Turkish navies had been sighted, the second, that there were nine ships in the convoy.

There was now no doubt in Ankara that this was a Greek military convoy with a destroyer escort heading for Paphos on the west coast of Cyprus. On 21 July, the Turkish Air Force and Navy were ordered to attack 'a convoy of 11 landing craft and transport ships, escorted by five destroyers, which is now 15 miles off the Paphos coast'. The Turkish destroyers *Adatepe, Kocatepe* and *Cakmak* were detached from the rest of the Turkish naval forces to intercept the convoy and to sink any vessels wearing the Greek flag which entered the prohibition zone.

The three destroyers were reported to have engaged three Greek MTBs, possibly sinking one, off the north coast of Cyprus. They were then informed that air strikes were to be made on the convoy and its escorts after 3 pm.

There then followed a most astonishingly confused series of events. A Turkish reconnaissance aircraft sighted two ships, said they were flying no flag, and read the name of one as 'Line Messina'. The pilot said he could see 'our own' destroyers and there were no, repeat no, other ships in sight.

The three Turkish destroyers could hear the radio operators of the two ships, talking to each other in Italian! Surely the convoy would have more than two ships, and their crews would speak Greek? And where was the convoy's destroyer escort?

The same aircraft then challenged *Kocatepe* with the password 'Senlik basladi mu?' ('Have the rejoicings begun?'). *Kocatepe* was baffled. Nobody on board knew the correct reply. Eventually *Kocatepe* said, simply, 'No'.

At 3 pm the first squadron of Turkish strike aircraft arrived, as expected. They saw three destroyers. No other ships were in sight. These must be the destroyers they had been ordered to attack. They dived on their targets and released their bombs, hitting *Kocatepe* with one bomb which exploded fatally in her funnel.

The three destroyers fired back furiously. *Cakmak* radioed Ankara that they were being attacked by enemy aircraft and asked for air cover.

The attacking aircraft were puzzled to see their targets flying Turkish flags. Had there been a ghastly error? But surely their own destroyers would not have subjected them to such a fierce barrage of fire? The Greeks had similar destroyers and were not above flying under false colours. The aircraft attacked for the second time, with rockets. *Cakmak* and *Adatepe* put up another barrage of anti-aircraft fire whilst retiring to the north.

Cakmak now realised that the attackers were Turkish, but when challenged could not give the correct password, so the ships were attacked again. *Kocatepe*, already on fire and lying almost stationary in the water, had her radar and radio destroyed. The other two destroyers were also slightly damaged but steamed off to the northward. The aircraft retired.

Kocatepe was so badly damaged she sank, but her Captain had already ordered her to be abandoned. Some 25 of her ship's company had been killed. The surviving 205 officers and men took to the liferafts and were swept to the south by a freshening northerly wind.

In Ankara there was wild rejoicing in the corridors of the Prime Minister's office when the news arrived that the convoy taking Greek reinforcements to Paphos had been attacked and stopped and an enemy destroyer had been sunk. But, in the Navy Operations Room, 'there was a deathly silence ...'

Rumours of the fiasco did not reach the outside world for twenty-four hours. On 22 July, 42 men were picked up from liferafts west of Cyprus by an Israeli naval ship which took them to Haifa, whence they were flown back to Turkey.

When *Andromeda* reached the search area, Gerken saw 'a Royal Air Force Nimrod who was the Commander of the operation, supported by RAF launches, two of *Hermes*' Sea Kings and a yellow RAF Whirlwind. I imagined that an aircraft had crashed and was surprised to see another warship, the Turkish frigate *Berk*. Two liferafts were sighted and I closed them to recover the occupants who turned out to be Turkish naval personnel from the destroyer *Kocatepe* who told us that the ship had been sunk by Greek gunboats on the previous Saturday 20th July (sic). The few men who spoke some English were engineroom personnel who had been below decks during the action and therefore were unable to give much information of where, why or how their ship had been sunk. There were 37 of them and some had minor injuries and nearly all were badly sunburned since they had little clothing and the canopies of the life-rafts were not inflated. However, they had survived nearly four days and many were able to climb unaided up the scrambling net and over *Andromeda*'s guardrail.'

Berk was seen to pick up a further 38 men. In all six dinghies were found, with a total of 111 survivors. Generally, they were in 'good shape' and although they claimed to have had no food or water since they were sunk there was no sign of parched lips or faces, but several did have salt sores.

Andromeda was ordered to disembark her survivors to Akrotiri by 814 NAS Sea Kings. Lt Cdr Mike Clark, Senior Pilot of 814, followed by Lt Richard Davey, landed their Sea Kings on *Andromeda* – possibly the first ever Sea King landings on a *Leander*'s flight deck.

But that night it was decreed, for political reasons, that the 72 Turks at Akrotiri should join *Berk*. They embarked in *Olna* to transfer outside Cypriot territorial waters. Gerken intended that *Olna* should stop beam on to the wind and *Berk* should close her lee side and take off the men by boat. But *Berk*'s Captain considered the sea too rough for boatwork (although Gerken took *Andromeda* close under *Olna*'s lee to show it could be done). A suggestion to transfer the men from *Olna* by jackstay was also turned down.

It was now 10.30 pm and nothing had been achieved. McKechnie, who had noticed that *Berk* had a flight deck (though no helicopter), now offered his services. The three ships steamed westwards, to give the Wasp the most favourable wind, with *Berk* leading, *Andromeda* (whose radar was controlling the evolution) half a mile on her starboard beam, and *Olna* a mile astern.

McKechnie launched at 11.55 pm and first took some of his own flight deck party to *Olna* and *Berk*. Lighting was provided first by pusser's (official issue) torches held by Turks standing in a line along *Berk*'s upper deck and later by jury-rigged flood lights. Although McKechnie had only this makeshift flight deck lighting and signalling (as he said, 'different sized, tiring Turks do not make for a very good horizon bar after two hours') and he himself began to tire and to lose his concentration at about 3 am, he successfully transferred all 72, including eight stretcher cases. He finally shut down at 4.15 am, after four hours, 20 minutes of non-stop flying, and 55 night deck landings.

The part played by the Royal Navy in rescuing *Kocatepe*'s survivors was not reported at the time, and was never properly publicised later, for fear of offending Greek political suceptibilities; it was thought the Greeks might misconstrue what the Royal Navy considered to be purely humanitarian acts as aid to the Turks.

But the sailors themselves recognised what they and their shipmates had done in Cyprus. When Captain Gerken told Leading Seaman Wakeling, who was Coxswain of one of *Andromeda*'s boats, that he was to receive the Commander-in-Chief's Commendation, Wakeling said 'It was the most worthwhile day of my life'.

Many heart-felt letters in the press at home also gave thanks where it was properly due to all who took part in the Cyprus evacuations: 'From the moment of sighting the ships we took for granted the superb efficiency and coordination with which the whole operation was carried out,' wrote Mr A. Storrs, of New Milton, Hants, to *The Daily Telegraph*, 'but what overwhelmed us completely was the fantastic kindness, courtesy and cheerfulness of every single person involved, with everything taken care of from the first welcoming cup of tea in the hangar of HMS *Hermes* to the final hospitality at Brize Norton. We were all made to feel such honoured guests that what started off as a nightmare ended as an enriching experience which we shall never forget'.

'I told them not to drip about paying their taxes this year,' said McKechnie, 'and they all smiled.' He himself won the Boyd Trophy for 1974, and the Turkish Distinguished Service Medal, only the 75th awarded in the history of the Turkish Republic and the first to a foreigner.

Meanwhile, at home, Culdrose's Sea Kings followed *Merc Enterprise* almost immediately with another notable rescue on 11 February 1974 when MV *Lutria*, about 100 miles south-west of Land's End, broadcast a 'May Day'

Lt Ian McKenzie's (Flight Cdr, HMS *Andromeda*) Boyd Trophy. Presented by FONAC (Flag Officer Naval Air Command) Vice Admiral Sir David Austin signal before her crew of 28 abandoned ship in very heavy seas. Sea Kings of the RNFTU and 706 NAS went out to the ship and found the crew in two life-boats. An SAR diver was dropped down to assist the survivors, and all 28 were winched up – the largest number rescued, so far, in any single SAR mission from Culdrose.

The Aircrewman's Branch was officially born at Portland on Monday 1 April 1974, 771 NAS being responsible for training crewmen and establishing the new branch. Admiral Sir Derek Empson attended Divisions that day and Lady Empson unveiled a stone obelisk, now at the Aircrewman's School at Culdrose, to mark the occasion.

The 1974 summer season opened with the familiar overture and beginners: man on surf-board drifting out to sea near Portreath; man fallen over cliffs, breaking ribs and wrist, at Mevagissey; civilian diver suffering from the 'bends' at Poldhu Cove; woman fallen over cliffs and swept out to sea at Land's End; three Frenchmen rescued after their trimaran broke up in a race off Portland; man with a strangulated hernia taken off the Greek freighter *Africa Lion*; cries for help heard from cliff at Culver above the wreck of the *Harry Sharman* – false alarm and possible hoax; explosion with extensive damage and injuries on board the Monrovian oil carrier *Asiatic*, attended by Sea King and the submarine *Opportune*; two swimmers in difficulty, one seen struggling ashore, the other face down in the water; man and a woman rescued, with the help of the SAR diver, from the 32 foot ketch *Ali Mhor* in danger of going ashore at Calshot.

As always, there were many reports of flares sighted, inflatable dinghies upturned, swimmers in difficulties, dismasted yachts and fishing boats, bodies in the water, voices crying out for help, climbers stuck on cliffs, rubber rings drifting out to seaward. Some reports were true. Some were false alarms. Some were genuine errors by onlookers. A few were deliberate hoaxes. But all had to be investigated.

With the onset of autumnal and winter gales, there were, as usual, more ships in difficulties: in September, *Ark Royal*'s Sea Kings of 824 NAS picked up four survivors and the skipper's body from the 420-ton coaster *Greta C*, sinking 25 miles south-west of Portland Bill; in October, off Malta, 824 winched up six of the crew from the sinking Italian merchant ship *Giovanni Sassenso*.

In the New Year of 1975, Culdrose's Sea Kings had another SAR mission which was to have repercussions. The 1,000-ton British coaster MV *Lovat* sailed from Swansea, bound for France with a cargo of anthracite coal, on Friday 24 January. There was already a full gale raging in the Western Approaches and as *Lovat* rounded Land's End the weather deteriorated still further, with very high seas and wind gusts up to 80 knots. Just before dawn on Saturday, 25 January, *Lovat*'s cargo began to shift and the ship took on a severe list. The Master, Captain Leslie Beeson, broadcast a 'May Day' signal at 6.22 am, giving his position as about 25 miles south of Land's End, and the crew of thirteen – twelve British and a Portuguese – abandoned ship.

Neither of *Lovat*'s two lifeboats could be launched because of the list. Her survivors had to make do with a rubber liferaft which was not large enough for them all; some crammed inside, with their heads sticking out through the canopy, the rest had to hang on as best they could to the sides.

A Whirlwind of 771 NAS (Lt Marsh, LACMN P. Mansell and P. Gibbs) took off from Culdrose at 7.43 am. At that range and in that weather, a Whirlwind would not have the capacity to rescue more than three people. At that time there was no Sea King specifically detailed or even at stand-by for SAR at Culdrose. Sea Kings for SAR emergencies were provided, as they had been for *Merc Enterprise*, for example, by whatever aircraft were available on the air station. In this case, the crews of FTU Sea Kings were called out from their homes.

Marsh arrived over *Lovat*'s survivors shortly before 8 am. Two merchantmen had closed the scene but had been unable to make a rescue in the heavy seas. LACMN Peter Gibbs (on his first operational SAR sortie, having completed his training only a week before) was lowered on the winch wire, to find that all of *Lovat*'s crew had been swept away except for six men actually in the life-raft. Of those, two were already dead. After two attempts, Gibbs managed to put one survivor, Mr Roy Hawley, into the rescue harness and gave the signal to Mansell to hoist.

'Just then,' said Gibbs, 'a huge wave washed out the raft and the fellow in the chopper lost sight of us. There was a huge loop in the wire which could have sliced off my arm if it had tightened, so he had to cut the winch wire. The two of us fell into the water, but we managed to swim back onto the raft, which was awash.'

'The tops of the waves were breaking across us. Two of the men looked desperate. I tried to keep one young fellow alive but he was too far gone and died in my arms. It must have been from exposure. The fourth fellow died, too. After what seemed like three quarters of an hour, two Sea Kings arrived and I knew they could handle it. I got the two survivors winched up, and then three of the bodies, but they were so heavy and took so much time we had to leave the fourth body as the survivors needed treatment badly.'

Gibbs deservedly won the Queen's Gallantry Medal, but it was not otherwise a very satisfactory episode. There was no overt criticism of Culdrose, but there was some public debate, in *The Times* and *The Guardian* and in the House of Commons, on the country's need for the regular establishment of long-range night-capable rescue helicopters at much shorter notice.

On 1 April 1975, a joint Royal Navy/Department of Trade and Industry contract was announced, providing for SAR Sea Kings to be stationed at ninety minutes' notice day and night at Culdrose and at Prestwick.

Thus by mid-1975 SAR at Culdrose had settled into the 24-hours-a-day, 365 days/year organisation which was to be maintained virtually unchanged for almost the next fifteen years.

Short range, quick reaction (fifteen minutes' notice but normally in two minutes or less) SAR in daylight was provided by 771 NAS, who had moved to Culdrose from Portland in September 1974 to join the Culdrose Training School, carrying out aircrewman training as well as providing the Station SAR Flight.

From 25 June 1975, 771 NAS had a dedicated SAR Flight of three Wessex Is which replaced the Whirlwinds. They had an endurance of two and a quarter hours, a speed of 90 knots, a thirty mile range, a 300 foot long winch wire, a crew of three – pilot, aircrewman and diver – and were capable of picking up eight survivors.

Longer range SAR, by day or by night, at ninety minutes' notice (but in practice often much more quickly) was provided by the Sea Kings of 706 NAS or Front Line squadrons disembarked to Culdrose.

The exceptionally fine summer weather of 1975 resulted in a drop in SAR sorties along the south coast. Culdrose sorties were down from 102 in 1974 to 85, Lee-on-Solent from 157 to 137. But the SAR crews still had to deal with the results of the eccentricities and irresponsibilities of human nature. 'One incident of man's lack of concern for the sea irritated me,' said Captain S. Leonard (the same Leonard rescued by helicopter in Korea) who was Captain of RNAS Culdrose that summer. 'Two men and a woman living in the Midlands had been studying sailing by post! Arrived at Penzance and took ownership of a converted life-boat and proceeded to sail it to Poole in Dorset. The engine failed after a short space of time before getting to the Lizard and they put into a cove and worked on the engine successfully! Went to sleep and next morning took the anchor up before starting the engine. It did not start and they drifted on to the rocks. One got ashore and raised the alarm. We recovered one alive and one body.'

In November 1975 Captain Leonard went up to London with the CO of 771 NAS, Lt Cdr C.P. West, to receive the Brackley Memorial Trophy from the Guild of Air Pilots and Air Navigators. It was the first time the Navy had won the Trophy, awarded annually in memory of Air Commodore Brackley who began his flying career in the Royal Naval Air Service in the First World War. 'For 25 years the Royal Navy has been a pioneer in helicopter search and rescue,' said the citation. 'R.N. Air Station Culdrose has been at the forefront in developing techniques contributing to this fine record.'

9 Worldwide SAR: From the 'Sailor' TV Rescue to the *Orion* Oil Rig

'... There were two US Navy personnel on the casing, attached to lifelines, who were to assist me with the stretcher. I grabbed one of the lifelines with one hand, holding the stretcher with the other. When the sick man came up on to the casing I began to strap him in. I had already got my feet wet with the occasional wave washing over the deck. While I was strapping him into the stretcher, the two men with me held the stretcher. Then it happened ...'

In February 1976, *Ark Royal* was on her way to Roosevelt Roads in Puerto Rico after taking part in Exercise SPRINGTRAIN, with the cruiser *Blake*, the destroyers *Hampshire* and *Kent* and Dutch naval ships. On 21st the carrier received a signal to divert to lift off a sailor suffering from appendicitis from the nuclear submarine USS *Bergall* and take him to hospital in the Azores.

Two Sea Kings of 824 NAS flew on ahead of the ship some 300 miles to Lajos in the Azores. Because of bad weather and because the man's condition had improved, they waited for daylight. Next morning, with a 30 knot wind and twelve foot swell, *Bergall* closed the island to make the transfer in calmer waters.

Sea King '050' (Lt Cdr David Anderson, CO of 824, Sub Lt Iain Moffat, observer Lt Bob Fewings, and CPOACMN Roy Withell) arrived over the submarine. Withell went down on the wire with the stretcher, and freed himself from the winch-hook so that the helicopter could stand off in a safer position.

'... Every now and again you get a big wave – we got one. The stretcher was lifted and thrown sideways from the casing. I held on as I presumed the two guys were holding on to the stretcher, but they couldn't hold it, so over we went, the sick man and myself.'

'We drifted aft rather quickly and were lucky not to get eaten by the propeller, which was just breaking the surface of the water. If the captain of the submarine hadn't put on full starboard rudder I dare not think what might have happened. Almost immediately we had cleared the stern, the winch hook was lowered to us and I hooked both of us to it and we were winched up into the helicopter.'

The patient was later reported to be 'comfortable' at the US base in Lajos. CPOACMN Withell received the Queen's Gallantry Medal for the rescue,

The 'Sailor' TV rescue

which was filmed in its entirety from the second accompanying Sea King and appeared in an episode of the BBC TV programme 'Sailor' in 1978.

The USS *Bergall* rescue, possibly the most celebrated of all SAR sorties to date, was one of a monthly series at the beginning of that year which showed the extraordinary variety of SAR work. It was impossible to predict SAR: the emergencies happened at any time, anywhere from the Arctic to the Mediterranean, over sea or land, involving one man or hundreds, one helicopter or several.

Early in March 1976, a fleet of French trawlers sailed from the port of Lorient bound for the fishing grounds west of the Scillies. By Thursday 11 March, when the trawlers were some 80 miles north-west of the Bishop's Rock lighthouse, about 130 miles west of Land's End, a gale of almost hurricane proportions approached them from the west.

The fishing fleet lay directly in the path of the storm and was unable to flee to shelter. The full force of the storm, with winds gusting up to 100 knots and waves 80 feet high, struck at about midday on 12 March. The first 'May Day', from the trawler *Gardestgue*, was received at the Land's End Coastguard

Station just before 2 pm: three of her crew had been washed overboard. Shortly afterwards another 'May Day' was received from a second trawler, the *Moussbihancoz*: a huge wave had pooped her and she was now in great danger of foundering.

Two Sea Kings of 706 NAS took off from Culdrose to fly the 100 miles out into the Atlantic and were joined in the search by a French Atlantique maritime reconnaissance aircraft. The 'Merc Enterprise problem', of salt ingestion in the engines, reoccurred in one of the Sea Kings, resulting in a loss of engine power and a near-stall. The pilot, Lt Cdr Richard Davey, had to fly higher 'with the power available and as rapidly as possible find a cloud, fly into it and let the deluge of rain wash it out'.

Shortly after 5 pm, a 'May Day' was received from a third trawler, the *Tamengo*, which was then about 70 miles west of Bishop's Rock: her engine room had been flooded by a giant wave, the crew were abandoning ship and taking to the life-raft. The Sea Kings gave up the search for *Gardestque* and went to look for *Tamengo*. But all that was found of her was the upturned life-raft. Four bodies were recovered some time later by the *Riquita*.

The first two Sea Kings had returned to Culdrose by 6 pm and when the doctors and medical assistants had been transferred, two more Sea Kings took off ten minutes later. From then on, for the next 30 hours, continuous relays of Sea Kings of 706 and 826 NASs took off to conduct a massive search operation, joined by Nimrods from RAF St Mawgan, French Atlantiques and Dutch Neptunes. The St Mary's lifeboat also put out from the Scillies.

The search went on all night – the SAR crews called it 'The Long Night'. Early on Saturday morning the trawler *Bruix* reported that she had recovered seven bodies over a period of two hours. By Saturday mid-day there were fears for yet another trawler, the *Krugan*, which had last reported on Friday afternoon, from a position some 75 miles west of the Scillies, that some of her crew had been swept overboard. Since then nothing had been heard from her. Two Sea Kings were launched from Culdrose at 3.30 pm to search the area. Some pieces of unidentified wreckage were seen.

Meanwhile, other ships were in trouble and broadcasting 'May Day' signals. At midnight on Friday the Master of the British cargo ship *Frendo Star* reported that her cargo was shifting, the ship had taken on a list of 25 degrees, and he was steering for the French coast. The list increased over the next few hours, until the ship was about to capsize. The crew abandoned her and took to the rubber life-rafts. French helicopters found them some time later and winched up the ten survivors.

On Saturday morning the 1,600-ton coaster *Steyning*, on passage to Germany, met a huge wave some 17 miles west of the Scillies. The ship's cook, who had very rashly gone on deck just then to ditch galley gash, was swept overboard and drowned.

The last helicopter search was called off at sunset on Saturday 13 March, in a general atmosphere of disappointment. One British seaman – *Steyning*'s cook – and at least fifteen French fishermen had lost their lives. Not one man had been rescued, in spite of the largest SAR operation ever mounted in the south-west of the United Kingdom. It had involved RNAS Culdrose, Royal Navy warships, the French warship *Savoyard*, merchant ships, RAF Nimrods, French and Dutch aircraft, Rescue Co-Ordination Centres at Plymouth and Brest, the St Mary's lifeboat, and the Coastguard (the Land's End Station alone handled 1,200 telephone calls and telexes during the emergency).

To keep two Sea Kings constantly on task throughout the 30 hours, 706 and 826 NASs had flown 16 sorties between them, averaging four hours per sortie, for a total of 66 flying hours, in very bad weather conditions which made for exhausting flying. They had been supported by over 200 people who had worked round the clock to refuel and repair (and wash the salt off) the helicopters. The Flag Officer Naval Air Command, Vice Admiral P.M. Austin, signalled Culdrose: 'I was very impressed by the enthusiasm displayed by all concerned during the rescue flights over the week-end. Although success did not crown your efforts, the number of sorties flown in the appalling weather conditions brought credit to air-crew and ground crew alike'.

Almost a month later, on 10 April, there was another flash emergency signal, several hundreds of miles to the north. The Norwegian research vessel *Harmoni*, some 370 miles inside the Arctic Circle, reported that one of her ship's company was seriously ill with a brain haemorrhage and desperately needed hospital treatment. *Harmoni* herself was frozen into a field of thick ice and could not move. Help would have to be brought to her.

One of the nearest ships was the RFA *Olwen*, supporting the Royal Navy's ships in the ongoing Cod War. She embarked the Wessex 3 of the destroyer *Antrim*'s Ship's Flight and, although she was not equipped to operate in the Arctic, her Master Captain Donald Averill took her through ice up to 15 feet thick so as to launch the Wessex from the shortest possible range.

Antrim's Wessex took off at 3.30 pm on a bitterly cold Arctic afternoon with the crew (Lt Cdr Keith Simmons, Lt Tim MacMahon, observer Lt Alastair Ross, and CPOACMN Anthony Butler) wearing extra layers of clothing to protect them from a temperature nearly 20 degrees below freezing. The wind was gusting up to 50 knots and visibility varied from about three miles down to a few hundred yards, but Simmons was guided by a USAF Hercules aircraft up above. He found the 'helipad' – marked out with planks of wood on a small ice floe – and landed in snow a foot deep 50 yards from *Harmoni*.

The sick man was brought across the ice on a stretcher and embarked in the Wessex which took off and was guided back by the same Hercules to *Olwen* who was circling in an open lead 46 miles to the southward. Advised by the Hercules on the best path out of the ice, *Olwen* reached open water an hour before midnight. The patient was flown to an airstrip on Jan Mayen Island the next day and then onwards to hospital in Tromso in northern Norway, where he later recovered.

Antrim's Ship's Flight won the Boyd Trophy for 1976. Simmons received an AFC in the 1977 Birthday Honours, and Captain Averill was the Royal Navy's Man of the Year.

Wessex MK3 on the ice close to the Norwegian vessel *Harmoni*. A party of men can be seen evacuating the sick crewman to the helicopter. March 1977

Some six weeks later, on 23 May 1976, the Ship's Flight Wasp of the frigate *Bacchante*, guard ship at Gibraltar, carried out the classical, almost archetypal, SAR helicopter cliff rescue. On the previous evening a Spanish climber, Senor Cesar Perez de Tudela, had had his leg broken by a falling rock when he was some 900 feet up on the 1,200 foot near-vertical north face of the Rock of Gibraltar. A rescue team had climbed 300 feet down from the top of the Rock but were unable to reach the injured man, or even see him, because of a cliff overhang.

Bacchante's Wasp pilot, Lt Christopher Chadwick, volunteered his services. After studying the North Face through binoculars, Chadwick took off with LACMN Jeff Coward as crewman, to reconnoitre the cliff. Knowing the dangers in the turbulent air conditions normally found close to cliffs, Chadwick made initial orbits over the North Front airfield, flying in a little closer each time at the level of the rescuers, who were perched on a small ledge 950 feet up, until he could hover some 25 feet from them.

After another circuit, Chadwick spotted the injured man, about 60 feet below the rescue team. He appeared to be conscious and had secured himself to the rock. Chadwick hovered alongside to indicate the man's position to the rescuers. He decided that a hi-line winch rescue was feasible, and returned to RAF North Front to refuel and rig the helicopter for the attempt, lightening the aircraft by stripping out flotation gear, seats and doors. To avoid any possible misunderstanding between himself and the rescue party, he also took the precaution of amending the chapter on hi-line transfers in his helicopter manual to cater for the unique conditions, added warnings for the rescuers, and put the papers in a weighted bag.

Chadwick then took off again, and manoeuvring close above the rescuers, succeeded in passing the weighted bag to them. Closing the cliff face again, he tried to swing in the weighted line, climbing higher all the time as he did so, until all 90 feet of line was out. Guided by Coward, who showed admirable coolness and excellent judgment of distances, Chadwick flew closer and closer, until the rotor blades were only inches from the rock face. But he could not reach the injured man. However, he believed that it could still be done if the full length of winch-wire was lowered. He flew back to North Front for more fuel and more line.

Meanwhile the rescuers decided that it was too dangerous to go on with the helicopter rescue from that position and that they would try and haul the injured man up to another small ledge above, where a helicopter rescue would be less hazardous. This they actually succeeded in doing, so that when Chadwick and Coward flew back for the third time they were able to lift the injured man off the rock and into the Wasp.

The rescue had taken a total of three hours' flying time, was watching by a vast crowd of spectators packed onto every vantage point, and made a half-hour programme on Gibraltar television that evening. Chadwick and

Bacchante's Wasp rescuing a climber on the Rock of Gibraltar, May 1976

Coward both received the Queen's Commendation for Brave Conduct.

Improvements in helicopters' military capabilities also enhanced their SAR techniques. For example, the Wessex HAS Mk 1 and the later Mark 3 were designed with a largely automatic Flight Control System to make them better anti-submarine weapon platforms. But it also enormously improved their night rescue ability.

For many years aircrew who ditched at night had to rely on rescue by sea-boat. In earlier helicopters it was not possible to hover low over the sea at night because of the lack of precision instruments and visual reference points for the pilot.But the Flight Control System enabled a helicopter to make an automatic descent from cruise altitude, reduce speed and, at the crucial moment, control height so that the helicopter could hover safely about twenty feet above the waves. The Wessex 3 had an automatic turn facility as an additional refinement.

In a night rescue the helicopter locates the survivor, ideally by homing on his radio beacon or his helmet light, and flies over him at 150 feet into the wind before making an automatic turn through 180 degrees and flying downwind, the distance down wind depending upon wind strength, and then turns back into the wind.

When steady, the auto hover buttons are pressed and the helicopter descends in a set pattern, losing speed, and eventually comes to the hover. The survivor will now be about 200 yards away, at two o'clock, and the crew take over. Conned by the back seat aircrewman, the two pilots work together to fly the helicopter on top of the survivor. They do not look out of the cockpit but rely solely on the instructions from the back seat and their own instruments. Once the helicopter is over the survivor, the aircrewman lowers the winch and hauls him to safety.

The advent of the Sea Kings increased the rang of SAR sorties some five or six-fold. On 14 May 1970, a Sea King of 700 'S' NAS, the Sea King Initial Flying Trials Unit from Culdrose, assisted by an RAF Shackleton, picked up an injured seaman from the Finnish tanker *Tiiskeri*, some 170 miles south-west of Land's End and 200 miles from Culdrose. 700 'S''s CO, Lt Cdr V. Sirett, won the Boyd Trophy for 1970.

But this and later long distance records were comprehensively broken on 5 March 1977 when a Sea King of 706 NAS from Culdrose responded to an emergency call to rescue a seaman with a serious arm injury on board the 3,170-ton Russian fish factory ship, *Vladimir Atlasov*, 130 miles off the west coast of Ireland.

The Sea King (Lt David Johnson, Fl Lt Peter Chadwick RAF, observer Lt Ray Doggett, CPOACMN Terry King, Ldg Wren (Phot) Clare Spence and Surg Lt Cdr Rick Jolly) took off at 5.55 am and flew first to Shannon airport to refuel. Taking off at 9.32, the Sea King reached the ship at 11.30. Jolly was winched down with a stretcher to render first aid. Doctor and patient, 23-year-old Vladimir Toystolex, were winched up and the Sea King returned 90 minutes later to Shannon, where the patient was taken to hospital by ambulance.

After refuelling, the Sea King took off again and landed at Culdrose at 3.55 pm, after a round trip of more than 800 miles and a total of eight hours, 40 minutes flying time, the longest SAR sortie from Culdrose. It was also the first time that an RAF pilot – Fl Lt Chadwick was attached to 705 NAS on exchange duty – took part in an SAR mission from Culdrose.

The long hot 'drought' summer of 1976 had produced a bumper number of SAR sorties – Lee-on-Solent's annual total shot up to 163 – and the summer season of 1977 got briskly underway with the usual crop of incidents: small boy in the Scillies with object lodged in throat, taken to hospital; bather in difficulties at Treyarnon Bay, dead on arrival at hospital; man reported missing at Bedruthan Steps, body found washed up by the tide in a cave; search for a Cessna 206 flying from Gander to Shannon, off course with only fifteen minutes fuel remaining, ditched 80 miles south-west of the Scillies, no sign of aircraft or pilot after 28 hours search; woman arriving at *Daedalus*' main gate in a taxi-cab, asking for assistance for her daughter and capsized dinghy off Lee Slip, helicopter found man up to his knees in the sea, dragging daughter and dinghy ashore; father and son rescued off Calshot after dinghy capsized, both visited operations room at *Daedalus*, given hot drinks and copy of 'How Safe is Your Craft'.

It was natural and understandable that the best helicopter crews in the

The SAR doctor goes down to see his patient on board the Russian fish factory ship *Vladimir Atlasov*, 130 miles west of Ireland, March 1977

Navy should wish to compete with the best of other Navies and to show off their best skills in front of the public. In 1973, for instance, the Royal Navy won for the third year running the Henri Dunant Trophy, named after the founder of the International Red Cross.

In a week-long contest of air-sea rescue skills and techniques, held by the Federal German Air Force at Uetersen near Hamburg, a team of two Wessex 1s of 771 NAS captained by Lt Cdr 'Jock' English beat ten other teams, from the Royal Air Force (a very close second), the Belgian Navy (third), the US Air Force, Belgian Air Force, Netherlands Air Force, Netherlands Navy, Danish Air Force, French Navy, Italian Air Force and the hosts. After three successive wins, the Royal Navy had won the trophy (a magnificent crystal bowl presented by United Aircraft International) outright and there was no further competition.

The success of display teams such as the RAF's Red Arrows encouraged others, the Hawker Hunters Blue Herons, and the Fleet Air Arm Helicopter Display Team, the Sharks.

It is probable that helicopter displays are not as naturally dramatic as those of fast jet aircraft and the general public never really appreciates the degree of skill and training needed to accomplish some of the Sharks' intricate manoeuvres.

But a high degree of skill and training certainly are demanded. On 13 June 1977, while flying in close formation and practising a complicated 'pass', two Gazelles of the Sharks' team collided off Praa Sands in Cornwall. Both two-man crews were lost.

As so often, a disaster was redeemed in part by the bravery of the rescuers. Wessex of 771 NAS and Sea Kings of 706 NAS flew 19½ flying hours to search for the bodies, and recovered three. It was through the skill, personal courage and perseverance of one of the SAR divers, LACMN Colin Rimmer of 771 NAS, that one of the Gazelles was quickly located on the sea-bed and two bodies were recovered. Rimmer was awarded the Queen's Commendation for Valuable Service in the Air. The reconstituted Sharks were in action again at that year's Culdrose Air Day in August.

SAR rescues sometimes involved enormous resources in ships, helicopters and flying hours, for very little result in terms of lives saved. At 8 am on 16 November 1977, the 500-ton MV *Union Crystal* left the sheltering lee of the island of Lundy and headed into a gathering south-westerly gale, bound for Portland with a cargo of salt.

At 7 pm that evening *Union Crystal* broadcast a 'May Day' message, in a position 12 miles north-west of Cape Cornwall, that her cargo was shifting, the vessel was sinking, and requesting helo assistance. Twenty minutes later the ship began to heel over and sink. Her crew of six jumped into the sea and tried to reach liferafts.

At Culdrose Sea King '593' of 706 NAS, which had only just landed after a night training sortie, took off again almost at once. '593' (Lt Phil Shaw, Commander Peter Voute, Culdrose's Commander (Air), observer Lt Henry,

CACMN Terry King and LACMN Martin Newton) was followed ten minutes later by a second Sea King, '595'. The two Sea Kings were joined, in what at first seems likely to be an unavailing search of the area, by a Nimrod from RAF Kinloss, by the frigates *Penelope* and *Diomede*, by the Sennen and St Ives lifeboats, and other merchant ships.

Good luck and good eyesight played crucial parts. The RAF Nimrod had no sooner entered the search area at 10 pm when its crew spotted a faint pinprick of white light, flashing among the waves, at least ten miles from the reported position of the sinking. '593' was diverted to the spot and at 10.37 pm found one survivor clinging to a water-logged raft.

Newton went down on the winch-wire and, despite being injured when his ankle became entangled with a rope attached to the raft, brought the survivor safely up. He was Mr Barry Wells, actually *Union Crystal*'s captain, who proved to be in remarkably good physical condition after his 3½ hours immersion. In Culdrose sick bay, he was able to tell his rescuers that the other five had very probably failed to reach a life raft and would be found upwind of his position, wearing lifejackets.

Two more Sea Kings, '596' and '593' for a second sortie with a different crew, took off to concentrate the search in this new datum area. Empty lifejackets, lifebuoys and other pieces of wreckage were sighted but there was no sign of life. The missing five seamen were presumed to have drowned.

The search was called off by HM Coastguards at 2 am on 17 November, but it was continued at first light by two Wessex of 771 NAS, with *Diomede*'s Wasp, in an area north of St Ives. One liferaft was recovered and brought back to Culdrose. A reported dead body floating in the sea turned out to be a black plastic sheet. A final search by two more Wessex ended at 11 am.

Helicopters from Culdrose had flown eight sorties, involving 31 crew and a total of 20½ flying hours. Warships, merchantmen, lifeboats, *Diomede*'s Wasp and an RAF Nimrod had also been involved in a fifteen-hour search, to save one life. But everyone concerned was in no doubt it had been a fair exchange.

No two SAR episodes are ever the same, but there were echoes of *Union Crystal* in 'The Christmas Eve Tragedy' a month later. Just before midnight on 23 December 1977, the 500-ton Danish coaster *Lady Kamilla*, en route from France to Manchester with a cargo of bulk sulphur, ran into heavy seas in a gale off St Ives. A hatch cover was forced open and tons of water poured into the exposed hold. Soon *Lady Kamilla* had to signal that she was taking in water fast, 15 to 20 miles off Trevose Head, and helo assistance was needed.

The duty Sea King, '595' (Lt Glen Tilsley), of 706 NAS took off at 1.40 am on 24 December but as it approached the scene it developed a gear-box fault and had to make an emergency landing in north Cornwall. Meanwhile, the St Ives, Padstow and Clovelly lifeboats were launched to look for the crew of *Lady Kamilla* – nine of them, including the master's wife, his son (aged three) and daughter (aged nine), and a female cook – who abandoned ship at 2.26 am and took to the life-rafts.

A second Sea King '593' with aircrew recalled from Christmas leave (Lt

Two boys trapped by the tide at Perran Sands, 9 August 1976

Nigel Arnall-Culliford, Fl Lt Peter Chadwick RAF, Observer Lt Chandler, Lt Ray Doggett) took off at 2.52 am and was at first diverted to investigate reported red flares off the coast at Portreath. Finding nothing, they joined an RAF Nimrod in the search for *Lady Kamilla*'s life-rafts.

A third Sea King of 706, '594' took off 'short-crewed' (Lt Cdr Roy Swales, Lt Cdr Kirby, Lt Spence) at 4 am and went first to RAF St Mawgan to collect two of the downed '595' crew, Lt O'Neill and Lt Williams, before joining the search. A relief Nimrod arrived at 7.30 am, so, too did an RAF Whirlwind from Chivenor at first light. '593' was relieved by '598' at 8.44 and a Wessex of 771 NAS arrived soon afterwards.

The search continued throughout the forenoon but nothing was found except a lifebelt from a vessel not involved and a 'body' which proved to be a canister. By noon the helicopter crews were growing weary, with nothing to raise their hopes, while Culdrose was sending out calls for fresh crews to come in from leave.

It was the HM Coastguard Inspector who insisted that the search should continue and his persistence was rewarded at 2.20 pm that afternoon when a Nimrod sighted a life-raft on which '598' (Lt Phil Shaw, Lt Rugg, Lt Phil Henry and Lt Ian Munday) found two survivors, Miss Lone Olsen, the Danish cook, and a Spanish crewman, Benjamin Pose. With Munday working the winch, Henry went down to recover first the girl and then the man, in a double lift. Both were very cold but surprisingly fit, considering the icy weather, the gale, and the length of time they had spent on an exposed raft.

These were the only survivors. The search was finally called off at 5 pm, with nothing further found, despite the best efforts of two RAF Nimrods, three lifeboats, and a total flying time of 22 hours and five minutes by five helicopters – not counting the Whirlwind from Chivenor.

The Sea Kings were busy until the end of the year. On New Year's Eve a French Atlantique reported a white rocket, and an RAF Nimrod sighted a partly-inflated life-raft, well out into the Western Approaches. The French authorities were anxious that the raft be recovered. A Sea King of 706 NAS investigated but found nothing. So ended the year, with 136 SAR sorties from Culdrose.

Lee-on-Solent, whose SAR Flight had exchanged its Whirlwind Mk9 for a Wessex 5 in April, flew 144 sorties in 1977. Their 'resident' SAR crew, Lt Ray Colborne and POACMN Roy Higginson, flew the usual sorties, to rescue fallen cliff climbers, crews of capsized boats, and swimmers in difficulties. They also flew out to the *QE2* on 30 September. The liner had been delayed by a gale and, to make up her cruise schedule, took a 'short cut' into the Solent through the western Needles passage. The sea was too rough for boat-work and the Southampton pilot was delivered to *QE2* by Wessex.

The New Year of 1978, which was to be an eventful one for the Navy's SAR teams and especially for Culdrose, began with a major rescue which was later described as a 'classic'.

After eleven years' service in the North Sea oilfields, the 19,000-ton exploratory drilling rig *Orion*, welded on top of the 3,500 ton barge *Federal 400-2* and towed by the German tug *Seefalke*, set off from Rotterdam on its 5,000 mile voyage to Recife in Brazil on 26 January 1978. At 6.40 pm on 1 February, when there was a Force 10 north-westerly gale blowing, the tow-line parted. At 8 pm *Seefalke*'s Captain reported that the line had parted, some 20 miles west-north-west of Guernsey, and that *Orion* was drifting at about 6 knots towards the coast to leeward.

The severe weather had already led to the cancellation of routine night flying at Culdrose. But at 8.08 pm that evening HM Coastguard at Land's End reported that the lightship guarding the notorious Seven Stones Reef in the Isles of Scilly was dragging its anchor. Two Sea Kings were brought to immediate readiness. However, when it was clear that the lightship could cope, the Sea Kings were offered to HM Coastguards at Brixham, to assist the helpless *Orion*.

Seefalke's crew were trying to take charge of the runaway rig but they had first to reel in and stow 3,000 metres of 2½-inch thick steel cable, while the rig was still drifting towards the rocks. At 10.40 pm *Seefalke*'s Captain decided that it was hopeless to go on and asked for the *Orion*'s crew of 33 to be taken off urgently.

At 10.26 pm Brixham reported that *Orion* was nearing the coast and the first Sea King '592' (Lt Glen Tilsley, Lt John Wingate, Observer Lt Bob Davidson, and CACMN Alf Tupper) was airborne at 10.55 pm. It was followed 20 minutes later by Sea King '594' (Lt Tony Eagles, Lt Len Mathews, Observer Lt Paul Crudgington, and CACMN Terry King). With the help of a gale force tail wind, the Sea Kings' 160-mile flight to the oil rig, by then very close to the Grandes Rocques off Guernsey, took only 50 minutes.

Meanwhile the St Peter Port lifeboat had put to sea and had met barge and oil rig about six miles from the shores. By superb seamanship the lifeboat had taken off two of the crew by 10.50, when *Orion* had only half a mile to go before running aground. *Orion* ran aground on the Grandes Rocques reefs, some 300 yards from the shore, at about 11 pm, and the lifeboat stood off.

When '592' arrived shortly before midnight, *Orion* was already aground and, with her own generators still working and all her lights blazing she looked, as Tilsley said, 'lit up like a Christmas tree'. The legs of the rig had been retracted for the voyage but they still stuck up some 278 feet into the air. Tilsley could see that the rig's own helipad was awash, with giant waves breaking across it, and there was no chance of '592' being able to land upon it. It would have to be done by winch.

Tilsley aimed his landing light at a fixed spot on the nearest rig leg and used that as a reference point. Watched by the crew of *Orion* and by spectators crowded on the nearest point of headland ashore, he brought the hovering Sea King nearer and nearer until the rotor blades were spinning only some ten

Orion oil-rig – Navy recruiting advertisement

to fifteen feet from the rig, with occasional gusts bringing the blades to within five feet.

Spray was lashing 80 feet into the air, with the possibility of the *Merc Enterprise* salt ingestion problem, so Tilsey had to keep the Sea King at least a few feet higher. Lt Bob Davidson had to go down on a winch-wire some 90 feet long and was caught many times by the buffeting wind and spun round and round.

The helipad itself presented its own problems. Every other plank on it had been removed for the sea voyage, leaving spaces between the slats big enough for a man to fall through. In the darkness and the wind-driven spray, with the helicopter roaring unseen somewhere overhead, *Orion*'s crewmen had to pick their way across the helipad one by one as Davidson signalled them to come forward.

At one point the rescue looked so dangerous for the Sea King that *Orion*'s Captain suggested that it be abandoned but Tilsley told him to shut up, because 'I'm busy right now'. After 11 survivors had been winched up, '592' wheeled away towards Guernsey Airport, a couple of miles away, while Lt Eagles brought '594' in to take its place.

Crudgington went down to rescue more survivors, in just as dangerous conditions, spinning around on the winch-wire as Davidson had done, and buffeted as violently to and fro. The oil rig crews were by now understandably chary of entrusting themselves to the helicopter and Crudgington had to dispel their fears of the breaking waves and dense spray before he could carry out the first double-lift rescue. But he eventually rescued twelve more survivors. As Eagles lifted up and away, Tilsley was back. One more man had been winched up and Davidson was strapping in a second when the barge slipped and began to turn on the rocks.

In strong and gusting cross-winds Tilsley had the greatest difficulty controlling the helicopter. With Davidson and the second survivor on deck in the rescue strop, Tilsley lost control over the tail-rotor. Only excellent crew co-operation saved the situation. Tupper had to call to Tilsley to climb away, whilst he winched up the two men 'on the run'.

The rig heeled in the wind and swung through 145 degrees, until its helipad was on the north-eastern side instead of the west and, worse still, was directly under the overhang of a leaning leg. The Sea King had to head into the wind to hover, which placed the winch and winchman on the seaward side away from the rig. Moreover, the rig continued to tilt and the helicopter's natural tendency to point upwind kept on spinning the aircraft round, so that Tilsley was presented with a view ahead of him of total blackness and no points of references.

What had before been a difficult and dangerous rescue enough now became virtually impossible. But Tilsley did his best. Facing away from the rig, he backed the Sea King in, flying 'blind' and controlled by instructions from Tupper, until his tail-rotor was only feet away from the nearest leg. As Tilsley said, 'we were perilously close to being out of control'. Reluctantly, he had to abandon the rescue for the time being, but waited beside the rig for a further 45 minutes, to see whether the rig was stable for men to stay on board, or as he said 'to see if it would topple over', before returning to the Airport, landing at 2.20 am.

Of the six men still on board the rig, two were hauled ashore by breeches buoy shortly after daylight. Then, when that method had to be abandoned, Tilsley took off in '592' at 10.09 am and winched up the last four. '594' had suffered a primary hydraulics failure after its first sortie to the rig. A Sea Prince of 750 NAS flew from Culdrose with ground crew and spares to make repairs. All aircraft had returned to Culdrose by 1.45 pm on 2 February.

'592' flew for a total of five hours, 30 minutes and rescued 17 persons, and '594' five hours 15 minutes for another twelve, for a total rescued of 29, which exceeded the previous highest SAR total from Culdrose: 28 from the freighter *Lutria*, some 100 miles south-west of Land's End, on 11 February 1974 (*Lutria*'s crew abandoned ship and took to the life-rafts although, in fact, their ship did not sink and was later towed in).

For the *Orion* rescue, Glen Tilsley, Bob Davidson, Paul Crudgington and Tony Eagles all won the Air Force Cross, CACMN Terry King and Alf

Tupper the Queen's Commendation for Valuable Service in the Air. Tilsley also won the Alan Marsh Medal for 1978, and was invited to the 'Man of the Year' lunch at the Savoy Hotel.

10 'Anything from a haemorrhage to a headache': SAR Medicine

On 10 February 1978 the Commanding Officer of HMS *Daedalus*, Captain A.J. Bastick, assisted by Naval Air Mechanic Douglas Davie, the youngest air maintenance rating on the Station, cut a large cake to celebrate the fifth anniversary of Lee-on-Solent's SAR Flight.

Compared with Culdrose's 771 and 706 NASs, Lee-on-Solent's 781 NAS did not have the same proportion of long distance and much-publicised sea rescues. Their dramas were domestic rather than epic. But theirs was, if anything, an even busier life. Seventeen pilots had served in the Solent SAR Flight since 1973. During those five years they had flown over 5,000 hours, for 710 SAR sorties and had rescued 277 people, including 50 medevacs. In the previous year of 1976 alone, the Flight had flown a record number of 163 SAR sorties, including 26 searches for missing boats, 24 capsized sailing dinghies, 14 cliff rescues, 18 swimmers in distress and 14 medevacs.

The Solent SAR Flight was complemented with three Wessex HAR Mk5s, four aircrews, and three watches of maintenance staff – some 40 men in all. It took ten man-hours of maintenance work to keep one Wessex flying for one hour. The 32 ground crew staff averaged 56 hours' work a week to keep two of the three Wessex available. It was calculated that flying an SAR Wessex cost £700 an hour.

As always, the SAR pilots, who would otherwise have been flying in anti-submarine or Commando-carrying roles, enjoyed their work, regarding it as the most exacting and rewarding experiences of their careers. Sometimes, there was the added satisfaction of the public's gratitude. On 4 August 1978, the *Daily Express* front page carried the headline BURIED ALIVE!: 'Youngsters in holiday mud horror'. 'A crowd of holiday-makers on a beach yesterday dug desperately to rescue three children buried by a cliff landslide ... '

The three children, Bryan Pearce, 13, his 14-year-old sister Debbie and Daniel Brown, 13, had been playing at the foot of the famous multi-coloured cliffs of Alum Bay near the Needles when they were buried by a landslide of tons of mud and sand loosened by recent heavy rain.

Remarkably, all three children were dug out alive, two of them from an estimated depth of five feet of sand. A SAR Wessex from Lee flew them to hospital in Ryde for a check-up. They were eventually discharged unhurt.

Two days later that Wessex pilot, Lt Ray Colborne, had a carefully hand-written letter: 'Dear Lt Colbourne and crew, This is just to thank you for getting to the beach quickly on Thursday 3rd Aug. and getting me and my cousins away from Alum Bay. Any other time I might have enjoyed a helicopter ride more, Thank you all very much Daniel Brown'.

By this time, the late 1970s, some three decades after the formation of 705 NAS at Gosport, there had been an SAR Flight of some kind at Culdrose for over twenty years, with an estimated 25,000 hours spent flying and perfecting life-saving techniques. The Navy's full range of helicopter techniques and procedures, for helicopters in general and SAR in particular, were all described, in print, in 'Search and Rescue Standard Operating Procedures' – SARSOPS – (later HELISOPS).

HELISOPS has become a kind of Flyway Code, which is periodically revised and brought up to date. It lays down, for example, the Standard Winching Circuit, with precise directions as to what the SAR pilot and his crewman should do, and say. The aim is to ensure that the survivor can be seen from the helicopter at all points in the circuit, while safe circuit heights, speeds and angles of bank are maintained.

After the survivor has been sighted, the helicopter flies over him, into the wind, until it is approximately 100 yards upwind of him, then makes a 180° turn to starboard, with 30° maximum angle of bank, and steadies on the downwind bearing. The pilot calls out 'Downwind', carries out downwind checks, and prepares for the lift.

The helicopter carries on downwind until the survivor is at four o'clock from it, and then makes another 180° turn to starboard, reducing height and speed as it banks, so that the helicopter rolls out into wind, downwind of the survivor, at a minimum height of 30 feet, and a ground speed of 30-40 knots, depending upon the type of aircraft.

During this turn on to the final heading, the pilot calls out 'Visual' when he can see the survivor, and 'Running In' when the final approach is established and he is ready for the con from the winch operator. The pilot makes the final approach to the survivor, guided by the winch operator, to achieve a steady hover over the survivor at a height of 15-40 feet, depending upon wind and sea conditions and the type of aircraft.

HELISOPS also lays down the proper hand signals to be used by the winchman, and standard voice procedures – 'UP' and 'DOWN' when referring to the helicopter, 'RAISE' and 'LOWER' for the winch, and never the twain to be mixed, so as to avoid confusion. There are set procedures to be followed when communications fail between pilot and winchman, or after an electrical failure, or when the winch malfunctions, or the wire fouls, jams, runs away, or, in a dire emergency, has to be cut.

There are procedures for everything a helicopter and its crew may be called upon to do at any time: for single lifts, when the survivor dons the strop himself; for (almost invariably in SAR sorties) double lifts, when a crew member goes down in the double harness with a rescue strop and helps the survivor into it; for cliff winching; for flying into confined areas or places where the pilot can see little or nothing of the surroundings; for transfers, by day and night, of personnel or stores to and from ships, or to and from the ground, where landing is not feasible; for stretcher transfers; for 'Hi-Line' transfers, when the weather, sea conditions or the layout of a ship's upper deck make a normal transfer impracticable, or when the height of hover would be 60 feet or more; for 'heave-ho' hoists, using a block and tackle; for using nets to scoop up objects or (very rarely these days) survivors from the sea; for dropping, working with, and recalling SAR divers; for external and internal load lifting; for co-operation with the RNLI; for air-launching of multi-seat liferafts; for in-flight refuelling; for using an underwater telephone; for recovering remotely piloted target vehicles from the sea; and for rescuing aircrew from a crashed or ditched Sea Harrier.

Rescuing aircrew from ditched helicopters and fixed wing aircraft is the main task of the SAR diver, who has always been one of the most highly trained and highly qualified specialist ratings in the Service. He is a volunteer and a qualified aircrewman who must have completed at least one front-line tour as an ASW Aircrewman. He must also be a qualified ship's diver, with at least 500 minutes underwater time completed after his ship's diving course.

Rescuing an injured cliff faller, Cornwall, July 1977

After being accepted, the would-be SAR Diver must first successfully pass a six-week navigation course and a four-week Search and Rescue Aircrewman's conversion course, before beginning the five-week SAR Diver's Course. There is never any shortage of volunteers and there is a very high wastage rate: over 50% fail for one reason or another.

The first two weeks of the course, held at Culdrose, involve physical fitness training, surface and sub-surface endurance swims, and jumping techniques, with about 100 jumps a week, from a jetty or a ship's bow, and from heights of between ten and twenty feet, followed by training in parachute disentanglement and rescues of fellow divers feigning unconsciousness on the sea-bed or panicking on the surface.

After some 200 training jumps, the trainees graduate to jumps from helicopters in flight. After four weeks comes 'The Dunker' at Yeovilton: the Underwater Escape Training Unit, with purpose-designed training areas and a pool which contains various mock-ups of fixed-wing and helicopter interiors. These are fully manned and then overturned so that their occupants are 'dunked' in the water. With the air full of blood-curdling screams and the water churned into a frantic froth by the 'trapped' aircrew, the trainee is then invited to rescue the occupants. Finally, the course visits Yeovilton for an introduction to ejector seats and canopy release systems.

The SAR diver jumps from the helicopter (maximum height for jumping 20 feet, maximum speed 5 knots) wearing a wet or dry suit, mask, fins, knife and an ABLJ (Adjustable Buoyancy Life Jacket) which can be filled from its own compressed air cylinder in 2-3 seconds and will not only produce positive buoyancy from 90 feet but also a limited air supply through the oral inflation mouth-piece. He also wears BASAR (Breathing Apparatus Search and Rescue) which is a lightweight (35 lbs) two-cylinder breathing apparatus charged to 250 bar, with enough endurance for – at worst – 30 minutes hard work near the surface or 15 minutes at 30 feet. The divers are cleared to carry out rescue work to 30 metres depth and, uniquely amongst naval divers, are free swimmers with no lifeline or any connection to a boat or attendant.

The decision to dispatch the SAR diver is made by the pilot after considering the aircraft's limitations, the sea state, visibility, tides, depth of water and any other rescue services available at the scene. Valuable life-saving time can be saved by an SAR diver jumping near a drowning person, instead of being winched down.

While the diver and the survivor are under the helicopter and being subjected to the noise and spray caused by the downwash, it was very difficult to assess a casualty's injuries. For some injuries sustained by crashed aircrew, such as compression damage to the lower spine (after using an ejection seat, for example) winching could actually be beneficial. But injuries to the upper shoulder girdle or to the rib cage could be aggravated by winching, just as injuries to back and leg might well be aggravated by hauling the casualty into the helicopter's cabin. Yet leaving a survivor dangling outside, on the strop, would subject him to severe cooling because of the strong airflow over his wet clothing. However, a casualty who appeared drowned might well revive if he were pulled inside and given artificial respiration.

Because there was, of course, a medical aspect to many SAR sorties, the Navy's doctors took a close interest in SAR from its earliest days. One of the very first 'Flying Doctor' SAR sorties was flown by Lossiemouth's Flight in 1956, the year two of their Dragonflies took off the crew of the *Dovrefjell*. The German trawler *Gerhardt Zimmermann*, 80 miles off the Buchan coast, had reported that a 15-year-old member of the crew, Wilhelm Jansen, had had his arm caught and seriously injured in a winch.

As always, the Dragonflies were constricted by a short fuel range. Two of them, one with extra fuel and the other with Surgeon Lt J. Laine on board, flew to a naval range at Rosehearty. There, one aircraft refuelled and, piloted by Senior Commissioned Pilot Arnold Webb, flew out to the trawler, while the other flew on to Dyce for more fuel. Laine was winched down to the trawler, put the boy on a stretcher and both were winched up again. After some anxiety over both helicopters' fuel states, Wilhelm was flown in Webb's Dragonfly to Aberdeen Royal Infirmary, where his life was saved, although his arm had to be amputated.

Since those early ventures, naval doctors have flown on hundreds of SAR sorties and, over the years, evolved their own codes of practice, with handy hints and useful tips gained from hard experience. It was sound practice, for example, to have as many responsible medical staff on the Air Station 'in date' for survival and safety equipment drills, so that they were available to provide airborne medical cover at short notice at any time. Experience taught that an SAR doctor had to be as fit as any other crewman or diver; going down on the end of a winch-wire to a ship tossing to and fro was physically very tiring and could inflict some fearful bruising.

They learned that it was wise to take with them a phrase book, and a copy of the International Code of Signals, and a notebook and pencil, also a small amount of paper money, identity card, toothbrush and a change of underwear, in case their helicopter had to leave without them. More than one doctor had to find his way home through a foreign airport, penniless, identity-less, unshaven and still dressed in his rubber immersion suit, lifejacket and ear-defenders.

Various conflicting factors have often to be weighed up while a rescue is in progress, and afterwards. Medicine, like politics, is always the art of the possible and the first decision is often where to treat the patient. 'The rear cabin of a Sea King vibrates tremendously, especially in the hover, and it is a cold, dark, noisy and often wet place in which to practise medicine', wrote Surg Lt Cdr Rick Jolly, a very experienced SAR practitioner. 'Yet it may be vastly better than the trawl deck of a small fishing vessel lying hove-to in a beam sea'.

The patient may be suffering from anything from a haemorrhage to a headache, from acute appendicitis to a grave rupture, from pneumonia to a strangulated hernia. There are head, back or leg injuries caused by machinery, and injuries caused by falls – down ladders, hatch-ways or cliffs. There are electrocutions caused by faulty electrical fittings, scalds, burns, divers with 'bends', premature births and gynaecological complications, not just in Dartmoor farmhouses in mid-winter but in ships at sea where an increasing number of women are crew members, or travelling wives.

Some ships suffered from what could be called 'overkill'. On 26 September 1975 the Master of the 65,000-ton Liberian registered tanker *Richard C. Sauer*, on passage from the Middle East to Belgium, signalled from off Cape Finisterre that one of his crew was suffering from Smallpox, Yellow Fever, Cholera *and* Typhoid. The French authorities prudently declined to help and so did Culdrose. When the tanker anchored off Brixham the following morning, the Port Medical Officer went on board and diagnosed a mild viral gastro-enteritis from which the patient had already recovered.

Sometimes, the symptoms were genuine enough. On the morning of 15 November 1974 the container ship *Asiafreighter* radioed from a position in the Atlantic some 210 miles from Culdrose that four crew members were very sick with suspected toxic poisoning and she was making 27 knots to reach the mainland as quickly as possible.

A Sea King of 706 NAS (Lt Fred Hatton, Lt Hugh Clark, Observer Lt David Keaney, LACMN Mike Langford, ACMN Colin Oxley, with the Principal Medical Officer at Culdrose, Surg Cdr Michael Boyle OBE) had taken off at 9 am, and was joined en route by a Sea King of the Royal Australian Navy's Flight at Culdrose (Cdr Edward Bell RAN, the Flight CO, Lt Tony Baker RAN, Observer Lt Patrick Arthur RAN, and Warrant Officer Aircrewman Fred Atkinson) who were diverted from another sortie. This Flight was a newly-formed training unit, their Sea King having been delivered from Westlands only the previous day.

The 706 NAS Sea King detected *Asiafreighter* on radar at 30 miles distance at 10.40 am and was overheard shortly afterwards. A high winching had to be done, from 60 feet, down to the only suitable point which was aft of the tall superstructure and the funnel emitting exhaust gases at a reported 700°C.

Cdr Boyle examined the four sick members of the crew and decided they needed urgent hospital treatment. All four were deeply jaundiced, and had been passing dark blood and bile-stained urine.

Although critically ill, the four were able to walk to the after-deck. But tension mounted as they were winched up one by one. The Sea King could remain over the ship for only 25 minutes, because of the long return flight and the extra weight of the four patients. But, with all four safely on board, the Sea King left at 11.25 and landed at Culdrose an hour later.

The operation had taken three hours and 25 minutes. The sick men were in the Royal Cornwall Hospital Treliske only five hours after the initial distress message. Throughout the SAR operation, top cover and a radio link with the mainland was provided by a French long-range maritime patrol aircraft which had also been diverted from a training exercise.

Later the same day the sick men were flown to London and taken to King's

College Hospital. They were suffering from arsine poisoning, caused by gas leaking from two cylinders stowed in No.2 Hold which they had been routinely inspecting.

Arsine gas, a compound of hydrogen and arsenic, attacks body tissues with a toxic effect on the kidneys, liver and blood cells, and can kill through the skin as well as the lungs; it was the basis of gases stockpiled by the Germans before the Second World War. It was so potent that Cdr Boyle, who had been on board the ship only twenty minutes and had not left the upper deck or superstructure, himself suffered minor symptoms of toxic poisoning.

Asiafreighter at first continued on her voyage but shortly afterwards the Captain and two other crew members exhibited the same symptoms, though less pronounced, and the ship diverted to Falmouth, where most of her crew were landed. In all, thirteen of the crew were affected.

Nine days later, *Asiafreighter* put to sea, with a volunteer relief Captain and crew, and escorted by the destroyer *Kent*, to carry out a controlled dispersal of the toxic gases. Even then, a Sea King of 706 NAS had to fly out to the ship, some 20 miles south-west of Culdrose, to pick up another doctor who became ill with the same symptoms and had to be relieved.

The attention of press, media and public tended to be concentrated upon SAR along the south coast. But meanwhile 819 NAS at Prestwick continued to provide an SAR service along the entire west coast of Scotland, as far north as the Hebrides, and as far east as the Grampians. On 14 September 1978, 819 NAS pulled off a rescue which was a classical example of how SAR should be done.

At 8.45 am an Atlantique maritime reconnaissance aircraft of the Royal Netherlands Navy, taking part in the NATO Exercise NORTHERN WEDDING, broadcast a 'May Day' from 2,500 feet over the Grampians that all power had been lost on one engine and the aircraft was unable to maintain height.

The aircraft was offered emergency landing facilities at Glasgow's airport at Renfrew but Lt P. Jongejan, the captain and navigator, declined because he was afraid the aircraft might descend upon houses during the approach. Instead he decided to attempt to ditch in the Clyde.

The pilot, Lt L. de Boer, achieved a good ditching in the Atlantic, south-west of Islay, on one engine, in a seven foot swell. The impact broke off the outer section of one wing, but all fourteen on board – Jongejan, de Boer, ten crew members and two RAF aircraftsmen on the flight for the experience – escaped unhurt. Ten of them got into the dinghy, two sat on the wing section and two more on floating debris.

A Sea King of 819 NAS was airborne less than twenty minutes after the 'May Day', followed after a minute by a Wessex, and by a second Sea King 17 minutes later. But unfortunately, a navigational error had sent all the rescue effort to look in the Kilbrannan Sound, between the Isle of Arran and the Mull of Kintyre, more than 100 miles from the actual ditching position.

It was not until 10 am that an RAF Nimrod, which had been scrambled from Kinloss in response to the 'May Day' and had also been searching in the wrong area, picked up a signal from a Search and Rescue Beacon (SARBE) and then, almost at once, sighted the Atlantique's dinghy. The Nimrod dropped a Sonar buoy to guide the helicopters.

With this datum, the rest of the rescue went perfectly. Lt Cdr Mike Lawrence, CO of 819 NAS, picked up two men from the wing section and four from the dinghy. Lt Ian Moffat, in the second Sea King, picked up the two on the floating wreckage and the remaining six from the dinghy. All 14 survivors were in the Southern General Hospital, Glasgow, only 2½ hours after the 'May Day' call.

SAR crews, by the very nature of their business, tend to think of SAR sorties as lasting an hour or perhaps ninety minutes. Some of the very shortest Solent SAR sorties were barely ten minutes. Even the Sea King crews thought in terms of a forenoon or afternoon, or at most an overnight, flight. But in October 1978 there was a prodigious Sea King SAR effort which lasted nearly three weeks.

In the early hours of Friday 13 October, the Greek-owned oil tanker *Christos Bitas* ran aground on rocks near Milford Haven. During the 18 days

Last moments of *Christos Bitas*, October 1978

the ship stayed afloat, whilst strenuous efforts were made to save her and her cargo, Sea Kings of 706 NAS, 826 NAS, RFA *Fort Grange* Flight, and the Royal Air Force Training Unit spent hours on task for the Department of Trade, ferrying DoT investigators, BP and salvage officials, oil pollution officers, A.S.W.E. scientists, *Christos Bitas*' Captain and ship's company, the press, mail and victuals to and from Culdrose, Plymouth, Brawdy, Pembroke Dock, the frigate *Eskimo*, the survey ship *Hecate*, the fishery protection ship *Orkney*, and the BP tanker *British Dragoon*, as well as carrying out oil pollution surveys in the Bristol Channel and around Lundy Island.

Between them the Sea Kings flew 42 sorties, for a total of 92 hours 35 minutes flying time, spread over 20 days. Finally it was decided to sink *Christos Bitas* in mid-Atlantic, to avoid further pollution. The frigate *Eskimo* joined the funeral cortège to the position where the tanker's sea-cocks were opened. The final and 42nd Sea King sortie on 1 November, after the ship had sunk, was to transfer TV crews and press from *Eskimo* to Culdrose.

The winter of 1978/79 was the hardest since the exceptional winter of 1963. Heavy snow fell all over the country, from Land's End to John O'Groats. Blizzards driven by gale force winds closed roads with drifts, brought trains to a standstill, and cut off remoter areas of moorland and mountain.

That Christmas 'leave period' was one of the busiest ever for the SAR crews at Culdrose. At 2.30 pm on 30 December, Mrs Chase of Perranporth reported that her daughter Joanne, aged 11, and her friend Michelle Rowse, aged 13, were missing. She thought they had gone rock-climbing on the cliffs nearby.

The two girls were spotted by Mrs Chase herself. They were cut off by the rising tide on the 100-foot Chapel Rock, a quarter of a mile offshore. At first, the local Coast Guards decided to wait for low tide, reassuring the girls through a loudhailer. But it was getting dark, the weather was worsening and spray was breaking over the ledge where the girls were sheltering. Culdrose was asked to send a helicopter, while the St Ives lifeboat was launched to stand by.

The duty Sea King manned by a crew from 814 NAS (Lt Laurie Williams, Lt Duncan Fergusson, Observer Lt Leslie Sim, POACMN Martin Newton and Surg Lt Dave Morgan) took off at 6.05 pm in winds gusting up to 40 knots and soon flew into a blizzard. Police and Coastguards illuminated the rock with car headlights, searchlights and flares. Even so, as Lt Laurie Williams said, 'We were very lucky. We moved in very slowly, and visibility along the north Cornish coast was by then down to only about fifty yards. But the weather cleared for about a quarter of an hour and we were able to move in slowly guided by coastguard flares.'

Lt Sim was twice lowered with the double lift, both girls were winched up and the rescue was over by 7.05 pm. But, clearing the area, 'we were lucky again,' said Williams. 'Once we had them on board we had to go straight up to clear the cliff'.

Both girls were in such good physical condition, despite their five-hour

Relief supplies delivered by 771 NAS in a hard winter, February 1978

ordeal on the rock, that Williams decided to take them to Culdrose rather than risk a night landing at Treliske Hospital. For 45 minutes he tried to reach Culdrose, but low visibility in blizzards driven by winds gusting up to 50 knots, compounded by power failures in the airfield's recovery aids, led him to put the Sea King down at 8.10 pm in a field of broccoli, close to the village of Marazion, some ten miles from Culdrose. Everyone was later taken to Culdrose by motor transport but the snow drifts and road conditions were so bad that the girls could not return to their homes for another two days.

Meanwhile, the stand-by Sea King had been in action. On that day, 30 December, the 450-ton Aberdeen trawler *Ben Asdale* was alongside the Russian fish-processing vessel *Antartika* in Falmouth Bay, transferring a catch of mackerel. In the Force 10 snow storm which had prevented Williams' Sea King returning to Culdrose, *Ben Asdale* broke adrift from the *Antartika* at about 11.05 pm and was driven helplessly with a jammed rudder across Falmouth Bay until she grounded at Newporth Head, near Falmouth. There were 14 men on board, including two Russians who had been assisting with the mackerel catch.

Guided by *Ben Asdale*'s faint flickering lights, coastguards, police and local volunteers quickly arrived on the scene. A rocket line was fired on board, and a breeches buoy was on its way down to the trawler, when she toppled over on to her side, rendering the equipment useless. Three men, one of them Russian, were washed overboard and drowned. Three more took to a life-raft and reached the shore, where the three brothers Billcliffe, from the Crag Hotel Maenporth, ran into the surf to help them.

That left eight men still on board, for whom there seemed no hope. One Russian could be seen clinging to the guardrails and being pounded by heavy waves. Culdrose was asked to provide a helicopter. Reluctantly, because of the experience of Williams' Sea King only a few hours earlier, but yielding to the Coastguard opinion that there was no other way to make the rescue, Culdrose called out the stand-by crew.

Manned by a crew of 814 NAS (Lt Tony Hogg, Lt Larry Jeram-Croft, Observer and Captain Lt Cdr Mike Norman, LACMN Chris Folland, and Leading Medical Assistant Brian Steele) Sea King '592' took off at 2 am in appalling weather and was over the place where *Ben Asdale* was reported to be some twenty minutes later. But for a time the ship was completely blotted out by a blizzard, so that even the watchers on shore could not see her.

Because of the wind direction, Hogg had to head out to sea while he let the Sea King down to winching height. But communications inside the helicopter deteriorated as the intercom began to fail, cutting Hogg off from Norman and Folland in the cabin. Having no point of reference, and knowing only that the Sea King was being blown perilously close to the cliffs, Hogg gingerly backed into the cove where *Ben Asdale* lay on the rocks, guided as he went by radio directions from Coastguard Officer Charles Robinson (ex-Fleet Chief and former Photographic Officer at Culdrose).

The rough seas and violent air turbulence caused extraordinary variations of pitch and roll but Hogg held the Sea King steady over the wreck, rotor blades whirling only feet away from the cliff face, while Norman and Folland began to winch the eight trawlermen up to safety.

The rescue would have been difficult enough in the weather conditions. It was made even harder and more dangerous by a complete cabin inter-com failure and a fault in the winch. One trawlerman was left swaying in the air for some minutes and finally had to be dropped back into the sea to take the weight off the wire-drum while the snag was cleared.

At last, after a rescue which one reporter said was 'Fantastic, I've never seen anything like it in my life!' the eight were winched up, all suffering from exposure and one from severe hypothermia. Because of the atrocious weather conditions, '592' flew back to Culdrose via a long roundabout route over the sea, Norman passing handwritten notes and directions to the pilots, and landed at 3.40 am. *Ben Asdale*'s survivors were taken to the sick bay, to join Joanne and Michelle.

For the *Ben Asdale* rescue, Hogg and Norman were awarded the Air Force Cross, Steele the Queen's Commendation for Brave Conduct, Jeram-Croft and Folland the Queen's Commendation for Valiant Service in the Air. Hogg also received the Royal Aeronautical Society's Alan Marsh Medal for 1978.

Only four days later, on 4 January 1979, the same Sea King '592' with the

Ben Asdale aground and capsized near Falmouth, December 1978

same crew, less LMA Steele, took off in a 60-knot gale at 10.05, followed at 10.15 by '594' (Sub Lt Gordon Jones, Sub Lt Frank Edwards, Observer Lt Ian Munday, LACMN Wally Waters) to answer a call for help from the 2,200-ton motor vessel *Cantonad*, in distress 30 miles north-west of Guernsey and 90 miles south-east of Culdrose.

In her first 'May Day' message, at 9.05 pm, *Cantonad* had reported 'Starboard side ripped out, listing to starboard 20 degrees'. A sequence of following signals recorded the ship's growing predicament: at 9.33 pm, the list 'is now 30 degrees', at 10.17 'Have 37 degree list', at 10.22 'My list is now 45 degrees'. At 10.38 another ship nearby, the motor bulk carrier *Eurosea*, reported 'They are trying to lower a lifeboat. They don't think they can hold more than a few minutes'.

Six minutes later, *Eurosea* signalled 'We cannot see *Cantonad* any more on radar'. At 11 pm another motor bulk carrier *Theomana* radioed that the last time they saw *Cantonad* had been at 10.35 when 'He said he was abandoning ship'.

It seems that *Cantonad* capsized and sank at about 10.50 pm. When '592' arrived at the scene at 11.20, they could see only debris – and three of the crew clinging to wreckage. With waves running over 50 feet high, efforts to lower a man from the Sea King had to be abandoned. But, miraculously, one man, a 19-year-old Greek steward Demetrius Petriphs, was saved. 'By the time we got there', said Gordon Jones, of '594', who arrived shortly after

'592', 'there was a lot of wreckage floating around and a partially submerged life-raft. We could see several of the crew bobbing about in life jackets holding on to a piece of wood and a barrel.'

'Conditions were pretty damn nasty. The waves were running as high as 50 feet, there was a long swell and winds were storm force ten. We lit up the scene with spotlights and Leading Aircrewman Walters went down on the wire, but it was hopeless. We couldn't get down too close because of the waves. At times we were literally five to ten feet above the water.'

'The man who survived did so because of animal will to live. He got the wire, simply tangled the harness around his legs, hung on to it with his bare hands and we pulled him to safety. He was very lucky. At any moment he could have slipped back to his death.'

'By the time we had got the one man out the others had let go of the wood and were drifting face down. It was pitiful to see'.

Always, in these rescues, the chances of saving a life had to be weighed against the risks to the helicopter crews. 'I stuck it until it was just tempting fate too far,' said Ian Munday, who also went down to see if anything could be done for the others. 'I kept landing up under the waves which meant the line went slack, and could have wrapped itself around any of my limbs which would have been very dangerous when I was dragged free again.'

'Every wave knocked the breath out of me as well, and the harnesses have a quick release panel which is very sensitive. The shock could have triggered that'. The survivor had been in the water for an hour and was suffering from severe hypothermia. Weighing up his chances, against those still in the sea, it was decided to rush him to hospital.

Demetrius was the only survivor of *Cantonad*'s 16-man Greek crew. Recovering in hospital, he said 'I was in my cabin playing cards when the captain ordered us on deck. The seas were huge and had ripped away the bulkhead on the bows. The captain ordered us into lifeboats, but just then a big wave swamped us and washed him overboard. We tried to launch the lifeboats but another wave made the ship roll over and we lost the lifeboats. She started to sink and we had no choice but to go over the side.'

'I was with the first and second engineers and my mate. The water was freezing and it seemed hours before we heard the helicopter in the darkness. We all cheered when the winch dropped. I grabbed it and the friction burnt my hand. I dropped back into the water and as I did so all three of my mates disappeared. I never saw them again.'

Leaving '592' to guide the lifeboat to the scene to recover bodies (two of them eventually), '594' flew north and landed in a car park at Berry Head, near Brixham, where a waiting ambulance took the patient to torbay Hospital.

'594' flew on to Portland to refuel, as did '592' at 2.15 that morning. From there Lt Cdr Norman telephoned Culdrose to say that in his opinion there was little hope of finding more survivors in those conditions. It was also found that the Sea Kings were affected by the '*Merc Enterprise* problem' of salt ingestion. Both Sea Kings' engines had to have a fresh water wash before they took off again to return to *Cantonad*.

By now, cold and fatigue were taking their toll of both crews, and as there seemed no prospect of finding further survivors, at 5.10 the crews asked permission to return to base, and landed at Culdrose at 6 am, after flight times of six hours, five minutes for '592' and six hours, 30 minutes for '594'.

A third Sea King '591' with the off-watch crew (Williams, Fergusson, Sim, and crewman Sub Lt Raymond Snook) had taken off from Culdrose at 12.35 am to join '592'. But an hour later '591' and an RAF Nimrod were diverted from the *Cantonad* search to investigate red flares, believed to be from a yacht or a fishing boat, sighted at 1.20 am by the German vessel *Mira* 30 miles south-west of the Lizard.

The RAF Nimrod and Sea King '591' arrived over *Mira* at 2.05 am on 5 January 1979 and began a search which, after about an hour, located a yacht wallowing in the very heavy seas, with people crouching in its cockpit. With 50 knot winds and waves 25 feet high, attempts at winching were soon abandoned. '591' needed refuelling, so *Mira* was left as escort for the yacht until a French aircraft and a warship arrived – before first light, it was hoped.

Mira lost contact with the yacht at about 4.45 and '591', having refuelled and cleared salt from engines and rotors with fresh water, returned to begin the search again. At 7.08 am '591' reported that it was returning to Culdrose, with the crew suffering from cold and fatigue after five hours' constant battling against the weather.

With three Sea Kings having been airborne for most of the night, Culdrose's long-range SAR resources were now severely stretched. At 3.30 am two more 814 NAS Sea King crews were contacted at home and warned they might have to fly a sortie at first light. The *Cantonad* search was taken over by surface vessels and Lee-on-Solent's SAR helicopter, while Culdrose concentrated on the search for the yacht.

Two more 814 NAS Sea Kings, '270' (Lt Keith Dudley, Lt Chris Jagger, Observer Lt Greg Lewis, Fleet Chief ACMN Norman Anning) and '273' (Lt Cdr Keith Hindle, Lt Jonathan Rich, Observer Lt Robert Faulks) took off at 8.25 and 8.45. Two hours later they found the yacht again, with her mast lowered, or possibly broken off when *Mira* had come too close whilst trying to rescue the yacht's crew. Anning went down with the double lift and by 11 am had recovered two women and a violin case belonging to one of them.

The yacht *Peacock* had left Salcombe in Devon for St Malo in France on New Year's Day with a crew of three: the French owner, his female companion Dominique Silhol and Miss Leonie Hutchings from Dartmouth who had met the French couple at a New Year's Eve party. With Dartmouth cut off by snow, she had hitched a lift in the yacht to return to her job in Paris. But *Peacock* had been caught by the ferocious storms in mid-Channel and driven westwards.

At 9.30 on Thursday 4 January the French skipper had been washed overboard and was not seen again. The two women had huddled in the

Clutching her violin case Miss Leonie Hutchings of Dartmouth arrives at RNAS Culdrose after her rescue from the yacht *Peacock*, January 1979

cockpit, loosing off flares and hoping somebody would eventually see them. They had been greatly cheered to see '591' and *Mira*, although *Mira* had damaged the mast in an over-zealous attempt at rescue. Both Sea Kings landed at Culdrose at 11.45. The two women were taken to the sickbay and treated for minor abrasions, cold and shock.

The gales continued, and the SAR events of this hectic 'leave period' were not over. At 5 pm on 6 January a Wessex of 771 NAS Culdrose recovered from a cove near Falmouth the body of one of the three men lost from *Ben Asdale* the previous weekend. Forty minutes later two Sea Kings of 814 NAS, '270' (the same team of Hogg, Jeram-Croft, Norman and Folland) and '273' (likewise, the same team of Williams, Fergusson, Sim, Newton and Dr Morgan) were recalled to Culdrose and were soon airborne again, '273' at 6.45 and '270' at 7 pm, to deal with a call from the 97,000 ton Japanese tanker *Daiko Maru*, 57 miles south-west of the Wolf Rock.

Daiko Maru had picked up two injured members of the crew of the yacht *Ile de Feu* and had asked for medical aid by helicopter. But when '273' arrived over the tanker and Morgan, Newton and a stretcher were winched down, they found not two but six people, five men and a woman, all French, who had been adrift in a liferaft for 30 hours.

Ile de Feu had sailed from St Malo bound for the Azores on Christmas Eve and had, like everybody else, been caught in the Force 10 gales. On the night of Thursday 4 January a giant wave ripped off the main cabin deckhead and swamped the yacht. The skipper's leg was broken and a second crew member had a broken jaw. They launched a liferaft and lit flares, but nobody saw them until *Daiko Maru* sighted their orange smoke and flares on Saturday afternoon and picked them up – a very fine feat of seamanship by the tanker in that weather.

'273' lifted the two injured men, and flew them to Treliske Hospital. '270' lifted the remaining four and took them to Culdrose sickbay. 814 NAS had rescued 19 people in five missions in one week.

By midnight, 7 January 1979, 814 NAS were nearly at the end of their SAR commitment for the Culdrose Christmas leave period. They were to be relieved at 8 am on the morning of 8th. But at 1 am, the 121,000 ton French oil tanker *Betelgeuse* exploded at Whiddy Island terminal in Bantry Bay. The Irish authorities appealed for help. The 'old firm' of '270' (Hogg, Jeram-Croft, Norman and Folland) and '273' (Williams, Fergusson, Sim and Newton) were airborne at 3.25 and 3.30 am respectively,

They arrived at 5.30 at an improvised landing strip at Bantry, illuminated by the headlights of the local Garda's cars. They could see flames from the tanker 20 miles away. Soon it was clear that there was very little chance of anybody still being alive. The Sea Kings carried out a search of Bantry Bay at first light, and recovered four bodies which were taken to Cork Regional Hospital. Both Sea Kings returned to Culdrose at 2.15 pm, having both flown over 20 hours, 40 minutes.

It had been a busy Christmas, after a very busy year. The aircrews of the Culdrose squadrons won the Boyd Trophy for 1978 for their outstanding record of rescues, medical and humanitarian flights during the year.

11 Fastnet 1979

The Fastnet Race has been run under the auspices of the Royal Ocean Racing Club every other year, except for the war years, since 1925. Latterly, the race has been part of the Admiral's Cup series. Over the years, 'the Fastnet' has become almost as famous a sporting event as the Grand National, a 'classic' amongst offshore races and very probably the only yacht race known by name to landlubbers who have never set foot in a yacht themselves.

But, unlike the Grand National, the number of Fastnet entries is virtually unlimited and no previous racing qualifications are strictly required. Despite its rugged, somewhat 'macho' image, or even because of it, the Fastnet attracts many who do not normally race offshore regularly. It is *The* Race many helmsmen and women and their crews like to pit themselves against, even though it may well be their only long distance race of the year. To 'do the Fastnet' is the ambition of many yachtsmen who have no hope of winning; just to finish is glory enough. Thus the entries have increased dramatically since the war. In 1955 there were 47 competitors, of whom 44 finished. In 1977, there were 288, and 229 finished.

Racing speeds have also increased noticeably. In 1957, the fifth boat to finish (the fifth boat being taken to represent an average for the large class) averaged 5¼ knots. In 1979, the fifth boat averaged 8 knots.

The race is run in the first fortnight of August, after Cowes Week. The start is at Cowes, and the course is outward and westward, passing either north or south of the Scillies, as the racing skipper decides, round the Fastnet Rock, off the southern coast of Ireland, leaving the Rock either to port to starboard. On the homeward leg, yachts must pass south of the Bishop Rock in the Scillies, to finish at Plymouth – a total distance by the most direct route, of about 605 miles. The race proper usually lasts between three and five days, although the time interval between the first and last to finish is often more than a week.

Until 1979, the Fastnet had an excellent safety record. Only one crewman had ever been lost – washed overboard in 1931. Most years, the weather along the Fastnet course in early August is reasonable. There were gales during the 1957, 1958 and 1961 races, but in the 1970s there was remarkably good weather. The 1971, 1973 and 1977 races were all sailed in light and variable winds, with calm patches, and the 1975 race had mostly brisk Force 3 westerlies. Possibly, this unusual sequence of fair weather years was responsible for the record number of 336 entries, of whom 303 started, in fine weather on the afternoon of Saturday 11 August, 1979.

The wind dropped away in the first twenty-four hours, and there were patches of fog. The press were soon bored. Bad visibility prevented photo-flights over the racing fleet and there was nothing to report. Hopes of a brisker racing pace than in the last three Fastnets began to fade. 'Slownet', one headline said.

Meanwhile, on Thursday 9 August, a 'weak disturbance' had moved eastward across the United States, and into the gulf of Maine on 10th. Although still small and weak, it soon spawned tornadoes and severe thunderstorms in the Ohio valley and over southern New England, before beginning to cross the Atlantic at what became a rapid rate of over 30 knots.

By 1200 GMT on Monday 13 August Low 'Y', as it was now called, was some two hundred miles off south-western Ireland. In the preceding twelve hours, this 'small wave depression' had given little sign of what was to come. It seemed quite possible it would fill and disappear in a few hours.

But in the next six hours from 12 to 6 pm, 13 August, Low 'Y' began to intensify and move rapidly north-east. By 6 pm its central barometric pressure had dropped to about 995 millibars and was still falling. One competitor, the Irish yacht *Sundowner*, had passed Land's End at 11 am on 13th when, as her skipper Barry O'Donnell said, 'the barometer began to fall and eventually fell an unbelievable 40 millibars in 24 hours. Our own readings were from 1025 to 985, and somebody suggested that we put a match under the needle because it was falling so fast. I could not believe the speed at which it was falling because after all a fall of one millibar/hour is dangerous, and this was almost double that. There was no other warning of the gale.'

The shipping forecast issued at 12.55 on 13th and broadcast at 13.55 for SOLE, LUNDY, FASTNET was unalarming: 'Southwesterly 4 or 5, increasing 6 or 7 for a time, veering westerly'. A gale warning issued at 13.55 and broadcast at 15.05 on BBC Radio 4 for SOLE, FASTNET, SHANNON was 'southwesterly gales force 8 imminent'. Even the shipping forecast, including gale warnings, issued at 17.05 and broadcast at 17.50 still gave no real indication of what was very shortly to come in LUNDY, FASTNET, IRISH SEA: 'Mainly southerly 4 locally 6, increasing 6 locally gale 8, becoming mainly north-westerly later'.

As Barry O'Donnell commented, with some justification, 'The meteorological offices and the BBC had arranged things in such a way that if you listened to the shipping forecast you got no warning of the gale, but if you listened to the BBC non-stop you did. But you have more to do on racing boats than listen to the BBC non-stop, and it was incredible that while a gale warning was being announced on some wavelengths it wasn't put out on the shipping forecast'.

The truth was that the 'Fastnet Low "Y" ' was an unusual weather system, with some aspects which are still mysterious. Towards midnight on 13 August the 'Low' slowed, though still moving north-eastward, and continued to deepen. At midnight it was close to the western Irish coast with a storm centre of 979 millibars. Without warning it swung the strongest winds in a narrow band south of Ireland, right across the strung-out Fastnet fleet.

Large waves normally required strong winds blowing over the surface of the sea for some hours before they can achieve their full stature. But on that night giant walls of water, up to 30 feet high but with very short wave-lengths, massively breaking tops and steep leading edges, were generated very swiftly.

At that time many yachts were crossing the Labadie Bank, between Cornwall and Ireland, where the sea shallows to a depth of about 200 feet. It was suggested later in some quarters that the Bank's 'shallow water effect' contributed to the size of the waves. If it did, it could only have been slight. Tides had no effect at all.

Very few yacht skippers – less than ten per cent, in fact – said later that they were aware that afternoon of the severity of the storm approaching them. Further gale warnings still did not convey a proper sense of urgency. One issued at 18.05 for FINISTERRE, SOLE, FASTNET, broadcast at 18.30 and again at 19.05 said: 'Southwesterly gales force 8, increasing severe gale force 9, imminent'. As late as 9 pm that evening Land's End was broadcasting for FASTNET 'Mainly southerly 4, locally 6, increasing 6 to gale 8 locally severe gale then becoming mainly north-westerly 6'. Finally, a forecast issued at 22.30 and broadcast at 00.15 on 14 August warned for FASTNET 'Southwesterly severe gales force 9, increasing storm force 10, imminent.'

But by then the Fastnet crews needed neither weather forecast nor the BBC to tell them they were in the midst of what Barry O'Donnell called 'the storm of all time'. By 11 pm, 'the wind was close on 50 knots and we were down to "bare poles" (all sails off) and streaming warps – that is, trailing all the heavy ropes over the stern to slow the boat down because we had decided to turn and run. And this is before we heard any forecast.'

Indications of real trouble in the Fastnet first became apparent on the late evening of 13 August, when a number of yachts reported problems with rudders and steering gear. By then the fleet was spread out over about 140 miles between Land's End and the Fastnet Rock. The Baltimore lifeboat (in south-west Ireland, one of the nearest lifeboat stations to the Fastnet Rock) was launched at 10.15 pm on 13th to search for and eventually find and tow in a rudderless yacht.

Sundowner overheard one 'May Day' call. With what O'Donnell called 'fantastic phlegm, the man said "This is the yacht *Magic*, and this is a May Day. We are in serious trouble. We have lost our rudder and we are out of control" and giving his position as if he were reading the news.'

During the night, as the storm centre moved north-eastward up the Irish coast, the wind veered from west to north, blowing across the original direction of the waves, and making it even more difficult for helmsmen to steer the safest course out of trouble in the darkness. 'The most frightening aspect,' said O'Donnell, 'was that so many things happened at night. The noise of the waves was incredible, as was their size, every oncoming wave blacked out everything else, you could not see beyond it. The speed of the boat was terrifying (I was afraid the rudder would come off), as was the whistle of the keel every time the boat surfed off a wave. There was no sleep, no hot food; we lived on chocolate.'

The yacht *Morningtown*, owned by Mr Rodney Hill, was at sea with the race, acting as the Royal Ocean Racing Club's representative and rescue ship and, with the Dutch destroyer HNMLS *Overijssel*, the Fastnet guard ship, as a communications link to undertake a radio 'round-up' of the 70 or so Admiral's Cup yachts and pass the list through Land's End MRSC twice a day.

Rodney Hill reported that at the height of the storm, with distress flares

Flying towards *Grimalkin*: the man lying on his back is already dead

going up in the vicinity of the Labadie Banks, it appeared as though *Morningtown* was in the eye of a hurricane, with bright stars above, and swirling clouds of mist and murk all around, and an 'impossible seaway' that was tossing yachts over and rolling them under, in some cases several times.

Between midnight and 2 am numerous red flares were reported and several 'May Day' calls were heard. Four more lifeboats were launched, from Courtmacsherry Harbour (at 2.40 am), Ballycotton (2.55 am), St Mary's (3 am) and Courtmacsherry (3.20am), to search for rudderless yachts.

At 2.16 am (GMT) on 14 August Land's End MRSC asked for Southern Rescue Coordination Centre help for several yachts in difficulty. Because of the very bad weather and the poor visibility, it was agreed to delay the air search until first light. Four lifeboats and the offshore fishery patrol vessel HMS *Anglesey* were already on their way, and *Overijssel* was also in the area.

An SAR Nimrod (Rescue 01) at RAF Kinloss was brought to advance readiness at 3.34 am (GMT), briefed at 3.53 am, and was airborne at 4.18 am. Rescue 01 arrived over the scene at 5.30, established communications with Southern Rescue Coordination Centre, assumed Scene of Search Commander, and co-operated with surface shipping, yachts and helicopters in locating yachts in distress and bodies in the water. The Nimrods, from 201 and 120 Squadrons, Kinloss, and from 42 Squadron, St Mawgan, were to fly consecutive sorties, sometimes with two Nimrods in the air simultaneously, for the next two days.

Meanwhile, the duty controller at RCC Mount Wise telephoned the Air Officer of the Day at Culdrose at 3.45 am (GMT) and told him there was concern for the safety of the crew of the yacht *Magic*, reported to be 75 miles north-west of Culdrose, taking part in the Fastnet. There were also reports of four people in a liferaft ten miles south of *Magic*'s position and a yacht running ashore on the Scillies (this last proved to have nothing to do with the Fastnet).

An SAR Wessex (Rescue 20) was scrambled at first light, at 4.35 am (GMT), on the first sortie of what was to be a very long day indeed, to assist the yacht aground in the Scillies. An SAR Sea King (Rescue 77) took off ten minutes later to look for *Magic*, reported rudderless and shipping heavy seas.

From now on, reports arriving thick and fast began to reveal the sheer scale of the emergency. It was becoming clear that a large number of yachts in the Fastnet Race were in the path of the storm, and that the normal SAR arrangements at Culdrose were insufficient. Air and ground crews living locally were recalled from leave. Aircraft were prepared and launched as crews became available.

At 5 am Land's End MRSC reported the yachts *Grimalkin*, capsized 30 miles north-west of Land's End, and *Mulligatawny*, in distress not yet clarified. By 5.30 four yachts were reported to be in serious difficulties – *Magic, Grimalkin, Mulligatawny*, dismasted, and *Tarantula*, reported sinking at 5.18 am.

Wessex Rescue 20 arrived over the Scillies at 5.30, tasked to pick up survivors from *Grimalkin*, but saw nothing and returned to Culdrose to refuel at 6.30 am. A second Wessex (Rescue 27) took off at 6.30 to look for *Grimalkin*. At 6.35 a second Sea King (Rescue 97) was tasked to look for *Mulligatawny*.

The first Fastnet survivor to be rescued was from *Tarantula*, by Sea King Rescue 77, at 7.45. When Rescue 77 arrived, the yacht's mast was whipping to and fro to such an extent that the aircrewman would be in danger. *Tarantula* was in touch with the Sea King by VHF. Her crew agreed to go into the water one by one and swim clear of the yacht, where they would be picked up by the aircrewman. The first man, M. Jacques Souben, was duly rescued by double-lift. But the rescue, with his and the aircrewman's lifejackets both inflated, took more than 30 minutes. The remaining five men of *Tarantula*'s crew decided to stay where they were – the French trawler *Petit Poisson* picked them up later and they all survived.

The next were all five of the crew of *Magic*, rewarded for their spokesman's R/T *sangfroid* by being picked up by Wessex (Rescue 20) at 9.25 and landed at Culdrose at 9.48. Rescue 20's pilot, Lt Jerry Grayson of 771 NAS, was in contact with *Magic* on R/T and asked them to let off a flare 'to help us locate them. Although they let off a smoke flare we went nearly over them without seeing anything. It was only when they crested a wave that we spotted them. I went into the hover alongside, with the waves about 40 feet or more.'

'There was no way we could lift people off the yacht, with the mast swinging something like 45 degrees each way. So we had to ask them to jump into the water one at a time. It is a drastic measure to take, because you are then totally committed to getting them out'.

Despite the waves breaking over his head and tossing his body up and down, the Wessex SAR diver, LACMN 'Smiler' Grinney, successfully caught hold of all the survivors and one by one they were winched up. *Magic* herself was next sighted, abandoned by Sea King (Rescue 77) at 10.35 the next day. She later sank under tow.

Two minutes before Rescue 20, Sea King (Rescue 97) had landed at Culdrose with three survivors from *Trophy*, and two from *Grimalkin*, including 17-year-old Matthew Sheahan, the skipper's son.

Grimalkin was a 30-foot glass fibre yacht built by Camper & Nicholson, owned and skippered by David Sheahan, an accountant. In the early hours of 14th the sea became so rough that the crew of six gave up the cabin and sat together in the cockpit, secured by safety harnesses. But the boat broached to six times between 3 and 6 am, rolling over each time so far that her mast touched the wave-tops and all six crew were thrown into the sea. They dragged themselves back on board but such a succession of knock-downs took its toll: the navigator Gerry Winks was almost unconscious from hypothermia, the helmsman Nick Ward had a badly injured leg, and Sheahan himself had suffered a severe head wound.

The sixth knock-down dismasted the boat and trapped Sheahan under the cockpit. The others freed him by cutting his harness. When the boat righted herself, Sheahan was swept away and was never seen again. By now *Grimalkin* was half-full of water and the others, except Ward and Winks who appeared to be unconscious if not already dead, decided to abandon her. The three survivors, Matthew Sheahan, Mike Doyle, and Dick Wheeler, rigged and inflated the dinghy, got into it and floated away down wind. They were picked up at 9.30 by Sea King (Rescue 97), who then went on to pick up *Trophy*'s survivors ten minutes later.

Trophy, a 37-foot boat by Holman and Pye, was owned by Alan Bartlett, a London publican, and had a crew of eight. At about 1 am on 14th they sighted a flare and went to help the other yacht which was dismasted and wallowing helplessly in the huge seas. *Trophy* stood by until the arrival of *Morningtown*, when Bartlett decided to 'get the hell out of here!'. But *Trophy* was hit by a giant wave which dismasted her and broke her rudder. While Bartlett and his crew were trying to fix a jury rudder, the yacht was hit by another wave and capsized.

Bartlett was swept over the side where he hung by his harness until two of

The yacht *Ariadne* found abandoned without rigging

his crew dragged him inboard again. *Trophy* righted herself but she had shipped a lot of water; survivors said later she was half full. They felt that with no mast or rudder she was entirely at the mercy of the sea and it would only be a matter of time before she rolled over and sank.

The decision to abandon the yacht seems to have been taken unanimously and instinctively. All eight succeeded in getting away. *Morningtown* sighted their raft and tried several times to lay alongside. The two were almost in finger-tip range more than once, with *Morningtown*'s crew unable to get a proper grip on the raft. After *Morningtown* had had problems with her own steering gear she lost contact. But in any case *Trophy*'s survivors were apprehensive that *Morningtown*'s heaving up and down might crush them. It seems they had decided to stay with the raft.

With hindsight, it was possibly the wrong decision. At dawn, they sighted a yacht and fired their last flare. To their dismay, they saw three more flares soaring up with theirs into the sky. Shortly afterwards, the raft capsized and both buoyancy chambers were torn open. The crew stayed in the lower half but there was only one attachment point to which one man was able to clip his safety harness. The eight men were repeatedly tipped out of the raft and about an hour later, after yet another capsize, two of them, Peter Everson and John Puxley, were separated from the rest. The others could still see them, some distance away, and tried to paddle the remains of the raft towards them, but they drifted away out of sight and were drowned.

Three hours later, at about 6.30, the raft capsized again and broke into two unequal sections. One survivor, Simon Fleming, was left clinging to a fragment while the other five held on to the lanyards of the upper buoyance chamber, which had become completely detached from the lower. One of the five, Robin Bowyer, was growing visibly weaker. The others encouraged him to try and hang on. But, said Bartlett, 'before he slipped away, he was dead'.

Rescue 97 picked up Fleming and Bartlett, but the other three were unable to extricate themselves from the raft. Luckily, *Overijssel* arrived shortly and rescued them, and also recovered two dead bodies. *Trophy* herself was found later, with two feet of water inside her, and was towed in. It seems her crew might have done better to have stayed with her, no matter how bad the situation might have looked.

The eight man crew of the 34-foot Buchanan North Sea Design *Camargue* were luckier, in the end. They were some 25 miles north-west of the Scillies when they were 'knocked flat' by a mountainous sea. Three of the crew were washed overboard as *Camargue* lay on her side. They all had lifelines and were washed back on board as the boat came upright, but the life-raft was swept away. An hour later *Camargue* was flattened again by another monstrous sea, and one man was washed overboard for the second time, being saved only by his lifeline.

'It was no longer a race,' said Mike Hackman, the man who was washed overboard twice. 'It had become a battle for survival. It was gear failure that got us. We just could not cope with it. We were being hit by tons of water.'

Wessex taking off last survivor from yacht *Camargue*

With rudder broken and radio out of action, the owner and skipper Arthur Moss decided to abandon ship. 'I remember trying to hold my breath as we rolled over and went under,' he said. 'My clothes were torn. My watch just disappeared. It must have been wrenched off. I never thought I would see a steering wheel complete with man attached soar into the sea!'

A 'May Day' was broadcast by the emergency radio, and Wessex (Rescue 27) arrived three-quarters of an hour later. With no liferaft, every man was winched up separately. 'That was the very worst moment of all,' said one crew member, Tony Lloyd. 'The helicopter winchman beckoned me to jump. It was terrible to have to leap into the sea. We were only in the water about a minute each before the winchman reached us.'

Rescue 27 had all eight of *Camargue*'s crew on board and was heading back for Culdrose by 10.35. At about the same time, Sea King (Rescue 98) was picking up from the water an injured man who had been one of the crew of the American yacht *Ariadne*. His condition was so serious he was flown direct to Treliske Hospital.

'We were told there were two men in the sea from the yacht (*Ariadne*),' said Rescue 98's observer, Lt Ray Winchcombe. 'She was dismasted and we saw one man hundreds of yards away. We went to him and he was clearly dead, and had probably been in the water some time. We then saw the second man. We had to abandon the body. We could do nothing for him. We went to the second man and lifted him in. The body just floated away. We pumped a great deal of water out of the second man and did mouth-to-mouth, but he died before we could get him to Treliske hospital.'

Ariadne, a 35-foot Carter Design owned and skippered by Frank Ferris, an American living in the UK, was to suffer the most casualties – four of a crew of six – of any yacht in the race. At dawn on 14th, after several mishaps which had already made Ferris decide to retire from the race, *Ariadne* was knocked over and rolled through 360°. The lifeline of one crew member, the American Robert Robie, snapped and he was washed out of the cockpit. The others saw him some 50 yards away but could not turn to pick him up.

Petty Officer Aircrewman Roy Henshaw, of 706 NAS, prepares to lift Frank Ferris, owner of *Ariadne*. Ferris, who had already been in the water for five hours, died during the flight ashore.

Two of *Ariadne*'s crew, Rob Gilders and Matthew Hunt, were later picked up by a West German ship, the MV *Nanna*. The German captain handled his ship with great skill, but three men, Bill Lefevre, David Crisp and Frank Ferris himself, were lost whilst trying to transfer from the dinghy to the ship.

At 11.37 Sea King (Rescue 97) and Wessex (Rescue 20) were tasked to look for five people who had been sighted in a dinghy. Rescue 20 found them, the entire Swedish crew of the Ballad Design *Skidblander III*, double-lifted them at 11.55 and flew them to Culdrose. Twenty minutes later Sea King (Rescue 77) reported double-lifting twelve survivors the six-man French crew of the Harle Design *Gan*, and five men and one woman (the skipper's wife) of the 37-foot Holman and Pye *Hestrul II*.

By 12.30, when Rescue 77 and Rescue 20 had both landed their passengers, the number of survivors taken to Culdrose had risen to 36, with one man taken to Treliske. The survivors were met at the helicopter hard standing by an ambulance with a medical assistant and, if deemed necessary, a doctor. They were treated, mostly for shock, given hot baths and hot drinks, and beds, and telephone calls to next-of-kin. When they were fit enough, survivors were either given Service clothing and taken by bus to Plymouth or Redruth, or they were collected by relatives and friends. Some were accommodated at Culdrose overnight.

By midday on 14 August, seventeen yachts were known to be in some degree of serious distress, either sinking, dismasted or abandoned. But it had become clear very much earlier in the day that, as events were unfolding, a potential major disaster was probable. At 7.15 Culdrose was asked to provide as many helicopters as possible. RNAS Yeovilton was asked to support Culdrose. SAR Wing at RAF Finningley had no assets available and it was decided not to take Sea Kings from RAF Coltishall at that stage, because similar emergencies might occur elsewhere around the coast. RAF St Mawgan and Kinloss were asked to prepare aircraft with SAR fit and to be ready for a protracted operation. RAF Odiham was asked to keep a Wessex on stand-by.

Between five and eight helicopters remained on task at any one time. An 819 NAS Sea King '304' with two crews arrived from Prestwick just after midday and took off for its first sortie at 12.50. Yeovilton contributed two more Wessex, Rescue 30 and Rescue 25, and two Lynxes, '463' and '747', which were disembarked Ship's Flights from HMS *Birmingham* and *Cleopatra*.

Several surface ships took part. The RMAS tug *Rollicker* was diverted to the scene at 8.50 am on 14th. Another RMAS tug *Robust* sailed at 2.33 pm to patrol between the Lizard and the Scillies. The frigate HMS *Broadsword* sailed from Plymouth Sound at 2.30 and proceeded at 21 knots to assume duties of Scene of Search Commander at 5.30.

Meanwhile, searches and rescues went on during the afternoon of 14 August. At 1 pm Sea King (Rescue 97) found the liferaft from the 33-foot Frers Design yacht *Gringo*. She had been knocked down three times, each capsize doing more damage, and dismasted during the night. One of the crew,

Adrian Hammond, had a broken rib. They put up a flare and as the skipper, Lt Cdr Richard Milward, said 'as if by magic a Nimrod appeared overhead. We left *Gringo* at 7.30 am and were in the liferaft for six hours before a Nimrod saw us again at 2 pm. We lost sight of *Gringo* after only twenty minutes and we presume she is lost (she did later sink). We were well aware that we might be in the raft for a very long time, even days. When the Nimrod came back we put up a flare and a smoke flare. The helicopter was with us 30 minutes later ...'. All seven of *Gringo*'s crew were saved.

That afternoon the weather moderated slightly, and the visibility improved, although another gale was forecast. Helicopters continued to quarter the sea, running down the bearings of yachts reported in difficulties. At about 3.30 pm Wessex (Rescue 27) picked up the ten-man crew of an Irish Admiral's Cup entry, the Holland Design *Golden Apple of the Sun*.

The crew included some yachting celebrities: Ron Holland, the boat's designer, the world-famous racing yacht skipper Harold Cudmore, and triple Olympic yachting gold medal winner Rodney Pattison. They had rounded Fastnet Rock, carrying a spinnaker, topping 14 knots and surfing across the mountainous seas, going faster than *Golden Apple* had ever sailed before, 'Rounding the Rock was an unbelievable experience,' said the skipper Hugh Coveney. 'The whole sea was white. It was all white as far as you could see. At one time we had winds of 62 knots on our instruments but afterwards the wind died down to storm force and we put up a little more sail.'

'We seemed to be through the worst when there was a crack as a particularly gigantic sea hit us, and the rudder started making creaking noises. Finally around midday the rudder went. We tried various jury rigs, but they failed in the seas. In answer to our distress call a Spanish coaster circled us. We discussed staying on board or leaving. I had to make the agonizing decision to leave. I had ten men to think about. I had no rudder, no control, and the crucial factor was a forecast of another storm force ten on its way in.'

'When the helicopter came, we abandoned *Apple* and got into the liferaft. The helicopter crew were incredible. Pure professionals who pulled off a marvellous job.'

The searches went on all afternoon. 'Flying out to the disaster area,' said Ray Winchcombe, 'we passed over empty liferafts drifting in the seas. We also saw the wrecked and abandoned yachts drifting by.'

Just after 3 pm, Wessex (Rescue 30) radioed that he was returning with a hypothermia case from the yacht *Festinia Tertia*. At 4.30 pm, Sea King (Rescue 96) reported that he was returning to Culdrose with another eleven survivors – five from the 34-foot Offshore One Design *Allamanda* and six from the 28-foot Mauric Design *Billy Bones*. This accounted for both crews.

Almost at the same time, Sea King (Rescue 98) picked up Mr Flowers, from *Gunslinger*, and Midshipman Jones, from *Flashlight*. *Gunslinger*, a 33-foot Stephen Jones Design, had lost one man, Paul Baldwin, who was blown over the side when he and three others were on the foredeck changing a headsail. 'From our helm position in the cockpit,' said the skipper, 'we watched in horror, praying and crying I think. We 'willed' those three men on the foredeck to survive. I was crying with grief, crying with terror for those men. And the wind was so strong it whipped my tears straight off my face. I have never cried without tears before ...' The remaining four of *Gunslinger*'s crew were rescued by the Dutch trawler, side-numbered *SCH 6, Alida*.

Flashlight, a 35-foot Ohlson Design with a crew from the Royal Naval Engineering College, Manadon, Plymouth, had already lost Sub Lts Russell Brown and Charles Stevenson, swept overboard during the night. The remaining four of the original seven were picked up by Wessex (Rescue 25) at 4.45 pm that afternoon and taken to Culdrose. The yacht was later towed into Penzance.

Helicopter rescues were almost over for the day, but not quite. *Grimalkin* had capsized again and Nick Ward, who had been left for dead, regained consciousness to find himself in an upside down cabin. He managed to extricate himself and saw Winks being dragged along through the water in his harness.

Midshipman Peter Harrison, of 819 NAS, being lowered down into the wrecked cockpit of *Grimalkin*

Ward pulled Winks on board. Amazingly, he was still alive, although only just. Ward tried artificial respiration but Winks murmured a last message to his wife before he died. Ward, and Winks' body, were recovered at 7.25 pm by Wessex (Rescue 21).

The total number of people rescued by helicopter on 14 August was 75, including Winks, and the dead man from *Ariadne* taken to Treliske earlier in the day. Another body was recovered from the sea near the yacht *Helstul II* by Sea King (Rescue 97) on the afternoon of 15 August. Three other men were lost during the race: Robert Watts from *Festina Tertia*, G.J. Williabey from the Dutch yacht *Veronier II*, and Peter Dorey from *Cavale*, making a total of fifteen crew lost in the 1979 Fastnet.

One other yacht, the Royal Ocean Racing Club's own 34-foot Offshore One Design *Griffin*, sank when she was turned completely upside down by a giant wave. Her seven man crew were picked up by the French yacht *Lorelei*. Other Fastnet yachts abandoned were *Callirhoe III, Charioteer, Bonaventure, Lipstick, Alvena, Polar Bear, Tiderace*, and *Maligawa III* – 25 sunk or abandoned, although the abandoned yachts were all recovered later.

Surface vessels also rescued a further 65 survivors. Apart from those already mentioned, *Overijssel* rescued six from *Polar Bear* and six from *Callirhoe III*; HMS *Anglesey* rescued eight from *Bonaventure*; the French trawler *Massingy*, seven from *Charioteer*; the yacht *Dasher*, six from *Mulligatawny*; a Gulf Fleet oil rig support vessel, seven from *Tiderace*; the French trawler *Sanyann*, six from *Lipstick*; and the yacht *Moonstone*, five from *Alvena*.

The main helicopter task on 15 and 16 August was that of accounting for the three hundred competitors, and searching for those who were reported as being in trouble – among them *Kalisana*, manned by a crew from HMS *Sultan*, who were eventually sighted rounding the Fastnet Rock – and very surprised to discover that anybody had been concerned about them.

But there were other casualties of the storm. One of the difficulties for the searchers had been to establish exactly who was taking part in the Fastnet. A number of yachts had been following the race, among them the trimaran *Buck's Fizz*, which had sailed from Yarmouth, Isle of Wight, with a crew of four, to take part in an event organised by the Multihull Offshore Cruising and Racing Association.

At some time on the first night of storm, *Buck's Fizz* capsized. The bodies of Richard Pendred, who owned a half-share in her, and Peter Pickering were picked up by a passing ship, *American Corsair*, and taken to Barry in South Wales. But the bodies of John Dicks and Olivia Davidson were missing.

A report that *Buck's Fizz* had capsized was received at Culdrose early on 17 August. A Sea King of 706 NAS located her and sent the SAR diver down to examine the hull, but there were no survivors or bodies on board. *Buck's Fizz* brought the total lost at sea to 19 (also during the storm a small girl was washed off a beach and drowned, and two men were killed by falling masonry).

Visibility deteriorated again on the afternoon of 16 August and aircraft had to be recalled. The final SAR sortie was at 7.45 pm on 16th, when the skipper of HMS *Dolphin*'s 35-foot Ohlson yacht *Bonaventure*, Captain Graham Laslett, who had a broken arm, was lifted off HMS *Anglesey* by Sea King (Rescue 77).

SAR flying from Culdrose finished at 9 pm on 16 August, when the Wessex had flown 27 sorties, for 62 hours 35 minutes flying time, the Sea Kings 25

The Culdrose Trophy Decanter, presented by Michael Campbell and the crew of *Allamanda II* in grateful recognition of the heroic rescue operations executed by RNAS Culdrose during the Fastnet Rescue 1979

sorties (112 hours 10 minutes) and the Lynx 10 sorties (20 hours, 20 minutes): a total of 62 sorties and 195 hours five minutes flying time. Whirlwind 'A' Flight from RAF Chivenor had also flown two sorties for four hours 20 minutes, and Whirlwind 'B' Flight from RAF Brawdy seven sorties for 12 hours, 50 minutes. A Whirlwind from Brawdy recovered one body on 17 August. There was one Sea King sortie from RAF Coltishall, and Irish helicopters made two sorties in four hours 20 minutes. The total for all helicopters was 74 sorties, 216 hours, 35 minutes.

Fixed wing aircraft also made a major contribution. Nimrod Mark 1s of 201 and 120 Sqs from RAF Kinloss and of 42 Sq from St Mawgan flew 13 sorties, averaging nearly nine hours each, for a total flying time of 109 hours, 25 minutes. A French Atlantique flew one sortie of eight hours, and an Irish Beech King Air six sorties of 18 hours, 30 minutes, for a fixed wing total of 135 hours, 55 minutes. This made total flying hours for the 1979 Fastnet Race 352 hours, 30 minutes, to cover a search area estimated at 20,000 square miles.

The frigate HMS *Scylla* and the RFA tanker *Olna* joined the search force on 16 August, and the Irish fishery protection ship *Deirdre* also took part. Thirteen lifeboats, from Courtmacsherry Harbour, Ballycotton, St Mary's, Courtmachserry, St Ives, Sennen Cove, Dunmore East, Padstow, Falmouth, Lizard-Cadgwith, Angle, Clovelly and Penlee, were launched 26 times between 13 and 16 August, spending a total of 169 hours and 40 minutes at sea, searching for, escorting and towing abandoned and rudderless yachts. In accordance with the traditions of the RNLI, no salvage claims were made for any yacht.

A total of 85 yachts completed the race and, almost unnoticed, the overall winner was the American Ted Turner in his 61-foot yacht *Tenacious*.

The Royal Ocean Racing Club organised a memorial service for those who lost their lives in the 1979 Fastnet Race at St Martin's in the Fields, Trafalgar Square, on 8 November. The congregation sang 'O God our help in ages past' and listened to Psalm 107, 'They that go down to the sea in ships ... these men see the works of the Lord'. In his address Sir Maurice Laing, Admiral of the R.O.R.C., said that many of those at sea that night had wanted to speak to the Lord but were unaccustomed to doing so and maybe were a little uncertain how to address Him.

Barry O'Donnell was struck by the number of widows and young children present at the service. Many of those who died were relatively young. 'I'll not forget the Fastnet memorial service,' he said, 'but I'll never forget the Fastnet '79. Close the hatch.'

12 Worldwide SAR: From *Fife* in Dominica to the Penlee Lifeboat Disaster

10 Downing Street
16 August 1979

'I should like to congratulate you, your crews and all those at Culdrose and the Plymouth Co-ordination Centre and elsewhere who contributed to the Fastnet Race operation, on your remarkable achievement over the past three days. Without your untiring efforts many more lives might have been lost. The whole country salutes the skill and courage of those who took part in the rescue. Margaret Thatcher'.

This letter of congratulation from the Prime Minister was only one of many received after the 1979 Fastnet Race by the Commanding Officer of Culdrose, Captain W.A. Tofts CBE AFC. There were ietters of praise from members of the general public, many of whom had previously served in the Navy or the Wrens. Many of the letters enclosed cheques, from £5 to £100.

There were letters from the Helston Branch of the Royal British Legion, Helston Town Council, the Director of the RNLI, and from the National Westminster Bank, whose Sailing Club yacht *Gunslinger* was one of the race casualties. There was an invitation to dinner with the Anchorites in London, and a present of two cases of Cordon Rouge Champagne from Mumms. An Endeavour Fund was set up, named in memory of Peter Dorey of Guernsey, lost from the yacht *Cavale*, to be awarded to Culdrose personnel.

There were letters from authors who intended to write books about the Race, and from BBC-tv who intended to screen a programme on it, and from reporters such as Peter Smith, of *The News*, Portsmouth, thanking Culdrose and especially CPO Peter Ferris, the deputy PRO, for their help.

International media attention had been intense throughout the three days of the emergency. All the national newspapers carried front page stories. The race was featured in *Newsweek* magazine. One Coastguard officer picked up the telephone at Culdrose and found himself taking part in a live phone-in programme in the United States. Culdrose's PR staff, like everybody else involved, worked for long hours under extreme pressure and pulled off a notable publicity *coup* for the Navy and the Fleet Air Arm.

There were letters from competitors. Lt Cdr Richard Milward, of *Gringo*, one of the yachts which sank, wrote 'We count ourselves very fortunate that we lost no one and that our injuries were all relatively slight. Eight hours of sitting in a small life raft was little discomfort to endure'. Mr Knox, also of *Gringo*, complimented the helicopter crew who rescued them, especially CPO Fowles who 'underwent several dunkings in order to winch us to safety'.

Some wrote returning the money they had been lent to get home. Rodney Pattinson, who had himself served in the Navy for ten years, also returned with his cheque the shirt and trousers he had been lent by Culdrose sick-bay. 'The aircrew,' he said, 'were nothing but superb'. The crews of some yachts, such as *Contentious Eagle* of Barclays Bank Yacht Club, wrote that they had spent some time hove-to, though not in need of immediate help, but they had been greatly cheered when they saw a helicopter and knew that there families would now know they were safe. Fl Lt D.J. McLement, of RAF Chivenor, skipper of *Black Arrow* who actually won Class IV, wrote that 'Victory was largely shadowed by the tragic events'.

The *London Gazette* of 4 March 1980 carried citations for Queen's Commendations for Valuable Service in the Air awarded to eight officers and ratings of 706 and 771 NAS for their parts in the Fastnet rescues. Another twelve officers and ratings were awarded Flag Officer Naval Air Command Commendations.

The Culdrose SAR crews must have been contenders for the 1979 Boyd Trophy. Possibly, the fact that they had just won the 1978 Trophy counted against them. But in any case there was stiff opposition. On 13 February 1979, the frigates HMS *Berwick, Antelope, Aurora* and *Arrow* were on passage to Gibraltar to take part in Exercise SPRINGTRAIN when the 1,000 ton German cargo vessel MV *Paaschburg* radioed that she had lost seven men overboard and was in need of urgent assistance, some 120 miles off the northern coast of Spain.

This first message was amended to say that she had a *crew* of seven men and there was a danger of her cargo of potatoes shifting in the 40 foot waves and 35 knot winds. Her Master requested that at least three of his crew be taken off.

Arrow had one of the new twin Rolls-Royce 'Gem' engined Westland Lynx helicopters, '326', (Lt Cdr Nicholas de Hartog, observer Sub Lt Ross Thorburn, crewman AA1 Victor Flemwell) which was launched to begin a search. With its own TANS (Tactical Air Navigational System) and the help of a French Atlantique aircraft, '326' found *Paaschburg*, some 60 miles to the southward, just after midday. The ship was indeed rolling through more than 30 degrees and pitching 60 feet at a time, in a wind which had increased to storm force 10.

The problem was that the ship had three masts and a tall radio aerial and no obvious place for a helicopter to land on or winch from. De Hartog finally decided to use a tiny space only eight feet by four on the port bridge wing. Using the Hi-line method and with Thorburn's navigation bag to weight down the line in the high winds, de Hartog had to maintain a safe hover while the ship's masts whipped to within ten feet of his rotor blade tips. But '326'

Lynx from HMS *Arrow* lifting a crewman from the German MV *Paaschburg* in the Bay of Biscay, 13 February 1979.

successfully winched up three men by single lifts and took them to *Berwick* some 12 miles away. He then flew on to *Arrow* 55 miles to the northward.

Paaschburg's Master now decided that he wanted to abandon ship. After refuelling, de Hartog flew back to *Paaschburg*, winched up the remaining four men, took them to *Berwick*, which had now closed to within a half a mile, and returned to *Arrow*, after nearly five hours airborne. *Berwick* stood by *Paaschburg* to warn shipping until a Dutch tug arrived to tow her into harbour.

This was the first Lynx SAR incident in the Royal Navy. De Hartog reported that the aircraft handled very well, in spite of the adverse weather conditions and incipient signs of the *Merc Enterprise* salt ingestion problem. De Hartog was later awarded the Air Force Cross, Thorburn the Queen's Commendation for Valuable Service in the Air, and Flemwell the Queen's Commendation for Brave Conduct.

But de Hartog and his crew did not win the 1979 Boyd Trophy. That went to the Ship's Flight of the guided missile destroyer HMS *Fife* (Captain H.G. 'Sam' Fry).

In August 1979 *Fife* was on her way home to pay off after a commission in the West Indies when Hurricane 'David' struck the Caribbean island of Dominica, and the ship turned back to give assistance.

'Memories: Dawn, off the coast of Dominica,' recalled *Fife*'s Principal Warfare Officer, Lt John Lippiett, 'having returned to follow the wake of the hurricane to see which island it would hit. There, beyond the waves crashing onto the shore, was an awe-inspiring horizon of jagged stumps – trees had been snapped off leaving a three foot stump of the trunk. Banana trees, a major crop, totally ruined.'

'A helicopter survey of the island by the Commander (John Wright) showed the extent of the damage. I landed to survey the island's hospital – walls still standing, roof largely blown off with flooding throughout. Wards full of frightened, soaked patients.'

'The islanders were "shell-shocked" – dazed and unable to contribute. The ship was there to give them the resolve to sort out the mess, but this took some four days to achieve. We would slave away whilst they watched. Looting, of damaged property, was a big problem. The scene in the island's capital of Roseau was as though a nuclear weapon had detonated overhead. Massive trees uprooted and houses blown down. No power, no fresh water, no telephones, roads blocked by debris and fallen trees, hundreds of casualties. Many roofs were corrugated iron – when flying through the air the corrugated sheets became flying knives and many of the injuries were from this. Limbs hacked off – decapitations – many nasty sights.'

Fife could not enter harbour at once because of the heavy swell running, but she came alongside in Roseau at midday on the second day. Of her 480 ship's company, *Fife* landed some 400 at a time, who worked up to eighteen hours a day in tropical heat and under the threat of another hurricane, 'Frederick', to clear the debris which had blocked the island's reservoir, re-open the road to the airport in the north of the island, reroof buildings, and bury bodies. *Fife*'s ship's company rationed their own food and water so as to provide for the people of the island.

The working party under Lt Lippiett restored the hospital to working order within hours of the ship's arrival, using the ship's medical staff and supplies. 'I had up to a hundred and twenty working on this – clearing the debris, making it watertight, providing power for emergency operations, providing blankets and fresh linen.' At first, the sailors used shovels and their bare hands. Later, a fleet of lorries was commandeered and fork-lift trucks converted into makeshift bulldozers.

'Humphrey', *Fife*'s Wessex HAS3, was not suitable for disaster relief because of its high basic weight, limited disposable load and cramped cabin arrangements. The whole Ship's Flight worked a total of about 150 man hours to convert it fully to the Short Range Transport role by stripping out entirely the sonar, radar, doppler equipment and their supporting structures, leaving a flat floor, two seats and not much else in the cabin. The long range fuel tank and underslung load hook were fitted throughout the operation.

Flown alternately by Lt Cdr John Passmore, the ship's Flight Commander, and by Sub Lt Colin Rae, with observer Lt Gordon Hall and POACMN Gary Callow, 'Humphrey' flew continuously for ten hours a day – a total of 23 sorties from the first at 6.30 am on 30 August to the last at 4.45 pm on 5 September – carrying out damage surveys, transporting working parties and 45,100 lbs of supplies, making 41 casevacs including ten stretcher cases, and ferrying medical staff including Surg Lt Ian Geraghty, *Fife*'s doctor, who inevitably became known as the 'Flying Doctor'.

'Humphrey''s internal start system was unreliable, so it could not be shut down away from the ship and all flying had to be carried out from on board. Flying conditions on land were not easy for a Wessex at high all-up weight, as 'Humphrey' almost always was. A central mountain range with deep ravines, running north-south, combined with a prevailing easterly wind to produce severe turbulence on the lee side.

The main landing zones were at Government House, Windsor Park sports stadium and a small football pitch next to the Princess Margaret Hospital. But almost every village and hamlet, no matter how remote or small, had its cricket pitch ('one great advantage of Empire', as Lippiett said) where a Wessex could land. But 'Humphrey' flew down steep-sided valleys to reach places which otherwise would have been inaccessible, sometimes landing with only two wheels on the ground in areas obstructed by debris and litter.

After *Fife* had made one trip to Barbados to pick up supplies, outside help had begun to reach the island. *Fife* finally sailed for home, ten days late, and Her Majesty the Queen passed on to the ship a message from Dominica's acting president, Mr Jenner Armour: 'They arrived on our ravaged shores at our darkest hour and lit the first beacon of hope. Their relief efforts were ceaseless and untiring, their devotion to duty a shining example of true

Aircrew of Wessex 'Humphrey' of HMS *Fife*, Dominica, August 1979. *L-R:* Lt Gordon Hall, POACMN Gary Vallow, Lt Cdr John Passmore (Flt Cdr)

friendship in our hour of need'. Lt Cdr John Passmore and Lt John Lippiett were both appointed MBE in the 1980 New Year's Honours.

The new decade of the 1980s opened with an unusual number of ships in trouble. On 7 March 1980, a Sea King of 706 NAS (Lt Alan Bell, Lt David Durston, observer Lt Bullock, POACMN David Jackson) flew in winds between 65 and 75 mph to assist a seriously injured man on board the Liberian freighter *Penta*. With visibility between five and seven miles, and waves up to 60 feet in height, the Sea King was 'homed in' by an RAF Shackleton to rendezvous with the ship 165 miles south-west of Land's End.

Penta was rolling and pitching dramatically and when Surg Lt Peter Waugh was lowered down, the violent movement of the ship, a thin coating of oil on deck and loose items of deck cargo made it very difficult for him to keep his balance. The ship's bosun, who had severe injuries to his legs, forehead and chest, had been placed in a Neil Robertson stretcher ready for the lift. But when Waugh examined him he found his patient was already dead. He and the body were winched up into the Sea King and returned to Culdrose.

In a separate incident later the same day a second Sea King of 706 NAS (Lt Lea, Lt Johns, observer Lt Carr, POACMN Gaskell) lifted two men with multiple injuries to head and limbs from the Panamanian *Grace V* and flew them to Landivisiau in France.

But domestic incidents also continued that summer. On 17 May a herd of cows stampeded over a cliff near Portholland, where they were in imminent danger of being drowned by the rising tide. In what became a race against time, twelve cows were lifted to the cliff top by a Wessex V of 771 NAS.

On 10 October, SAR divers from *Daedalus* carried out what they themselves called 'a pretty scarey' rescue after a barge had turned turtle in the Solent. One man was thrown overboard and was picked up by a passing fishing vessel, but the other member of the crew, Mr Stephen Devereux, was trapped below in an air pocket, where he tapped on the upturned hull, hoping somebody would hear him.

A Wessex of 781 NAS (Lt Bill Sample, LACMN John Spencer) arrived in thirty minutes and after Spencer had jumped into the sea to try and locate the trapped man Sample returned to Lee to pick up a second diver, CPOACMN Dave Brown. Spencer dived on the barge again, smashed a hatch open and felt his way through the pitch darkness to find and reassure the trapped man. By the time Spencer returned for another breathing set, Brown was also in the water and both divers entered the barge to help Mr Devereux to the surface. Spencer found his way out blocked by flotsam and had an anxious time clearing it before he could wriggle through and get clear.

Brown and Spencer later visited RN Hospital, Haslar, where Mr Devereux thanked them, saying they 'were magnificent', which was certainly not an exaggeration. Brown received the Queen's Commendation for Brave Conduct and Spenser the Queen's Gallantry Medal.

There were several spectacular SAR episodes in the autumn and winter of 1981. On the night of 19 September, a Sea King of 706 NAS and the Sennen lifeboat combined to carry out what was described as 'an almost perfect rescue'.

In gale force winds and a very heavy swell, the cargo shifted in the 1,300 ton Icelandic ship *Tungufoss*, about four miles south of the Longships, and the ship began to list violently. It seemed that she was about to founder at any moment. A Sea King of 706 NAs (Lt Cdr Ray Winchcombe, captain and observer, Lt Nick Houghton, Lt Phil Sheldon, second pilot, and POACMN 'Jumper' Collins) responded to the 'May Day' call.

Having rescued three of her crew, the Sea King illuminated *Tungufoss* with its powerful searchlight whilst the Sennen lifeboat rescued a further seven men from liferafts and the ship. The lifeboat had to back off as the ship began to turn turtle, but the Sea King went in again and winched up the last man as the ship literally sank beneath him.

This rescue touched the hearts of the Icelandic people. The Sea King and lifeboat crews were presented with the Icelandic Silver Medal, Iceland's highest award for bravery. Instituted in October 1950, it was awarded to Icelanders and foreigners who, at the risk of their own lives, saved an Icelander in danger of death. It had only been awarded once before, in 1952, and the President of Iceland, Mrs Vigdis Finnbogadottir, came over in February 1982 to present the crews with their medals at the Hyde Park Hotel. The lifeboat coxswain also won the RNLI's Silver Medal.

The Culdrose SAR helicopter tended to monopolise the rescue reports and the headlines. But over the years helicopters from the Royal Naval Air Station at Portland also achieved some notable rescues. Six weeks after the *Tungufoss* incident, on 8 December 1981, the helicopter support ship RFA *Engadine* picked up a distress message from the 5,000 ton cargo ship MV *Melpol*, reported on fire in bad weather 35 miles off St Catherine's Point, Isle of Wight.

Engadine had embarked two Sea Kings of 737 NAS from Portland. The first '274' (Lt Martyn Reid, captain and observer, Lt John Connell, Sub Lt Richard Churchley, second pilot, and POACMN Kevin Matthews) was launched and found *Melpol* some fifty minutes later. She was heavily ablaze amidships. The fire had engulfed her entire superstructure. She was lying across wind, wallowing in the heavy seas, with a pall of thick acrid smoke streaming down to leeward. Two groups of survivors could be seen, one on the forecastle and a larger group at the after end.

The second Sea King, '271' (Lt David Larmour, captain and observer, Lt Andrew Healey, Lt Matthew Jennings, second pilot, and LACMN Paul Newman) arrived ten minutes later and the two aircraft captains had a radio conference. They decided to go ahead despite the conditions. '274' manoeuvred to begin winching from the ship's stern.

'274' first winched up six seamen and took them to the container ship MV *Europic* which was at that time nearer than *Engadine*, before returning to pick up the rest. The rescue, which lasted three and a half hours, was extremely risky. During the critical phase when the Sea King was hovering directly over the ship, only Churchley the second pilot was in a position to judge whether there was enough margin of clearance between the rotor blades and the wildly pitching after mast. Encouraged and advised by Connell, Churchley managed to maintain a steady and precise hover in very wet, gusty and inhospitable conditions.

Even so, the poor visibility and the violent rolling and pitching of the ship meant that the position where survivors could be picked up had to be changed several times. PO Matthews on the winch had to face high winds, smoke and rain, and had to be relieved after twelve survivors had been picked up. Nevertheless, '274' finally winched up a total of seventeen survivors and took them to *Europic*, before beginning a search for one crew member reported missing.

Meanwhile, '271' had begun a 'double lift' rescue of survivors from *Melpol*'s forecastle. When LACMN Newman reached the pitching and slewing deck, he received a discharge of static electricity so violent it knocked him off his feet. Although he was dazed and in a great deal of discomfort he successfully double-lifted two survivors. '271' then went to the after end, where it had the same difficulties as '274'. Healey had to manoeuvre the Sea King so as to provide a stable platform for rescue while the ship was still rolling and pitching, and there was a rigged jack-staff directly beneath him.

A typical Medevac: a Sea King of 706 NAS from Culdrose picking up a crewman of MV *Josefa* with a dislocated arm and possible fractures, March 1981

Jennings was the only one who could judge the safety margin between the rotor blades and the after mast while the Sea King was hovering immediately over the stern area and he took direct control during this phase, while another nine seamen were picked up. '271' then joined in the search for the missing man.

In all 28 were rescued; the missing man was never found and it was later considered he had died in the engine room. For the *Melpol* rescue, Larmour, Connell, Healey, Jennings, Reid and Churchley all received the Queen's Commendation for Valuable Service in the Air. Matthews and Newman both received the Queen's Commendation for Brave Conduct.

A few days later, on 13 December, Culdrose SAR crews were in action again for a double rescue in which POACMN Spencer won a Bar to his Queen's Gallantry Medal. A Sea King of 814 NAS and a Wessex of 771 NAS took off to assist the Ecuadorean freighter *Bonita* which was reported to be sinking in heavy seas whipped up by 60 knot winds in the channel. The

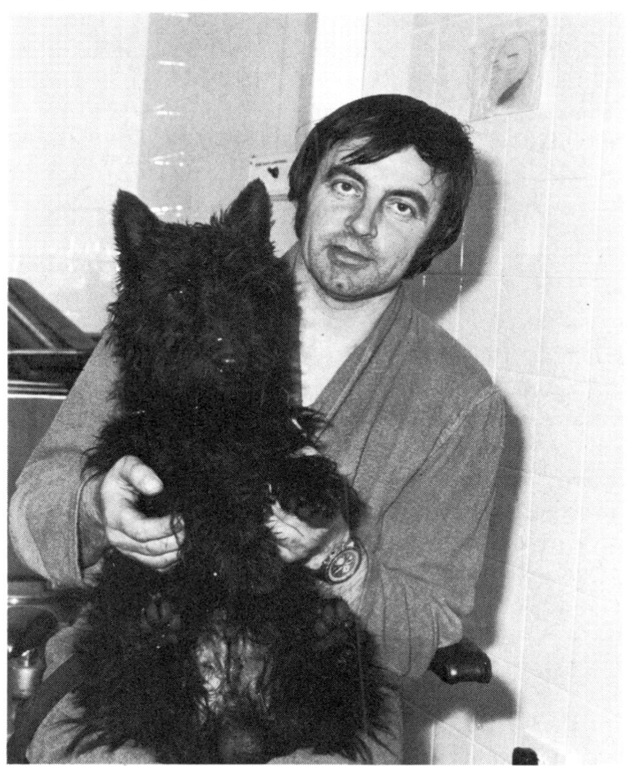

SAR incident, teatime 9 June 1981: Scramble Wessex of 771 NAS from Culdrose to assist fishing vessel *Julieanne* reported on fire, Lamorna Cove. On arrival found vessel burnt out and Mr Ian Southard and Scottie dog in liferaft. Both double-lifted and taken to Culdrose sickbay for check-up

Wessex was damaged in a snowstorm and had to land at Dartmouth. But the Sea King reached *Bonita* and provided illumination while the St Peter Port lifeboat from Guernsey took off 29 of the crew. Another helicopter and a French tug rescued six more.

Having been airborne for more than six hours, the Sea King then diverted to assist the coaster *Bobrix* which had developed a list and was sinking some 40 miles to the west. The six-man crew were taken off and the Sea King returned to Culdrose after a total flying time of nine hours.

Only a week later, on 19 December, a Sea King of 820 NAS (disembarked ashore to Culdrose) took part in a celebrated SAR incident which was to be widely known as 'the Penlee Lifeboat Disaster'. The Sea King captain's report, with its official format and technical descriptions of the techniques and equipment used, nevertheless gives an exciting mental picture of the difficulties and dangers which helicopter and lifeboat crews had to try and surmount in appalling weather and poor visibility:

UNION STAR – DUBLIN 19 December 1981
SORTIE 1

1820 Bleeper Recall

1835 '016' Ranged and spread. All crew mustered in (captain, Lt Cdr Russell Smith USN (on exchange posting), observer Lt Stephen Marlow, second pilot Sub Lt Kenneth Doherty, LACMN Martin Kennie)

1900 Formal brief
Met
Air Traffic Control
Situation – Position updated from 8 nm. south of Wolf Rock to 8 nm. east of Wolf Rock (1815 position)
Aircraft at stand-by only
1400 ton *Union Star* loss of engine and possible cargo shift
1901 position 126° Gwennap Head 4.5 nm.
8 people on board, 1 woman, 1 child 14 years, 1 child 15 years (step-daughters of *Union Star*'s captain)
Two way communication with salvage tug in Mounts Bay
Penlee Lifeboat at standby
Communications: UHF Ch.3 Culdrose Ops
HF 3885 Culdrose Ops
Pye VHF Ch.16 SAR – Falmouth Coastguard

1920 Scrambled: Took blankets
SAR Bag (Aircraft's own)
DTI (Dept of Trade and Industry) SAR Bag
ATLJs and Ear Defenders
NO Stretcher

1937 Airborne, transited to area. Wind velocity greater than 50 knts
Sea state 40′-45′ swell from SSW
Rain (heavy)

Low cloud, visibility poor
No moon

Good communications with *Union Star* and Falmouth Coastguard Channel 16

1945 Arrived at the Scene. Identified *Union Star* by requesting a flare
Made Recce of ship
Ship lying beam onto the swell
Wind 60-65 kts, gusts 75-80 kts
Discussed winching possibility
Requested intention from Falmouth coastguard
Was asked if happy to commence transfers

1950 Ran in for first transfer at Starboard Aft Quarter
Attempted 3 normal double lift transfers (with LACMN Kennie)
Wind velocity/sea state/ship movement/aircraft movement made this method impossible
2nd one winchman (Kennie) came within 15 feet of the deck
Aircraft was between 120 ft and 60 ft
Aircraft became very dangerously close to the mast
Backed off, reassessed and decided to attempt a high line transfer
Ship was briefed over radio
Attempted six high line transfers
100ft of high line proved unsuccessful with aircraft in such a high position
Tried lowering the winchman (Kennie) with the high line to extend it
At one attempt line got caught in mast rigging but was safely recovered (Winchman 15ft below aircraft)
On three occasions line dragged across deck within 3-4 ft of ships crewman
No attempt was made to chase after the line
At one stage ships crewman actually got the line but we were unable to keep it on the deck – with ship/aircraft movements
Backoff/reassessed and decided to attempt a high line using two high lines tied together
Ship now veered suddenly, bows into the sea
Union Star stated they would put people in the life raft to attempt pick up from there
We acknowledged this
At this point the RNLI Lifeboat was sighted running in and made a number of attempts to come alongside
At this stage the ship had put out and lost 1 anchor and put out a second and was then riding bow into the sea
Lifeboat made at least 5 attempts to come alongside – unsuccessfully
At the rear port quarter of the ship, the ships crew put out a rope ladder from the port bridge wing
Life boat also tried to transfer at the port midships position
Wind now indicating 65-70 kts, gust to 85+

We decided two high lines tied together was not a good idea as the second line was of very light gauge

2105 Then observed that ship was now within 200 yds of coast and informed all units that we had only 10 minutes left before grounding

Aside from a ship's crewman putting ladder over side, no persons came out of bridge except to occasionally open port door and wave at RNLI crew who had been gesturing to crew to come out since arriving on scene. There seemed no sense of urgency from Ship's crew

As ship was now into sea and in better position from transfer we ran in for a normal high line while lifeboat worked at midships

We also hoped this would entice some crew out of bridge

High line 250 lb breaking strain was snapped by wave taking weight

Then we decided to make immediate normal double lift transfer to port bridge wing (lifeboat still working amidships)

Two attempts made (Lt Marlow and LACMN Kennie taking turns on the wire and operating the winch gear)

Swing on winch and ship movement totally unacceptable

By now within 50 yds of beach. Too close for us due to gusting winds and confused violent sea

We were unable to see the cliffs

A white line of breakers (60 ft high) could be seen and then a dark silhouette of the coast above

There was no delineation between the cliffs and the distant horizon

Ship was now lay beam onto the swell again

We then cleared to keep clear of the cliffs

Lifeboat commenced more runs at the midships

Lifeboat picked up by a wave onto ships hatch covers and then slid off stern first

People were now seen to be running down the catwalks to where the lifeboat was coming alongside

Saw 4 people jump onto lifeboat and possibly an orange object fall between ship and lifeboat

2125 Ship started to go into the breakers

Lifeboat was bashed against the ship a number of times in the breakers and during entire rescue evolution

At this point we departed due to proximity of cliffs/breakers as lifeboat pulled away bows into sea

Lifeboat reported 4 persons recovered from the ship after it broke away but was seen to return to starboard. Presumed it would survey situation and possibly make another run.

Tug was still in attendance ½ nm of the coast

2130 Radio transmission from tug: 'saw all lights go off'

2135 We landed on. Communications heard to be lost with the lifeboat

Assumed antenna damage

SORTIE 2

Debriefed all concerned
Waited at standby
Sorted out SAR kit
Called in Sobs
2245 Scrambled
2310 Take off
Transited to Penzance
Commenced search ½nm-1nm from coast round to SW
Investigated two surface contacts ½nm and 1nm south of Tater Du
Also investigated two buoys, one 1½nm SE Penzance and the other was Runnel Stone buoy
Continued the search between 450 ft and 200 ft
Very bad visibility/turbulence, even worse than previously experienced
Was calling blind for the lifeboat
Then instructed to call blind for a flare
Instructed to open search out to 1nm-2nm
Accurate search flying impossible in the conditions
0010 Turbulence/visibility impossible, called to recover
0022 Land on

The wreck of the *Union Star*, 20 December 1981

The message from the salvage tug *Noorde Holland* at 2130, 'saw all lights go off' and the loss of communications between the lifeboat and the Sea King five minutes later, did not, as Russell Smith had supposed, merely mean damage to an antenna. The Penlee life boat *Solomon Browne* was lost with all hands – eight crew members and four rescued from the *Union Star*. The remaining four left on board the *Union Star* were also lost.

The tragedy understandably aroused much public interest. It seems that the *Solomon Browne* was either dashed on shore or against the side of the *Union Star* whilst trying to claw its way out through wind and sea to safety. The 56-year old coxswain, Trevelyan Richards, had been coxswain since 1970 and had served in the crew for twenty years before that. He had won the RNLI Bronze Medal for his service during the *Lovat* rescue of January 1975, when other members of his crew had also been honoured.

Evidence at the inquest on the bodies which were recovered suggested that the *Union Star*'s Master, Henry Moreton, was not entirely blameless. He had never broadcast a 'May Day' signal. There had been a two-hour discussion with the salvage tug over terms and conditions of rescue, while *Union Star* drifted ever nearer the rocks. And, as Russell Smith had noticed, there had been little effort on the part of *Union Star*'s crew to save themselves.

Afterwards, there were some recriminations in the press and even an accusation by a private maritime investigator that a Wessex should have been used in the rescue – because its rotor blades were shorter than a Sea King's! The general public subscribed £2.75 million to a fund for the families of the dead lifeboat crewmen, who all came from Mousehole and left five widows and 12 children, some of them grown up.

Russell Smith, by then back in the United States, provided written evidence to the inquest in which he paid his tribute to the lifeboat men, a tribute which could have been echoed by other helicopter crews down the years: 'Throughout the entire rescue the Penlee crew never appeared to hesitate. After each time they were washed, blown or bumped away from the *Union Star* the lifeboat immediately commenced another run in. Their spirit and dedication was amazing considering the horrific hurricane seas and the constant pounding they were taking.'

'The greatest act of courage that I have ever seen, and am likely ever to see, was the penultimate courage and dedication shown by the Penlee lifeboat when it manoeuvred back alongside the Union Star in over 60-foot breakers and rescued four people shortly after it had been bashed on top of Union Star's hatchcovers. They were truly the bravest eight men I have ever seen … '

13 South Georgia and the Falklands, 1982

'Ian's flying today has been quite remarkable, although he is too modest to admit it himself,' wrote Lt Chris Parry in his diary, of what had indeed been one of the most remarkable SAR sorties of all time. 'I hope that when they hand out the 'goodies' at the end he will receive something. All this excitement and we haven't seen an Argentine yet!'

It was April 1982. The Argentinians had invaded the Falkland Islands and South Georgia. The United Kingdom had dispatched a task force to the South Atlantic. Parry was Flight Observer on board the guided missile destroyer *Antrim* (Captain B.G. Young) which, with a small task group of the frigate *Plymouth* (Captain D. Pentreath), the RFA tanker *Tidespring* (Captain S. Redmond RFA) and the Antarctic research ship *Endurance* (Captain N.L. Barker), was approaching South Georgia to begin Operation PARAQUAT, the recovery of the island.

It was decided as a preliminary move to land initial reconnaissance parties on South Georgia: the Special Boat Squadron (SBS) at Hound Bay, towards the eastern end of the island, for surveillance of Grytvyken, and the Mountain troop of D. Squadron, Special Air Service (SAS), on Fortuna Glacier, in the north, some ten miles west of Leith Harbour.

Early on 21 April, *Plymouth* and *Endurance* headed east down the coast of South Georgia to carry out the insertion of the SBS, while *Antrim* and *Tidespring* were off the north coast, preparing to launch the SAS in helicopters.

The SAS were to be carried in *Antrim*'s Ship's Flight Wessex HAS3 of 737 NAS, and two Wessex HU5s, of 'C' Flight 845 NAS, from *Tidespring*. *Antrim*'s Wessex 3, known as 'Humphrey', was an anti-submarine aircraft, fitted with radar, sonar and a computerised Flight Control System (FCS) which enabled the pilot to programme the aircraft to fly to a particular position over the sea and to hover over it, while maintaining constant height, heading and position, regardless of darkness or low visibility.

The two Wessex 5s, being 'utility' aircraft primarily used for transporting personnel such as Commandos, had comparatively unsophisticated Automatic Stabilisation Equipment which would maintain the aircraft's altitude but not its position. In bad visibility, such as they were bound to meet up on the Glacier, the pilots could determine altitude by radio altimeter but would have to rely on visual reference points, or keep Humphrey constantly in sight, to know whether they were flying forwards, backwards or sideways. This difference in equipment between the Wessex 3 and the Wessex 5s was to prove crucial on the Fortuna Glacier.

By 8 am on 21 April, *Antrim* and *Tidespring* were some 30 miles off the South Georgia coast. The weather was discouraging, with a half-gale blowing from the north-east, visibility down to less than two miles, continuous cloud below 400 feet, and the barometer still falling ominously.

Lt Cdr Ian Stanley, *Antrim*'s Flight Commander, persuaded Captain Young that in view of the weather conditions, it was worth making a reconnaissance of the proposed landing site before committing all three helicopters.

Antrim's Wessex (Stanley, second pilot Sub Lt Stewart Cooper, Lt Chris Parry, POACMN David Fitzgerald) was launched at 9.30. Nobody had yet seen an Argentinian but as a precaution Fitzgerald cocked the General Purpose Machine Gun (GPMG) in the starboard window as Parry directed Stanley through gaps in the swirling cloud and snow.

'The geography of South Georgia is staggering,' wrote Parry. 'The huge mountains which rear up like jagged teeth are themselves dwarfed by the enormous glaciers which grow down to the edge of the sea. The whole spectacle had an eerie, other world atmosphere about it – the predominant colours were the green of the sea, the brilliant white of the snow and the ethereal blue of the old ice in the glaciers.'

Lt Cdr Ian Stanley (seated centre), Lt Chris Parry on his right, and members of HMS *Antrim*'s Ship's Flight, 1982

After a short reconnaissance, Stanley was satisfied that conditions were acceptable and there were no Argentinian ships or military forces in the immediate area. He returned to *Antrim* to report and it was decided that the SAS insertion could go ahead. After a delay for a snow storm, Humphrey embarked four SAS and took off, while the two Wessex 5s, piloted by Lt Mike Tidd and Fl Lt Andy Pulford RAF, came over from *Tidespring* and embarked their passengers.

All three Wessex then set off, in 'echelon port', with Stanley in the lead. But as they crossed the land they met a snow storm, and visibility dropped almost to nothing. As Stanley said, 'We hit a solid wall of snow'. The three helicopters turned back and landed on again.

Major Cedric Delves, of the SAS, now asked for a personal look at the ground. After yet another delay for a snow storm, Humphrey took off again with Delves and Captain John Hamilton, the SAS troop commander. When they came to the massive edge of the Glacier, there did not seem a way up amidst what Parry called 'the encircling gloom', but fortunately a break occurred in the weather and they were able to climb up to the proposed landing site.

'The weather was better this time,' said Stanley. 'I worked my way up the slope of the glacier – hover-taxying about thirty feet above the ice – and got onto the top without difficulty. We cruised around for a while to get the feel of the place and let Delves and Hamilton have a look ... John Hamilton didn't seem too enthused at the prospect.'

Hamilton's lack of enthusiasm was understandable. 'As we climbed the glacier the prospect which greeted us was quite alarming,' wrote Parry. 'The glacier was deeply pitted with crevasses about 300 feet deep every 100 yards or so and the SAS were proposing to cross some three miles of this terrain.'

Parry particularly remembered the exchange of comments between Delves and Hamilton: 'What do you think, John?' 'It's not good.' 'Well, you've got to get on John.' 'Okay, we'll do it.' ('You've got to get on, John' became a popular catchphrase in *Antrim*).

The three helicopters took off once again, with the SAS once more embarked, but after trying the same route up the Glacier they were baulked by thick low cloud and driving snow storms. Again they had to return, to refuel.

At 1.15 pm they had yet another try and this time reached the landing site. 'There was plenty of snow flying around,' said Stanley, 'but no real problem apart from severe buffeting. I had the advantage over the other two pilots because, apart from FCS, I also had three other pairs of eyes – Chris Parry's, Stewart Cooper's and Fitz Fitzgerald's. They were looking out of the windows and door while I concentrated on the instruments. They were giving me directions as I descended and it was slightly depressing to hear their steady chant in my headphones – 'You are going down, you are going down!'. Even with their help, I still nearly got into trouble. At the last moment, Fitz shouted that I was putting one of the wheels into a crevasse.'

'Today has not been pleasant,' Parry wrote, without understatement. 'We certainly would not have considered doing that sortie in anything short of operational or SAR conditions. Ian did really well to get the 'cab' through the gloup. Certainly I've never worked so hard on the radar in my life. It's not designed for the terrain following role which we were called upon to perform and the 30° blind arc through the nose doesn't help when you are running towards a mountain.'

With ice, cloud and snow all whipped into one blinding swirling white smother, there was no proper horizon and the other two Wessex pilots got down largely by using Humphrey as a reference. All sixteen SAS and their equipment were finally landed on the Glacier. 'Rather them than me, I thought,' said Parry. 'Even with three layers of clothing under my immersion suit I was absolutely chilled to the bone. None of my chinagraph pencils would work and the windows had icicles forming on them. Just as we lifted, the snow was falling all about us and Fitz noticed that we had in fact landed on an ice bridge between two crevasses which was rapidly disintegrating.'

That night the weather worsened. The gale increased to Force 11, with the barometer falling like a stone. In *Antrim* they had to leave Humphrey on deck all night with rotor blades spread, because nobody was allowed or dared to go out on deck. As people tried to eat their evening meals, plates on their knees, whilst they and the ship were tossed from side to side, many had thoughts for the SAS, 3,000 feet up on the Glacier.

Next morning, 22 April, Hamilton realised that his Troop's situation was untenable and signalled *Antrim* asking if evacuation was possible. The three helicopters loaded first aid kit and blankets for the expected exposure victims and took off again, in worse weather conditions than the day before. Thick low clouds driven by raging snow storms swept across the Glacier. There was violent air turbulence in the mountains, caused by winds gusting up to 70 knots, suddenly dropping away to 10 knots, and changing direction by as much as 120°.

While the two Wessex 5s circled below, Stanley tried to find a way up on to the Glacier. After three attempts, while the Wessex 5s landed on a spit of land at sea level, Stanley gave it up and all three aircraft returned to refuel.

The next attempt was successful. All three helicopters climbed upwards and found the SAS about half a mile further up the Glacier from their landing site. The weather closed in yet again as the SAS were embarking. Lt Mike Tidd, the pilot of Wessex 5 'Yankee Foxtrot', saw another snow storm approaching and asked Stanley's permission to lift off. He was heading north towards safety when the snow squall enveloped him and he suffered a 'white out' – a wellknown and much dreaded condition in which a helicopter pilot can see nothing and has no horizon to fly by.

Tidd knew there were mountains to left and right of him: 'All aviators try to steer clear of cumulo-granite,' he said, 'and I was keen not to wander too far off track. However, I knew that I had passed over a cluster of rocks shortly before. If I could find it, it would give me a reference. I was flying with one eye on the altimeter and the other looking ahead. I had about forty feet of height. As the snow swept over me and I lost sight of the ground, I shouted "Tug (LACMN D. Wilson) we've got a problem." He was in the back serving out a Thermos of coffee to the SAS guys. He jumped to the door, looking down for a sight of the ground. I was banking hard to the left, looking for the rocks. Then I saw the altimeter unwinding very fast and I knew we must be close to the surface. I put on full power and that softened the impact, but we hit at about thirty knots.'

'The left undercarriage was torn off and then she thumped down on her port side. I was hanging there in my straps, thinking "Mrs Tidd isn't going to like being a widow", while seven tons of helicopter went bashing across the glacier for about eighty yards with bits flying off in all directions and the cockpit rapidly filling with soft snow and broken Perspex. It was lucky we went down on the port side – the left hand side of the cockpit was smashed. If I had had a second pilot, he would have been killed.'

Stanley and Lt Ian Georgeson, who was flying the other Wessex 5, 'Yankee Alpha', took off together and hover-taxied the half mile to the crashed 'Yankee Foxtrot'. Amazingly, nobody was killed or even seriously injured; the worst were cuts and bruises. The survivors were divided between the two helicopters. Humphrey and Yankee Alpha lifted off, Georgeson dumping fuel to compensate for the extra weight and, with Stanley leading at thirty feet and Georgeson following in line astern at seventy feet, both headed hopefully down the Glacier.

All went well for some minutes until another snow squall arrived just as Stanley was about to cross an ice-ridge, short of the glacier's edge, and running parallel to it. Humphrey with FCS flew over it, and down the other side, vanishing from Georgeson's sight.

Humphrey's disappearance deprived Georgeson of his main point of reference. 'I had no way of knowing why the other helicopter had disappeared so suddenly,' he said. 'It was just engulfed somewhere in the whiteness. I continued to fly in the same direction, trying to maintain level flight. Then my altimeter indicated that I was about to hit rising ground ahead. There was a sort of fateful inevitability about it. I reduced speed and prepared for an involuntary landing. The wheels touched and the whole aircraft shuddered for several seconds.'

'I almost got away with it. What I didn't know was that the wind had slewed me round so that I was broadside on. It was gusting to forty knots or more. It pushed the aircraft broadside across the ice until a wheel caught in a small crevasse and over she went onto her starboard side.'

Yankee Alpha, like Yankee Foxtrot before her, crashed in a tangle of smashed rotor blades and shattered perspex. Stewart Cooper, who had been looking out astern from Humphrey and giving Stanley a running commentary, suddenly had to change from 'Fine, steady, steady all OK' to 'Oh God, he's gone in!'

Again, miraculously, there were no serious casualties. 'Tug' Wilson, after his second helicopter crash of the day, found himself 'lying on top of Jan Lomas

Helicopters and HMS *Plymouth* going to the assistance of HMS *Ardent*, hit and damaged, 21 May 1982

(LACMN Lomas, Georgeson's crewman) with an SAS soldier across my back. At first neither Jan nor I could move because our legs were trapped under ammunition boxes and weapons. The troops seemed stunned – they were making no move to evacuate the aircraft. Jan shouted to them to jettison the port cabin windows and get out. They quickly did so and then Jan said that he could see the pilot's legs jerking around in the cockpit. I disentangled myself and went around to the front.'

Georgeson was trapped in the harness of his personal liferaft. Some SAS saw that he was not with them and, although they believed the wreck was about to catch fire, ran back to help. Lomas reached in and freed Georgeson who was able to crawl out through the smashed cockpit window.

Stanley now had no option but to leave Yankee Alpha and carry on with his own survivors to *Antrim*.

Taking on a half load of fuel, medical supplies and blankets. Stanley took off to search for the Yankee Alpha survivors. 'I hover-taxied up the side of the glacier and managed to get up to the top,' he said. 'Conditions were very violent. It was impossible to attempt a landing – I couldn't even find the wreck – but I raised Ian Georgeson on the 243.0 distress frequency and he told me that everyone was safe.'

'We had two tries at it,' said Parry. 'The first attempt nearly ended in disaster as we flew out of a cloud to find a huge white mountain rearing up in front of us, which we avoided thanks to a spectacular "flare" by Ian. On the second, we totally lost tail rotor control and spiralled down towards the glacier. Luckily, we pulled out before striking the surface. After these fruitless efforts, we returned to the ship to wait for a break in the weather.'

'I went back to *Antrim*,' said Stanley, 'was debriefed, and tried to decide what to do next. The weather was showing no sign of improvement. All we could do was wait and hope.'

Stanley and his crew had done as well, or better, than anybody could possibly have expected, but he now had time to think over what had happened and have his doubts. 'I must admit to feeling depressed and bombed out,' he said. 'We had lost two helicopters. I was in charge and the whole thing had gone wrong. I asked myself if it was my fault, if there was anything I could have done to avoid the disaster. Was I right in authorising Mike Tidd to take off when he did? Should I have told him to stay on the ice until that particular squall had passed? Should I have followed a different route off the glacier? I suppose it was natural to have a period of doubt but, the more I thought about it, the more I realised that everyone had tried their hardest and it was simply the weather which had defeated us.'

'The main thing was to concentrate on the next phase – getting the survivors off. I certainly didn't relish the prospect. The "jungley" Wessex – the Mark 5 – has two engines, but the Mark 3 – like "Humphrey" – had only one. The Mark 3 did not have a good reputation for engine reliability and, with only one of them, I would have no margin of safety when we went back up there.'

'Earlier in my flying career I had twice experienced sudden and total engine failures with the Wessex 3. On one occasion I had to make an emergency landing in Dorset, and another time I ditched in the sea and two of the aircrew were injured. With all this in mind, I was somewhat nervous about having a third engine failure in the conditions in which we were now operating. "Humphrey" had been up there five times in the past twenty-four hours and now we were faced with trip number six. You tend to wonder how long your luck will hold out.'

Late in the afternoon it was decided there was time to have two more tries before darkness fell. Parry wrote a letter to his wife, enclosing his wedding ring, before the 'sombre briefing. We climbed back into our trusty 'cab', wondering if our luck would hold out just once more. We all, almost subconsciously, shook hands before we manned up the aircraft.'

This time, instead of going up the Glacier at low level, Stanley climbed through the clouds to 3,000 feet, accepting the risk of ice. This gave him 600 feet clearance over the Glacier, but nothing over the mountains. 'I stooged around for a few minutes,' he said, 'and then, in a sudden break, we were looking straight down at the crashed helicopter and the bright dayglo of the liferafts (which the survivors had erected to shelter in). I dived down through the gap and landed alongside. The wind was not only strong, it was shifting direction every few seconds. I had a quick talk with Ian Georgeson and assessed the situation. It wasn't good.'

Stanley now realised there was no chance of a second sortie that day. He decided he would take everybody in a single lift. Bergen rucksacks and other equipment had to be abandoned, although the SAS insisted on keeping their sidearms. 'We had to pile twelve weary, battered survivors one on top of each other in the back,' said Parry. 'I will always remember their shocked, ice-fringed faces huddled together.'

Stanley took off with arms and legs sticking out of Humphrey's door and windows. Parry watched his radar screen sitting on the chest of an SAS man who was lying across the seat with his head in the side blister. Three SAS were in the sonar well. Fitzgerald flew back hanging halfway out of the door.

The normal maximum all-up weight of a Wessex 3 was 13,600 pounds. Humphrey left the Fortuna Glacier for the last time weighing over 15,000 pounds. But Stanley's main problem was not weight but 'how many bodies we could jam into the space available. The engine produced all the drive I needed and the high wind helped to create lift. The only limitation is the amount of torque you can safely apply to the rotor-head gearbox. I didn't need to dramatically over-torque for the lift-off, but I knew I would have problems landing on.'

'When I got back to *Antrim*, the air would be slightly warmer, there would be less wind, and I would be contending with the movement of the ship. Consequently, when she came in sight, I didn't go through the usual manoeuvre – hovering alongside and gradually moving in sideways – I simply

Chief Petty Officer 'Alf' Tupper

Lt Cdr Hugh Clark, CO of 825 NAS in the Falklands

came down in a long descending slide over the port quarter. The landing was a bit heavier than usual, but nothing broke.'

None of the survivors was severely injured, although some of them had been involved in two crashes, but all were very cold. They were also very relieved. It was unlikely that any of them would have survived that night up on the Glacier.

The relief was shared generally in *Antrim* and at home in Whitehall. The loss of a whole SAS troop and two helicopter crews at such an early stage would have been a tremendous blow to morale and a very ominous portent for the future recovery of the main Falkland Islands.

That night the SAS presented Stanley's crew with a bottle of whisky and shared it with them. 'The SAS are a strange lot,' Parry commented. 'Before the events of the last two days, they barely spoke to us. Just now, all of them, including the troopers, invaded the wardroom and insisted we had a drink with them. There they were, toasting the Fleet Air Arm and our good luck, with bandages around their heads, dressings on their faces.'

As Parry had hoped, Ian Stanley was remembered when the 'goodies' were distributed, being awarded the DSO for his flying skill. Parry himself, Stewart Cooper and POACMN David Fitzgerald were all mentioned in dispatches. Not least, Chief Air Eng. Artificer (M) D.J. ('Fritz') Heritier, who led the maintenance team who kept Humphrey serviceable, was awarded the British Empire Medal.

But in his elation at his own crew's success, Parry did not forget the two *Tidespring* pilots. 'I feel sorry for Mike Tidd and Ian Georgeson,' he wrote in his diary that night. 'They are very depressed about the loss of their 'cabs' and are currently filling out their accident reports. However, I think that it took a lot of guts to go up to the glacier today, having seen how bad it was yesterday. I suspect that all that will be remembered is that they crashed their helicopters, not that they went on a very difficult SAR, with the odds against them.'

Early on 23 April, Humphrey was in action again, on an SAR sortie to look for an SAS Boat Troop Gemini, one of five reconnaissance parties which *Antrim* had lowered in Stromness Bay during the night. The outboard motors on three of the Geminis had refused to start and they began to drift to the east. Two managed to get ashore but the third was carried some miles out to sea. Its crew were reluctant to use their radio for fear of alerting the Argentinians and compromising the whole operation. But eventually, when their situation was getting desperate, they did transmit and their transmission was picked up and passed to *Antrim*.

Stanley took off at 8.10 that morning with only an approximate briefing of where the Gemini might be. Parry plotted its likeliest position from calculations of wind strength and direction, and Stanley began a box search. They could not use radar because of the nearness of the Argentinian base at Leith Harbour, so they would have to rely on visual sighting.

After an hour and a half, when fuel was running low and they were on the last leg of the search before having to return to *Antrim*, Parry heard the faintest tone of an SARBE homing beacon. Visibility was very poor indeed but Fitzgerald suddenly saw the Gemini about one and a half miles away.

The SAS had heard and seen the helicopter flying around, obviously searching, about a mile away from them, but they were not sure whether it was Argentinian. When they recognised the shape of a Wessex they 'knew it was one of ours. We switched on the beacon and set off an orange smoke flare. The pilot came hurtling over and winched us up. The last man out slashed the rubber and the boat went down like a rock. We were very glad to get back to *Antrim*. We were more tired than cold, even after seven hours in the Gemini. The Navy had loaned us some divers' dry suits before we launched from *Antrim* and these kept us dry and reasonably warm. Without those suits, and plenty of underwear and gloves, we might well have been in a bad way.'

Humphrey, piloted by Stewart Cooper, carried out the third rescue in four days on 26 April, the day Operation PARAQUAT was accomplished with the surrenders of the last Argentinian garrisons on South Georgia. It had been decided to transfer a party of SBS, who had been embarked in the nuclear submarine *Conqueror*, to the frigate *Plymouth*.

Conqueror surfaced that morning in a rough sea, with winds gusting to forty knots. When the SBS and their gear assembled on the submarine's casing, a larger wave washed a quantity of SBS stores and arms over the side. One of the SBS and a member of *Conqueror*'s casing party were knocked off their feet, their lifelines snapped and they were both swept into the bitterly cold sea.

Fitzgerald saw the accident from the helicopter's open door above: 'I alerted the pilot and conned him back over the two survivors. I could see that the marine was swimming strongly, but the sailor was not moving or attempting to swim. I got a strop and lowered it down to them. It actually hit the sailor but he made no attempt to grab it. By now I was very concerned, so I guided us over to the marine who inserted himself into the loop. I then conned Lieutenant Cooper back to the sailor, dragging the marine across the surface of the water. I gestured for him to lasso the other guy and, once he caught on to what I was trying to tell him, I managed to winch them both up to the door in a single lift.

Surg. Cdr Rick Jolly goes down from a Wessex with a stretcher to HMS *Plymouth*

I had a hell of a job getting them both inside the aircraft because the sonar was in the way. Eventually I got them into the back of the fuselage and made them beat their arms around their bodies to combat the intense cold. The submariner didn't look too good.' (However, both men recovered in *Antrim*).

Meanwhile, the political and military events leading to the British counter-invasion of the Falklands rolled onwards: the establishment of a total exclusion zone on 30 April, the first SAS and SBS raids, the first Vulcan raid on Port Stanley, the first Sea Harrier raids and ship bombardments, all on 1 May, the sinking of the *General Belgrano* on 2nd, and the Exocet hit which crippled *Sheffield* on 4 May.

At sea, two Sea Kings of 826 NAS from *Hermes* ditched, on 12th and 17 May, both four-man crews being picked up by SAR helicopter. Two days later, on 19 May, a Sea King of 846 NAS, who were then embarked in *Hermes*, struck a large bird and crashed in the sea while transferring troopers of D Squadron SAS from *Hermes* to the assault ship *Intrepid*. Of the thirty men on board, both pilots, the aircrewman and five passengers were rescued by *Brilliant*'s seaboat and *Intrepid*'s Landing craft, but twenty-two others were lost, including a member of the Royal Signals and Fl Lt G.W. Hawkins, the RAF's only casualty of the Falklands conflict.

The landings by 3 Commando Brigade at San Carlos Bay began at dawn on 21 May. Helicopters had been allocated for casualty evacuation: a Sea King to take wounded from the ships out to *Canberra*, and a Wessex 5 of 845 NAS, with a medical team on board, for duties inshore and overland.

The Wessex (Lt Mike Crabtree, Lt Jonathan ('Hector') Heathcote, crewman Cpl Kevin Gleeson RM, and Surg Cdr Rick Jolly, 3 Commando Brigade's Medical Officer) was soon making the first casevac of the campaign, picking up a paratrooper of 2 Para with a badly twisted back from Blue Beach near San Carlos and taking him to *Canberra*.

The Argentinian Air Force reacted to the landings during the forenoon and the ships in San Carlos soon came under air attack. Early in the afternoon the Wessex was scrambled from *Canberra* to go to the assistance of the frigate *Argonaut* (Captain C.H. Layman) which had been strafed and rocketed by an Argentinian naval Macchi MB339 armed trainer from Port Stanley, with some damage to her upper deck and two men wounded.

Jolly had put on the strop and was ready to be winched down to *Argonaut*'s empty flight deck when he was puzzled, and somewhat put out, by the behaviour of the Flight Deck Officer, who stubbornly refused to beckon him down. Instead, the FDO stood with his bats firmly crossed against his chest in a gesture of dismissal.

At last, after some delay, Gleeson tapped Jolly on the shoulder and swung him up and out of the aircraft to begin the descent to the deck. But as Jolly did so the Wessex suddenly dipped its nose and flew out across the water at some speed, with the doctor still hanging on the end of the wire.

When he regained the helicopter cabin and plugged in his helmet lead, Jolly realised that the reason for the Wessex's violent evasion and for *Argonaut*'s cool welcome was that *Argonaut* was again under air attack. She was bombed by six Skyhawks, suffering several near-misses and two direct hits by 1,000 lb bombs, which failed to explode but still did very severe damage.

Crabtree flew the Wessex ashore and took shelter in a gully on Fanning Head overlooking Falkland Sound, from where he and his crew watched four Mirages attacking *Antrim* out in the Sound. As they watched, the fourth Mirage suddenly turned towards them on what was clearly an attacking run. While Gleeson fired his GPMG at the aircraft, Jolly decided that discretion was the better part of valour and jumped out of the Wessex into a ditch. When Jolly somewhat shamefacedly climbed back into the Wessex and plugged in his helmet again, he heard Crabtree saying 'Oh, you back with us, Doc?' 'He and his crew had to remain strapped in throughout the incident,' said Jolly. 'I felt very ashamed and humbled at my terror in the face of the enemy'.

They watched the dramatic and spectacular events unfolding in the Sound, as the frigates tried to beat off the air attacks, until they saw 'this huge plume of smoke down at the southern end off the Sound and realised a ship had been hit, and when we got the call-sign (*Ardent*) we instinctively said to each other "Let's go help".'

Crabtree and Jolly were debating whether it was safe to get into the air again when their minds were made up by the sight of a Wasp flying past them, 'nose down for maximum speed', obviously taking a casualty from *Argonaut* to *Canberra*. If he could do it, so could they. 'We flew down to *Fearless* to refuel, and I borrowed a couple of stretchers. We then went back out to *Ardent*, slid in alongside her and saw this breath-taking sight, of a ship on fire.'

Ardent (Cdr A.W.J. West) had been attacked and hit by at least five 500 lb bombs which destroyed her hangar and her Lynx helicopter, caused extensive damage aft, and killed twenty-two men and wounded thirty more.

Now, as the Wessex arrived alongside her, *Ardent* was an awe-inspiring sight, lying still in the water, 'listing and drifting,' as Jolly said. 'Her lovely classic lines had been obscenely defaced by some demented giant who had smashed her hangar in and opened up the flight deck edge with a huge tin opener. Deep inside the enormous blackened hole with its ragged edges, the fires of Hell were burning. The flames had a bright orange intensity that was painful to look at directly.'

'I reached for my camera again, to photograph the blazing wound, and found that there were no exposures left. While I was looking for another film, Mike Crabtree and his crew noticed that *Ardent*'s survivors were grouped on the upper deck forward of the bridge. Some of them were already in their Day-Glo emergency survival suits, but almost all of them were pointing at the sea off the port quarter.'

'I was still feeling in my pocket for another film when I realised we were above a survivor in the water. Corporal Gleeson was lowering a strop down to him, but there seemed to be a problem. I went across the cabin deck on my knees, and looked down, and saw the man was drowning. The down wash from the rotor blades was blowing water into his face.'

'I put my camera in my pocket. I was still smarting from my disgrace at Fanning Head. Because I had some forty SAR sorties under my belt from my Culdrose experience I was familiar with winch-hooks and belts and things, so I volunteered to go down. Gleeson gave me a very strange look but he winched the strop back up. I put it round me and before I knew it I was descending towards the sea. I had no immersion suit on, nor any trailing wire to earth the static electricity charge from the helicopter as crewmen usually do, so I got a violent shock when I hit the water. The sea was numbingly cold, which made me gasp for breath as Mike, with marvellous precision, towed me across to the survivor. That desperate look on his face, his frantic thrashings, and his punctured lifejacket, said it all.'

The drowning man was Able Seaman (Radar) John Dillon, one of *Ardent*'s after damage control party, stationed in the junior rates' dining hall. He had been knocked unconscious when the ship was bombed. When he came to, he found himself pinned down by wreckage, a large fire was raging nearby, and the dining hall was flooding and filling with smoke. He could hear cries and screams from wounded and dying men all around him. Although he had a bad shrapnel wound in his back and one ear was burned, he made his way towards the ship's side, where he found Chief Marine Eng. Artificer Ken Enticknapp, who was in charge of the damage control party.

Medevac scene, Ajax Bay, Falklands 1982. Air Raid RED in force at the time, pilot Mike Crabtree told the medics that the air battle was 10 miles distant and would they kindly load him quickly, please

Enticknapp was also wounded, with one of his fingers almost severed, and a deep cut on his scalp. When Entiknapp fell into a hole in the deck, Dillon helped him out and both men went over the side into the sea. Still supporting Enticknapp, Dillon began to swim away from the ship. 'But I was so tired and my arm was killing me,' he said. 'I couldn't hold on to the Chief any longer – I was slipping under the water and dragging him down as well. I thought 'I'll let him go because at least he's got a lifejacket so he'll be all right for a while.' So I let him go and he just started drifting away but he was almost unconscious by then. I started swimming by myself but I was really tired now.'

'Then I looked up and saw this helicopter and saw it was lowering this strop. I tried to reach the strop but couldn't. They lowered it down a little bit more, and I was just about to reach it, and they flew off. I thought "Oh no, this is it. After all I've been through, I'm just finally going to die', and I just started going under. I began to sink – all I could see above was water. I didn't feel any pain or anything, just kind of relaxed. I wasn't even frightened as I quietly waited for myself to go right to the bottom. It was all over.'

From above, Jolly had seen Dillon resigned to drowning. 'He had just swum away from the other man, to die. Our outstretched hands touched, grasped, and suddenly I had him in a fierce bear hug. There was no other way to secure him, and up we went.'

'The next minute,' said Dillon, 'this hand grabbed me from behind and it just lifted me out of the water. It was magic! This bloke had come down the hawser; he wasn't supposed to, but he did. He just picked me up and grabbed me. I thought, "What a relief". He just lifted me out of the water. He was a really good bloke, he was. I owe him my life. He was surgeon Commander Rick Jolly. It was a very brave thing to do. I couldn't believe it, I was safe.'

But Dillon was not safe all at once. When Jolly reached the level of the helicopter cabin he still hugged Dillon close to him. 'I could not make any move to help. I knew if I tried to make the least extra movement I would drop him and that would be that. I had to rely on the crewman. I knew enough about the sport by then to know what a *magnificent* job Gleeson did, making the most delicate adjustments, inches at a time, up or down on the winch motor control with one hand, whilst grabbing us both with the other hand and dragging us into the helicopter cabin with a tremendous tug.'

'Exhausted, I collapsed on top of the survivor. Then I remembered there was someone else down there. Gleeson looked at me anxiously as I put the winch strop on again. Then he grinned and gave me an encouraging pat on the shoulder as I went down again. A twist had developed in the wire and I spiralled slowly down, a mad Cinerama projection unfolding before me; the burning outline of *Ardent*, her crew watching me, *Yarmouth* putting her bows alongside *Ardent* for survivors to step across, *Broadsword* close to us for air protection, Grantham Sound, the Falkland shore, *Ardent* again.'

'I watched, stunned and chilled, until just above the surface when a new sight appeared on the merry-go-round. Lying there quietly in the swell, arms outstretched and blood streaming downwind from a large cut in his forehead, the second survivor watched me with uncomprehending eyes. Bang! The static voltage discharged again and I was in the water alongside him. I was too weak to lift him bodily so I put the hook on the strop in a small nylon becket on the front of his lifejacket. It was not supposed to take any weight but the Navy always has belt *and* braces in its designs and the stitching held.'

Enticknapp had watched Dillon being lifted up to safety and shouted to try and attract attention to himself, without much hope of succeeding. 'But the guy did come back down again,' he said, 'and just hooked on the blue tag that came out of the front of my lifejacket. His rank badge was visible on the front of his smock. I thought "Oh no, it's a Surgeon Commander". Every Surgeon Commander I had known was old and I thought "I've had it; he won't have the strength to get me into the helicopter". But I underestimated this particular doctor. He just hooked me onto the tab, wrapped his legs around me and hauled me up into the helicopter. I've since done a survival course and the instructor said that no way should you hook onto the lifejacket, it wasn't designed for that.'

Jolly put his hand in his anorak pocket and found his camera. 'It was ruined. We delivered our customers to *Canberra*, then Mike Crabtree said "Well *done* Doc! Bloody marvellous!". After Fanning Head I felt a lot better. We were all square.'

'The thing about the *Ardent* affair was that it gave me tremendous satisfaction. When I went down the second time, I knew I was going to have to risk my life for this guy and I was quite happy about it. I was at peace with myself that I was willing to die for him if necessary. It is very strange to look into one's soul and like what you see. My love and concern for him meant that I just had to get him up somehow. How do you explain that?'

John Dillon was later awarded the George Medal, Ken Enticknapp the Queen's Gallantry Medal. For Jolly, the war was only just beginning.

14 The Falklands: *Coventry*, *Atlantic Conveyor* and *Sir Galahad*

It seems that Lt Cdr Glen Robinson-Moltke, the First Lieutenant of the Type 42 destroyer *Coventry*, must have had some premonition of what was to happen to the ship. 'I have certainly not been away as long as has been the case in the past,' he wrote to his wife Christine, on 21 May, 'but I have not left three of you before and I have never thought before that I would never see you again.'

Four days later, on 25 May, the National Day of Argentina, *Coventry* (Captain David Hart Dyke, LVO) was one half of a 42/22 'Combo' with the Type 22 frigate *Broadsword* (Captain W.R. Canning). The two ships were on patrol off Pebble Island, near the northern entrance to Falkland Sound, acting as a 'Missile Trap' to direct the Sea Harrier CAPs who intercepted incoming Argentinian aircraft.

The Trap was highly successful and had been instrumental in the destruction of five Argentinian aircraft in the previous twenty-four hours. There had been two air raids already that day when, just before 6 pm in the evening, *Broadsword* was attacked and hit by one of four 1000 lb bombs which ricocheted off the sea, bounced up through her ship's side and flight deck, wrecked a Lynx helicopter (belonging to *Brilliant*) in its path and then pitched back into the sea, without exploding.

In a second attack a few minutes later, *Coventry* was less fortunate. She was hit by three out of four 1000 lb bombs which were released at very low level and perhaps should not have had time to arm themselves. But at least two and very possibly all three exploded deep in *Coventry*'s machinery spaces.

At once, the ship began to list to port, heeling over so suddenly there was no real possibility of saving her. Lt Cdr Timothy Fletcher, the ship's Supply Officer, went onto the upper deck and 'aft, stepping over a neat bomb crater in the upper deck to direct some fire-fighting effort. The ship began taking on an appreciable list indicating the fire-fighting was likely to be academic, so abandoned fire-fighting and started 'uphill' across the midships cross-passage to where preparations were being made to abandon ship.'

'There was a rapid and orderly movement of men over the starboard side into the liferafts. After putting on my lifejacket and survival suit I too jumped over just before the list was beginning to get too prohibitive. (I have never been addicted to swimming from the ship's side for recreation – a flippant remark in an earlier letter to my wife that I considered swimming from the ship's side to be an occupation to be reserved for emergencies flashed through my mind en route to the water).'

'Brisk swim to the 25 man raft which I boarded to find another 35 inside with one man in some distress from shock and burns. I gathered four other liferafts to my own to make a more visible nest of them. This caused no great problem except for an unplanned altercation with the starboard propellor (stopped) which was well clear of the water at this stage. Rapid search of brain to recall Sea Survival film – issued sea sick pills for starters and then looked at manual! We all eventually got clear and drifted down to leeward, until the helicopters appeared and their down wash split up the group of rafts sending mine the furthest to leeward.'

Radio Supervisor Sam Macfarlane, whose action station was below in the Main Communications Office, managed to get through the hatch on to the port bridge wing, to what he recalled as 'a scene of devastation and a list so bad it was difficult to stop yourself going over the side as you tried to get aft. A voice said 'over to the starboard side and make your way down to the starboard waist'. It was easier than I thought; bent, ripped and twisted metal was piled upon the boat deck and I literally walked down it. I think shock had set in by now as we all followed like sheep and stood (or rather laid) back against the bulkhead. An officer said to get down the liferafts and prepare to abandon ship. With such a list on, and with the liferafts being very heavy and in cradles it proved near damned impossible. One fell short and nearly fell on some of us, bending the guardrail like a piece of plasticine.'

' "ABANDON SHIP" – My God, it's really happening. Get your "once only" suit on, that water is bloody cold, no time the ship's sinking, you'll die of the cold if you don't. Jesus how the hell do you get this on when the list is so bad you can't even stand to attempt it. Try again, fall over, try again, fall over again. Another lurch, further over. Sod it! Chuck it in the water and try to pick it up when you get in there yourself (stupid bugger!). Right, suit in water, lifejacket on, climb over the guardrail, stand by to jump. Hang on, remember your training, slightly fill life-jacket with air, few puffs not enough, just a few more, echoes of "if you over inflate you'll break your neck when you hit the water", let some out, is it enough? Well, it's now or never, hang on to guardrail, crouch down, push like hell and away, one giant leap for mankind and down you go, and down, and down.'

'All you can see are bubbles going up, you're still sinking like a rotten stone and then you start to panic. Suddenly up you go like a rocket, you break the surface and choke like the clappers on the gallon or two of south Atlantic cocktail you decided to scupper.'

'Looking for and locating a liferaft is easy, but everyone else seems to go for the one you have decided on. After being spoilt for choice I saw a friendly face saying "give us your hand mate and climb in, standing room only but the beer's good". So I got in. (The bar must have been shut, 'cos nobody was

Sea King 4 'VT' of 846 NAS after crashing with SAS on board from *Hermes* to *Intrepid*, 19 May 1982

drinking!). When we were all settled down (all twenty odd of us) we started bailing out, and then came the first laugh. We had started to use shoes to do it and somebody passed a steaming boot to (Petty Officer) Paddy Burke. 'That's no good it's full of water' he said, promptly emptying it inside the liferaft!'

Captain Hart Dyke made his way from the Operations Room up broken and twisted ladders to the upper deck and finally to the bridge. 'I moved from the port wing of the bridge as the ship began to roll over,' he said, 'and climbed the steeply sloping deck to the starboard side and saw the ship's company abandoning ship. It was quite remarkably orderly and calm, looking just like a peacetime exercise. I am still trying to discover who gave the order to abandon ship. Perhaps no one did. People just very sensibly got on and did it. It was the only thing to do.'

'All the starboard side liferafts were in the water and people were helping each other to put on their liferafts and 'once only' suits. Someone helped me with mine because it was then I realised I had been burnt. Some flesh was hanging off my right hand, but it did not worry me at all, nor did it hurt very much. There were more important things to worry about – like surviving! When I had watched everyone jump into the sea and get in to their liferafts I walked down the ship's side, jumped the last two feet into the water and swam to a liferaft. My war was over.'

Even before *Coventry* had turned over, Sea Kings of 846 NAS and 826

NAS, Wessex 5s of 845 NAS and *Broadsword*'s boats were all on the scene picking up survivors. One Sea King of 846 NAS, flown by the squadron CO, Lt Cdr Simon Thornewill, closed in to the ship and its aircrewman CPO 'Alf' Tupper was winched down into the water. He unhooked himself and swam from raft to raft assisting the injured. He was credited with saving some fifty lives (and was later awarded the DSM, Thornewill winning the DSC).

'The liferaft I was in,' said Hart Dyke, 'was sucked against the overhanging port side of the ship and was punctured by the sharp nose of a Sea Dart missile which was still in the launcher. About 35 men, some badly burnt, ended up back in the water when the liferaft sank underneath them. The injured who were unable to swim were held up above the sea by their courageous colleagues until helicopters arrived and were able to lift them to safety. One helicopter actually landed on the ship's side to pick up people who had had to scramble back on board. By this time the ship was burning red hot inside. These men were all rescued.'

Hart Dyke himself was one of those winched up after the liferaft sank. But the neck seal of his 'once only' suit leaked and admitted a large quantity of water which drained down to his feet, so that when he was hoisted up he looked and felt 'like the old-fashioned deep sea diver with huge bulbous and heavy feet. When I arrived on board the Sea King I could hardly move for the weight and size of my feet and floundered on the helo deck like an exhausted whale! The crewman quickly spotted the problem and took a knife to my swollen feet, slashing a hole so as to release the gallons of sea water. The helo deck was awash with water from the outflow! But at least I was then able to stand up and walk forward to a seat in the helo.'

Within fifteen minutes of being bombed *Coventry* was lying on her beam ends, and then quickly rolled right over. ' "She's going," Macfarlane heard somebody say, watching out of an airhole and we looked. Coventry was well on her side poor old girl and going further by the minute. Suddenly we heard aircraft, maybe they've come to finish us off. "They're ours, helicopters, bloody hundreds of 'em", shouted someone, and *Broadsword*'s seaboat and Gemini ... Rescue ... what a lovely word.'

'The "armada" of helicopters was a cheering sight," said Fletcher, 'as they started to carry out the recovery in their usual professional way. An MEM emerging from the inside of the raft to be put in the strop was clearly impressed by the scene and said to me "All those f*****g helicopters; looks like f*****g Air Days". Eventually the liferaft was cleared with a Commando squadron aircrewman and me going up in a double lift (after a final drag through the South Atlantic for good measure).'

'The helicopters proved to be invaluable,' said one eye-witness in *Broadsword*. 'Time and again aircrewmen were winched down to pluck men from the icy sea and at one stage a Wessex landed on the hull of the stricken COVENTRY to pick up survivors. One extremely brave piece of flying occurred when one pilot hovered above the Sea Dart magazine, and his winchman recovered 17 men from a group of liferafts which were trapped

HMS *Coventry*, 25 May 1982: Sea King 4s of 846 NAS arrive from San Carlos to join the rescue

alongside the ship's hull. At any moment the magazine could have exploded.'

'The raids cleared,' said a member of *Broadsword*'s Flight Deck team, 'and we went to pick up survivors from the now capsizing COVENTRY. She lies on her side, a Wessex 5 resting his front wheels on her port side winching men out of liferafts trapped by her Sea Dart launcher. There are a total of ten helos dotted round the sky, picking up survivors who have drifted away in bright orange liferafts, checking pieces of flotsam to see if anyone may be clinging to them.'

The helicopters were assisted by *Broadsword*'s rubber outboard Gemini dinghies, one of them crewed by Able Seaman Andy Coppell and Marine Wilson. 'We were told to go and look for survivors floating in the water,' said Coppell. 'When we were heading towards the COVENTRY we noticed two 30 man liferafts stuck alongside. By this time the ship was almost on her side and threatening to crush the liferafts, so we went to the rescue.'

'The first one was amidships, which was in the most danger. The men inside were badly burnt, some of them panicked and jumped out but we pulled them into the Gemini. We thought the ship was going to explode at any moment; there were flames and heavy black smoke coming out of the funnel but we carried on with the job and somehow managed to get them to safety. We used a small nylon line to tow one liferaft clear of the ship and we left them our paddles to stop them floating back into the sinking ship as we returned to drop off survivors.'

'We then went back for the liferaft at the forward end of COVENTRY which contained her Captain. About 16 of them came aboard the Gemini (which was only made for 7 people) and 10 more were hanging onto the side. We couldn't pull ourselves away from the ship as there was not enough power in the engine. The helicopters used their down draft to blow us off until we could make some headway, and we tried to tow the liferaft but the line snapped, and there was no going back to rig another one without endangering ourselves and the other people in the boat. It took about 45 minutes to get 100 yards; the boat had six inches of water in it; the engine was straining, and some of the people clinging to the side were freezing to death so we had to drag them aboard. We were then badly overloaded and threatening to capsize, but we managed to reach our seaboat which was straining its engine pulling another liferaft. Our first job was to get the men out of the water. These were winched up by helicopter and flown to safety, and another Gemini came alongside and took half our survivors.'

'We thought our day was over until we got the propellor fouled with some rope which had to be cut off. We finally cleared the prop and returned to BROADSWORD and the warmth within the ship. The Gemini had eight inches of water in it, the motor was almost worn out and the boat had broken its back. Our thanks to the helicopter pilots who probably saved our lives and the lives of many others.'

'We were passed a rope by the seaboat to try and tow us away from Coventry,' said Macfarlane, 'but we got nowhere fast. Then the roof caved in, 'what stupid bugger's up there?' It was an aircrewman getting us into harnesses and away to a helicopter. We decided to forgive him.'

'When I got into the helo there was only me left and I was freezing. The aircrewman pulled off my anti-flash and tried to warm up my hands. 'Clap your hands,' he said, and I couldn't. After three or four attempts I wrapped my hand in. He told me to get on the deck and crawl to the door. For some inexplicable reason I thought they were putting me back in the liferaft 'cos I couldn't clap my hands, and told him to go to hell. When he asked me again using his boot as gentle persuasion how could I refuse such an offer. Still convinced, his instructions of "you'll go out in the harness and then down" got a swift "cheers for ****all" reply.'

'Out I went and down, cursing my hands for refusing to clap. When I looked down searching for the nearest liferaft I saw this great big grey thing, Broadsword. Looking up, thumbs up, screaming sorry and a pile of thanks I nearly slipped out of the harness and fell twenty feet astride the Seawolf launcher. Talk about ride'em cowboy!'

Macfarlane was shocked and distressed to count only 78 *Coventry* survivors in *Broadsword*. In fact, in what had been a gigantic (and impromptu) rescue operation, 263 unwounded survivors were flown by helicopter or taken (from *Broadsword*) in Landing Craft to San Carlos and put on board the RFA *Fort Austin*, which was due to leave that night. Sixteen minor wound cases were taken to the Field Hospital at Ajax Bay. Four badly burned men went to the hospital ship *Uganda*, in the 'Red Cross Box', north of the Falklands.

HMS *Coventry*, 25 May 1982

Coventry herself continued to float upside down, her keel a few feet above the sea, until she sank the following day.

In all, nineteen of *Coventry*'s people were lost. There were 283 survivors. Robinson-Moltke was not among them. He did have a premonition of death. 'I was shocked,' said Hart Dyke, 'when a day or two before the end my First Lieutenant came into my cabin and without hesitating said "You know, Sir, some of us are not going to get back to Portsmouth". Although it disturbed me to hear him say that, it was very brave to admit to his Captain what he really felt and we now no longer had to pretend to each other about the risks we were taking. He included himself amongst those that would not return and in his last letter home he told his wife so. She received the letter just after she heard the news of his death.'

Meanwhile, miles to the north and east of *Coventry*, another rescue drama was taking place. The 14,946 ton Cunard Steam Ship Company Roll-on Roll-off container cargo ship *Atlantic Conveyor* (Master, Captain Ian North, MN, Senior Naval Officer, Captain Mike Layard, RN) had been taken up from trade and converted at Devonport into an aircraft ferry. She had come south with the amphibious group carrying a total of 25 aircraft: six Wessex 5s of 848 NAS (formed on 19 April) and five CH-47C Chinooks of No.18 Squadron RAF which had embarked in Devonport, and eight Sea Harriers of the reformed 809 NAS, and six GR3 Harriers of No.1 Squadron RAF, which had embarked at Ascension Island on 6 May. She also had stores, aircraft ordnance, spares and ammunition, rations and a tented camp for 4,500 men.

By 25 May, when *Atlantic Conveyor* received orders to enter San Carlos, the Sea Harriers and GR3s had been flown off to bring the carriers' squadrons up to strength. But the Wessex and the Chinooks would be disembarked when the ship anchored in San Carlos. Two Chinooks were unbagged and rebladed, and in the evening of 25th one of them, and one Wessex, were airborne on task around the force.

As *Atlantic Conveyor* closed the land on 25 May, the carrier battle group were necessarily drawn further than usual to the west, to provide air cover for her and for the rescue operations around *Coventry*. That evening the battle group was attacked from the north by two Super-Etendards, who fired Exocet missiles at what appeared on their radar sets to be the largest targets.

Atlantic Conveyor was turning to port, following the standard procedure of presenting the ship's stern to the likeliest direction of threat, when she was hit on her port quarter by two Exocet missiles which penetrated her hull some six to eight feet above the water-line.

Neither missile exploded, but the unexpended fuel and the heat generated by the destruction of the missiles' kinetic energy caused an explosion and fire ball and started huge fires below decks. Within ten minutes the machinery spaces below had to be evacuated because of smoke and heat, the ship lay dead in the water, and there was no firemain pressure, so firefighters had to start auxiliary pumps to provide water for their hoses. Attempts were made to extinguish the fires with sprinkler systems and 'one-shot' carbon dioxide drenching, and by shutting down fan vents and pumping water through hoses into every access in the cargo decks.

'Only twenty minutes after being hit it was clear that our ship was doomed,' said Captain Layard. 'Already the whole of the upper deck was becoming too hot to stand on despite drenching with fire hoses. Night was drawing in and the sea state beginning to worsen. I knew the fire was creeping forward and would reach thousands of gallons of kerosene and 75 tons of cluster bombs which could blow us to pieces at any moment. Captain North (who had been sunk twice in World War Two) and I both reached the conclusion to abandon ship together. The decision was a dreadful one for a Master to make but Ian's calm and good sense prevailed.'

The life rafts were released, 'once only' suits donned, and *Atlantic Conveyor*'s mixed Royal and Merchant Navy ship's company began with what Layard called 'extraordinary calm and discipline' to climb down into the water. The problem was that in a container ship there is only one limited space where one can abandon ship, just opposite the superstructure where, of course, the freeboard was a massive forty feet.

'By now the decks were smoking,' said Layard, 'and there were loud explosions from inside the ship and yet because ladders and ropes were at a premium, like good Englishmen, the company were forming orderly queues to take their turn to abandon the ship. John Brocklehurst (*Atlantic Conveyor*'s First Officer) had a large part to play in this operation.'

The danger was particularly grave up forward, where the forward firefighting team and the flight deck party reported that they were cut off by flames and smoke and were unable to get aft to the liferafts. 'For a dreadful moment I racked my brains over what we could do for them,' said Layard, 'when, to my delight, first a Wessex followed by a Sea King emerged out of the smoke and gloaming, landed, took them all aboard and then lifted safely away.'

Layard climbed down just below Ian North, with the ship's side 'literally glowing red in places and the paint peeling off in others. The descent seemed interminable, the more so as pieces of shrapnel from the explosions inside the ship were coming out through the side and singing past my ears. I was half expecting that she and I would blow up at any second. I felt a quite unwarranted sense of relief as I dropped the last ten feet into the water'.

However, Layard's relief was short-lived, for he discovered that *Atlantic Conveyor* apparently intended to take her survivors to the bottom with her. She 'had a rounded stern section and as she rose and fell in the swell we were first sucked in under the overhang as she rose then firmly pushed under water as she fell. To make matters worse the bulky liferafts were in a clutch together and tending to buffet and squash us against the ship's side'.

Time was running out for Ian North who, as Layard said, 'was no chicken nor greyhound'. The last Layard saw of his 'dear old friend' was when he gave him a strong shove in the small of the back in the direction of the nearest raft. Layard himself went under again, thought his number was up, surfaced to find no sign of Ian North, only an empty life raft and a body (not Ian North) floating face down beside him. 'I caught hold of him, swam to the liferaft and to my delight found two others in it who relieved me of my body and hauled me aboard'. In the event, three of *Atlantic Conveyor*'s company were lost on board and nine, including Captain North, in the sea.

The frigate *Alacrity* (Cdr Christopher Craig) came to the rescue by closing the burning ship which was now 'glowing like a beacon' and firing lines across the seven liferafts and then whilst going slowly astern herself pulling them and the survivors in them and clinging to them safely away. Meanwhile, Sea Kings from *Hermes* and *Invincible* and *Atlantic Conveyor*'s own Wessex flew round the hulk looking for anyone who might have been missed. Survivors from six of the liferafts were taken on board *Alacrity*. The seventh, commanded by John Brocklehurst, broke away from the rest, survived an unpleasant moment or two around *Alacrity*'s bows, and drifted away, but it too was rescued two hours later by *Brilliant*.

Layard watched from *Alacrity*'s bridge as *Atlantic Conveyor* 'burnt like a torch all night'. Her cargo was so important that it was hoped to get at least a small party on board her, but a further explosion blew off her bows. She finally sank while under tow by the tug *Irishman* early on 28 May. So passed, in Layard's words, 'a distinguished old lady' – called the '30 day wonder' because it had been 30 days from sailing to sinking.

The loss of *Atlantic Conveyor*, with most of her aircraft and stores, was as serious a setback for the Task Force as the loss of a major warship. But by 25 May over 5,500 troops and 5,000 tons of supplies, armaments and equipment were ashore at San Carlos. The 'long yomp' which was to end in Port Stanley began with the break-out from the beach-head on 27 May. The ground troops were accompanied, transported, resupplied and evacuated by the tireless helicopters, while the Harriers flew CAPs and armed reconnaissances in support.

Of course there were losses. On 29 May, 801 NAS suffered a bizarre accident when a Sea Harrier was taxying after landing on *Invincible* in bad weather. The ship rolled heavily and the aircraft slid over the side. But the pilot, Lt Cdr Mike Broadwater, ejected and although his dinghy did not inflate properly he was close to the ship and was recovered safely by helicopter.

A day later, two RAF GR3 Harrier pilots of No.1 Sqn, Sqn Ldr Jerry Pook and Fl Lt John Rochfort, were on a sortie over Port Stanley when ground fire hit Pook's Harrier in its main fuel and hydraulic systems. Pook tried to reach *Hermes* but the fuel leak was so serious he was forced to eject some 50 miles west of the ship. However, he had only been in his dinghy for about ten minutes when he was picked up by a Sea King.

Much less fortunate was Fl Lt Ian Mortimer RAF, the Air Warfare

Atlantic Conveyor abandoned and burning after two Exocet missiles hit port side aft

Instructor of 801 NAS, flying a combined CAP and armed reconnaissance sortie south of Stanley on 1 June. He was alone, his No.2 having had to return to *Invincible* with a defect (one of only three sorties lost in almost 600 launches). He was looking for likely targets along the Darwin-Stanley road as well as keeping a radar watch out to seaward for incoming Argentinian C-130s, when he was locked up by a 'Pulse India' radar from the direction of Port Stanley town.

At 10,000 feet and outside six and a half kilometres, which he had been reliably informed was out of SAM range, Mortimer was not unduly concerned by this, even when he noticed a bright flash to the south of the town 'just as if someone had shone a giant mirror at me' and actually saw the light grey smoke trail, already about 2,000 feet and coming rapidly towards him. He could see the (Roland) missile clearly, about 2,000 feet below him and seemingly almost horizontal.

Still quite convinced he was out of range, Mortimer rolled left to watch the missile fall away into the sea. 'The violence of what happened next is indescribable,' he said. 'I only remember that my overriding impression was one of doing front somersaults under extreme g. Being a bright lad, however, I quickly assessed the problem and came to the conclusion that not only was I not in control of the situation, I wasn't in control of the aircraft. I pulled the handle. The violence continued and for one horrible second I thought the seat hadn't fired, but then, just as suddenly as my world had turned upside down, I was hanging in a parachute.'

After a parachute drop of nearly seven minutes, Mortimer was plummetting towards the sea. 'Even if you have never parachuted you will have heard that in the last 1,000 feet or so the surface rushes up at you. Boy, does it! It was definitely time to turn the ... time to turn the ... time to take off the stupid immersion mitt ... CRASH. I hit the water with my left hand (complete with immersion mitt) fervently trying to turn the Quick Release Button and my right hand tucked under my left arm trying to pull off the other immersion mitt. This is not the landing posture taught ... '

Mortimer's right leg was entangled in the lines of his parachute, but he inflated his dinghy, climbed into it, and collapsed face down, totally exhausted. When he had had time to recover and 'think things out in slow time', he crested the top of a twenty-foot swell 'and saw Cape Pembroke lighthouse two miles to the north. Two miles from enemy held territory – oh great!'

Having cut himself free of the parachute lines, Mortimer put out a Mayday call. 'The reply was almost immediate, totally garbled and unreadable, but at least someone had heard me. Things were looking up. I began doing the basic dinghy drills until cresting yet another swell, I saw the Chinook'.

It was Argentinian, searching the sea under the point where the Harrier had been hit. But the wind had carried Mortimer some two miles to the east during his descent. He put out another call to say the enemy was looking for him, but had no reply. Meanwhile, the dinghy was attracting attention from seagulls who threatened to give Mortimer away.

The Chinook was joined by a Bandeirante which flew overboard at 200 feet and then broke sharply away. The Chinook then came so close that Mortimer could see faces looking down at him. Just as he was trying to reconcile himself to being captured, both aircraft turned away (having been warned from shore of the approach of a Sea Harrier section) and set off to the north at speed.

Mortimer put out another call to say he was still in the dinghy. 'The reply might have been in Chinese for all I could tell but at least someone knew I was still there and in need of help. I completed the basic dinghy drills, took a sea-sickness tablet (I was beginning to feel just a touch queezy) and settled down for a long, cold wait.'

It was to be a wait of nine hours, after which a very cold and cramped but not dispirited Mortimer, 'definitely heard the noise of an aircraft. I pulled the canopy open and there, about half a mile away, I could see the dark shape of a helicopter. (Unbeknown to me the crew had already seen the shape of my dinghy even though I was not showing any light and were coming back for another look). I pulled out the PLB and muttered something friendly into it. At last it leapt into life. Totally garbled and unreadable but at least it was life. I asked it if I should show a light and it answered in Chinese, although I later discovered they had heard me. China sounded an awful lot better than the South Atlantic so I switched on the Firefly. In seconds the dark shape switched on its light and became a Sea King of 820 NAS. More seconds and my old buddy (Leading Aircrewman) Mark Finucane appeared out of the side and came down the winch to get me. We had a short grinning competition which I won, followed by a short swim which activated the McMurdo light – not now – and then I was sitting in the back of a Sea King on my way back to Mother. The journey home took one hour 15 minutes, John Trotman poured me enormous cups of coffee and I laughed the whole way.'

As the Falklands campaign developed, it was clear that helicopters were priceless. There could never be enough of them. At home, fresh squadrons were formed in haste. An extra Commando squadron, 848 NAS (CO, Lt Cdr David Baston AFC) reformed at Yeovilton on 17 April from 707 NAS and elements of 772 NAS. The squadron's thirteen Wessex HU.5s were embarked in *Atlantic Conveyor*, RFA *Olna* and RFA *Regent*.

825 NAS (a very famous Fleet Air Arm squadron number) formed at Culdrose on 7 May from a nucleus of 706 NAS, the Sea King training squadron, under Lt Cdr H.S. Clark who had until recently been CO of 706 NAS. Although 706 NAS's pilots were basically anti-submarine pilots, or 'pingers', the new 825 NAS was to be a Commando squadron, equipped with ten Sea King HAS.2As, eight of which embarked in *Atlantic Causeway* and two in *Queen Elizabeth II*. A further Commando squadron, 847 (CO, Lt Cdr M.D. Booth) was hurriedly formed from 771 and 722 NASs and commissioned 'quietly and efficiently amidst a wave of "Pinger" hysteria' (according to the Squadron's own account) at Culdrose, also on 7 May. Within seven days the squadron's twenty four Wessex HU.5s were embarked

(twenty in *Atlantic Causeway*, four in RFA *Engadine*) and on passage for the South Atlantic.

Atlantic Causeway, Atlantic Conveyor's sister ship, sailed south with 28 helicopters and the Rapier missiles of 63 Squadron RAF Regiment on board. She was one of a small convoy – *Baltic Ferry, Atlantic Causeway* and RFA *Blue Rover*, escorted by the frigate *Brilliant* – which left the Carrier Battle Group bound for San Carlos on 31 May and flew off four of 825's Sea Kings to Port San Carlos that afternoon. She anchored that night and began to fly off the remaining four Sea Kings and 847's twenty Wessex at dawn the next day.

847 NAS had originally been intended as the Garrison Squadron, but after the loss of *Atlantic Conveyor* with several of 848 NAS's Wessex, 'B' Flight of 847 NAS landed at Port San Carlos on 1 June to operate from a Forward Air Base along with elements of 845 and 825 NAS and a Chinook of 18 Sqn RAF.

The 'Pinger' pilots took a little time and a few sorties to adjust to their Commando role and there was some early rivalry between the converted 'Pingers' and the 'genuine Junglies'. But under the pressure of war conditions lessons were very quickly learned. The serviceability rate was high and all the helicopters were soon hard at work ferrying prodigious quantities of ammunition, stores and personnel from ship to shore and then overland to the advancing ground troops, as well as bringing back casualties to Ajax Bay. This inevitably meant flying near the front line. Some helicopters felt mortar and shell blast at close range. A few had shrapnel damage.

Helicopter bases were set up at Teal Inlet and at Fitzroy as the troops moved onward. The LSLs (Landing Ships, Logistic) RFA *Sir Tristram* (Captain G.R. Green, RFA) and RFA *Sir Galahad* (Captain P.J.G. Roberts, RFA) anchored in Port Pleasant, the inlet leading to Fitzroy Cove, early on the morning of 8 June: *Sir Galahad* had on board a Sea King of 825 NAS, some vehicles and 470 Army personnel including 16 Field Ambulance, a Rapier missile troop, the Prince of Wales Company and 3 Company, a mortar platoon and other elements (350 men, or about half the battalion) of the 1st Battalion, Welsh Guards.

The Sea King flew the Rapier troop ashore, while other Sea Kings of 825 NAS and a Wessex of 847 NAS began to transfer loads from both LSLs to various 5 Infantry Brigade ammunition dumps and artillery positions already ashore. It would surely only be a short time before the Guards were landed.

But it seems the Welsh Guards were given a low priority for disembarkation. The signal announcing their arrival in *Sir Galahad* had not been correctly passed. Some 250 Welsh Guardsmen had already gone ashore at Bluff Cove in *Fearless*' landing craft the previous day. Possibly Brigade HQ believed the whole battalion was at Bluff Cove.

Thus *Sir Galahad*'s arrival off Fitzroy had not been expected, nor was it known that 350 Welsh Guards were on board her and would need some means of disembarking. Only one LCU (Landing Craft, Utility) and one Mexeflote (motorised pontoon platform, operated by the Royal Corps of Transport) were available at Fitzroy. These were already loaded with ammunition from *Sir Tristram* but the Welsh Guards were offered whatever room was available on them to land on Fitzroy.

The Guards had been ordered to join the rest of their battalion, already at Bluff Cove, which was a sixteen mile march away (or so they understood; in fact, 2 Para's engineers had repaired a bridge at Fitzroy, reducing the march to about six miles). The Guards preferred to wait until LCUs were available to take them and their equipment ashore.

The single LCU disembarked 16 Field Ambulance to Fitzroy first. It did not return until 12.30 pm. Its ramp was defective, so loading had to be carried out over *Sir Galahad*'s ship's side, using rope ladders. This caused yet more delay.

As a result of this whole unfortunate train of circumstances, the Welsh Guards were still on board *Sir Galahad* when, at 1.15 pm, without any warning, five Argentinian Skyhawks flew up the inlet towards Fitzroy from seaward at wave top height. Neither LSL had any chance to open fire and hardly had time to broadcast warnings to take cover before *Sir Tristram* was hit by two 500 lb bombs, and also suffered a near miss under her stern, while *Sir Galahad* was hit by at least three 500 lb bombs.

Both ships caught fire at once, *Sir Galahad* so seriously that Captain Roberts immediately gave the order to abandon ship. One bomb went through an open hatch in *Sir Galahad* and exploded on the tank deck causing heavy casualties among the Guardsmen waiting to go ashore. A second exploded in the galley, killing the ship's butcher Sung Yuk Fai and injuring several others.

The third bomb went into the engine room, killing 3rd Engineer Officer A.J. Morris, and trapping other engineer officers in the Machinery Control Room. Junior Engineer Officer Bagnall tried to escape without breathing apparatus but was driven back by smoke. Second Engineer Officer P.A. Henry gave him the only available breathing set and told him to get out. He did so, but Henry and 3rd Engineer Officer C.F. Hailwood, who was with him, were not seen again.

It was clear in *Sir Tristram* that *Sir Galahad* was very badly damaged. Captain Green sent his lifeboats to assist, and assessed his own ship's damage. Neither bomb which hit *Sir Tristram* had exploded, but the near-miss blew off her stern ramp. Her Bosun Yu Sik Chee and a sailor Yeung Shui Kam were killed. The ship caught fire forward, near ammunition and explosives. There was a report of an unexploded bomb in the steering flat, where a fire had started. Above the flat were several pallets of ammunition. Captain Green decided to abandon ship.

Helicopters were very quickly on the scene. Lt John Boughton and Lt Philip Sheldon, both of 825 NAS, had gone to Fitzroy that morning to move equipment from *Sir Tristram* and *Sir Galahad*. They found other aircraft already doing it so flew back to Goose Green to carry on ferrying the rest of the Guards' equipment forward. Boughton had one of their Land Rovers slung under his Sea King and was flying along at fifty feet when he saw four Skyhawks very low down and following each other. He broadcast a contact report, saying that four Skyhawks were inbound towards Fitzroy, went into 'a quick hide'

Sea King recovering a survivor from a liferaft astern of RFA *Sir Galahad* at Fitzroy, 8 June 1982

himself in a small gorge for a few minutes, and then heard on HF radio that there had been an attack at Fitzroy. He put the Land Rover down in a field where he could find it again, called Sheldon, who he thought was some ten miles away, asked him to join him and then headed to Fitzroy where he could see smoke already rising.

When Boughton arrived there were survivors in dinghies, and smoke pouring out of the ship. The men in the dinghies looked OK, so he went straight on over the fo'c'sle. As soon as he was within fifty yards it was clear that some of the soldiers were 'pretty badly off'. Some of their clothing was smouldering. Others were jumping up and down to keep their circulation going. Many of them had badly burnt hands. A few were just lying quietly on the deck.

Boughton could see 'a few able bodied men who definitely knew what they were doing medically and they were trying to sort out the soldiers who were injured. There was also the Captain of the *Galahad*, who was excellent. He'd organised people to search the ship as best they could and was controlling everything'.

Boughton and his crew began to winch up casualties, but dispensed with the usual routine of strapping people in because 'there wasn't time so we just got them moving down the bus. I said to my crewman (LACMN Roy Eggleston), 'As soon as someone comes in who looks badly injured, we'll take him directly ashore,' because it was only twenty seconds' flying home to a patch of fairly flat grass, which had been used for a landing point for ammunition. As soon as we picked up a badly injured man we went straight to the shore as fast as the aeroplane would go. We'd land them next to anybody we saw and call them in to help carry the casualties out. By that stage 2 Para were already organised and a few stretchers had appeared. They would take the injured out of the aircraft, and that set the pattern'.

'From then on, it was just straight off from the beach back into the fo'c'sle. Radio-wise, it was very quiet among the aeroplanes and the only thing you'd hear was someone saying 'Next', which was to tell anyone waiting that they were getting the last bloke in. Everyone had decided individually that as soon as they got a badly injured guy on board they'd go and then call 'Free space up here' or something similar. It was a bit chaotic, but calm.'

Eggleston had his hands full, so Boughton sent the second pilot back aft to become another 'dragger in' – safe enough, provided there was no emergency. After four or five runs, it was discovered that a first aid post had been opened in Fitzroy settlement and later casualties were taken there.

The fire in *Sir Galahad*'s vitals had been out of control from the outset and by now it was spreading, with what Boughton called 'a few large explosions, which was a bit hairy. We were sitting there in the hover, winching up these poor blokes. Hovering is all an art of watching for changes in your depth of field, or your perspective movement, and as soon as you see a change, you automatically correct to stop it. This is fairly easy if you're sitting over a nice big area where you can see all round you, but all we had was three or four feet of deck, because we were right over the fo'c'sle. The door of the Sea King, which is quite a long way back in the aeroplane, was the focal point. The door was over the bows while the cockpit was over the sea, out in front, which made it slightly difficult because I had to crane round to see.'

But Boughton had the utmost confidence in Roy Eggleston – 'probably one of the best to have there at the time. He kept the whole operation going very well, telling me what was going on, with the occasional 'Ugh' because obviously the sights were pretty gruesome.'

Philip Sheldon had arrived to find *Sir Galahad* on fire and 'surrounded by quite a few helicopters. John was there and also my boss and there was a Wessex (of 847) helping to rescue people'. Short of fuel, he landed on *Sir Tristram* and had actually refuelled, taken off and cleared the ship before he realised she had also been hit and was on fire.

Meanwhile, below him Boughton could see some horrific sights. 'As the fire set in more and more, it just got worse, and you could see right down into the hold. The pillars that were supporting the deck down in the hold were completely wrecked. The whole thing was just like looking into a furnace. The ammunition started to cook off and that was, I think, probably the worst bit of the lot, because Eggleston was leaning out of the aeroplane, and he'd be shaken by those blasts – but he kept going. I had my window open and the first explosion was quite a smack against my face so goodness knows what it was like to be on the deck, because a lot of hot debris was flying out of the hold'.

Captain Roberts was walking up and down the fo'c'sle, organising the exodus, and indicating to Boughton the distance between the bottom of the Sea King and the deck. 'But of course Eggleston was indicating our height all the time. "You're four feet above the deck. You're in a good position', or "You're fifteen feet over the deck – good position, hold that there." I would ask him if we could move in a certain direction and he would "talk" us into the best position ... I'd told him that we'd go as low as we could so the men wouldn't have to spend a long time being winched, so we were definitely quite low at times. It was the quickest way to get those poor devils into the aircraft'.

For Sheldon and his crew *Sir Galahad* was an eerie mixture of everyday technique and the most appalling horrors. 'The rescue of survivors was not a difficult flying exercise,' he said, 'it was very straightforward and we'd been thoroughly trained to do it – but I'd never been so close to flames before. As we worked away, every now and again there would be an explosion within the hold and you'd find yourself looking down at these balls of fire and the shock waves would physically move the aircraft. Tug Wilson, my crewman in the back, was unbelievable. He was incredibly calm, and suppressed his anxiety at what he was both seeing and touching. In a reassuring voice he'd say, "That's a good hover, boss, nice hover, got one coming up now who's got no arms, badly burned, face has disintegrated. I'm going to push him down in the front". I felt him verbalizing his emotional reactions to what he was seeing. There was the standard pukka Naval chat, necessary to position the aircraft, interspersed with, "Oh, fuck me, this guy's got no face". I couldn't see because I was sitting ahead trying to keep the aircraft steady. Suddenly this injured person got pushed up to the front and I felt quite ashamed of myself, because I had to bring myself to actually look down at him and I thought, 'Christ – what a mess.' I felt cowardly that I was having to try and pluck up the courage to actually look at this poor chap and yet here was this guy, suffering agonies.'

'At one point we got a big blast – ammunition in the hold went off – which was frightening. It sounds corny, but I prayed. I think a lot of people who'd never prayed before said them that day. I just said, "If you're on my side, just hang in for the next hour or so." Bits were flying everywhere and I was very aware of the fact that any second the *Galahad* could blow itself to pieces and after one big blast I closed my little window thinking, "That will protect me!" '

Both Boughton and Sheldon particularly noticed the disgusting smell of burnt flesh in their aircraft. Boughton could hear casualties shouting with pain but thought that no bad thing, because if they could shout they must be in a reasonable condition. 'It was the guys who were really quiet that worried me.'

With the helicopters, *Sir Galahad*'s own lifeboats and emergency liferafts, and two lifeboats from *Sir Tristram*, all able-bodied survivors and those wounded who could help themselves were evacuated in about thirty-five minutes. The last two men winched up from *Sir Galahad* were Sgt Peter Naya RAMC, who had behaved with surpassing coolness and gallantry to render medical aid to the stricken men on the fo'c'sle although he was himself a casualty, and, last of all, Captain Roberts who left his ship at 2.15, an hour after the attack.

Boughton, who had winched Naya up, was somewhat taken aback after he had landed when 'Naya came up and gave me a smacker of a kiss on my cheek. I was a bit surprised. He was the one guy I remember vividly. There was nothing I could say – he said it all. He'd done all he could and more, and I think he was overwhelmed with the thought that he had survived – not only that, but that others had survived because of our teamwork.'

It was certainly true that many had only survived because of the helicopters. The total casualty list – the majority from the Welsh Guards – was fifty men killed or missing, and fifty-seven wounded. Army casualties were forty-three killed and forty-six wounded. Two of *Sir Tristram*'s people were lost. *Sir Galahad* had five killed and eleven injured.

But without the helicopters the disaster at Fitzroy might have been much worse. The helicopters had been on the scene quickly, to rescue men from the ships and from the sea, and had used the downdraught of their rotors to waft liferafts away from the burning ship.

Totally overshadowed by the events at Fitzroy, and now almost completely forgotten, was the loss of another ship that day, followed by more Sea King SAR sorties. At 3.40 pm that afternoon a flight of four Skyhawks sighted and attacked the landing craft LCU F4 in Choiseul Sound, the inlet leading to Goose Green and Darwin. LCU F4 had been sent from Bluff Cove to Darwin the previous night to collect 5 Infantry Brigade HQ's vehicles and drivers and was now on her way back to Bluff Cove.

The Skyhawks scored one bomb hit which did not explode, but killed three marines and two naval ratings, among them LCU F4's CO, Colour Sgt Brian Johnston (who later was awarded a posthumous Queen's Gallantry Medal for his gallant part in the rescue of *Antelope*'s ship's company on 23 May).

LCU F4 was badly damaged but still afloat. She was found by Sea Kings who winched off the eleven survivors of the sixteen men who had been on board. Attempts were made to take the landing craft in tow but she sank later that night.

Captain Roberts was awarded a DSO, and Lt Cdr Hugh Clark, CO of 825 NAS, and Lt Cdr Mike Booth, CO of 847 NAS, were awarded DSCs. Lt John Boughton and Lt Philip Sheldon both won the Queen's Gallantry Medal, and Sgt Peter Naya the Military Medal. But there was nothing, not even a Mention in Dispatches, for Eggleston or Wilson.

15 Worldwide SAR: Ajax Bay to the Scillies, Antarctica to the Solent

'Slowly, things degenerate into a nightmare,' wrote Surg Cdr Jolly. 'As night creeps over the horizon, load after load of helicopter casualties begin to arrive at Ajax Bay. Each patient seems worse than the last, until soon the triage and resuscitation areas are completely choked. Helicopters continue to clatter in, and stretcher-borne casualties keep appearing in the main door. No one knows how many are coming, only that we've had over 120 victims of the bombing, mostly with burns.'

Jolly had already had an eventful day. Early that afternoon the frigate HMS *Plymouth* had been about to start a bombardment of Mount Rosalie on West Falkland when she was attacked by five Daggers and was hit by four bombs. None of them exploded, but one detonated a helicopter depth charge on the flight deck, causing casualties and starting a fire.

Jolly was on board the assault ship HMS *Fearless* when *Plymouth* arrived, listing and smoking, in San Carlos Bay. At his suggestion to the Captain, *Fearless* summoned by radio a Wessex just flying by, like hailing a passing taxicab. This took fire-fighting gear, Jolly and a stretcher out to *Plymouth*.

There were ten casualties in all, the most seriously wounded being a stoker who had a piece of metal bracket embedded in his skull. He and the others were taken to the temporary field hospital set up in an abandoned refrigeration plant at Ajax Bay. Known as the 'Red and Green Life Machine' from the colours of the medic's berets, it had been established by Jolly and his medical teams when they landed from *Canberra* on the night of 21 May.

As the casualties from *Sir Galahad* and *Sir Tristram*, many of them horribly burned and mutilated, continued to pour in, it became clear that the 'Life Machine' was going to be tested to the limit.

But the sheer scale of the disaster at Fitzroy was still in the realms of rumour. Nobody yet knew the full details, not even General Moore's headquarters. Jolly ran down to the Logistic HQ by the shore and tried to explain over the radio to an incredulous duty staff officer at Division HQ that he urgently needed accommodation on board the ships for over a hundred casualties. Eventually arrangements were made to take some of the less badly burned men, by landing craft and a few by helicopter, out to *Fearless, Intrepid* and *Atlantic Causeway*, each ship receiving about thirty casualties.

The Welsh Guards took the news of a further delay stoically and bravely. 'I felt morally obliged to apologise to these young Welsh Guardsmen that I couldn't treat them,' said Jolly. 'They stood near the doorway, blowing on their tattered and painful hands to keep them cool. The skin on their fingers hung like thin white rags. Their faces were blistered and raw and their hair was singed short. I was going round with a cigarette, holding it up to their faces so that the glowing tips didn't sting them.

'I said "I'm sorry I can't treat you here because we haven't got much space and because you're only lightly burned – I know you're seriously burned, but only lightly compared with the others – I'm going to have to take you to one of the ships and there's transport coming". But they all accepted the bad news of another half an hour in a landing craft cheerfully and willingly. Every one of them seemed to know about someone else in the building more badly injured than himself and wanted him treated first. They *all* said in their sing song Welsh voices "Doan' you worry about me, sir, you look after my mate". I only have to hear the word *mate* pronounced that way, and it takes me straight back.'

For most of that night the devoted staff of the 'Red and Green Life Machine' laboured to treat the worst burns. 'For each patient there is one attendant, sometimes two,' wrote Jolly. 'It's a heartening sight. The fused and charred clothing is cut away and the total percentage of burned skin area assessed and recorded. Where necessary an intravenous infusion is set up. Then carefully and lovingly, Flamazine is spread over the affected areas. The cool white cream contains a silver and sulpha drug mixture which is pain-killing, antiseptic and promotes healing. Hands and fingers are enclosed in sterile plastic bags to avoid the risks of bandaging. If a scar forms under a dressing it will probably remain undetected until too late, and a contracture might be the severe and unwelcome penalty.'

'Come the dawn, I knew I was going to have to get them out to the hospital ship quickly because we had run out of burns dressings and almost everything else. We were chock-a-block and we couldn't nurse them properly. We didn't have that sort of facility. I ran down to the radio again and told HQ "I need helicopters". They said "Sorry, there aren't any".'

A medical staff officer then came ashore and Jolly showed him the main dressing station. 'He just couldn't believe it. He looked at these burns and these spectral figures and said, I see your problem, then went away to see what he could do.'

The staff officer wanted to be helpful but he was not hopeful. It seemed there would be no casevac helicopter service that day. Everyone wanted to get the war over as quickly as possible. Resupply of the battle line understandably came first.

When the daily Wessex tasked for Ajax Bay arrived it was sent to find *Uganda*. It came back shortly, reporting that she was in Grantham Sound, just over the ridge. Then a Sea King arrived, quite unexpectedly, with familiar faces on board whom Jolly recognised from his time at Culdrose.

Shown the burns cases in the dressing station, the pilot offered to take some casualties out to *Uganda* – if he could be loaded quickly. 'Could we load him quickly!' said Jolly.

Officially, there were no further helicopters available. But that Sea King was followed by another, and then by a third. None of them had been summoned. All had heard of the situation at Ajax Bay on their radios and came to volunteer their services, creating time for flights out to *Uganda* from their normal resupply sorties.

Throughout that forenoon, the helicopters came and went. Thus, in a marvellous example of flexible flying operations, those untasked and unbriefed helicopter crews maintained an impromptu but highly effective and speedy casevac service. By noon, Ajax Bay had been cleared of burns cases. By 2.30 in the afternoon the casualties in *Fearless, Intrepid* and *Atlantic Causeway* had also been taken to the hospital ship.

When the medical staff officer returned to report that there were no helicopters and the casualties would simply have to be held at Ajax Bay until resupply was completed, Jolly was able to show him a 'completely empty dressing station, with all the debris and mess cleared and swabbed away, everything wrung out and hung up to dry, stretchers stacked and everybody having lunch'.

'He couldn't believe it. He said, "How did you do it?". I just tapped the side of my nose, simply busting with pride, and said "My Fleet Air Arm family". I would say almost every helicopter flying that day came to Ajax Bay at some time to help.'

'SAR is an occasional welcome relief from more prosaic flying duties. Every pilot welcomes it. What it did on that day was enrich their vital but boring sorties flying up ammunition to the front line. All aircrew know it's important, so you do your duty and you get the combat supplies to the right place. But it's a sort of *inert* thing, very important but rather impersonal. Whereas, with six hundred pounds of fuel remaining and you know you've got to refuel anyway, you just put a little 'loop' in your circuit and go out to the hospital ship – then look back into the cabin, and all you can see are the grinning faces of the wounded saying "Thank you, sir" ... Every single Falklands casualty who entered into the evacuation chain – 778 injured is the official total – spent some part of his life in a helicopter.'

The success of the 'Red and Green Life Machine' was remembered in the Falklands honours. Surg Cdr Rick Jolly and Lt Col Bill McGregor, RAMC, were appointed OBE, Surg Lt Cdr Phil Shouler, Major Charles Batty and Captain Terry McCabe RAMC, MBE, and Medical Technician 1st Class Stuart McKinley the BEM. Four others received C-in-C Fleet's Commendations.

For the Fleet Air Arm, the Falklands conflict was a brief but very hectic period of operations; for example, on a single day, 21 May, a detachment of Sea King Mk 4 Commando helicopters of 846 NAS lifted 912,000 lbs of stores and carried 520 troops. This intensity of flying was made possible by a very high serviceability rate – over 90 per cent for the Sea King squadrons, whilst the Sea Harriers lost only one per cent of planned sorties through unserviceability.

During the months of April, May and June 1982, Sea Harriers of 800, 801, 809 and 899 NAS, Sea King Mk 2s of 824 and 825 NAS, Sea King Mk 4s of 846 NAS, Sea King Mk 5s of 820 and 826 NAS, Wessex Mk 3s of *Antrim* and *Glamorgan* Flights, Wessex Mk 5s of 845, 847 and 848 NAS, Lynx Mk 2s of 815 NAS, and Wasp Mk 1s of 829 NAS, flew a total of 23,725 hours, 35 minutes, carried out 12,757 sorties and made 21,953 deck landings.

The effort of the helicopter crews was recognised in the Falklands Honours List, published in *The London Gazette* of 11 October 1982. Apart from the DSCs to Clark and Booth, COs of 825 and 847 NAS, and the QGMs to Boughton and Sheldon, of 825 NAS, Lt Cdr Hugh J. Lomas, CO of 845 NAS, Lt Cdr Simon C. Thornewill, CO of 846 NAS, and Lts Alan R.C. Bennett, Richard Hutchings, Royal Marines, and Nigel J. North, all of 846, also won the DSC.

Major Charles P. Cameron, Royal Marines, the CO of 3 Commando Brigade Air Squadron, won the Military Cross and two of his Royal Marine helicopter pilots, Captain Jeffrey P. Niblett and Lt Richard J. Nunn (posthumously), won the Distinguished Flying Cross. Lt Cdr Douglas J.S. Squier, CO of 826 NAS, and Lt Cdr Ralph, J.S. Wykes-Sneyd, CO of 820 NAS, both won the Air Force Cross. CPO ACMN Malcolm J. ('Alf') Tupper, LACMN Peter B. Imrie, and Cpl ACMN Michael D. Love, Royal Marines (posthumously), all of 846 NAS, won the Distinguished Service Medal. Sgt Williams C. O'Brien, Royal

Sea King approaches the seaward end of the glacier before beginning the ascent to Waghorn Camp at 3,800 feet

Marines, of 3 Commando Brigade Squadron, won the Distinguished Flying Medal.

Lts Peter C. Manley (845 NAS) and Frederick W. Robertson (826 NAS), Sgt Thomas A. Sands Royal Marines (845 NAS) and LACMN Stephen W. ('Shiner') Wright (826 NAS) were all Mentioned in Dispatches.

Other awards followed. 846 NAS, embarked in *Hermes*, had mounted 26 secret night missions to infiltrate, resupply and extract special forces operating on the enemy-held islands, with DSCs to Thornewill, Bennett, Hutchings, and North, and DSMs to Tupper, Imrie and Love, was the most decorated helicopter squadron (Bennett, Hutchings and Imrie won their decorations for a sortie by a Sea King which crashed near Puntas Arenas, Chile – while ferrying an SAS advance party to attack Argentine mainland bases on 20 May 1982).

Thornewill and 846 NAS were awarded the Johnston Memorial Trophy by the Guild of Air Pilots and Air Navigators and received it from HRH The Duke of Edinburgh at the Mansion House on 26 October 1983. Ian Stanley and the crew of 'Humphrey' – Parry, Cooper and Fitzgerald – won the 1983 Prince Philip Helicopter Rescue Award presented annually by the Court of the Guild to an individual member or a complete crew for an act of outstanding courage or devotion to duty in the course of land or sea SAR operations.

Meanwhile, at home, the 'silly season' opened as usual at Easter and continued through the summer with the customary crop of SAR incidents. Towards the end of the year there was a remarkable rescue by 819 NAS at Prestwick. On 9 November 1982, the Rescue Co-Ordination Centre at Edinburgh asked for assistance for the fishing vessel *Poseidon* which was reported to have suffered a mechanical breakdown and to be taking in water north of Skye.

Another fishing vessel, *St Kilda*, was towing her but the tow was continually parting and *Poseidon* was on a lee shore. The Duty Sea King, 'Rescue 701', (Lt Nigel King, second pilot Sub Lt A.J. Read, observer Lt Stephen Westwood, LACMN S. Revell, POACMN R. Gardiner) took off at ten minutes to midnight. The wind was gale force 9, gusting from 45 knots to 56, visibility about three miles in heavy rain, with thick cloud cover down to 500 feet. Because of the weather, a second Sea King, 'Rescue 707', took off twenty minutes later to provide mutual SAR.

Rescue 701 was first directed to another fishing vessel *Sea Otter* to pick up a pump, while Rescue 707 located *Poseidon*. Screen 'clutter' caused by the storm obscured 707's radar picture and the datum position given was five miles in error. While 707 was searching, *St Kilda* broadcast: '*Poseidon* is on the rocks and sinking – men are in the water'.

St Kilda fired four red flares and 701's crew were able to identify two faint white lights, abut two miles to the north of them, as *St Kilda* and *Poseidon*. 701 closed the scene at Fladda Chuain on the coast flying into wind from the north and letting down about half a mile from the coast. All land was lost on the radar due to clutter at ranges of less than half a mile.

701 was being buffeted by wind, rain and spray and would not turn out of wind. King had to 'crab' his helicopter backwards and sideways towards where he guessed *Poseidon* was lying. Westwood was lowered four times, into the water or on to wave-swept rocks, to bring up four crewmen in the double harness. All four were intensely cold and in shock. One, a non-swimmer, clinging spreadeagled to a partially submerged rock, was very near death from hypothermia.

The fifth and last survivor was nowhere to be seen. 701 moved sideways across the rocks in each direction for about ten minutes and King was thinking of abandoning the rescue, because of the deteriorating condition of the three who had been rescued, when the fifth man suddenly walked into view on the shore line.

701 joined 707 and together they flew to Stornoway, by which time it was clear that the non-swimmer would not have lasted much longer. After refuelling, the two Sea Kings returned to Prestwick after nearly seven hours in the air.

King was awarded the Queen's Commendation for Valuable Service in the Air and Westwood the Queen's Commendation for Brave Conduct. The whole crew won the Edward and Maisie Lewis Award for 1983 from the Shipwrecked Fishermen and Mariners' Royal Benevolent Society. This award, instituted in 1980, for the most outstanding air/sea rescue of the year, was set up with a donation from a Family Trust by Mr Richard Lewis in memory of his father and mother, Sir Edward, Chairman of Decca Ltd, and Lady Lewis. The trophy, kept for one year, is a replica of a Decca Navigator MK21 Receiver originally given to Sir Edward by his work force to mark the production of the 10,000th set.

Sometimes, the actions of SAR aircrew went well beyond the limits of what could reasonably be called their duty. In December 1983 *The London Gazette* announced the award of the Queen's Gallantry Medal to PO Aircrewman John Coleman, of HMS *Osprey*, Portland. On 22 February 1983 Coleman was the SAR diver in a Wessex of 772 NAS which went to the assistance of the trawler *Petit Forban*, reported as sinking with three of her crew missing, some 25 miles off Beachy Head.

When the Wessex arrived, the trawler was almost vertical in the water with only about three feet of her bow still showing above the surface and even that was disappearing frequently under the waves. Weather conditions were bad, with Sea State 5, an eight to thirteen foot swell, and the wind gusting from 30 to 40 knots.

It seemed very unlikely there would be any survivors, but Coleman elected to try and search the vessel. He was lowered into the sea with a 90-foot heaving line, with the helicopter crewman tending the other end. But the line was not long enough, so Coleman signalled for it to be let go, and he fastened it to a guard rail on the trawler.

Coleman entered through the wheelhouse and began his search, trying to find his way forward where it seemed most likely any survivors would be. The visibility was very poor because of oil, fuel and debris and Coleman became disorientated inside the trawler's hull. Not knowing the layout, he could not find a way forward. While he was still trying to feel his way up into the bows, the aircraft dropped a sound signal to warn him that he had been in the water for fifteen minutes and he only had another five minutes' air supply left.

On being recovered back into the Wessex, Coleman talked over the problem with the pilot and it was decided to look for a vessel which had already picked up three of *Petit Forban*'s survivors. It was possible they knew more about the ship's layout and the likelihood of survivors still being on board. But, perhaps fortunately for Coleman, who would certainly have made another attempt, *Petit Forban* sank before anything more could be done.

As well as the QGM, Coleman also won the Prince Philip Award. He was presented with it by the Grand Master himself, HRH The Duke of Edinburgh, in the Merchant Taylor's Hall, London. At the same ceremony His Royal Highness presented the Sir Barnes Wallis Memorial Award to Lt Cdr John White and Lt Gary Hunt, of HMS *Endurance*'s Ship's Flight, representing all their predecessors, in recognition of the Flight's achievements in improving the standard of rescue and survival equipment in the Antarctic over a period of more than 30 years.

It was an autumn for SAR awards. In November, CPOACMN Richard Foster was honoured at the Access 'Men of the Year' lunch at the Savoy Hotel in aid of the Royal Association for Disability and Rehabilitation. In October Foster had been the SAR diver in a helicopter from Lee-on-Solent which was scrambled to assist a badly injured yachtsman in gale force winds twelve miles off St Alban's Head, Dorset.

As Foster was being lowered onto the deck, the yacht's wildly swinging mast smashed itself against him, breaking his left arm in four places. Foster then became trapped as the winch wound itself round the mast and rigging. Finally, the wire snapped and Foster fell fifteen feet into the sea.

Rescued by his own helicopter, Foster was flown to the Royal Naval Hospital, Haslar, where he underwent extensive surgery, had a steel plate inserted in his wrist and several skin grafts. Yet he amazed his doctors and his physiotherapists by recovering so rapidly he was back in action again as an SAR diver only four months later.

The early SAR sorties of 1983 included one of the most bizarre of all, on 19 January, when a Wessex of 771 NAS was scrambled from Culdrose to evacuate a crewman from the fishing vessel *Lady Hamilton* who had been bitten by a dogfish and needed treatment for injuries to his left hand and shock.

The 'Season' proper, of what was to be a long, fine summer, began with a major rescue when all the emergency services were summoned in the early hours of 2 April to go to the aid of the 4,700 ton Britanny Ferries liner *Armorique* which was some ten miles north of the Seven Stones light ship,

Petty Officer Aircrewman Larry Slater, GM

between Land's End and the Scilly Isles with 700 passengers on board. Fire had broken out in the accommodation deck and one passengers, a Brittany school teacher, had died in the blaze.

By 6.30 am a massive coordinated rescue operation was underway. A Wessex of 771 NAS (Lt Morton, POACMN Wallace) took a fire-fighting team, breathing apparatus and foam extinguishers. The fire-fighters were winched down, and two casualties, a girl of six and her father, were stretcher-lifted off and taken to hospital. A second Wessex of 771 NAS (Lt Kirby, LACMN Eggleston) arrived and another eleven passengers were winched up and flown to Penzance hospital suffering from toxic fumes and burns.

Throughout the day the Sennen and Penlee lifeboats ferried people, fire-fighting equipment and medical supplies to and fro between the ship and Penzance. Almost 80 passengers and crew were taken ashore before the fire was brought under control.

A second major emergency occurred on 16 July when a British Airways S.61 helicopter G-BEON ditched into the sea on a routine passenger flight between Penzance and the Scillies. A Wessex of 771 NAS (Fl Lt Crouchman RAF, LACMN Fileman) and a Sea King of 706 NAS (Lt Chapman, Lt Taylor, Observer Lt Ward, LACMN Keen) were scrambled, and the St Mary's lifeboat was launched.

When the helicopters arrived on the scene they found a calm sea but thick fog, making it very difficult to locate the exact position where the aircraft had crashed. The lifeboat picked up six survivors on the surface, including the pilot and co-pilot of the ditched helicopter, and one seriously injured woman, but twenty people were still missing. An SAR diver did a circling dive down to the sea-bottom in an effort to find the wreck. But the aircraft sank quickly in 200 feet of water and was swept away by strong underwater currents. A major salvage operation recovered the wreckage three days later and the victims' bodies were flown to Penzance.

The long hot summer of 1983 came to a very abrupt end at the beginning of September with gale force winds and driving rain storms over much of the country. As expected, it was not long before the first call for help arrived at Culdrose. On 2 September, the yacht *Adfins Rival*, was some 60 miles south-west of the Scillies on the last leg of the Portugal to Plymouth Race when she began to take on quantities of water in mountainous seas whipped up by sixty knot winds. The two man crew sent out a 'May Day' and then abandoned ship.

Two Sea Kings of 706 NAS were scrambled from Culdrose. Meanwhile an RAF Nimrod found the survivors in their damaged and only partially inflated life-raft and dropped two more life-rafts to help them keep afloat until the Sea Kings arrived. One man was winched up, utterly exhausted and suffering from shock. The second crewman was also recovered, but was pronounced dead on arrival at Culdrose.

The day's events were not over. A second yacht *St Patrick II* was in difficulties and was taken in tow by the Falmouth lifeboat. A third yacht *CS Aradis* also broadcast a 'May Day' from a position 30-40 miles south-west of the Scillies. Sea Kings of 706 and 826 NAS were launched from Culdrose and searched for the rest of the day. A Sea King from RAF Brawdy and a Nimrod from RAF Kinloss searched through the night and were relieved by Culdrose's Sea Kings at first light. They searched that day 3 September until 1 pm when the yacht was found off Ushant, its crew 'shattered but alive', and the search was called off.

As so often, a good summer was followed by a bad winter. There were fierce blizzards in Scotland and the Borders over New Year. 819 NAS at Prestwick were kept busy flying rescue sorties – hover taxying along the A9 road at 50 feet with 50 yards visibility, and 100 foot cloud base, searching for missing cars and trains, transporting police and mountain rescue teams, medevacs, and the unpleasant duty of carrying bodies down to the lower slopes. Much of their work was in conditions naval helicopter crews dislike most – hilly country, poor visibility and low cloud, with always the risk of flying into a 'rock-filled cloud', or 'cumulo-granite' as the aircrew describe it.

Earlier, in December 1983, three of 819 NAS's six Sea Kings joined with Wessex of No. 72 Sq from RAF Aldergrove, Belfast, to rescue everybody on board the 3,600 ton Sealink ferry *Antrim Princess* which had had a serious engine room fire off the Antrim coast. The Master, Captain Thomas Cree, ordered the ship's electrical system shut down and anchored his ship only half a mile from the rocks of the Magee Island peninsula. By then, the wind was reaching 60 knots and heavy seas swept five life-rafts off the ferry's upperdeck and prevented the lifeboats being launched. But within two hours of the alarm being given, the naval and RAF helicopters had between them taken off all twenty crew and 108 passengers.

Early in the New Year, there was yet another example of the personal risks taken by any aircrewman who was lowered down to a ship in rough weather. In this case, the crewman involved was dubbed, rather unkindly, the ' "Upside Down" Rescuer' by *Navy News*. On 23 January 1984, reports were received that the 10 metre yacht *Oggie* with two people on board, was in some difficulty. Her auxiliary engine had failed and the weather was getting worse. HMS *Orkney* responded and headed towards the yacht.

By about 11 pm that evening, *Oggie* had been repeatedly knocked over 90 degrees, had been turned full circle and her mast had been broken. She broadcast a 'May Day' signal from a position some 60 miles south-east of Culdrose where two Sea Kings of 706 NAS were scrambled in weather conditions candidly described as 'abysmal'.

When the first Sea King (Lt Fred Robertson, Lt Doug Sealy, Observer Lt Stephen Marlow, and LACMN Martin Scott) reached the scene, *Oggie* was being illuminated by searchlights from *Orkney* and from the MV *Columbialand*. Marlow went down on the wire but was accidentally dunked in the sea and winded. He was lowered again and actually hit the yacht, landing with unexpected force on its deck where the skipper, Mr John Hathaway, who was not hurt, helped him to recover his balance.

Marlow put the winch strop around the second crew member, John Scragg, and, to avoid either of them getting caught in the yacht's loose wires and rigging, leapt into the water with him. The yacht's hull was plunging up and down in the swell, threatening to crush both men, so Marlow wasted no time in giving the 'thumbs up' signal for hoisting.

Unfortunately, Marlow was unaware that his leg was entangled in a wire. When winching began it could be seen that he was being hoisted feet first and might well be injured when he reached the helicopter. However, it was also probable that John Scragg, already in a semi-hypothermic condition, might not survive being put back into the water while Marlow tried to free his leg. So the winching continued and both men were recovered safely, although Marlow suffered bad bruising and back injuries.

The winch wire was found to be defective through its contact with the yacht's rigging, so Robertson flew back to Culdrose, leaving the second Sea King to recover Hathaway which it successfully did fifteen minutes later. A third Sea King was launched to provide air cover but was not required.

Marlow, who had taken part in the Penlee lifeboat drama and also served with 820 NAS in the Falklands, won the Queen's Gallantry Medal. Robertson, Lt Ian Galway, the pilot of the second Sea King, and Lt John Ward, his observer, were all awarded the Queen's Commendation for Valuable Service in the Air.

706's Sea King crews had barely reached their homes after the *Oggie* rescue when they were recalled. *Orkney* was responding to a call for help from the Greek MV *Radiant Med* which reported she was taking in water. Five Sea Kings were launched from Culdrose. Several ships including *Orkney* and the RFA *Green Rover* assembled on the scene. *Orkney* signalled at 2.44 am on 24 January that the ship had sunk. There had been 26 people on board. Guernsey lifeboat picked up nine survivors from a liferaft. The Sea Kings recovered fourteen bodies and various debris, liferafts and belts.

The last major rescue of the year from Culdrose was on 23 November, when a 'May Day' was received from the MV *Gulfstrom*, on passage from Portugal to Liverpool and in difficulties north-west of St Ives. Her cargo of timber had shifted and her engine room was flooded. A Wessex of 771 NAS (Lt Miko, US Coast Guard on an exchange posting, LACMN Allison) was launched, with a Sea King of 706 NAS (Lt Yearsley, Lt Sambrook, observer Lt. Gibson, LACMN Humphries) as air cover.

When the helicopters arrived, the ship was seen to be listing some 20 to 30 degrees in heavy seas. Allison was winched down to supervise the lifting of each crew member. The crew of six was brought up and flown to Culdrose sick bay. MV *Gulfstrom* sank an hour later.

It had been a busy year. Naval SAR helicopters had been scrambled on 304 occasions in 1984 and had saved 219 people – and seven cows. In detail, Lee-on-Solent SAR Flight made 151 sorties and rescued 114 people, ending on Christmas Eve with the rescue of ten men from the tug *Implacable* which sank in heavy seas off the Isle of Wight while on its way to the Falklands. Culdrose made 110 sorties in the year, rescued 73 people (and the seven cows) and recovered twelve dead bodies; 819 NAS at Prestwick rescued 22 people in 35 sorties; and Portland helicopters scrambled nine times and saved ten lives.

The year of 1985 demonstrated, perhaps more dramatically than any other, the worldwide extent of Search and Rescue. There were some notable rescues, not just around the coasts of the United Kingdom, but as far afield as Antarctica, Puerto Rico, and in the Norwegian Sea.

On 5 March 1985 the RFA *Olna* with two Sea Kings of 826 NAS embarked was despatched from the Falklands to join HMS *Endurance* and her Wasp Flight who were already heading for Brabant Island, a remote and desolate place on the north-west tip of Antarctica, to attempt to rescue Lt Cdr Clive Waghorn, the leader of a Joint Service Expedition to Brabant.

Waghorn had broken his leg in a fall from an 'ice-bridge' over a crevasse on 3 March. He was now lying in considerable pain in a tent shared with Corporal Kerry Gill, Royal Signals, another member of the Expedition. The two men were nearly 800 miles from civilisation, and 3,500 feet up a snow-covered glacier which was swept by blizzards in temperatures down to minus 30°C. Two attempts to reach them by aircraft from the British Antarctic Survey team and a group of Chilean scientists had already been thwarted by appalling weather.

The 826 NAS crews were 'pingers' who had been on anti-submarine patrol duties around the Falklands. Neither crew had much experience of mountain and arctic flying overland and the maps available, they found, were 'so poor as to be useless'. In the event, the unsatisfactory maps were to be compounded by grid reference errors.

There was no spare deck or diversion field, so ditching in the icy sea or a forced landing on Brabant could be fatal. During the 36-hour transit to Brabant the two Sea Kings were stripped of equipment to reduce their weights by some 300 lbs and give more space in the rear.

By the time *Olna* arrived off Brabant on 7 March, the two crews had a plan of action. It was decided to launch the Sea Kings as a pair, both fully SAR capable and with maximum endurance to effect casevac, at a range of about 100 nautical miles from Brabant. They would fly first to Metchnikoff Point, a small rocky outcrop on the island, where they would pick up two members of the Joint Service Expedition to act as guides and show them where Waghorn was. One Sea King with a light weight stretcher would attempt the actual rescue while the second provided mutual SAR back-up.

The 7 March was what Lt Cdr Nigel Thomson, the Sea King Detachment Commander, was to call 'a difficult and most frustrating day'. It began when a planned early launch was delayed by the hangar door jamming shut with both aircraft inside, and then by a fuelling system defect which eventually reduced the fuel flow to a trickle.

Olna was lying beam on to a very heavy swell so as to give the helicopters ideal wind direction for take-off. But this meant that the deck was rolling beyond permitted limits for flying (plus or minus ten degrees roll). So a compromise was reached, to give an 'adequate' wind and an 'adequate' deck movement.

The first Sea King, 'Rescue 529' (Thomson, observer and captain, Lt Gurney Hickey, first pilot, Sub Lt Phillip Reed, second pilot, POACMN Kevin Weller and Ldg Medical Assistant M. Phillips) launched at 7 am followed by 'Rescue 537' (Lt Andy McKie, pilot and captain, S/Lt Alex Atrill, second pilot, Lt David Naismith, observer, LACMN J.J. 'Scouse' Doyle and Lt David Issit, Senior Pilot of *Endurance*'s Wasp Flight). But within ten minutes '529' called *Olna* with a message that a transmission chip light caption was showing in the main gearbox and they were returning for a precautionary landing (the Sea King crews' motto, that day and the next, was 'Don't add to the casualty list').

Rescue 529 took off again at 11.30 am and, with 537 leading (because Issit had used the landing site before and knew the way) by noon were approaching Metchnikoff Point. The landing site was only big enough for one Sea King, with high ground on one side and 300 foot rock pinnacles on the other. Air turbulence was so severe that Hickey had to make two precautionary passes before landing. Two Expedition members climbed on board and said that Waghorn was lying at about 2,500 feet on the north west side of Mount Cushing.

The Sea Kings now began a methodical search of the lower slopes and the glacier valleys. From the start, the helicopter crews were awed by the sheer size of the island's features. 'One of our biggest problems,' said McKie, 'was coping with the scale of things. Brabant Island is in excess of 8,000 feet high which would put the safety altitude outside the Flight Envelope for the aircraft. Without any familiar visual cues such as houses and people the whole place seemed to shrink. It is only when going in to pick people up that the whole environment grows again and you realise just how big the place is. Small icebergs were spotted from the air which, in actual fact, on closer inspection proved to be in excess of 300 feet high.'

As the aircraft worked upwards towards the higher slopes, it became impossible for the crews to tell the difference between snow and cloud. There was no real horizon, no way of estimating scale or distance and no depth perception, so flying was entirely by instruments. The outside air temperature was minus 8°C and visibility decreased markedly anywhere near the cloud base at 2,500 feet. The surface wind was about 40 knots but the local katabatic winds, roaring down the slopes, reached 55 knots with gusts even higher, whipping up violent turbulence and strong down draughts as well as equally sudden updraughts so that the aircraft were often forced to turn back. At one point the Air Speed Indicator in 537 went from 90 knots to zero and back to 90 knots in two seconds. On occasions, even under full power the Sea Kings were still descending at a rate of 700 feet a minute.

All in all, it was an environment totally strange to all the aircrew except

Weller, who had served in *Endurance* Ship's Flight for some eleven months, and conditions could not have been more testing for crews more used to flying over the sea. But the search continued all afternoon, the aircraft pushing higher and higher.

At 2.05 pm 537 returned to *Olna* to refuel and then went directly to a Joint Service Expedition outpost at Minot Point on the west coast of the island to pick up a JSE doctor, Captain Tony Williams RAMC, so that when the casualty was eventually found there would be a doctor immediately available to attend to him.

The pick up gave a dramatic insight into the scale of the terrain. 'The doctor was to be picked up by winch transfer from a rocky outcrop at the base of a 500 foot cliff,' said Naismith, 537's observer. 'We spent several minutes looking for him, and in fact had almost flown past the briefed pick-up point when a relatively minuscule figure, waving a smoke grenade, was spotted against the megalithic backdrop.'

By now it was clear that the casualty was not at 2,500 feet and the contours on the maps were inaccurate. At about 4 pm the cloud base thinned and both aircraft flew higher. At 5 pm, 537 spotted what looked like a tent at about 3,800 feet. The precise position was recorded in the aircraft's TANS (Tactical Aid to Navigation System) and McKie began some dummy runs. Smoke markers were dropped to try and establish local wind directions but the markers all vanished in the snow or fell down into deep crevasses.

529 joined and also made a number of dummy runs, and then actually achieved a doppler hover at about 150 feet above the casualty with approximately another 200 yards to run. However, the air turbulence was so violent that Hickey was unable to maintain controlled flight even with maximum permissible torque applied and maximum left pedal. 529 began to descend and yaw uncontrollably and Hickey had to break away involuntarily to the right, although his pre-planned escape route was to the left.

529 and 537 returned to *Olna* in deteriorating weather. Ice formed on both helicopters during the transit but with no landing field ashore for two aircraft and no spare deck there was nothing to be done. Both made radar controlled approaches to land on with visibility down to less than a quarter of a mile. They had flown beyond the aircrafts' design limits in almost every way for fourteen hours that day.

On the next day, 8 March, the helicopter crews briefed on *Olna*'s bridge at 4.45 am, hoping to launch at first light at 6 am. But at dawn the ship was enshrouded in thick icy fog. Visibility was less than forty yards, and in fact was never to be more than two to four hundred yards around *Olna* throughout the day.

537 (with 529's crew of the day before) launched at 7.15 when the visibility had improved just enough and flew to Metchnikoff for a weather reconnaissance and to transfer three JSE personnel to *Endurance* for briefing. 529 (with 537's crew of the previous day) then launched to fly round the north of the island in very poor visibility to Bulls Bay, on the south-eastern coast to

pick up a second doctor, Captain Martin RAMC. Both helicopters now had a doctor.

529 had stripped the tape from her main rotor blades whilst 'flogging around in the murk' and returned to land on *Olna* with 'some nasty vibration'. But the maintenance party did an excellent job in replacing all the tape in an hour and twenty minutes. The work was hardly done when there was a pipe to emergency stations for a fire in *Olna*'s funnel. 529's crew had to man up their aircraft and launch in a hurry.

It had been decided to land a party of Royal Marines and JSE members as near as possible to the casualty's camp site and attempt an overland rescue on foot. 537 tried to land this party, but had to abandon the sortie and turn back because of low cloud and 'white-out' conditions. Then (at POACMN Weller's suggestion) it was decided to land a two-man radio team at Metchnikoff Point to report on weather conditions and this 537 successfully achieved.

Meanwhile, *Endurance* had arrived about five miles off Brabant at 11 that morning in thick fog and a heavy swell. At about 12.30, the cloud cover over the coastline began to disperse, and the tops of the mountains could be seen. As often happens in those altitudes there was a magically rapid clearance in the weather. In twenty minutes almost the whole coast could clearly be seen in bright sunlight.

When *Endurance* informed *Olna* of the weather clearance, *Olna* reported both Sea Kings on deck and shut down with the ship still in thick fog and unable to launch. The fine weather could disappear as quickly as it had arrived. At 1.05 pm it was decided to launch *Endurance*'s Wasp and locate the survivors.

The Wasp '435' was launched at 1.30 (Lt Cdr J.J. White, pilot and Ship's Flight Commander, Lt Cdr K.W. Terrill, observer), with a stretcher, the ship's doctor Surg Lt J.P. Miell and the Detachment Sergeant Major, Sgt C.R. Henderson, Royal Marines, on board. The weather was still fine with brilliant sunlight but extensive banks of stratus cloud were covering the search area and moving north. It was estimated that this cloud would reach the survivors' camp site in about thirty minutes.

435 flew upwards, hugging the mountainside, for about 15 minutes until at about 1.40 pm the camp site was seen through a gap in the clouds at a height of about 3,400 feet. The tent was well dug in and surrounded by a snow wall, with the letters HELP dug out along-side. When 435 made its first pass overhead, Corporal Gill appeared from inside the tent, waving, and apparently in good health and spirits.

The area was then completely clear of cloud, but the camp site was in a precarious position, situated on a jagged rock face between two wide crevasses at the top of a three mile long glacier, with a one-in-three slope making a landing very risky.

435 made two low level approaches and dropped a smoke grenade 50 yards from the tent. During the second approach, Sea King 529 called 'Inbound' from a range of about 10 miles and was given a Sitrep of the site, weather and

approach. 435 now had only ten minutes' fuel left and White decided to hold off winching down the Doctor and the Sergent Major and wait for the Sea King and the full rescue team to arrive.

529 approached at low level from the west and flew straight in below 435 to hover about 100 yards north of the camp site. At that point, with 435 on 'Chicken Fuel', and feeling confident that the evacuation would now go ahead, White flew back to *Endurance*.

Olna was still fogbound when the Wasp's call was received but the fog bank was estimated to be no more than 150 feet high and the two Sea Kings were launched. 529 achieved a high hover, at between 80 and 100 feet to avoid disturbing the surface snow and causing a 'white-out', and winched down a stretcher and team of five before the creeping cloud forced a retreat. 537 had also arrived and the two Sea Kings orbited the peaks at about 5,000 feet for the next twenty minutes, waiting and hoping for another gap to appear in the clouds.

When this occurred, 529 established another high hover and Naismith went down in the double lift to winch up Waghorn and the doctor. 'As we picked him up,' said Naismith, 'Lt Cdr Waghorn was smiling and he said "Bloody nice to see you" and then "I'm looking forward to a beer on board".'

537 winched up the remaining five men, and the Sea Kings returned to *Olna*, where the fog was as thick as ever. Both helicopters had to make emergency low visibility ship-controlled approaches to find the deck and, with the ship still rolling more than ten degrees each way, had to pick their moments carefully to land on.

It had been a tense and tiring 36-hour rescue operation in which, as everybody realised, the aircraft had frequently been operated outside limitations. It was the highest stretcher lift 'Scouse' Doyle, a very experienced aircrewman, had ever achieved. 'I was proud to be involved with a team who showed such professionalism in what I can only describe as an alien environment,' he said. 'I would not have missed it for the world!' said Gurney Hickey.

RFA *Olna* began the return to the Falklands the next day. The two Sea Kings were launched at a range of 150 miles to casevac Waghorn and his JSE companions to the local hospital at Stanley. But 529 suffered a transmission oil leak en route and had to make a 26-mile emergency dash to land on Lively Island. 537 picked up the passengers and took them on to Stanley.

Thomson and his 826 NAS colleagues, and *Endurance*'s Wasp Flight, together received Commander-in-Chief's Commendations and the Guild of Air Pilots and Air Navigators Prince Philip Helicopter Rescue award for 1985 for what the Guild called 'their splendid efforts' in Antarctica.

16 The Late Eighties: Russian Forgers and Royal Yachts

While Cdr Waghorn was being flown home to the United Kingdom where he made a complete recovery (although 529, the Sea King which rescued him, was destroyed in a mid-air collision on patrol off the Falklands on 27 June) the season at home was well under way. In April 771 NAS polished their skills with the highly professional rescue of seven men from the 400-ton coaster *Caroline*.

Caroline was a somewhat accident-prone vessel, having been rescued off Portland the previous November by the frigate HMS *Active* when she was taking in water and had suffered engine failure. On 7 April *Caroline*, with a cargo of fertiliser, was about three miles south of the Lizard when she developed a leak in her starboard bilges and began to list so heavily she put out a 'May Day' call.

'Rescue 77', a Wessex 5 of 771 NAS (Lt Andy Marshall, POACMN Roy Eggleston, and diver POACMN Larry Slater) was already airborne and was sent to the scene. Six crew members were double-lifted up from their liferaft by Slater who then went down again to recover one more man from the vessel's stern.

An eighth man, who had insisted on staying on board, then took to a dinghy secured to the coaster and only let go the line as she was actually turning over. He was eventually taken on board the Lizard lifeboat. Then, as though to bring the whole episode to a neat and proper conclusion, *Caroline* sank,

At 7.13 am on Sunday 23 June, an Air India Boeing 747 'Jumbo' jet, Flight Number A1 182, with 329 people on board, suddenly disappeared from the radar screens at Air Traffic Control, Shanwick, in Ireland. Flight AI 182 was then over the Atlantic some 160 miles west of Cork, bound for Bombay and Delhi, via Heathrow.

A major rescue operation went into action, controlled by the RAF Rescue Co-Ordination Centre at Plymouth, which eventually involved more than twenty fixed wing aircraft and helicopters of the Navy and the RAF, ships of the Irish Navy, and the seabed operations vessel HMS *Challenger*.

The first Sea King of 706 NAS (Lt Gordon Jones, second pilot Lt Tansey Lea (of 810 NAS), observer Lt Rod Cox, CPOACMN Tony Dunmore, with

Surg Lt Richard Cribb and MT1 Kemp) took off soon after 9 am, quickly followed by a second (Lt Jim Laird, Lt Hugo Stacey, observer Lt Chris Sutton, CPOACMN Roy Henshaw, with Surg Lt Lawrence Roberts, and POMA 'Taff' Lander). Both Sea Kings flew to the forward base at Cork airport. Two more 706 NAS Sea Kings arrived later in the day.

The scene of the crash was easy to find. Debris and bodies were strewn over a wide area. 'Once there,' said Lt Gordon Jones, 'it was no difficulty spotting them. It was a grim task for the aircrewmen, who did a fine job.'

As the day went on and the helicopters quartered the sea, it became clear there were no survivors. By the end of that day, a total of 139 bodies and some floating wreckage had been recovered. The first two 706 NAS Sea Kings recovered 22 bodies and the two later Sea Kings another two. The bodies were landed on the container ship MV *Normand Astel* and taken to Cork.

Challenger, whose flight deck the helicopters had used for refuelling, remained in the area for some time to locate wreckage on the sea bed, some 6,000 to 7,000 feet below.

A curious SAR incident took place in July 1985, when the Type 42 destroyer HMS *Newcastle* (Captain P.J. Erskine, RN) and RFA *Olna* (Captain J.M.M. Wilkins, RFA) were taking part in a NATO effort to monitor Soviet naval exercises in the Eastern Atlantic and off Norway. Both ships were in the Norwegian Sea in company with the Russian *Kiev* Task Group, consisting of up to ten Soviet warships including the aircraft carrier *Kiev* herself and the cruiser *Kirov*.

On the afternoon of 21 July, *Newcastle* witnessed *Kiev* launch eight VSTOL 'Forger' fighter aircraft. The Forgers returned in two groups of four. The first group were recovered successfully, but the last aircraft of the second group approached much too fast so that it rapidly closed on the third aircraft which was still on its final approach.

Trying to reduce speed, the last Forger increased its nose-up angle and seemed to attempt to use its ability to hover, like a Sea Harrier. But either through equipment failure or pilot error the aircraft assumed too great an angle and stalled. The pilot ejected successfully, while his Forger continued to rotate and hit the water, intact, on its back and sank at once.

Newcastle manoeuvred to close and launched her Tornado (rigid inflatable boat) to help if needed. Meanwhile, *Kiev*'s SAR helicopter approached and tried to winch the pilot up. But he was caught in his parachute lines and could not reach the strop. The Tornado (Coxswain AB J.I. Cresdee, bowman AB N.C. Sinclair, and CPO(D) M.J.S. Mason as diver) went alongside the pilot, freed him and helped him into the strop.

Again, *Kiev*'s SAR helicopter tried to winch. Again, the pilot became entangled in the parachute harness and had to be cut free by the Tornado crew before he could be winched up. As the helicopter flew back to *Kiev*, the Tornado crew recovered the parachute and inflatable dinghy and returned them to one of *Kiev*'s boats. The Forger pilot was seen to walk from the helicopter to a stretcher on *Kiev*'s flight deck.

POACMN Slater going down on the wire to rescue members of the crew of the coaster *Caroline* off the Lizard, April 1985

Later, *Kiev*'s SAR helicopter was relaunched and came to the hover close to *Newcastle*'s port bridge wing. The pilot clapped his hands and waved to men on *Newcastle*'s upper deck, before wheeling away back to *Kiev*.

Newcastle signalled 'We all regret your aircraft accident and hope the pilot is not hurt', to which *Kiev* replied, 'Health of pilot is well. Thanks for help.'

As usual, at home August was the peak month of the season and August 1985 included two Culdrose rescues which occurred within hours of each other. Both were difficult and dangerous. Both demanded equal skill and courage of the SAR helicopter crews. But whereas one rescue achieved world-wide publicity, because of the personalities involved, the other passed almost unnoticed.

Very early on the morning of 11 August, Falmouth Coastguard asked for helicopter assistance for the 36-foot yacht *Mister Cube*, disabled in severe weather some 55 miles south-east of the Lizard. The yacht was returning to Britain after a two-week holiday with nine people on board, three adults and six children, aged from six to fourteen.

'Rescue 77' Wessex of 771 NAS (Lt David Marr, POACMN Mike Palmer, diver POACMN Larry Slater) took off knowing that flying conditions were marginal. The weather was appalling, the cloud base often down to 150 feet, with low visibility in periodical squalls of torrential rain, the sea state 7, and the wind gusting 50 knots.

Lack of radar cover meant that they had to make an ultra low level visual departure from the Lizard which added to Palmer's navigational problems. Palmer had to work out their own and the yacht's positions largely from dead reckoning, updated by information passed from a merchantman.

When the Wessex arrived over the yacht in very poor visibility, *Mister Cube* was beam on to the sea and being pounded by 25 foot waves, her sails blown to shreds, her masts whipping through arcs of more than 90 degrees, while her hull was plunging up and down like a maddened animal in the swell.

Marr decided on a Hi-line transfer and, aided by a flawless commentary over the intercom from Palmer, succeeded in putting Slater down on to the yacht's foredeck to supervise the transfers. Slater, a very experienced SAR diver on his third tour of duty with 771 NAS, fought his way aft through a mess of sails and thrashing rigging to reassure the nine survivors and brief them on the method used to rescue them.

The three eldest children were Hi-line single-lifted and the three youngest – Lucinda Bell, aged six, and the twins Justin and Crispin Sykesball, aged seven, were Hi-line double-lifted with Slater. Two adults were Hi-line single-lifted. Twice during the rescue the Hi-line snapped when the yacht was thrown onto its beam ends. Each time Palmer calmly rerigged and went on with his work.

Slater had now completed three double lifts and supervised five single lifts, and there was only one survivor and one double-lift to go, when the yacht was knocked down onto its side again by a giant wave. Miraculously, he and the last survivor hung on long enough for Marr to position the Wessex and lift them clear. As they swung away from the yacht, Slater coolly cut the Hi-line and he and the survivor were winched into the Wessex which then recovered safely and with no more ado to Culdrose. It was, as the official report later made clear, an exceptional rescue by an exceptional helicopter crew.

The day was by no means over for 'Rescue 77' which was scrambled again just after 2 pm that afternoon (Lt David Coles, Palmer and Slater again). Falmouth Coastguard had asked once again for helicopter assistance: the yacht *Drum England*, one of the contestants in that year's Fastnet Race, had capsized about 1½ miles off the small Cornish village of Portscatho.

Again, the weather was marginal for rescue, with sea state 5, low cloud and low visibility in frequent heavy rain showers, and wind gusting over 35 knots. When the Wessex arrived, the crew saw an upturned hull, 77 foot long, with no keel, and no less than eighteen people crouching on top. The survivors made signs to indicate that there were more people below, trapped under the hull. Coles decided to dispatch the SAR diver and, guided by Palmer, established a hover close to the yacht.

Slater, who had taken part in the 1979 Fastnet Race rescues, jumped from

Mister Cube survivors with their rescuers, POACMN Larry Slater, POACMN Michael Palmer, and Lt David Marr RN

the helicopter and after free swimming to the vessel climbed on board to reassure the people on top of the upturned hull. Slater dived under the hull and, making his way underwater through a snarl of tangled wires and rigging and blockages caused by torn sails, he discovered a rope locker and a white hatch cover which was shut. He returned to the surface where those sitting on the hull assured him the hatch was the entrance to the cabin below.

Slater dived down again, slid back the white hatch and felt his hands grabbed from above. He was pulled upwards and found six more men, including the yacht's owner, Simon Le Bon, the lead singer of the pop group

Duran Duran, still alive in an air pocket. They were standing waist deep in water mixed with fuel and battery acid. The atmosphere was thick with the smell of diesel and whiffs of chlorine gas.

Slater's first task was to reassure the six that if they did exactly as he told them they would be safe. He told them he would first return to the helicopter and get breathing sets for them. As he ducked under the water, somebody said 'Don't be long'.

But having obtained more breathing sets, Slater decided the gear was too bulky and cumbersome and he would do a 'free escape' after all. He told the survivors each to take a deep breath, then lower themselves one at a time through the open hatch where he would be waiting for them. He would take charge of them and do the rest.

Six times Slater dived down to the hatch, grabbed the emerging figure by the ankles, pulled him down through the hatch and guided him to the surface. It all went very well. Only one survivor 'got a little excited' and struggled, knocking Slater's face mask off. As for the rest, 'once out,' Slater said, 'they could see sunlight and knew which way to go!'

Slater then stayed on the yacht's deck to supervise the winching of twenty of *Drum England*'s crew who were then shuttled ashore in the Wessex. The remaining four were taken off by the Falmouth lifeboat. All survived, although some had to go to hospital for check-ups. Le Bon said later, 'We all owe our lives to the helicopter crew, the lifeboatmen and the coastguards.'

Next day, Simon Le Bon and three of his crew were back on *Drum England*'s hull inspecting the damage, although the weather was still rough. 'Rescue 77' (Coles and POACMN Roy Eggleston) happened to be passing after answering a call to lift off three people trapped fifteen feet up a cliff by the incoming tide at Caerhays Beach. Coles saw Le Bon waving and after consulting base decided to lift the four off. So, for the second time in two days, Simon Le Bon was rescued by Rescue 77.

The *Drum England* incident caught the nation's imagination and media attention. The rescue of the nine people from *Mister Cube* attracted much less attention. But the Fleet Air Arm was in no doubt of the skill, courage and dedication required to carry out the *Mister Cube* rescue. Marr and Palmer both received the Queen's Commendation for Valuable Service in the Air.

For his part in both rescues that day, in which 29 people were rescued by helicopter, Larry Slater was awarded the George Medal. He was understandably proud and delighted, but was quick to give credit to his peers. 'Don't forget,' he told the press, 'I was in the right place at the right time – it could have been any one of six duty divers at Culdrose. I regard the medal as recognition of them as well.' That was well said.

On the same day as Le Bon's rescue, but on the other side of the Atlantic, there was a classical demonstration of the way in which an SAR incident could develop from normal operational flying and how helicopter crews had to be prepared to drop whatever they were doing at any time and undertake an SAR sortie.

On 12 August, the Lynx of the frigate HMS *Alacrity*'s Ship's Flight had disembarked to the US Naval Air Station at Roosevelt Roads, Puerto Rico, to carry out day and night flying practise. The weather forecast for night flying was pessimistic, with the approach of a tropical squall, but Lt Martyn Reid, observer and Ship's Flight commander, decided to continue the flight as long as possible. Reid and his pilot Lt Michael Burrows had completed one more circuit to the runway, and were about to taxi back to the hangar when a 'May Day' call was heard from a light aircraft which had ditched off the island of Vieques, about ten miles away.

Reid and Burrows took off again at once. Heavy rain and low cloud forced them to stay in visual contact with the sea but they reached the search area and found the ditched aircraft some twenty yards off a beach, with two survivors on the beach.

The rain now became a torrential tropical downpour, with strong gusting winds and flashes of lightning. Despite the heavy rain, and the panicking state of one of the survivors, Reid successfully winched them both up. Burrows' initial approach to Roosevelt Roads was thwarted by low cloud and drenching rain, so he had to fly around the coast of Puerto Rico before making a safe landing at the airfield.

Reid and Burrows were both awarded the Queen's Commendation for Valuable Service in the Air. (Reid had previously been awarded the QCVSA for his part in the MV *Melpol* off Portland on 8 December 1981, and shared with his crew the Edward and Maisie Lewis Trophy for 1982).

Waghorn's rescuers in the Antarctic must have been strong contenders for the Boyd Trophy. Instead it went to the Lynx Ship's Flight of the Type 22 destroyer HMS *Beaver* for a rescue in home waters. On 6 October 1985, the newly completed *Beaver* was some 300 miles out in the Western Approaches in the course of her Operational Work Up after first commissioning. Just before 7 pm, she received a signal from CINCFLEET that the Japanese ship *Reefer Dolphin*, four hundred miles south-west of Land's End, had been hit by a freak wave, with one man dead and two seriously injured. The Dutch frigate HNMLS *Banckert* was on her way to help with a helicopter and a doctor. *Beaver* was told to report if she was able to assist.

Beaver assessed that she was within 80 miles of *Reefer Dolphin*, scrambled her Lynx, and signalled CINCFLEET that she was heading north and offering medical assistance. The Lynx (Lt Cdr Tim Williams, observer Lt Philip Needham) was launched with PO Medical Assistant Martin on board just after 7.30 pm and headed for the likeliest intercept point with *Reefer Dolphin*. The French weather ship *France 1* was also proceeding to give medical help.

A revised position for *Reefer Dolphin* was received at 8.45 pm and *Beaver* altered course to the west and increased speed to 28 knots. The Lynx was recovered at 9.30 having failed to find *Reefer Dolphin*, but communications were established with *Reefer Dolphin* herself at 10.10 pm. It was learned shortly afterwards that *France 1* had failed to transfer her doctor because of the weather.

Beaver was in touch with *Reefer Dolphin* on VHF just after midnight and actually sighted and positively identified the ship herself at 12.25 am. The night was very dark and clear, but there was little horizon. *Reefer Dolphin* was steering east-north-east, rolling and pitching as she ran before a heavy, confused swell and a strong westerly gale force wind gusting to 30 knots.

Reefer Dolphin slowed down to about 5 knots and at 1 am *Beaver* turned in under her stern to assess the situation. Despite the darkness and the weather, and *France 1*'s earlier failure, it was decided to send a boarding party across to assess the medical condition of the two casualties. *Beaver*'s rigid inflatable boat was launched at 1.10 am, with a crew of three and PO Martin and AEM Evans on board. Although *Reefer Dolphin* was rolling violently and the boat itself was plunging up and down unpredictably, the boat was held against *Reefer Dolphin*'s side while the rescue team boarded her.

Martin's examination showed that one patient had two broken legs, and the other a broken jaw, multiple abrasions, and internal bleeding. For this man the only hope was urgent transfer to hospital, and the only way to achieve that was by helicopter.

The Lynx was launched at 2.10 am to assess conditions. It was decided to use a modified Hi-line transfer method. A transfer position was chosen on *Reefer Dolphin*'s fo'c'sle, between a stump mast and a gantry. To approach it, the Lynx had to fly backwards, very close to wildly swaying masts and with the rotors only a few feet from obstructions. Brilliant white lighting below, necessary for those on deck to see what they were doing, denied Williams any stable reference points for his hover.

In spite of these very difficult and dangerous conditions, Williams accomplished five separate approaches and winchings. A stretcher was lowered at 2.30 am and the first casualty lifted off at 2.45. In the next hour, the Lynx made three more sorties, to lift off the second very badly injured patient, Evans and Martin.

At 3.45 *Reefer Dolphin* resumed her course for Brest. *Beaver* recovered her Lynx a few minutes later and headed towards Land's End and HNMLS *Banckert* (who had been warned to expect *Beaver*'s Lynx) at 28 knots. The Lynx was launched at 5.10 am with the two casualties and PO Martin, landed to refuel on *Banckert* at 6.20, relaunched ten minutes later and arrived at Treliske Hospital, Truro, at 8.05. But, sadly, the man with severe internal injuries had died during the flight an hour earlier.

Beaver's Lynx refuelled at Culdrose and flew on to Portland, landing there at 10.20, after fifteen hectic hours in action. Besides the Boyd Trophy, Williams and Needham both received Queen's Commendations for Valuable Service in the Air.

The New Year of 1986 opened with a major rescue operation in an unexpected locale and with some unusual participants. In January there was an uprising against the government of South Yemen which soon developed into a civil war. Much of the city of Aden was burning and there was gunfire in the streets. As in Cyprus in 1974, several hundred foreign nationals were caught up

Surg. Cdr Jolly entangled in the rigging of the foremast of the French fishing vessel *Menkar*, April 1987. He was lucky not to fall to the deck, but managed to improvise a jury hoist for himself and his patient

in the turmoil and needed evacuation and, again as in 1974, the cry was 'The Navy's here!'

At the time, the destroyer HMS *Newcastle*, the frigate HMS *Jupiter*, the survey vessel HMS *Hydra* and the RFA *Brambleleaf* were all on deployment in the Indian Ocean and all became involved in the rescue. However, the operation was not to be a simple rescue from the beaches. Rebel leaders would not allow warships inside the twelve mile territorial limit, not even for humanitarian purposes.

This situation of seeming impasse was unexpectedly resolved by the arrival on the scene of HMY *Britannia*, on passage to New Zealand. She was patently not a warship and was eminently suitable for rescue. *Britannia* sent her boats ashore to pick up some 430 people, including mothers, children and grandmothers, who waded out from the beach to embark in the boats.

When the people waiting on the beach saw the Royal Yacht all lit up, 'there was a lump in everybody's throats,' one man said. 'When the boats came ashore there was a wonderful feeling.'

'As *Britannia* was waiting just off the coast,' said one evacuee, 'the whole town was enveloped in black smoke as if everything was burning. And then they decided to have a deck party and the Band came up and played 'Somewhere Over the Rainbow'. We had two Soviet warships each side observing it all with complete disbelief, and all the while there was Aden burning. It has to be said we do it in style.'

On board, the evacuees were amazed by their reception. They were welcomed with towels, blankets, hot soup and 'tiddy oggies'. They were put into cabins and Royal Yachtsmen took it in turns to babysit while parents bathed and showered. For some it was the first change of clothing for at least a week. Those who were wearing only T-shirts or bathing costumes were kitted out with naval gear. Meanwhile, the Royal Marine band played Glenn Miller and selections from musicals and light opera on the quarterdeck.

'In one Royal room,' said another, 'we had to step over 64 bodies sleeping beneath a signed photograph of the Queen Mother. Ship's flags and buntings were laid over the floor to protect the deep-pile carpets. The contrast was bizarre – the very room where the Queen entertains was simply full of people dossing down! I cannot speak too highly of the crew. They were marvellous.'

'We were expecting some old jalopy from Djibouti to turn up,' said another, 'but it was magic seeing the *Britannia* – like a fairy story. The crew were absolutely fantastic.'

'What we would have done if the *Britannia* had not appeared,' said Mr Arthur Marshall, the British Ambassador in Aden, 'I shudder to think. It would have been a bloodbath of unspeakable proportions.'

Britannia took the first evacuees 150 miles across to Djibouti on the East African coast and then returned for another 209, many of whom were transferred to *Jupiter* and also landed at Djibouti. *Britannia* embarked a third party of another 450 people and ferried them to Djibouti. In all, *Britannia* evacuated about 1,000 people of 50 nationalities, including some 100 British. Her boats were also used to ferry Soviet citizens to waiting Soviet ships.

In fact, there was, as the Flag Officer Royal Yachts, Rear Admiral John Garnier, said at the time 'a fine atmosphere of international co-operation here – the French, Soviets and us. We are talking regularly and pooling our information.' The Admiral said later that although *Britannia* had received most of the publicity, *Newcastle* and *Jupiter* had 'played a blinder'.

Newcastle was detached to the north of Aden to try and evacuate a large number of refugees who had gathered on the beaches there. After two days of negotiations, the rebel chieftain in control of the area gave permission for evacuation to begin but insisted that, once again, no warships were to be used. This ban even included *Brambleleaf*, who was painted grey (and had already been fired on).

Fortunately, the P&O offered the services of one of their merchant ships, the *Diamond Princess*, which was in the area. *Newcastle* and *Diamond Princess* rendezvoused some twenty miles off the coast at dusk on 22 January. The Lynx (Sub Lt Stephen James) was launched to transfer *Newcastle*'s Operations Officer and a radio operator to co-ordinate and control affairs on board *Diamond Princess*.

At dawn on 23 January *Diamond Princess* went inshore and evacuated most of the refugees. One party had assembled some distance away and the ship went back for them later. *Newcastle* and *Diamond Princess* rendezvoused at 7.30 am twelve miles offshore to transfer the evacuees by boat to *Newcastle* so that *Diamond Princess* could continue on her business. But the sea was too rough for boatwork and after one attempt the boat transfer was called off.

Newcastle's Ship's Flight then suggested transferring at least some of the refugees in the Lynx, winching them up from the *Diamond Princess*'s small fo'c'sle and landing them on *Newcastle*'s flight deck, and taking food across to *Diamond Princess* on the return flights.

The Lynx, with all its seats removed, was launched at 8.20 am, beginning what was to become a marathon flight transfer by taking six more of *Newcastle*'s ship's company across to *Diamond Princess* to join the two already there in organising the evacuees and their baggage. The Lynx then returned for the first sack of food, and transfers of food went on during the first half of the operation.

Six people were transferred on each trip, and in all 248 refugees were transferred, of all nationalities including Swedish, French, Filipino and British. Evacuees were winched up by single strop, except for the children who were double-lifted with the aircrewman. Each evacuee was allowed one bag or suitcase.

The Lynx flew for eight hours and twenty minutes that day, with two fifteen minute stops, to check aircraft oil levels etc., allow the aircrew a rest from the concentration of flying (and to give the observer's knees relief from the weight of children sitting on them). Refuelling was done with rotors running when dropping evacuees. In all, 308 winch transfers were carried out, including the transfer of *Newcastle*'s crew members back and forth and the transfer of food – very possibly a daily record for the Fleet Air Arm.

At home, in very different conditions of weather and temperature, 819 NAS experienced in one sortie, which was really three SAR sorties in one, most of the difficulties and problems of flying helicopters in the Highlands and islands of Scotland.

The afternoon of Saturday 11 January 1986 was raw and blustery at Prestwick, with a strong wind blowing in off the Irish Sea. It was the sort of afternoon when any sensible person would be sat with feet up in front of a

Jolly with improvised hoist after *Menkar* incident

roaring fire watching the telly. But at 3.25 the Rescue Co-Ordination Centre at Pitreavie requested a helicopter to assist in the search for a man reported lost overboard from a French trawler thirty miles south of the Outer Hebrides.

The duty Sea King (Lt G.R. Lewis, second pilot Lt C.P. Maude, observer Lt M.P. Davis, LACMN A.J. Cooke, LMA E.G. Batchelor) launched at 4.05 pm in poor visibility, with the wind gusting over 45 knots from the north-west and occasional showers of sleet, and arrived at the scene at 5.35. Two other trawlers were already searching for the lost man, and the Barra lifeboat was on its way, but was being hampered by bad weather.

Shortly after the Sea King arrived, it was reported that another trawler, the *Magdaleine*, had an injured seaman on board. As it was now dark, Lewis decided to abandon the search for the man overboard and take off the injured man instead. But *Magdaleine* had lost steerage way and radio communications and three attempts to winch the injured man off by hi-line failed.

Meanwhile, the weather had been steadily getting worse, with the wind rising to over 80 knots in gusts, and the snow showers becoming heavier and more frequent. After a particularly heavy snow shower had forced Lewis to abandon the third hi-line attempt, he decided to fly to the island of Barra to inspect the aircraft. A landing was made, assisted by the cross headlights of two police vehicles, in a field on Barra. A visual inspection was made and the Sea King was then flown on to Benbecula for refuelling, landing there just before 8 pm.

While the Sea King was being refuelled, *Gannet* received a further report from Pitreavie of a road traffic casualty on the island of Mull – a woman who needed urgent transport to Glasgow hospital if her severed leg was to be saved. With the wind still in the north-west, at 55 knots with gusts of over 70, the quickest way to do this was for the Sea King to pick up the casualty on the flight from Benbecula to Prestwick.

The Sea King was launched just before 9 pm and reached Glenforsa at half past, after a low level radar transit through the one-mile wide Sound of Mull. Another landing was made in a field, lit only by police vehicle headlights. The woman was stretchered into the aircraft and flown to Glasgow airport through the Crinan Canal route – a flight which in low visibility required a very high degree of crew cooperation between both pilots and observer.

The Sea King landed at Renfrew airport at 10.45 pm and the injured woman was taken to Southern General Hospital where her leg was successfully re-attached to her body. Meanwhile, the Sea King returned uneventfully to Prestwick, landing on at 11.45, after a total flight time of over seven and a half hours, all of it in extreme weather conditions.

It had been an admirable performance by Lewis and his crew. They had responded to one change of plan and situation after another, and had supported each other and kept alert and cheerful throughout a long day of miserable weather.

In 1986 the Alan Marsh Medal was awarded to Lt Wayne Taylor of 706 NAS for an SAR sortie which once again showed the Sea King's surpassing ability to fly in almost blind conditions.

In the early hours of Saturday 15 February 1986, the Duty SAR Sea King at Culdrose, Rescue 88 (Taylor, observer Lt Kevin Wesley), launched to recover a Royal Marine who had fallen on Dartmoor and was lying unconscious in freezing weather. It was reported that an RAF Wessex had already made several unsuccessful attempts, being thwarted by severe gale force winds and poor visibility in driving rain and low cloud.

After letting down and approaching Plymouth using a 'blind pilotage' technique, Rescue 88 made three low-level attempts to rescue the man, but was forced back each time by low cloud and very poor horizontal visibility. As the vertical visibility was much better, the Sea King then tried high-level approaches. In spite of the proximity of Princeton Mast (which was never actually sighted during the rescue) and by the very rugged high ground where the Marine was lying, the Sea King let down successfully at the third high-level attempt. The injured man was lifted up and taken to hospital in Plymouth.

771 NAS at Culdrose had already been in action in January when the duty Wessex 5 was scrambled at 11.35 am on 27th to look for the yacht *Double Cross*, reported to be taking in water some 18 miles south-west of the Lizard. Once on the scene, the Wessex began a search and found the yacht, with one person on board, three miles from the datum position given.

LACMN/Diver Ian Penhaligon was lowered on to the yacht, followed by a pump to help bail the vessel out. A second Wessex joined the rescue, together with the container ship MV *Atlantic Song*, the cable ship *Alert*, HMS *Upton* and the Penlee lifeboat. The yacht was eventually towed into harbour.

The same diver, Ian Penhaligon, carried out a very brave rescue attempt on 6 April, after a report that a 16-year-old youth had been swept into the sea at Mullion Harbour in Cornwall. The weather was appalling, with very poor visibility, high winds and huge waves rolling through the harbour entrance. Having established that the boy was believed to be still somewhere in the harbour, Penhaligon dropped from the Wessex into the water.

After a dive of about three minutes, he surfaced to indicate that underwater visibility was zero. However, he went on with the search in extremely dangerous conditions. Shortly afterwards, a Coastguard patrol sighted some clothing in a sea cave, and the Wessex went to investigate. With the tail rotor turning only feet from the cliff face, Penhaligon was lowered to just above wave height. Guided by Penhaligon, the Wessex was manoeuvred until he could see inside the cave.

There was nobody in the cave but the rescue attempt was not over. There was a report that a boy's body had been washed ashore in Mullion Harbour. The Wessex flew back and Penhaligon was lowered down once more. He found the boy, began heart massage, placed the casualty on a portable ventilator, and continued the heart massage while they were both being winched up.

Unfortunately, in spite of all Penhaligon's efforts, the boy was pronounced

Sea King of 820 NAS from *Ark Royal* winching up a survivor of the 998-ton West German trawler *Hessen* in the Pentland Firth, 26 June 1987

dead. Penhaligon was later awarded the Queen's Gallantry Medal.

There were at least two more outstanding rescues, at opposite ends of the country, later that year. At dusk on 31 October the duty SAR 819 NAS Sea King launched to evacuate two casualties from the Liberian tanker *Don Humverta*, some 30 miles west of Tiree and 110 miles from Prestwick. When the helicopter arrived the night was pitch black, with occasional lightning flashes, cloud at 1,000 feet and heavy showers of hail. The tanker was rolling heavily, so that her tank deck was regularly swamped, in a forty foot swell and winds rising to 60 knots.

Both casualties – one with an open leg fracture, the other with a broken collar-bone – had been caused by falls in the heavy seas. A Medical Assistant was lowered down to assess the injuries, followed by LACMN Anthony Gardiner with a stretcher.

As Gardiner was releasing himself from the winch-hook, the ship gave such a heavy roll to port that the deck edge sank beneath the swell. The tank deck was immediately submerged and the stretcher was washed away into the darkness towards the ship's side. Gardiner jumped after it, caught it, and held the stretcher and himself against the guard rail until the water level had subsided. Although he was pinned to the guard rail again by another wave, he put the first casualty into the stretcher and they were both winched up.

With the casualty safely in the Sea King, Gardiner came down again for the second man and completed the winching with no further excitement. Gardiner himself was awarded the Queen's Commendation for Brave Conduct.

On 20 November, as night was falling on a dreary autumn day in the Solent, a vehicle with two women on board went into the water at Fishbourne ferry terminal on the Isle of Wight. When the SAR Wessex from Lee-on-Solent arrived at dusk twenty minutes later, its crew – Lt John Humphries and POACMN Bob Murdoch – did not know how long the jeep-type vehicle had been underwater and believed there was still a chance of saving life.

Although underwater visibility was only a few inches and the sea-bed was littered with debris and obstructions, Murdoch found the vehicle on his first dive. It was upside down and a strong tide was rocking it dangerously from side to side. Murdoch managed to get both front doors open, but the tidal flow kept shutting them as he went inside. After about fifteen minutes he found one of the occupants, who showed no sign of life.

Murdoch surfaced and was winched back into the aircraft. It was now quite dark, although the water surface was lit by the ferry terminal floodlights. Murdoch told Humphries that he thought it just possible there was a second occupant still alive in an airpocket and another dive would be worthwhile.

Humphries, himself a qualified SAR diver, decided that in these hazardous conditions two divers were needed. He flew the aircraft back to *Daedalus*, handed it over to another pilot and, returning to the scene fifteen minutes later, jumped into the water with Murdoch. When they found the vehicle again, Humphries tried to get in through a door but the tide prevented him as it had Murdoch.

The vehicle had a soft top, so Humphries then cut his way through from underneath. The bodies of the two women were recovered after a dive of about 30 minutes. Humphries and Murdoch were both awarded Queen's Commendations for Brave Conduct.

Early in 1987 the winter turned suddenly severe, with a sharp freeze, and fierce gales and blizzards sweeping over much of the country. 819 NAS at Prestwick were once more in the front line. In January they carried out a dramatic and newsworthy sortie to save the life of an 11-year-old girl with suspected meningitis. Her own doctor could not get through the deep snow to her home near Airdrie, so police, prison officers and inmates of a nearby local remand centre cleared a landing pad for the Sea King, piloted by Captain Don Henry, Canadian Armed Forces, which took the girl to hospital, and eventual recovery, in Glasgow.

At Culdrose, high winds and four foot deep snow drifts brought traffic to a standstill in the roads leading to the Air Station. The Captain, Commander (Air), heads of departments and over 100 ratings turned out to clear the main runway, so that the Wessex and Sea Kings could take supplies to communities cut off from water, heat and electricity, delivering coal to isolated villages and heating oil to a cliff top nursing home.

In 1987 Culdrose celebrated its 40th anniversary since its first commissioning as HMS *Seahawk* on 17 April 1947, when it was known as the 'Naval Fighter School'. After divisions that first day, there was an aerial display by Fireflies from RNAS St Merryn, and a low level formation flypast by five Seafire F17s from the School of Naval Air Warfare.

On the Air Day that year, 29 July 1987, the only Firefly was in the Historic Flight, with a Sea Fury and a Swordfish. There was no Seafire but a Spitfire from Shuttleworth. Also in the fly pasts, as signs of how things had moved on in forty years, were Concorde, Sea Harrier, Phantom and Super Etendard. Helicopter displays were given by the Sharks' Gazelles, and by the 'Piranhas' – RNAS Culdrose Sea King Display Team.

In the late 1980s, there was a spate of well publicised incidents, almost as though the whole country was enduring an epidemic of transport disasters and high profile rescues. These, of necessity, also involved helicopter SAR crews. Their traditional and seasonal work went on as usual, as it had for the past forty years. But now they were linked with headline names – *Herald of Free Enterprise, Virgin Atlantic Flyer*, Piper Alpha, Lockerbie. There was also to be a major reappraisal of the national organisation, resources and financing of Search and Rescue.

17 The Way Ahead

In December 1985, the fishing vessel *Bon Ami* went aground on the north-west coast of Scotland and six fishermen lost their lives. There was no SAR helicopter at Stornoway, the official view at that time being that military SAR requirements in Scotland were adequately covered from Leuchars and Lossiemouth. It was true that SAR was established, and maintained, for military purposes. But in peacetime more than 90% of SAR call-outs are on behalf of the civil community, and these civil emergencies provide valuable training for SAR crews. The *Bon Ami* incident brought to public and painful notice a deficiency in the country-wide SAR coverage along the north-west coast of Scotland, where military SAR helicopters could not respond in time to a civil emergency.

After the *Bon Ami* incident, the UK SAR Committee appointed a Helicopter Coverage Group (HCG) to review SAR helicopter cover round the UK as a whole, but with special reference to north-west Scotland. In December 1986 the HCG reported its findings, noted that SAR cover in north-west Scotland was lacking and recommended that night/all weather cover be improved in the central part of the English Channel (because Lee-on-Solent's Wessex flew only by day), the South-west Approaches and the north Irish Sea.

As a result of meetings and deliberations in Whitehall, improvements were made over the next two years. In May 1987, Bristow Helicopters began to operate a Sikorsky S-61 on behalf of the UK Coastguard at Stornoway. By the beginning of 1988 there were suggestions that the whole of the UK SAR service be thrown open to commercial tender for eventual privatisation. But in February 1988 it was decided upon a mixed military/commercial service.

The Wessex HU5 was withdrawn from SAR service at Culdrose and at Lee-on-Solent in April 1988. The emphasis of military flying along the south coast having shifted to Portland, the detached SAR Flight of 772 NAS at Lee-on-Solent was closed down on 1 April, after fifteen years' service during which it was concerned with the rescue of more than 1,000 people. 771 NAS at Culdrose was re-equipped with the Sea King Mark 5, to provide military and Department of Transport SAR cover from Tregonnick Point in Cornwall to Start Point in Devon. 772 NAS at Portland provided a Sea King Mark 4 for SAR cover between Start Point in the west and Bournemouth Pier in the east.

By the end of 1988, Bristows were operating three Sikorsky S-61Ns under contract to the Department of Transport for SAR purposes under Coastguard control, based at Sumburgh in the Shetlands, Stornoway, and Lee-on-Solent.

819 NAS at Prestwick provided a Sea King specifically for SAR at fifteen minutes notice from 31 July 1989. From then onwards, helicopters formally declared by the Ministry of Defence for SAR duties were deployed at eleven locations: Sea Kings at RNAS Culdrose, Portland and Prestwick, and at RAF Lossiemouth, Boulmer, Manston, Leconfield, and Wessex at RAF Leuchars, Coltishall, Chivenor and Valley. The helicopters were at 15 minutes notice in daytime and 45 minutes by night – although, in practice, they were often airborne within two or three minutes of a 'Scramble'.

These helicopter facilities took their place within a country-wide organisation in which the Ministry of Defence coordinated its military operations and those involving civil aircraft from Rescue Co-Ordination Centres (RCC) at Pitreavie, near Edinburgh, and at Plymouth. Civil Maritime SAR operations were co-ordinated and controlled by HM Coastguard through continuously manned Maritime Rescue Co-Ordination Centres (MRCC) at Aberdeen, Yarmouth, Dover, Falmouth, Swansea and the Clyde, and eighteen Maritime Rescue Co-ordination Sub Centres (MRSCs) spread around the country.

The passing of the Wessex from front-line service was marked by fly-pasts at Culdrose, Portland and Lee-on-Solent on 31 March, 1988. The same day also marked the end of twenty-five years of front-line service of the Wasp, when 829 NAS at Portland – who had taken delivery of the first Wasp in 1963 – said goodbye (985 Wasps later) with a formal farewell.

A few days earlier, the Wasps of two frigates, HMS *Achilles* and *Ariadne*, had had their final flights. *Achilles*' Wasp was actually older than the ship, being built in 1966. The last take-off was made by Lt David Edward, the flight commander, with LACMN Steve Truick in the left hand seat. Edwards completed 2,000 flying hours on Wasps during the trip and also made his 1,000th deck landing.

Perhaps the very last Ship's Flight Wasp was the frigate HMS *Ariadne*'s which, piloted by Sub Lt Mike Langley – the most junior (and only) sub-lieutenant Flight Commander afloat – escorted the ship into Portsmouth for refit in May 1988. This aircraft took part in one of the very last major Wasp rescue operations.

Early on 5 December 1987, *Ariadne* (Captain John McAnally, RN, Captain 6th Frigate Squadron) was on passage to the Clyde exercise areas when she answered a 'May Day' call from the Irish fishing vessel *Salve Regina*, flooded and apparently drifting some fifteen miles north-west of Malin Head and 73 miles from *Ariadne*. The Wasp was launched with the ship's Marine Engineer Officer, Lt Cdr Keith Smith, on board to survey the damage. Smith found the fish hold flooded to a depth of fifteen feet, but there were no casualties and the vessel was still able to manoeuvre.

A Rover gas turbine pump and seven men from *Ariadne* were winched

Sea King 'Rescue 177' – HMS *Argonaut* and *Virgin Atlantic Flyer*

down to the vessel by *Ariadne*'s Wasp and by the Bristow Coastguard Sikorsky S.61 from Stornoway. After two hours, Captain McAnally, now in personal charge on the spot, decided to bring the *Salve Regina* alongside *Ariadne* and boost the pumping with the ship's electric submersible pumps, capable of over 400 tons an hour.

But *Salve Regina* was rolling and bumping heavily against *Ariadne*'s ship's side and was eventually slipped with another three of *Ariadne*'s crew on board. With shoring timbers and splinter boxes, and ships' divers who went down and repaired a split in the hull, *Ariadne*'s damage control party stemmed the flooding. The Portrush lifeboat escorted *Salve Regina* to Lough Swilly, in the Irish Republic.

The Wasp's crew, Sub Lt Langley and LACMN Mitchell, flew thirty sorties between the fishing boat and the lifeboat.

National rescue co-ordination was fully tested on the night of 6/7 March 1987, when the Townsend Thoresen ferry *Herald of Free Enterprise* overturned in the entrance to Zeebrugge harbour with great loss of life. The stand-by SAR Sea King 'Rescue 196' (Lt Cdr Roger Harrison, CO of 706,

Lt Paul Crudgington, and Lt David Lee) of 706 NAS scrambled from Culdrose, followed by 'Rescue 197', and by 'Rescue 199' from the Culdrose RAF Sea King Training Unit.

These three (of a total of seven Navy and RAF Sea Kings who rendered assistance) flew non-stop from 2.15 to 7.15 am on the morning of 7th, to Roborough near Plymouth, to Lee-on-Solent and to Portland to collect divers and their equipment and take them to the scene. Among the naval divers who took part were an SAR team of four, CPOACMN 'Smiler' Grinney, LACMN Martin Dodd, LACMN Ian Penhaligon, and LACMN Gary Davies.

819 NAS came to 15 minutes' notice for SAR at 4.15 pm on 3 July 1987, as the giant balloon *Virgin Atlantic Flyer*, owned by Mr Richard Branson, was nearing the Irish coast after its crossing of the Atlantic. At 6.10 the balloon was reported by Scottish Military Air Traffic Control, Prestwick, as being 28 nautical miles north of Portrush, Northern Ireland. The balloon touched the water but returned to the air under its own power.

The duty SAR Sea King 'Rescue 177' (Lt Martin Rayner, Lt Chris Highton, Lt Martin Tilley, LACMN Robert Yeomans, LACMN (Phot) Phillip Ball and LMA Mark Stephenson) was scrambled and airborne in eleven minutes. A second Sea King already airborne on an anti-submarine exercise but nearing the end of its fuel endurance was also diverted to the scene and by 6.34 had the balloon in sight, at an estimated height of 2,000 feet.

At 6.41 the balloon was reported to have lost some flotation gear and VHF antennae. At 6.50, the diverted Sea King had to leave to refuel at Machrihanish. Two minutes later, there was a report that one person was believed to be in the water. This was actually Branson's co-pilot, Per Lindstrand, who had jumped (from a height of 70 feet, according to Branson) out of the balloon's underslung capsule after it had first struck the sea.

Lindstrand was picked up by a local privately-owned high speed inflatable launch which had been guided to him by 'Rescue 177' and was taken ashore to Portrush. He was suffering from slight exposure after spending some 40 minutes in the water wearing only his trousers. Meanwhile, Branson himself had also jumped after the balloon's second bounce, some twenty-five minutes after Lindstrand, and had been picked up by the frigate HMS *Argonaut*'s Lynx by 7.15.

Sea King 'Rescue 177' was tasked to pick up Lindstrand from Portrush and Branson from *Argonaut* at 7.30, had them both aboard by 7.45, and took them 75 miles to Crosshouse Hospital, Kilmarnock, landing there at 8.20.

During the flight, when both men were treated for shock and exposure, Branson inscribed Chris 'Hagar' Highton's knee board: 'To Hagar Chris – thanks for another life – a very good friend – Richard Branson.' The whole SAR operation, from 'Rescue 177's' scramble to landing at Crosshouse Hospital, had lasted one hour and thirty-five minutes.

A year later almost to the day, in July 1988, 'Rescue 177' took part in another major rescue operation, one of the largest ever mounted in the North

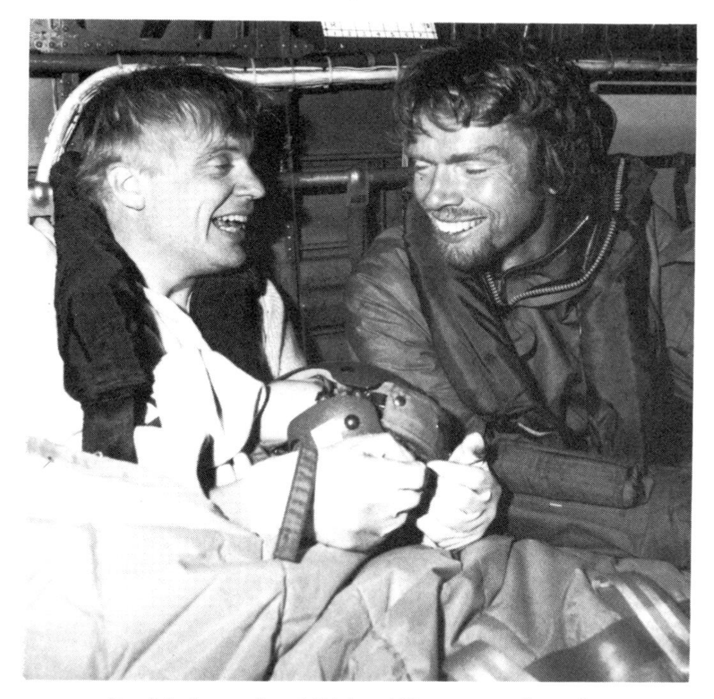

Per Lindstrand and Richard Branson on board
'Rescue 177'

Sea. The first 'May Day' was terse: 'Explosion at Piper Alpha'. Royal Navy, RAF and civilian helicopters were scrambled and warships from six NATO countries eventually took part. One of the first ships to arrive was the fishery protection vessel HMS *Blackwater* who guided eight civilian ships to the scene.

'Rescue 177' (Lt Stuart Alexander, second pilot Sub Lt Steve McArdell, observer Lt Paul Shepherd and LACMN Robert Pheasant) was scrambled from Prestwick within thirty minutes, tasked to pick up the Burns Unit at Aberdeen Royal Infirmary and fly them 120 miles north to the Claymore Platform. They returned with only a few walking wounded and stretcher cases.

'Rescue 177's crew had expected many more survivors, until they actually saw the burning oil rig, when the full magnitude of the disaster became plain. 'The glow from the fires on the platform was clearly visible from at about ten miles ... ' said Shepherd. 'What little remained of Piper Alpha was ablaze from top to bottom.'

'We had expected to be picking up a large number of people, but when we got there I was surprised that anyone at all had survived. Oil and debris littered the surface out to several miles from the burning platform and during the next few hours we found only one body.'

819 NAS also provided a Sea King at RAF Lossiemouth while their SAR

Sea King was heavily involved in the Piper Alpha disaster. While they were there the Sea King (Lt John Newell, Lt John Sime, Sub Lt Dave Nicholson and POACMN Douglas) was scrambled to rescue two fishermen stranded by flood waters.

Although everybody welcomed the Sea King's extra speed, range and carrying capacity over the Wessex, some pilots thought it a large aircraft for SAR. At ten tons, it was heavy, with a great deal of inertia to be overcome before it could stop and hover. A Sea King could not be brought to a dramatically 'flaring' stop like a Wessex and possibly it might be a trifle big for intricate work between the rocks and beside the cliffs along the Cornish coast. In March 1989, the Sea King's handling qualities in a confined space were put to a decisive test.

The weekend of 11-12 March was very quiet at Culdrose, with good weather all Saturday and Sunday morning. But on Sunday afternoon the Duty Sea King SAR crew of 771 NAS (Lt Darrell Nelson, US Coast Guard, Lt Jim Pollard, Lt Kevin King, CPOACMN 'Smiler' Grinney and LACMN Chris Hart) were scrambled to medevac an injured crewman from a Spanish fishing vessel 195 nautical miles south-west of Culdrose. As was usual practice, the stand-by Sea King crew were called in from their homes by 'bleeper' to provide 'back-up' and subsequently flew to St Mary's in the Scillies to refuel and await further instructions from the RCC at Plymouth.

The Spanish fisherman was winched up after some considerable difficulty, in stormy conditions, with winds gusting to 50 knots and a sea state of 6 or 7. Meanwhile the stand-by crew, who had been expecting to be recalled to Culdrose, were tasked to respond to a 'May Day' call from the 2,500 ton Panamanian registered ship *Secil Japan*. Her cargo of timber had shifted and she was reporting to be heading for a sheltered anchorage off the north shore of Cornwall – actually a lee shore.

When the stand-by Sea King (Lt John Bishop, Lt Doug Sealy, Lt David Cook, POACMN Martin Dodd, LACMN Kevin Bruford) reached *Secil Japan*, her Master refused the offer to take off all or some of his crew and decided to make for a safe anchorage. All might have been well, had not the ship's engines failed while she was trying to anchor less than half a mile from a place called Hell's Mouth, near St Ives, with a tremendous surf running, a strong swell and a north-westerly gale blowing onshore.

By this time Lt Darrell Nelson's Sea King had delivered the injured Spaniard to Treliske Hospital near Truro and at once received another tasking, to go to the assistance of *Secil Japan*. When Nelson arrived, *Secil Japan* was drifting stern first towards the rocks, with huge waves battering her upper decks and sheets of spray being flung 150 feet into the air. Two lifeboats were in attendance but had been unable to get near the vessel in the unpredictable surf although they had tried the dangerous tactic of anchoring and allowing themselves to drift down wind and sea towards her.

The Sea Kings tried unsuccessfully to carry out hi-line transfers but two lines parted because of the vicious skewing motion of *Secil Japan*'s deck and the violent air turbulence close to the 200-foot cliff faces. Nelson thought it was too dangerous to lower his diver, 'Smiler' Grinney, but guided by Hart he manoeuvred the Sea King so as to lower a hi-line and a rescue strop down on deck.

At that point the ship swung round and Nelson deftly relinquished control to his second pilot, Lt Pollard, who had a better view of the rocks and a visual reference point on the cliffs. At last, as *Secil Japan*'s stern was grounding on the rocks, Nelson managed to pluck four Korean crewmen off before the hi-line parted again.

Nelson took the four survivors to Culdrose while Bishop tried again. But during his attempt the ship was lifted almost completely out of the water and slammed on to the rocks at the foot of the cliff face. The ship was now wedged in a cleft of rock with huge green waves sweeping over her. Nevertheless, Bishop achieved a hover above the ship and managed to keep it, with the hi-line actually resting on the bridge wing, for nearly twenty minutes. But the remaining twelve of *Secil Japan*'s crew refused to leave the shelter of the wheelhouse.

At 12.30 am an RAF SAR Sea King of B Flight 202 Squadron, RAF Brawdy (Fl Lt J.E. McLeod, Fl Off L.D. Calderwood, Flt Sgt P.D.G. Soundy, Fl Sgt V.G.S. Dodsworth, and Cpl K. Barnett) arrived to relieve Bishop's crew, who had been airborne for some six hours. Nelson then returned and, after some of *Secil Japan*'s crew had been seen by Coastguards on the cliff top to emerge from the wheelhouse, moved into a winching position, between the cliff face and the ship's main mast, and passed a hi-line on to the deck, followed by the rescue strop.

A fifth crewman put on the strop and was being winched up when he was seen to raise his arms, slide out of the strop, and drop more than a hundred feet back into the sea. Nelson was too close to the cliff face to have room to carry out a search between the ship and the rocks, and although the Coastguard shone a powerful light down on the water, the man was never seen again.

Having parted yet another hi-line, Nelson was relieved by a third Sea King of 706 NAS, and returned to Culdrose. Some forty-five minutes later, McLeod managed to get his crewman, Fl Sgt Dodsworth, onto the *Secil Japan*'s deck. With some very skilful flying by McLeod and Calderwood and winching by Soundy and Barnett, and at great risk to themselves, McLeod's Sea King crew took off the remaining eleven men. Dodsworth stayed on deck until everyone had been rescued, organising the survivors to go up in pairs.

Calderwood was at the controls throughout this part of the rescue because the best hover references were on his side. He had to maintain his hover accurately in the appalling conditions for even longer at the end while Dodsworth had to climb the mast to free the winch cable, which had become entangled with the radio aerial, before he himself could be winched up.

On the following day a third 771 NAS Sea King crew (Lt Cdr Mike Lawrence, Lt Chris Wildish, Lt Keith Blount, POACMN 'Shiner' Wright, and POACMN 'Ginje' Tyler) who had been in Guernsey exercising with the Guernsey lifeboat, were tasked to go to the assistance of the container ship *Perintis* which was sinking close to the Channel Light Vessel, some 20 miles north-west of Guernsey. All eleven members of the crew were winched up from their liferafts as the vessel capsized and were taken to Torbay hospital suffering from exposure and hypothermia, from which one of them died.

Nelson and McLeod and their respective crews won the Shipwrecked Fishermen & Mariners' Royal Benevolent Society's Edward and Maisie Lewis Award, and the Silk Cut National Rescue Special Award, for 1988/89.

The decade of the 1980s closed for Culdrose with a major SAR incident which epitomised so many others – the appalling weather, the risks run by the rescuers, the gratitude of the rescued, the dangers and the successes.

The weekend of 28-29 October 1989, ironically when British Summer Time ended, was one of the stormiest of the whole year. In the West Country there were winds gusting to 100 mph and numerous accidents on land and sea.

On Saturday, 28 October, the 18,000 ton Pakistan-registered ship *Murree* was in the English Channel, on her way from London to Egypt with a cargo of building material and forty people, men, women and children on board. On Saturday afternoon, when the ship was about 25 miles south of Start Point in

Waiting for business: Search and Rescue Crew in the SAR Ready Room, Culdrose

Devon, some of her deck cargo of containers shifted in the gale and knocked a hole in her bows.

Two Sea Kings of 771 NAS from Culdrose and one from 772 NAS at Portland were scrambled to assist. The ship was listing twenty degrees and the bows were already awash when POACMN Dave Wallace and POACMN Steve ('Shiner') Wright, of 771 NAS, were winched down on the deck to begin lifting off the first thirteen survivors, including two women and babies.

One mother and her child had to be lifted together. 'I had the mother on the rescue strop,' said Wright, 'and the baby in the grip next to me and I just prayed that the baby would stop struggling to get out with eighty feet still to go. It seemed to take ages to get them both into the safety of the aircraft.'

All forty survivors were rescued by the three Sea Kings before the ship sank, but it was a very near thing for the rescuers themselves. 'As we started sending them up two at a time we could see the ship was going down fast,' said Wallace. 'With four still to go there was an almighty crashing sound underneath and both Steve and I thought we were going down. As the last two went away Steve and I were very worried that we wouldn't have time to get off, and then she gave an almighty lurch and went 90 degrees.'

'There was an enormous bang and we could see the boys in the aircraft signalling to us to jump. By this time we were slipping down the deck and I got my foot caught in a rope which stopped me. As soon as I got free I jumped and Steve went over the rail at much the same time. I had no idea how high we were until I was in mid-air.'

'I knew it was a long fall (it was, in fact, ninety feet) and I went very deep into the water. It felt like an age before I came up again. When I did, I could see the ship's stern towering above us.'

Both men had to swim frantically to avoid being sucked under with the ship. 'I have never been so scared in my life,' said Wallace. 'I thought this was the end. We could see the screw turning as the ship lifted out of the water and we had to clear that.' Wallace and Wright were both winched up into their own Sea King. 'We are lucky to be alive,' said Wallace. Both aircrewmen were awarded the George Medal.

The CO of 771 NAS, Lt Cdr Ian Domoney, concurred. 'They could have been taken down by the ship and the sea was also extremely dangerous with containers being washed away all the time. They did an extremely good job. They were very professional and very brave in those conditions.'

When *Murree*'s Second Officer, Ifran Jafri, was landed at RAF Mount Batten, Plymouth, he presented his lifejacket to the crews who made the rescue, having inscribed on it: 'To the angels who came in the guise of men. The Lord hath chosen thee to perform the most profound of his miracles – save life. You are what the world was made for.'

771 NAS were profoundly impressed by this tribute. 'This message has touched the hearts of the rescue crews involved very deeply,' said Domoney. 'To think that this man wrote this on his life jacket in the middle of his rescue is unbelievable. It makes it all the more worthwhile.'

The Search and Rescue team, Culdrose

towards their jobs. 'We do get a rewarding feeling from rescuing people,' they say, 'and we can't help being moved and pleased that it all went well and we were in the right place at the right time. But with increased experience we get more of a technical satisfaction from the way the rescue went, the balance of all the factors involved, the way the right solutions evolved. But then there are all the times when the rescue didn't go well, when we missed them or we found them already dead. That's awful.'

There seems a proper, almost biblical fitness, in that rescue arrives from the sky. There is often a dramatic contrast between the SAR diver descending on his wire, in his shining flying helmet and his sleek and smooth rubber wet suit, all competent and collected, and those he has come to rescue – soaking wet, stained with blood, or mud, or tears, shocked by their personal injury or predicament.

But even the SAR divers get used to it. 'There are times when we're on a real high,' they say, 'but it is amazing how often you feel a little bit let down. You just feel flat. It's our job. It's over and that's that.'

SAR crews do not paint insignia on the sides of their aircraft, in the manner of wartime fighter pilots recording their kills. The sides of the helicopters would soon be covered if they did. But they do log every incident, even uneventful sorties and false alarms, in a kind of SARspeak in which human dramas are rendered into crisp stereotyped phrases, initials and abbreviations: 'Scramble to pick girl out of the water. Arrived on scene to find girl floating face down. Despatched diver and recovered girl. Commenced EAR (Expelled Air Resuscitation – 'kiss of life' as the SAR crews explain it) and CCCM (Close Chest Cardiac Massage – 'basically a thump on the chest') *en route* to Treliske but girl DOA (Dead On Arrival).'

One of the oddest sensations in the whole SAR experience for the general public is the extraordinary quiet, the peculiar feeling of absence, almost of loss, when the rescuing helicopter has gone. That great noisy flashing machine has been thundering overhead for some time, causing a rushing mighty wind which blasts everything movable away for a hundred yards all around. Men have lowered themselves down from the sky on wires. Somebody has been whirled upwards and away. And then, the helicopter suddenly roars off, leaving behind a curious silence on the ground.

Those who are left behind look at each other. Could that furious thrashing machine really have been here? Did it all really happen, just above here? There are many thousands now who are grateful it really did.

Appendix I: *Honours and Awards*

Abbreviations

AFC	Air Force Cross
AFM	Air Force Medal
BEM	British Empire Medal
BEM(Gall)	Award of BEM specifically for Gallantry
CGM	Conspicuous Gallantry Medal
Commendn	Commendation
DFC	Distinguished Flying Cross
DFM	Distinguished Flying Medal
DSC	Distinguished Service Cross
DSM	Distinguished Service Medal
DSO	Distinguished Service Order
GM	George Medal
L.G.	*London Gazette*
MBE	Member of the Order of the British Empire
MBE(Gall)	Award of an MBE specifically for Gallantry
MBO	Most Blessed Order
MC	Military Cross
MID	Mention in Dispatches
NAS	Naval Air Squadron
Not Gaz	Not in *The London Gazette*
OBE	Officer of the Order of the British Empire
QCBC	Queen's Commendation for Brave Conduct
QCVSA	Queen's Commendation for Valuable Service in the Air
QGM	Queen's Gallantry Medal
RHS	Royal Humane Society
RNAS	Royal Naval Air Station

In compiling this List of Honours and Awards I am much indebted to *Seedie's Roll of Naval Honours & Awards 1939–1959* (Ripley Registers, 1989) and later supplementary information.

Name	Unit	Action	Award	L.G.
Lt Vernon Beauclerk George CHEESMAN RM	710 NAS HMS *Albatross*	Rescue of ss *Eumaeus* survivors off W. Africa 14 Jan '41	MBE	16-5-41
TSub Lt(A) Walter Claude BROADBURN	"	"	MID	"
CPOAirmn Michael Wyndham DALE FAA/FX77285	"	"	BEM	"
Captain John Edwin WATSON MN	Master ss *Eumaeus*	"	OBE Lloyds War Medal for Bravery at Sea	13-5-41
Sub Lt Patrick Michael Cay WILLIAMS RNR	ML 141	Air-Sea Rescue Dover	MID	2-12-41
Lt "	ML 141	Air-Sea Rescue and action against enemy A/C Dover 15 July '42	DSC	29-9-42
Ch Mtr Mech Leslie Charles Thomas ADAMS C/MX 68801	ML 139	Air-Sea Rescue 15 July 42	CGM	29-9-42
AB Guy Andrie SANDFORD D/JX 133162	ML 139	Air-Sea Rescue 15 July 42	CGM	29-9-42
Lt Cdr Anthony Foster COLLETT	CO HMS/M *Tactician*	Rescue of US Airman off Sabang, 19 Apr '44	Commander, Legion of Merit (USA)	3-4-45
Lt Cdr Peter CANE	HMS *Triumph*	Rescue of US Corsair pilot off Korea, 19 July '50	Air Medal (USA)	1-5-56
CPO ACMN Gilbert Charles Edward O'NION L/FX 77297	"	"	MID	2-2-51
Lt Col John C SHUMATE USAF	3rd Air Rescue Squadron USAF	Helo rescue of Lt Leonard RN in Korea 10 Oct '50	MC	Not Gaz
Capt David C McDANIEL USAF	"	"	MC	Not Gaz
Cpl Carl William POOL USAF 16315056	"	Helo rescue of pilot from *Theseus* in Korea 28 Jan '51	DSM	Not Gaz
Avtn Pilot Henry CARDOSA	*USS Manchester*	Helo rescue of pilot from *Theseus* in Korea 13 Apr '51	DSM	Not Gaz
AM3 James Herbert HICKS USN 347-87-51	"	"	DSM	Not Gaz

Lt Roger James GILL USNR	*USS Manchester*	Helo rescue of pilot from *Theseus* in Korea 14 Apr '51	DSC	Not Gaz
Avtn Mchn Mt Thomas Cornelius ROCHE 710-03-54	"	"	DSM	Not Gaz
Avtn Devce Chf Arlene Keith BABBITT USN 300-20-77	HMAS *Sydney*	Helo rescue of crashed aircrew in Korea 26 Oct '51	DSM	Not Gaz
Avtn Mt Callus Calvert GOODING USN 568-24-19	"	"	DSM	Not Gaz
Lt Cdr Denis Theodore John STANLEY	HMS *Campania*	Helo flying Monte Bello Atomic Tests	MBE	1-1-53
Lt Richard Denison Rowan HAWKESWORTH	HMS *Ocean*	Flying operations in Korea	DSC	19-5-53
Lt Cdr "	CO 847 NAS	Cyprus Jan-Jun '59	MID	14-7-59
Lt Cdr Horace Robinson SPEDDING	CO 705 NAS	Helo rescues in Dutch floods Feb 53	MBE	1-6-53
	HMS *Siskin* (Gosport)	"	Officer, Order of Orange Nassau (Neth)	24-6-53
CPO ACMN Sidney CRAIG L/FX77747	705 NAS	Service in Dutch floods Feb '53	BEM	1-6-53
	HMS *Siskin* (Gosport)		Bronze Medal, Order of Orange Nassau (Neth)	
Captain Hugh Shenfield BARBER	CO HMS *Alacrity*	Rescue of 7 US airmen off Korea 16 July '50	Bronze Star Medal (US)	30-10-53
Lt Cdr Brian PATERSON	HMS *Falcon* RNAS Hal Far	Helo rescues in Greek earthquake Aug '53	MBE	16-2-54
	CO 848 NAS	Helo operations in Malaya	DFC	31-5-55
Lt Cdr Sydney Hal SUTHERS	CO 848 NAS	Helo operations in Malaya	DFC	4-5-54
Lt Cdr John Edward BREESE	848 NAS	"	DFC	"
Lt(E) Andrew William LLOYD	"	"	MBE	"
CAA William George KEEN L/FX75037	"	"	BEM	"
AA3 Peter James HUNT L/FX87967	"	"	BEM	
Lt Cdr Gilbert Charles Joseph KNIGHT	848 NAS	Helo operations in Malaya	DFC	29-10-54
Lt Cdr Geoffrey Donovan LUFF	"	Malaya Dec '53-May '54	DFC	"

Ldg Airmn Peter COOPER L/SFX772140	”	Malaya	MID	”
LEM(A) David Henry RETALLICK L/SFX850089	”	”	MID	”
NA1 Raymond George THACKER L/SFX83701	”	”	MID	”
Lt Ronald LEONARD	848 NAS	Helo operations in Malaya	DFC	31-5-55
	HMS *Vidal*	Helo exped to Rockall	MBE	31-5-56
Lt Cdr ”	A&AEE Boscombe Dn		AFC	1-1-63
Lt Cdr(L) Kenneth Stanley WILSON	848 NAS	Malaya	MID	31-5-55
Lt Andres Ivan Robert JAMIESON	”	”	MID	”
ACMN James Jeremiah HAYBALL L/FX114950	”	”	DFM	”
AA2 Reginald Royston FERRIS L/FX100216	”	”	BEM	”
Lt Cdr Donald Frank FARQUHARSON	CO RAN Helo Unit	Rescue Ops NSW Floods Feb-Mar ’55	OBE	22-1-55
Lt Cdr Gordon McPHEE RAN	RAN Helos	”	OBE	”
Lt Cdr Matheson William WOTHERSPOON	CO 848 NAS	Helo operations in Malaya	DFC	6-12-55
Lt Jack Rex PALMER	HMS *Fulmar*	*Dovrefjell* Rescue in Pentland Firth 3 Feb ’56	MBE	22-2-56
	RNAS Lossiemouth	”	Chevlr, Order of St Olav (Norway)	19-2-57
Sn Cd Pilot Richard Harold WILLIAMS	”	”	MBE	22-6-56
Lt ”	”	”	Medal for Heroism (Norway)	Not Gaz
CPO ACMN Alexander JAPP L/FX79405	”	”	Commend	22-6-56
			Medal for Heroism (Norway)	Not Gaz
APO Tel Roy MONEYPENNY C/SSX836087	”	”	”	”
NA1 Roger MITCHELL L/FX927006	HMS *Eagle*	Rescue of a pilot, Med., Sept ’56	RHS Bronze Medal	

CAA Harold James FRANCIS L/FX667388	848 NAS	Malaya	MID	11-9-56
Lt Kenneth MITCHELL	848 NAS	Malaya May-Nov '56	DFC	11-6-57
AA2 Dennis Robert AUSTEN L/FX82494	"	"	MID	"
Lt Cdr Peter Everard BAILEY	HMS *Eagle*	Suez Ops Nov '56	MID	13-6-57
Lt Cdr John Claud JACOB	HMS *Theseus* CO 845 NAS	"	MID	"
Lt John Arthur Charles MORGAN	HMS *Theseus* 845 NAS	"	MBE	"
CAA Russell George KING FAA/FX75251	HMS *Theseus* 845 NAS	"	BEM	"
Lt Cdr Roi Egerton WILSON	848 NAS	Malaya	DFC	3-12-57
Lt Cdr John Robert Tenison BLUETT	CO 719 NAS HMS *Gannet* Eglinton	Rescue of *Argo Dilos* survivors off Irish coast 22 Oct '60	Min of Mercantile Marine Silver Medal 2nd C1 (Greece)	
"	HMS *Centaur* CO 815 NAS	Radfan Operations Apr-Oct '64	MID	27-4-65
Lt Frank Harvey SIMPKIN	719 NAS HMS *Gannet* Eglinton	Rescue of *Argo Dilos* survivors of Irish coast 22 Oct '60	Min of Mercantile Marine Silver Medal 2nd Cl (Greece)	
Lt Geoffrey Robert FYLEMAN	"	"	"	
Lt Philip Russell LLOYD	"	"	"	
PO(SE)1 Stanley Pearson MUSGRAVE L/FX849563	"	"	"	
LSeaUC1 Arthur Louis BARKER P/J 925647	"	"	"	
LSeaUC2 William Frank HALL P/J928043	"	"	"	
AB(UC)2 Donald John WOODSELL P/JX908951	"	"	"	
Lt Cdr Douglas Walter Frederick ELLIOTT	HMS *Seahawk*	Services to Search and Rescue	MBE	31-12-60
Lt Cdr Digby John LICKFOLD	HMS *Albion* 845 NAS	Operations in Brunei 1962	M.B.O. of Stia Negara di Brunei	21-13-63

"	HMS *Albion* 845 NAS	Helo rescue of Gurhka soldier, Borneo Sept '63	MBE (Gall)	21-8-64
Lt Cdr Peter John WILLIAMS	HMS *Albion*	Brunei	M.B.O. of Stia Negara di Brunei	21-12-63
Lt Cdr Alan Anthony HENSHER	CO 845 NAS HMS *Albion*	Helo operations in Borneo	MBE	1-1-64
Lt Cdr David Frank BURKE	CO 846 NAS HMS *Bulwark*	Helo operations in Borneo	MBE	1-1-65
"	"	Govt Sarawak Award 5 Oct '64	Pegawi Bintang Star of Sarawak	
Lt Cdr Geoffrey James SHERMAN	CO 845 NAS HMS *Bulwark*	Helo operations in Burma	MBE	1-1-65
"	"	Govt Sarawak Award 5 Oct '64	Pegawi Bintang Star of Sarawak	
Ch Air Ftr(A/E) Robert Clifford Steele KENTSBEER L/FX643667	HMS *Albion*	Operations in Borneo	BEM	1-1-64
	707 NAS HMS *Seahawk*	Rescue of SAS canoeists off S. Wales 18 Mar '65	QCBC	10-9-65
Lt Anthony Peter WOODHEAD	845 NAS HMS *Albion*	Operations in Borneo Terr Sep '63	QCBC	7-8-64
Lt Geoffrey de Salya ATKIN	"	"	QCBC	7-8-64
CAA Anthony Wilfred FRANKCOM L/FX 670075	845 NAS	Borneo	BEM	1-1-65
Lt Malcolm Stanley KENNARD	HMS *Bulwark* 845 NAS	Rescue of Iban boy, Nanga Entebai, Borneo 19 Aug '64	QCBC	19-1-65
CAA John Lawrence KINGSTON	"	Borneo	BEM	12-6-65
Lt Cdr Bryan Collier SARGINSON	HMS *Bulwark* 845 NAS	Borneo Jun-Dec '64	MBE	22-6-65
Lt Timothy Peter Thomas DONKIN RM	HMS *Bulwark* 845 NAS	Borneo Jun-Dec '64	MBE	22-6-65
Cadet Jeremy John Donnell KNAPP	HMS *Venus*	Rescue in Plymouth Sound Oct '56	RHS Bronze Medal	
Lt "	845 NAS HMS *Albion*	Borneo	QCBC	
Lt David Robert Bruce STORRIE RM	845 NAS	Borneo Ops Jun-Dec '64	MID	22-6-65

Name	Unit	Details	Award	Date
Eng Sub Lt Richard Ernest VAN KEMPEN	845 NAS HMS *Bulwark*	Borneo Ops Jun-Dec '64	MID	22-6-65
Lt Richard Edward SMITH	HMS *Seahawk* 707 NAS	Rescue of SAS canoeists off S. Wales 18 Mar '65	MBE (Gall)	10-9-65
Lt John Harold ADAMS	"	"	Commndn	"
Lt Cdr John Trevor RAWLINS	848 NAS	Evacuation of Commandos Khurban 13 May '65	QCBC	19-11-65
"	HMS *Albion*	Malaysia Dec '65-July '66	MBE	13-12-66
Air Mech 2 Colin Leslie THORNE L/FX951607	RNAS Culdrose	Rescue on Perran Sands 13 Aug '65 13 Aug '65	QCBC	17-12-65
RE Mchn(A)4 Harry John WILSON L.057057	845 NAS RNAS Culdrose	Rescue of crew of ss *Kremsertor* off Lizard 20 Jan '66	QCBC	17-5-66
LAirman David Robert KINCAID L/F965827	HMS *Victorious*	Rescue of aircraft observer in Far East 20 Jan '66	RHS Bronze Medal	
Lt David BLYTHE	706 NAS	Rescue of injured man from Longships Lighthouse 16 Apr '68	MBE	17-12-68
Lt Cdr(E) Michael CUDMORE	RNAS Culdrose	"	QCBC	"
Cdr "	Staff COM AW	Op CORPORATE, Falklands '82	OBE	11-10-82
Lt Richard Giles SAKER	706 NAS RNAS Culdrose	Rescue of injured man from Longships Lighthouse 16 Apr '68	QCBC	17-12-68
POAirman Anthony MILLS L/FX883441	"	"	QCBC	"
MA Barry NORTON PO83875	"	"	QCBC	"
Lt Cdr Graham Pierce STOCK	HMS *Fife*	Rescue of survivors from MV *Tui Lau* in Fijian waters, 23 Oct '68	QCBC	1-4-69
Lt Neville Gordon TRUTER	"	"	QCBC	"
Lt Fraser HUGHES RM	"	Floods rescue in Malaya 10 Dec '69	QCBC	9-6-70
Lt John Boyes FROST RM	"	Rescue in jungle, Trengganu, 5 Jul '70	AFC	3-11-70
Lt Cdr Nigel Hawkesly BURBURY	HMNZS *Waikato*	Rescue in Cook Strait, N.Z., 15 Mar '70	AFC	1-1-71
LAM Peter Richard HAMMOND L083113		Rescue of pilot trapped in crashed aircraft 29 Jul '72	BEM (Gall)	9-1-73
NAM1 Anthony Hugh WAREING D104274P		"	BEM (Gall)	"

Name	Unit	Details	Award	Date
Lt Richard Paul SEYMOUR	HMS *Yarmouth*	Rescue of crew of ss *Oriental Falcon* S. China Sea, 12 July '72	AFC	20-2-73
Lt Cdr David Sumner MALLOCK	RNFTU Culdrose	*Merc Enterprise* Rescue, 16 Jan '74	AFC	19-11-74
Lt Anthony Roydon BAKER RAN	HMS *Ark Royal* 824 NAS	"	AFC	"
PO ACMN David John Dudley FOWLES DO72561M	706 NAS Culdrose	"	AFM	"
PO ACMN David John JACKSON J976002S	706 NAS Culdrose	"	AFM	"
PO ACMN Adrian John WILLIAMS D094384P	HMS *Ark Royal* 824 NAS	"	AFM	"
[Mallock, Baker, Fowles, Jackson and Williams were also awarded the Royal Medal of Reward 1st Class with Crown (Denmark) in July 1977)				
Lt Ian McKECHNIE	829 NAS HMS *Andromeda*	Rescue of Turkish destroyer *Kocatepe* survivors off Cyprus Jul '74	QCVSA DSM of Armed Forces of Turkish Republic	20-1-75
LSea(Aircrw) Raymond Anthony HIGGINSON D053589F	HMS *Ark Royal* SAR	Rescue in Channel 7 Sep '74	QGM	18-3-75
Lt Peregrine William David COPE	771 NAS Culdrose	Rescue, Cornwall Jan '75	RHS Bronze Medal	Awarded Apr '75
CACMN David Hughes CARTER K955470S	"	"	"	
LACMN Anthony James MOSSMAN D104087T	"	"	"	
ALACMN Peter Nicholas Andrew GIBBS D129476X	771 NAS Culdrose	Rescue of survivors of MV *Lovat* 25 Jan '75	QGM	6-5-75
ACPDACMN Roy WITHELL D0667295	HMS *Ark Royal* 824 NAS	Rescue of crewman of USS/M *Bergall* 22 Feb '76	QGM	17-8-76
Lt Cdr Keith Martin Cologne SIMMONS	HMS *Antrim*	Birthday Honours 77	AFC	11-6-77
Lt(E) Christopher John CHADWICK	HMS *Bacchante*	Rescue of injured climber, Gib. 23 May '76	QCBC	31-8-77

LACMN William Jeffrey COWARD D113268N	”	”	QCBC	”
LACMN Colin Geoffrey RIMMER D103643A	771 NAS Culdrose	Recovery of Gazelle crew after collision 13 June ’77	QCVSA	1-11-77
POACMN Tudor Wyn DAVIES J944355H	771 NAS Culdrose	Helo Rescue	QCVSA	14-3-78
Lt Glen James TILSLEY	706 NAS Culdrose	*Orion* Oil Rig rescue off Guernsey 2 Feb ’78	AFC	28-11-78
Lt Robert George DAVIDSON	”	”	AFC	”
Lt Paul CRUDGINGTON	”	”	AFC	”
Lt Anthony James EAGLES	”	”	AFC	”
CACMN Terence Anthony KING D0557746N	”	”	QCVSA	”
CACMN Malcolm John TUPPER D083002	”	”	QCVSA	”
”	846 NAS	Op CORPORATE, Falklands ’82	DSM	11-10-82
Lt Ian Vernon MUNDAY	706 NAS Culdrose	Rescue of survivors of ss *Cantonad* 4 Jan ’79	QCVSA	31-7-79
LACMN Raymond John WALTERS D097527E	”	”	QCVSA	”
Lt Cdr Michael John NORMAN	814 NAS Culdrose	*Ben Asdale* Rescue 31 Dec ’78	AFC	4-9-79
Lt Anthony John Marsden HOGG	”	”	AFC	”
Lt Lawrence Maynard JERAM-CROFT	”	”	QCVSA	”
LACMN Christopher John FOLLAND D105603U	”	”	QCVSA	”
LMA Brian David STEELE	RNAS Culdrose	”	QCBC	”
AB(S) Terence Patrick LOFTUS D109327S	HMS *Jupiter*	Rescue of survivors of MV *Iris* 15 Feb ’79	GM	11-9-79
Sea(S) Jason GARLICK D166720S	”	”	QGM	”
AB(R) Simon William HUTT D162257N	”	”	QGM	”

PO(R) Norman WILLIAMS D095538Y	”	”	QGM	”
LACMN David Smith WALLACE D130808C	829 NAS HMS *Jupiter*	”	QCBC	”
Sea(R) Mark Sinclair THOMAS D162904G	HMS *Jupiter*	”	QCBC	11-9-79
Lt Cdr Nicholas Jan DE HARTOG	829 NAS HMS *Arrow*	Rescue of crew of MV *Paaschburg* 13 Feb '79	AFC	18-9-79
AA1(A/E) Victor Charles FLEMWELL D0850480	”	”	QCBC	”
Sub Lt Ross THORBURN	”	”	QCVSA	”
Lt Cdr John PASSMORE	HMS *Fife* CO Ship's Fit	Hurricane 'David' Dominica Aug-Sep '79	MBE	31-12-79
Lt Richard John LIPPIETT	HMS *Fife*	”	MBE	”
Lt Cdr Graeme John Patrick WINGATE	706 NAS	Fastnet Race helo rescues Aug '79	QCVSA	4-3-80
Lt Cdr Bernard Michael BROCK		’	QCVSA	”
Lt Jeremy GRAYSON	RNAS Culdrose	”	QCVSA	”
”	771NAS	New Year Honours 1981	AFC	31-12-80
Lt Albert M FOX	771 NAS	Fastnet Race helo rescues Aug '79	QCVSA	4-3-80
”	”	New Year Honours 1981	AFC	31-12-80
Lt Robert Charles SIMPSON	706 NAS	Fastnet Race helo rescues Aug '79	QCVSA	4-3-80
Mid Stephen George LAPTHORNE		”	QCVSA	”
APOACMNDvr Julian Patrick Rodmell GRINNEY D106848C	RNAS Culdrose	”	QCVSA	”
CACMN ”	771 NAS	Rescue Spanish trawler *Ivan Antonio* and Korean *Secil Japan* survivors 12 Mar '89	AFM	23-1-90
LACMN Richard BURNETT D138082C		Fastnet Race helo rescues Aug '79	QCVSA	4-3-80
Lt Cdr David Edward Penrose BASTON	781 NAS Lee-on-Solent	Birthday Honours	AFC	14-6-80
POACMN Tudor Grenville WILLIAMS D070213N		Attempted rescue of Wessex crew	QGM	23-12-80
CACMN David Edward BROWN F974315J	781 NAS Lee-on-Solent	Rescue of man trapped in upturned barge in Solent 10 Oct '80	QCBC	24-2-81

ALACMN John Pettinger SPENCER D12520S	781 NAS Lee-on-Solent	”	QGM	”
APOACMN ”	SAR Flt Portland	MV *Bonita* rescue off Portland 13 Dec ’81	QGM*	27-2-82
Lt Cdr Raymond Allan WINCHCOMBE	771 NAS	Rescue of *Tungufoss* survivors 19 Sep ’81	Silver Medal for Valour (Iceland)	
Lt Nicholas Gran HOUGHTON	”	”		”
Lt Philip James SHELDON	”	”’		”
’	825 NAS	*Sir Galahad* rescue, Fitzroy, 8 June ’82	QGM	11-10-82
POACM W R COLLINS D106885X	771 NAS	Rescue of *Tungufoss* survivors 19 Sep ’81	Silver Medal for Valour (Iceland)	
Lt Andrew Timothy HEALEY	737 NAS Portland	MV *Melpol* rescue 8 Dec ’81	QCVSA	20-4-82
Lt Matthew Paul JENNINGS	”	”	QCVSA	”
Lt John Desmond CONNELL	”	”	QCVSA	”
Lt David Rutherford LARMOUR	HMS *Osprey*	”	QCVSA	’
Lt Martyn REID	737 NAS Portland	”	QCVSA	”
		”	QCVSA	”
”	HMS *Alacrity*	Rescue of crew of crashed aircraft Puerto Rico 12 Aug ’85	QCVSA	29-4-86
POACMN Kevin John MATTHEWS D1292500	737 NAS Portland	MV *Melpol* rescue 8 Dec ’81	QCBC	20-4-82
LACMN Paul Thomas NEWMAN D149501E	”	”	QCBC	”
Lt Cdr Ian STANLEY	HMS *Antrim*	Op PARAQUAT, S. Georgia 1982	DSO	4-6-82
Lt Cdr John Anthony ELLERBECK	HMS *Endurance*	”	DSC	”
Lt Christopher John PARRY	HMS *Antrim*	”	MID	”
Lt David WELLS	HMS *Endurance*	”	MID	”
Sub Lt Stewart COOPER	HMS *Antrim*	”	MID	”
LACMN David FITZGERALD	”	”	MID	”
Lt Cdr Michael Dennison BOOTH	CO 847 NAS	Op CORPORATE, Falklands 1982	DSC	11-10-82
Lt Cdr Hugh Sinclair CLARK	CO 825 NAS	”	DSC	”
Major Charles Peter CAMERON RM	CO 3 Cdo Brigade Air Squadron	”	MC	”

Lt Cdr Hugh John LOMAS	CO 845 NAS	”	DSC	”
		Gallantry in ops in Lebanon	QCVSA	12-6-84
Lt Cdr Simon Clive THORNEWILL	CO 846 NAS	Op CORPORATE, Falklands 1982	DSC	11-10-82
Lt Alan Reginald Courtenay BENNETT	846 NAS	”	DSC	”
Lt Richard HUTCHINGS	”	”	DSC	”
Lt Nigel John NORTH	”	”	DSC	”
Lt Richard James NUNN RM	3 Cdo Brigade Air Squadron	”	DFC(Post)	”
Lt Jeffrey Peter NIBLETT RM	”	”	DFC	”
Lt Cdr Douglas John Smiley SQUIER	CO 826 NAS	”	AFC	”
Lt Cdr John Stuart WYKES-SNEYD	CO 820 NAS	”	AFC	”
Lt John Kenneth BOUGHTON	825 NAS	*Sir Galahad* rescue Fitzroy 8 June 1982	QGM	”
Act Cpl ACMN Michael David LOVE RM P035079S	846 NAS	Op CORPORATE, Falklands 1982	DSM(Post)	”
LACMN Peter Blair IMRIE D134900T	”	”	DSM	”
Sgt William Christopher O'BRIEN RM P030684R	3 Cdo Brigade	”	DFM	”
Lt Peter Charles MANLEY	845 NAS	”	MID	”
Lt Frederick William ROBERTSON	826 NAS	”	MID	”
”	814 NAS Culdrose	*Oggie* rescue off Plymouth 23 Jan '84	QCVSA	13-11-84
Sgt Thomas Arthur SANDS RM P027627C	845 NAS	Op CORPORATE, Falklands 1982	MID	11-10-82
LACMN Stephen William WRIGHT D155244K	825 NAS	”	MID	”
Ch Air Eng Art(M) David John HERITIER D063192F	HMS *Antrim*	”	BEM	”
AEA(L)1 Robert Anthony John MASON D063242M	845 NAS	”	BEM	”
Lt Nigel Alan KING	819 NAS Prestwick	Rescue of survivors from *Poseidon* off Skye 9 Nov '82	QCVSA	3-5-83
Lt Stephen John WESTWOOD	”	”	QCBC	”

POACMN John Stephen COLEMAN D074677K	HMS *Osprey* Portland	Rescue attempt on *Petit Forban* 22 Feb '83	QGM	4-10-83
Lt Ian Philip GALWAY	814 NAS Culdrose	*Oggie* rescue off Plymouth 23 Jan '84	QCVSA	13-11-84
Lt Stephen William MARLOW	810 NAS Culdrose	"	QGM	"
Lt John Emlyn WARD	814 NAS	"	QCVSA	"
LAirmn(AH) Michael John PIERCE D154749P	HMS *Osprey*	Attempted rescue of crashed helo 3 Dec '84	QGM	10-9-85
Lt Peter Charles RICHINGS		Rescue of sailing vessel *Liseul* 26 Jan '86	US Coast Guard Medal	Not Gaz
Lt David Charles Worth MARR	771 NAS Culdrose	Rescue of 9 persons from yacht *Mister Cube*12 Aug '85	QCVSA	11-3-86
APOACMN Michael Charles PALMER D146020W	"	"	QCVSA	"
POACMN Laurence SLATER D114895W	"	"	GM	11-5-86
Lt Michael John BURROWS	HMS *Alacrity*	Rescue of crew of crashed aircraft off Puerto Rico 12 Aug '85	QCVSA	29-4-86
Lt Cdr Timothy Nicholas Edward WILLIAMS	HMS *Beaver*	Casevac of 2 men from *Reefer Dolphin* 6 Oct '85	QCVSA	24-6-86
Lt Philip David NEEDHAM	HMS *Beaver*	"	QCVSA	"
Lt John Edward HUMPHRIES	HMS *Daedalus*	Rescue in Solent 20 Nov '86	QCBC	23-6-87
POACMN Robert Andrew MURDOCH D134017J	"	"	QCBC	"
LACMN Anthony GARDINER	819 NAS Prestwick	Casevac of 2 men from *Don Humverta* 31 Oct '86	QCBC	14-7-87
LACMN Martin Philip DODD D152710B	771 NAS Culdrose	Rescue of person trapped in car 20 Mar '87	QCBC	1-9-87
LACMN Ian PENHALIGON D153773Y	771 NAS Culdrose	Attempted rescue Mullion harbour 6 Apr '86	QGM	1-12-87
APOACMN Adrian ROGERS	772 NAS Portlnd	Recovery of missing diver off St Catherine's Point 13 June '89	QCBC	5-12-89

Lt Darrel NELSON US CstGrd	771 NAS Culdrose	Rescue Spanish trawler *Ivan Antonio* and Korean ship *Secil Japan* survivors 12 Mar '89	QCVSA	23-1-90
QCVSA				
POACMN David WALLACE	771 NAS Culdrose	Rescue of Pakistan ship *Murree* survivors off Start Point 28 October '89	GM	24-7-90
POACMN Stephen William WRIGHT	"	"	GM	"
CPOA (Phot) Keith STURGE	Joint Services PR Unit Hong Kong	Rescue of survivor from oil rig, S. China Sea, Aug '91	AFM	26-5-92

Appendix II: Winners of the Boyd Trophy

1946 Lt Cdr D.B. Law and Lt Reynolds for formation aerobatic display in Seafires at St Merryn.
1947 Lt Cdr H.J. Mortimore, CO of 733 NAS, for leading a flight of three Expeditors from Trincomalee to Lee-on-Solent in adverse weather conditions.
1948 Lt Cdr E.M. Brown, of RAE Farnborough, for trials with rubber deck.
1949 1830 NAS, RNVR, for 205 accident-free deck landings during embarked period in HMS *Illustrious*.
1950 17th Carrier Air Group, HMS *Theseus*, for operations in Korea.
1951 814 NAS for night flying in HMS *Vengeance*.
1952 802 and 825 NAS for operations in Korea.
1953 848 NAS for operations in Malaya.
1954 Naval Test Squadron, Boscombe Down, for improvements to RN aircraft.
1955 806 NAS for pioneering the Sea Hawk at sea, and for contributions to tactical investigation in night strike role.
1956 Search and Rescue Flight at Lossiemouth for *Dovrefjell* rescue.
1957 Not awarded.
1958 845 NAS for operations in the Persian Gulf and salvage of ss *Melika*.
1959 781 NAS, Lee-on-Solent, for efficiency in communications flights.
1960 831 NAS for efficiency in training with the fleet.
1961 HMS *Protector*'s Ship's Flight for efficiency in Antarctica.
1962 815 NAS for bringing the Wessex HAS.1 into service, pioneering night and all-weather ASW tactics and Wessex SAR procedures.
1963 846 NAS for operations in Borneo.
1964 845 NAS for services in the defence of Malaysia.
1965 759 NAS for fine record in converting Jet Provost pilots to Hunter aircraft.
1966 849C Flight for outstanding performance in HMS *Ark Royal* during Mozambique patrol.
1967 801 NAS for bringing the Buccaneer S.2 into service.
1968 814 NAS for bringing the Wessex HAS.3 to a high state of operational effectiveness at sea.
1969 Lt Cdr P.C. Marshall, AFC, for exceptional skill and personal courage in bringing a badly damaged Phantom safely back to base.
1970 Lt Cdr V. Sirett for the work of 700S NAS, the Sea King IFTU.
1971 826 NAS for *Steel Vendor* rescue from HMS *Eagle*.
1972 Lt Cdr Davis, Lt C.D. Walkinshaw, Lt Park and Lt Lucas for flying 2,000 miles from HMS *Ark Royal* to Belize.
1973 Not awarded.
1974 Lt I. McKechnie, HMS *Andromeda* Flight, for evacuation of refugees from Cyprus.
1975 Not awarded.
1976 Lt Cdr K.M.C. Simmons, Lt T.J. MacMahon, Lt A.B. Ross and CPO ACMN E.A. Butler, *HMS Antrim* Flight, for rescue off Iceland.

1977 700L NAS, the Lynx IFTU, for introducing the Lynx into Naval service.
1978 Aircrews of Culdrose squadrons for the outstanding record of rescues, medical and humanitarian flights during the year.
1979 HMS *Fife*'s Ship's Flight for outstanding performance in Dominica following the devastation caused by Hurricane David.
1980 Not awarded.
1981 801 NAS pilots for their outstanding achievements in operating the Sea Harrier embarked in HMS *Invincible*.
1982 Cdr T.J.H. Gedge for his leadership on the ground and in the air, perseverance, skill, professional knowledge and courage.
1983 705 NAS for its excellent overall performance, training achievement, outstanding airmanship, and exceptional contribution to the prestige of Naval aviation.
1984 846 NAS in recognition of its outstanding contribution to naval aviation in support of the Lebanon operations.
1985 815 NAS HMS *Beaver* Flight in recognition of its outstanding Rescue and subsequent evacuation of casualties from the freighter *Reefer Dolphin* in October 1985.
1986 849 NAS for its outstanding success in reintroducing AEW into the fleet.
1987 Not awarded.
1988 815 and 829 NAS for the contribution made by their flights to the undoubted success of the Armilla Patrol. They operated in extreme conditions, far from home in a hostile environment and all tasks were completed in an exemplary manner, entirely within the finest traditions of the Royal Navy and the Fleet Air Arm.
1989 HMS *Alacrity*'s Lynx Ship's Flight for their skill, stamina and professionalism in providing immediate life-saving and disaster relief to the Caribbean island of Monserrat in the aftermath of Hurricane Hugo, 18-21 September 1989.
1990 HMS *Sheffield*'s Lynx Ship's Flight for their professionalism, enthusiasm and stamina in achieving an outstanding flying rate, with the highest standards of serviceability under arduous conditions, in Operation Nickleby.
1991 845 NAS, a support helicopter unit, for their performance during Operation Granby in the Gulf, and other work.

Sources and Bibliography

1 Shoes … and Ships … and Shagbats

Barker, Ralph, *Down in the Water*: True Stories of the Goldfish Club, London: Chatto & Windus, 1955

Brown, Lt (A) W.N., RNVR, Letter of 25 June 1989 (Naval Walrus with 275 Sq RAF)

Cheesman, V.B.G. Cheesman, Major, DSO MBE DSC RM, *From the Diary of a Fleet Air Arm Royal Marine Pilot*, in typescript

Chartres, John, *Fly for their Lives*, Shrewsbury: Airlife, 1988, Ch.4, 'Rescues by flying boats'

Dale, CPO Michael, BEM, 'A Walrus And The *Albatross*', *Experiences of War: The British Sailor*, Kenneth Poolman, London: Arms and Armour Press, 1989

Fuller, Lt Cdr Neil, RN, Letter of 17 October 1989, (Sub Lt Blatchley and U-331)

Harris, John, *The Sea Shall Not Have Them*, London: Hurst & Blackett

Ministry of Information, *Air-Sea Rescue*, London: HMSO, 1942

Mortimer, Bill, *The RAF's Navy*: The History of the Royal Air Force Marine Branch, SEASCAPE International Maritime Magazine, No.23, March 1989

Nethercott, Iain, 'Underwater Rescue (*Tactician*, April 1944)', *Experiences of War: The British Sailor*, Kenneth Poolman, London: Arms and Armour Press, 1989

Nethercott, Iain, DSM, Letter of 25 January 1990 (*Tactician*)

Nicholl, Lt Cdr G.W.R., *The Supermarine Walrus*, London: G.T. Foulis & Co Ltd, 1966

Pilborough, Geoffrey D., MIRT, *The History of Royal Air Force Marine Craft 1918–1986*, Volume One, 1918–1939, Volume Two, 1939–1945, London: Canimpex, 1986

Roberts, Cdr Gordon, OBE RN, 'Notes on the Rescue of 8 RAF Personnel by Sea Otter Aircraft 23rd–24th July 1948', 14 June 1989, in typescript

Scott, Lt Cdr Peter, MBE, DSC*, RNVR, *The Battle of the Narrow Seas*, London: Country Life Ltd., 1945, Ch. VII, 'Air/Sea Rescue'

Warner, Oliver, *The Life-boat Service*, London: Cassell, 1974

Waterman, Lt Cdr Jack, RD, RNR, Letter of 15 February 1989 (SAR from *Owl* 1944)

Winton, John, *The Forgotten Fleet*, London: Michael Joseph 1969, Ch. 3, 'Palembang', Ch.4, 'Iceberg One', Ch.8, 'Submarine Operations'

2 From Da Vinci to Dragonfly

ADM 1/12189, Autogyros for merchant ships, 1942–43

ADM 1/13538, R5 Helicopter

ADM 1/13589, Helicopter for ASW, 1943

Brie, Reginald A.C., 'Practical Notes on the Autogiro', *Aeronautics: a Complete Guide to Civil and Military Flying*, Volume IV, Routine and Special Applications, London: George Newnes Ltd. c.1938

Bristow, Alan, Letter and draft of 11 July 1989 (Early RN helicopter days)
Brown, Captain Eric, CBE, DSC, AFC, MA, FRAeS, *The Helicopter in Civil Operations*, London: Granada, 1981
Chartres, John, *Helicopter Rescue*, London: Ian Allan, 1980, Ch.1, 'Early beginnings and principles'
John, Rebecca, *Caspar John*, London: Collins, 1987
Myall, Eric, ARAeS, Letters of 19 June and 12 August 1989 (HMS *Thane*)
Popham, A.E., (Compiler), *The Drawings of Leonardo da Vinci*, London: Jonathan Cape, 1946
Reed, Ken, Letter and draft of 1 July 1989 (Early RN helicopter days)
Richter, Irma A., (Editor), *Selections from the Notebooks of Leonardo Da Vinci*, Oxford University Press, The World's Classics No.530, 1952
Sikorsky, Igor, *The Story of the Winged S*, London: Robert Hale, 1940
Spedding, Lt Cdr H.R., 'The Helicopter', *The Naval Review*, 1953
Turner, John Frayn, *Hovering Angels*, London: George G. Harrap & Co., 1957, Chs. 1–4
Wells, Captain John G., CBE, DSC, RN, *Whaley*: The Story of HMS Excellent 1830 to 1980, Portsmouth; HMS Excellent, 1980, Ch.12, 'Back To Normal 1945 to 1950'
Walker, Lt Cdr V.A. RN, Letter of 9 July 1989 (Sea Otter/*Affray*)

3 Dutch Floods, Malayan Bandits and Greek Earthquakes

Crayton, Lt Cdr R.R., RN, Interview with Sub Lt Snell, 4 April 1989
Dragonfly Photo Album, (FAA Museum)
Elliott, Lt Cdr D.W.F., MBE, RN, Interview with Sub Lt Snell, 3 April 1989
'Greek Earthquake Rescue', *Flight Deck*, Winter 1953
History of Gosport Airfield: Extract concerning 705 Squadron
Hoverfly Photo Album (FAA Museum)
Line Book, 848 NAS., 1952–63 (FAA Museum)
Spedding, Lt Cdr H.R., RN, 'Naval Helicopters in Holland', *The Aeroplane*, March 20, 1953
'Helicopter Rescue', *Flight Deck*, Summer 1953
Spedding, Cdr H.R., MBE, RN, Interview with Sub Lt Snell, 6 April 1989
Squadron Record Book, 705 NAS, 1952–71, (FAA Museum)
Squadron Record Book, 848 NAS, October 1952–December 1956, (FAA Museum)
Suthers, Lt Cdr S.H., DSC, DFC, RN, 'Helicopters in Malaya', *Flight Deck*, Autumn 1953 'Troop-lifting in Malaya', *Flight Deck*, Spring 1954; Letter of 30 June 1989 (848 NAS in Malaya)
The Battle of the Floods, Amsterdam: Netherlands Booksellers & Publishers Association, London: Newman Neame Ltd, 1953
Turner, op. cit., Ch.5, 'Fighting the Floods', Ch.6, 'Magnificence in Malaya', and Ch.8, 'The Earth erupts'
Turpin, Cdr R., MBE, RN, Interview with Sub Lt Snell, 5 April 1989
Letter of 25 June 1989 (Dutch Floods)

4 Korea: Triumph, Theseus, Glory, Sydney and *Ocean*

'ARS 'Copter Pilots Duck Red Sniper Bullets To Save British Pilot 90 Miles Behind Lines (Leonard)', *The Sikorsky News*, Bridgeport, Connecticut, February 9, 1951
Barker, Lt Edward L., US Naval Reserve, 'The Helicopter in Combat (in Korea)', *US Naval Institute Proceedings*, Vol.66, November 1951

Bolt, Captain A.S., DSO, DSC, RN, 'H.M.S. Theseus in the Korean War', *Journal of the Royal United Service Institution*, Vol.XCVI, No.584, November 1951
Bolt, Rear Admiral A.S., CB, DSO, DSC, Letter of 4 July 1989 (*Theseus*' helicopter SAR in Korea)
'British Commonwealth Naval Operations During the Korean War', *Journal of the Royal United Service Institution*, 'Part I: June 1950–February 1951', Vol.XCVI, No.583 May 1951; 'Part II: February 1951–June 1951', Vol. XCVI, No.584 November 1951; 'Part III, June 1951–November 1951', Vol.XCVII, No.585, May 1952; 'Part IV, November 1951–June 1952', Vol.XCVIII, No.586, February 1953; 'Part V, July–December 1952', Vol.XCVIII, No.587, May 1953; 'Part VI, January–June 1953', Vol.XCVIII, No.589, November 1953; 'Part VII, Conclusion and Summary', Vol.XCIX, No.590, February 1954
Cagle, Malcolm W., and Manson, Frank A., *The Sea War in Korea*, Annapolis: 1957
Carver, Captain Edmund, DSC, RN, 'The R.N. in the Korean War – Helicopters and S.A.R. 1950–1952', in typescript, 22 August 1989
Clapin, Major B.P.W., DFC, R.E., commanding 67 C.B.G.L. Section in HMS *Glory*, 'A Report of Operations in KOREA', *Flight Deck*, Winter 1952
Field, James A. Jr. *History of United States Naval Operations – Korea*, Washington: Naval History Division 1962
Hastings, Max, *The Korean War*, London: Michael Joseph, 1987, Ch.14, 'The Battle In The Air' (Jacob and Hearnshaw)
H.M.S. 'Theseus' Goes East, Portsmouth: Acme Printing Co., 1951
Holly, Lt Cdr David C., USN, 'The ROK Navy', *US Naval Institute Proceedings*, Vol.78 November 1952
Lansdown, John R.P., *With The Carriers in Korea*: The Fleet Air Arm Story 1950–53, Square One Publications, 1992
Leonard, Lt S., Flying Log Book Extract, 10 October 1950
Michener, James A., *The Bridges at Toko-Ri*, London: Secker & Warburg, 1953
Ocean Saga, H.M.S. OCEAN from May 1951 to October 1953, Devonport: Hiorns and Miller, 1953
Scutt, Jerry, *Air War over Korea*; Warbirds Illustrated No.11, London: Arms and Armour Press, 1982
'The "Inchkilda" Incident', *Flight Deck*, Spring 1954

5 Sproule Net and Suez 1956

Bailey, Cdr Peter, RN, '*Eagle*'s SAR at Suez', Letters of 30 July and 12 September 1989
Conway, Sub Lt D.G., RN, 'Helicopter Rescue' (*Dovrefjell*), *Flight Deck*, Spring 1956
Couchman, Vice Admiral W.T., 'Award of Boyd Trophy for 1956', for *Dovrefjell* Rescue
Fergusson, Bernard, *The Watery Maze*, Ch.XVI, Tria Juncto in uno: Port Said 1956, London: Collins, 1961
Flight Deck, Winter 1956, 'Operation Musketeer'
Flintham, V., 'Suez 1956: A Lesson in Air Power', Parts I and II, *Air Pictorial*, August and September 1965
'HMS Eagle In The Mediterranean', *Spreadeagle*, HMS *Eagle* Ship's Magazine, No.4, January 1957
Jackson, Robert, *Suez 1956: Operation Musketeer*, London: Ian Allan, 1980
'Kynance Cove Rescue', *The Coastguard*, Vol. 7, No.2, Summer 1953
The Naval Review, Vol.XLV, No.1, January 1957, 'The Seaborne Assault on Port Said', No.2, April 1957, 'The Aircraft Carrier Aspects of "Musketeer" ', 'The Amphibious Assault on Port Said'

Sproule, Lt Cdr John, RN, 'Over the Mountain, over the Sea', *Flight Deck*, Winter 1954
'Pioneering Search And Rescue', *Aeroplane Monthly*, May 1982
Turner, op.cit., Ch.10, The Iron Lung saves a Life, and Ch.16, Tragedy and Triumph
Williams, Lt R.H., MBE RN, Private Scrapbook and Album

6 *'The most savage, bloodthirsty, treacherous tribe in Borneo'*

Burke, Cdr D.F., MBE RN, '846 in Borneo', Letter of 9 August 1989
Burns, Ken, and Critchley, Mike, *HMS Bulwark 1948–1984*, Liskeard: Maritime Books, 1986
Flag Officer Air (Home), Special Order Of The Day of 11 January 1962, Lt Cdr J.R.T. Bluett RN, and Lt P.J. Judd RN, *Steintje Mensinga* Rescue, 4 December 1961
Lickfold, Mrs Mary, Letter of 7 February 1990 (Lickfold MBE)
Marriott, John, *Disaster At Sea*, London: Ian Allan, 1987, Ch.17, *Torrey Canyon*
Pocock, Tom, 'Jak (On Active Service) Meets a Savage Tribe', *Evening Standard*, 11 August 1964
Sherman, Cdr G.J., MBE RN, '845 in Borneo', Letter of 6 August 1989
Sirett, Cdr V.G., RN, Interview of 27 June 1989
Smith, Cdr Richard, MBE, RN, 'SAS Rescue off Castlemartin, March 1965', Letter of 16 September 1989
The London Gazette, Friday 10th September 1965, Citation for MBE for Lt Richard Edward Smith, Royal Navy, Commendations for Lt John Harold Adams, Royal Navy, and Chief Air Fitter (A/E) Robert Clifford Steele Kentsbeer

7 *Into the Seventies: Merc Enterprise*

Citation of 12 December 1972 for Alan Marsh Medal, for Lt R.P. Seymour Royal Navy, 'Rescue of Crew from SS Oriental Falcon'
Fleet Air Arm Museum: Ship's Flight Records, *Ajax, Dido, Fife, Gurkha, Hermione, Juno, Jupiter, Sirius, Yarmouth; Ark Royal* SAR Records January 1970–December 1977: HMS *Seahawk*, Culdrose SAR 1975–85; HMS *Fulmar*, Lossiemouth SAR; HMS *Goldcrest*, Brawdy SAR; 820 NAS 1965–70; 824 NAS 1970–75; HMS *Daedalus*, Lee-on-Solent, Search and Rescue Incident Log, 1973; RNFTU Records; 706 NAS 1962–76
'FGN Helicopter Crews' Courage in Dramatic Rescue in English Channel' (*Merc Enterprise*), RNAS Culdrose Press Release, 22 January 1974
HMS *Eagle*, Commission Book, 1970–72 (*Steel Vendor*)
Mallock, Lt Cdr D.S., RN, 'Merc Enterprise: The Experience Of One Crew', *Cockpit* FAA Safety Review, No. 67, Second Quarter 1974
Van der Plank, Lt Cdr R.E., RN, (CO 826 NAS) 'SAR Incident 7 October 1971 – SS Steel Vendor/826 Sea Kings', report of 11 October 1971
Pearce, Frank, *Mayday! Mayday! Mayday!*, Falmouth: Bantam, 1977
'Royal Tour Tragedy In Cook Strait', *The Evening Post* (Wellington N.Z.), 16 March 1970

8 Cyprus 1974: 'Bottles, nappies and nippers ... '

Branson, Rear Admiral Peter, CBE, '*Theseus* in the Evacuation of Cyprus July 1974', in typescript, 24 August 1989
Commander-in-Chief's Commendation, Citation, 'Lt T.J. Yarker Royal Navy HMS Rhyl'
Dyson, Lt Cdr Tony, RN, *HMS Hermes 1959–1984*, Liskeard: Maritime Books, 1984
Henn, Brigadier F.R., CBE, (Chief of Staff, UN Forces, Cyprus, 1974), *A Business Of Some Heat*, Chs. 44, 'Fiascos by Sea and Air' and 47, 'The Kyrenia Evacuation', in draft typescript, 12 September 1989
HMS *Daedalus*, RNAS Lee-on-Solent, SAR Incident Logs 1974 and 1975
HMS *Seahawk*, RNAS Culdrose, SAR 1975–85
Leonard, Captain S., OBE, RN, Letter of 2 August 1989
McKechnie, Lt I., RN, 'With 829 in Cyprus', *Flight Deck*, No.4, 1974
McKechnie, Lt I., RN, Letter home of 23 July 1974
Pearce, op.cit.
Yarker, Cdr T.J., RN, Letter of 27 September 1989 (*Rhyl* in the Cyprus Emergency)

9 Worldwide SAR: From the 'Sailor' TV Rescue to the Orion Oil Rig

Citation for QCBC for Lt C.J. Chadwick and LACMN W.J. Coward
'Flying In The Face Of Danger' (*Bacchante*'s Wasp/Gibraltar), *Navy News* June 1976
'Helo lifts two from Atlantic' (*Ark Royal*/USS *Bergall*), *Navy News*, April 1976
HMS *Seahawk*, RNAS Culdrose, SAR 1975–85
Pearce, op.cit.
Prigant, Dave, *Runaway Rig*, St Peter Port, Guernsey: Guernsey Press Co, 1979
'Sailor', BBC-TV, 1978
Tupper, Alf, 'The *Orion* Oil Rig Rescue', in typescript
Vladimir Atlasov, 5 March 1977, Culdrose Press Release
'Wessex ice dash wins top award (*Harmoni*/Boyd Trophy)', *Navy News*, June 1977

10 'Anything from a haemorrhage to a headache': SAR Medicine

'Asiafreighter – Arsine Incident', 'Rescue by Helicopter', *Denholm News*, Magazine of Denholm Ship Management Ltd, Spring 1975
BURIED ALIVE!, *Daily Express*, 4 August 1978
Calnan, Cdr Denis, RN, 'Flying Divers', *The Sunday Times of Malta*, 14 December 1969
Colborne, Lt Ray, RN, Private Scrapbooks, 1977–79
Culdrose Press Releases, 3 November 1978, the CHRISTOS BITAS Affair; 30 December 1978; Rescue of Two Girls from Chapel Rock, Perranporth; 31 December 1978; *BEN ASDALE* Incident; 4 January 1979: *CANTONAD*; 5 January, the *PEACOCK* Rescue; 6 January, **ILE DE FEU**; 8 January 1979, The *BETELGEUSE* Explosion
Culdrose SAR 1975–85 (FAA Museum)
'Flying Tigers (814 NAS) to the rescue;: "Missions Impossible" ', *Navy News*, February 1979
HELISOPS, Edition 8, November 1988
H.M.S. *Daedalus*, RNAS Lee-on-Solent, SAR Incident Logs 1976–79

Jolly, R.T., 'Search and Rescue – The Medical Viewpoint', *Journal of the Royal Naval Medical Service*, Vol.64, Spring 1978
Lockey, Lt Alan, RN, 'Techniques of Inshore Search And Rescue', *Shell Aviation News*, No.447, 1978
Milne, Lt Ivor, RN, 'Scramble the SAR', *Navy News*, April 1976
Pearce, Lt Cdr David, RN, OIC Aircrewman School, Culdrose, 'SAR Divers Branch', Letter of 20 July 1989
'Rescue flight celebrates', *Southern Evening Echo*, 11 February 1978
Winton, John, 'Scramble, search and rescue', *The Illustrated London News*, May 1978

11 Fastnet 1979

Bond, Jennifer E., Browning, K.A., Collier, C.G., 'Estimates of surface gust speeds using radar observations of showers' (Fastnet 1979), *The Meteorological Magazine*, No.1303, February 1981, Vol.110
Brown, Pritchard Russell, (Deputy Regional Controller, Brixham SSR), 'Fastnet Race 1979', *Coastguard*, Vol.13, No.4, October 1979
Culdrose Press Release, 23 October 1979, Royal Navy Rescues Fastnet Yachtsmen
Culdrose SAR 1975–85
Day, A.P., 'Revised analyses and their effect on the fine-mesh forecast for the Fastnet storm', *The Meteorological Magazine*, No.1303, February 1981, Vol.110
Flag Officer Plymouth, Report on 'Fastnet Race Search And Rescue Operation – 14–16 Aug. 79' and Annexes, 23 August 1979
Gardner, L.T., *Fastnet 1979*, George Godwin
Jeffrey, Tim, 'The Recovery', *Yachting World*, November 1979
Marriott, John, op.cit., Ch.19, The Fastnet Race 1979
Morgan, Surg Lt D., RN, (Deputy Medical Officer Culdrose, 14 August 1979), 'Air Sea Rescue at the Fastnet Race 1979'
O'Donnell, Barry, 'The Fastnet Race 1979', *British Medical Journal*, Volume 281, 20–27 December 1980
Page, Frank, Nicholls, John, and Crookston, Peter, 'Pitch-Poled In the Fastnet: How Thirty-four Fathoms Doomed The Fastnet', *Observer Sunday Magazine*, 25 November 1979
Rousmaniere, John, *Fastnet Force 10*, Lymington: Nautical Publishing, 1980
Rowlings, Bill, 'The Horror of Fastnet', *Australian Sea Spray*, 7 September 1979
Royal Naval Air Station, Culdrose, 'Report of the Fastnet Race Rescue Operation 14–16 Aug 79' and Annexes, 6 September 1979
Royal Yachting Association and Royal Ocean Racing Club, *1979 Fastnet Race Enquiry*
Smith, Peter, Portsmouth News, various issues, August & September 1979
Watts, Alan, 'The Storm', *Yachting World*, October 1979
Woodroffe, A., 'The Fastnet storm – a forecaster's viewpoint', *The Meteorological Magazine*, No.1311, October 1981, Vol.110

12 Worldwide SAR: From Fife *in Dominica to the Penlee Lifeboat Disaster*

Crace, Jim, 'High Wire Heroes', *Sunday Telegraph Magazine*, c.1980
Culdrose Press Release, 7 March 1980, *MV PENTA*
Culdrose SAR 1975–85
'Daedalus Divers Free Trapped Seaman', *Navy News*, November 1980

'Helicopter Search and Rescue Operations in the South West', produced by RNAS Culdrose, in typescript, 1987
Lippiett, Captain John, MBE, RN, Letter of 16 October 1989 (*Fife* in Dominica)
'Lucky Seven Get A Lift In A Lynx: Coaster Crew Winched to Berwick in Biscay Rescue', *Navy News*, April 1979
'Mission Impossible: Fife Brings Order Out Of Chaos in Dominica', *Navy News*, October 1979
Passmore, Lt Cdr John, MBE, RN, Letter of 29 October 1989
'Humphrey in Dominica': An account of the part played by HMS FIFE and her aircraft in the disaster relief operation on the island of Dominica in August 1979, *Flight Deck*, 1980
'Helicopter Operations in Dominica', in typescript

13 South Georgia and the Falklands, 1982

Arthur, Max, *Above All, Courage*: The Falklands Front Line First-Hand Accounts, 'Bomb Attack on HMS *Ardent*, 21 May', London: Sidgwick & Jackson, 1985
Brown, David, *The Royal Navy And The Falklands War*, London: Leo Cooper, 1987
Cameron, Norman, Lt RN, 'HMS ANTRIM in the South Atlantic – a Personal Story', in MS
Enticknap, Ken, Fleet Chief, interview of 6 June 1984
Flight Deck, Falklands Edition, 1982
Jolly, Rick, *The Red and Green Life Machine*: A Diary of the Falklands Field Hospital, London: Century Publishing, 1983
Jolly, Surg Cdr Rick, OBE RN, Interview of 24 October 1989
Morgan, Cdr M.R. RN, *Antrim's War*: A Photographic Record of HMS ANTRIM's contribution to the Falklands Campaign April–June 1982, Gosport: Prontaprint, 1982
Parry, Lt C.J., RN, Diary, HMS *Antrim*, 2 April 1982–14 June 1982, in MS
Perkins, Roger, *Operation Paraquat: The Battle for South Georgia*, Chippenham: Picton Publishing, 1986
The London Gazette, Supplement of Friday 8th October 1982, Falklands Honours and Awards

14 The Falklands: Coventry, Atlantic Conveyor, Sir Galahad

Arthur, Max, op.cit., 'The Sinking of *Sir Galahad*, 8 June'
Brown, David, op.cit.
Castle, Cdr John, RN, (Editor), *HMS Broadsword Falklands 1982*, ship's souvenir publication, privately produced
Ethell, Jeffrey, and Price, Alfred, *Air War South Atlantic*, London: Sidgwick & Jackson, 1983
Fletcher, Lt Cdr Timothy, RN, 'Disconnected Jottings' (*Coventry* in the Falklands), in typescript
Hart Dyke, Captain David, MVO RN, 'H.M.S. Coventry – Her Part in the Falklands Conflict', written for press release in QE2, in typescript, 9 June 1982
'HMS Coventry in the Falklands', lecture for naval and civilian audiences
'HMS *Coventry* in the Falklands Conflict – A Personal Story', *The Naval Review*, Vol.71, No.1, January 1983'
'Personal Thoughts on the Effects of War at Sea', in typescript
'Lessons from the Falklands – An Operator's View', *The Naval Review*, Vol.72,

No.1, January 1984
Letter of 13 November 1989
Layard, Captain Michael, CBE, RN, *How Should A Merchant Ship Be Adapted To Join A Task Force?: Design Factors To Be Built In*, Address to the Honourable Company of Master Mariners, 13 April 1983
Recollections of the Falklands Campaign from the Senior Naval Officer SS ATLANTIC CONVEYOR, 1983
Macfarlane, Radio Supervisor Sam, 'Everyone needs something to believe in, Right now, I believe I'll have another beer', HMS Coventry May 1981–May 25th 1982, in typescript
Monn, Lt A.G., RN, 'HMS *Coventry*', *The Naval Review*, Vol.71, No.3, July 1983
Mortimer, Sq Ldr Ian, RAF, Part I: 'Shot Down in the Atlantic, or How I Carried Out a Perfect 90 Degree Intercept on a SAM', Part II: 'Nine Hours in a Dinghy: I Get My Own Command in the South Atlantic But Still No DSO', *Air Clues*, August and October 1988
Roberts, Captain P.J., DSO RFA, 'RFA Sir Galahad – The Demise of a Gallant Knight' (*The Naval Review*, Vol.72, No.1, January 1984)
Robinson-Moltke, Lt Cdr Glen, RN, Letters to his wife Christine, April–May 1982
Tupper, Alf, 'Coventry', in MS, 30 May 1990
Villar, Captain Roger, DSC, RN, *Merchant Ships At War: The Falklands Experience*, London: Conway Maritime Press and Lloyd's of London Press, 1984

15 Worldwide SAR: Ajax Bay to the Scillies, Antarctica to the Solent

'Antarctic Rescue', *Flight Deck*, No.4, 1985
ap Rees, Elfan, 'Antarctic Rescue', *Helicopter International*
Butcher, Richard, 'Rescue in The Antarctic (Brabant Island)', *The Rolls-Royce Magazine*, Number 27, December 1985
'Casevac: Lt Cdr Waghorn, Brabant Island, by 826 NAS A Flight', tape of Presentation by Lt Cdr Nigel Thomson and others who took part
Citation for Guild of Air Pilots and Air Navigators Prince Philip Helicopter Rescue Award for 1983–84 to POACMN John Stephen Coleman QGM
Culdrose SAR 1975–85
'For 819 Squadron ... It's All In A Year's Work ... ', *Navy News*, April 1984
'Helicopter crews rewarded for rescue (Brabant Island)', *Flight International*, 5 October 1985
'Helicopter Search and Rescue Operations in the South West'
'Honour for Poseidon Rescues', *Navy News*, December 1983
Jolly, ops.cit.
'Queen's Gallantry Medal for Stephen Marlow', Culdrose Press Release, 12 November 1984'
'Richard (Foster) is a "Man of the Year" ', *Navy News*, December 1984
'The Brabant Island Rescue (Lt Cdr C. Waghorn RN) 7–10 March', Citation for Guild of Air Pilots and Air Navigators Prince Philip Helicopter Rescue Award for 1985, FONAC's Letter of 17 April 1985
'The Edward and Maisie Lewis Award 1982/83 (*Poseidon*'), Appendix to the Shipwrecked Fishermen and Mariners' Royal Benevolent Society Annual Report 1982/83
Thomson, Lt Cdr Nigel, 'Brabant Island Rescue Report of Proceedings', March 1985, with narrative of events, sortie details, list of personnel, and meteorological report
" 'Upside-Down' Rescuer Wins Medal", *Navy News*, December 1984

16 The Late Eighties: Russian Forgers and Royal Yachts

'Alan Marsh Medal Nomination – Lt W. Taylor, Royal Navy', Enclosure 1 to FONAC's M6031/1/7 of 16 January 1987

Culdrose SAR 1975–85

'Danger dive after jetty car plunge (Humphries and Murdoch)', *Navy News*, September 1987

'Drama In The Snow', *Navy News*, February 1987

'Forger Pilot Rescue', Press Release, HMS *Newcastle*, 14 August 1985

'Gallantry Award For Navy Diver (Penhaligon)', *Flight Deck*, No.1, 1988

'Grim task for aircrews off Cork', *Navy News*, July 1985

'Helicopter Search and Rescue Operations in the South West'

'Helo crewman in deck ordeal (Gardiner)', *Navy News*, September 1987

'Helo saves 29 in two incidents' (*Mister Cube* and *Drum England*), *Navy News*, September 1985

'HMS *Alacrity* Flight – Puerto Rico Rescue', Fleet Air Arm Press Release

'HMS *Newcastle* Flight – Evacuation of Refugees from South Yemen, 23 January, 1986', Fleet Air Arm Press Release

'MV *Reefer Dolphin* – Search and Rescue', and Narrative of Events, Annexes to *Beaver*'s letters of 18 November 1985 and 3 March 1986

'Report on 819 NAS SAR Mission – 11 January 1986', Enclosure 3 to FONAC's M603/1/28 of 13 June 1986'

'Rescue Mission: DRUM ENGLAND (Yacht) 20 Personnel Rescued', FONAC's M603/1/28 Enclosure 2 of 13 June 1986

'Rescue Mission: MISTER CUBE (Yacht) 9 Personnel Rescued', FONAC's M6031/1/28 Enclosure 1 of 11 June 1986

Royal Naval Air Station Culdrose 1987, 40th Anniversary Souvenir Brochure

'Storm Rescue Award For Lynx Fliers' (*Alacrity* – Puerto Rico), *Navy News*, June 1986

'Trophy For Beaver', *Navy News*, May 1986

'Tunes of Glory' (*Britannia* in South Yemen Rescue, January 1986), *Navy News*, February 1986

17 The Way Ahead

Allen, Patrick, 'Reaching undreamt of heights: The UK's SAR service', *SEASCAPE International Maritime Magazine*, No.15, July 1988

'Ariadne in flood boat rescue', *Navy News*, January 1988

'Ark To The Rescue', *Flight Deck*, No.3, 1987

Beech, Eric, 'UK improves SAR coverage', *Flight International*, 26 November 1988

'Branson And Lindstrand Rescued', *Flight Deck*, No.3, 1987

'Flying Finale: farewells to the Wessex and Wasp', *Navy News*, May 1988

'Hell's Mouth!', *Navy News*, April 1989

'Hell's Mouth Rescue: Stormy Baptism for Sea King SAR', *Flight Deck*, No.2, 1989

'Horror Of Rig Blaze', *Navy News*, August 1988

Jolly, Rick, 'A Life In The Day of Rescue 20', *The Sunday Times Magazine*, 31 January 1988

Jolly, Surg Cdr R.T., OBE, 'Any Hangups, Doc?' *Cockpit*
'Design For Life', *Defence Helicopter World*, December 1987–January 1988

'Piper Alpha': 167 die in Oil Rig explosion', *Flight Deck*, No.3, 1988
'S & R Flight Closure At Lee', *Flight Deck*, No.1 1988
'The Edward And Maisie Lewis Award 1988/89 (*Secil Japan*)', Appendix to the Shipwrecked Fishermen & Mariners' Royal Benevolent Society, Annual Report 1988/89
'Zeebrugge', *Flight Deck*, No.2, 1987

General

Chartres, John, *Fly for their Lives*, Shrewsbury: Airlife, 1988
Chartres, John, *Helicopter Rescue*, Ian Allan 1980
Friedman, Norman, *British Carrier Aviation*: The Evolution of the Ships and their Aircraft, London: Conway Maritime Press, 1988
Grove, Eric J., *Vanguard To Trident*: British Naval Policy since World War II, London: The Bodley Head, 1987
Milne, Lt Cdr J.M., RN, *Flashing Blades over the Sea*: The Development & History of Helicopters in the Royal Navy, Liskeard: Maritime Books, 1980
Popham, Hugh, *Into Wind*: A History of British Naval Flying, London: Hamish Hamilton 1969
Rodrigo, Robert, *Search & Rescue*, London: William Kimber 1958
Seedie's Roll of Naval Honours and Awards 1939–1959, Tisbury, Wilts: Ripley Registers, 1989
Seedie's Naval Honours and Awards, post 1959
Sturtivant, Ray, *The Squadrons of the Fleet Air Arm*, Tonbridge: Air-Britain (Historians) Ltd, 1984
Swanborough, Gordon, & Bowers, Peter M., *United States Navy Aircraft Since 1911*, London: Putnam, 1983
The Life-boat Service & The War: The First Thirty Months, London; RNLI, 1942
Thetford, Owen, *British Naval Aircraft Since 1912*, London: Putnam, 1982
Turner, John Frayn, *Hovering Angels*: The Record of the Royal Navy's Helicopters, London: George G. Harrap, 1957
War In Peace, 10 Volumes, 120 Issues, London: Orbis Publishing Ltd. 1984–86
Whittle, Peter, and Borrisow, Michael, *Angels Without Wings*, Angley Book Co., 1966
Winton, John, *Air Power at Sea 1945 to Today*, London: Sidgwick & Jackson, 1987

Index